Missouri Genealogical Gleanings

1840 and Beyond
Volume 9

Sherida K. Eddlemon

HERITAGE BOOKS
2008

HERITAGE BOOKS
AN IMPRINT OF HERITAGE BOOKS, INC.

Books, CDs, and more—Worldwide

For our listing of thousands of titles see our website
at
www.HeritageBooks.com

Published 2008 by
HERITAGE BOOKS, INC.
Publishing Division
100 Railroad Ave. #104
Westminster, Maryland 21157

Copyright © 2004 Sherida K. Eddlemon

All rights reserved. No part of this book may be reproduced or transmitted in any form or by any means, electronic or mechanical, including photocopying, recording or by any information storage and retrieval system without written permission from the author, except for the inclusion of brief quotations in a review.

International Standard Book Numbers
Paperbound: 978-0-7884-2544-8
Clothbound: 978-0-7884-7183-4

PREFACE

Missouri was a gateway to the west. Both the Santa Fe Trail to the southwest and the Oregon Trail to the northwest began at Independence, Missouri. Settlers and new immigrants from Germany, Switzerland, Ireland, England, Poland, Bohemia and Italy flooded into Missouri when statehood was granted in 1821. Many of these new arrivals often did not list a destination on the ship passenger list. If a destination was indicated, it may mean that there were other relatives already there or that the family had already purchased property in advance.

Kansas was part of the Missouri Territory until 1821, but it was not until 1854 that the territory of Kansas was created luring new immigrants and settlers from Illinois, Ohio, Indiana and Missouri. So many Missourians relocated to Kansas that in 1855 Kansas was voted into the Union as a slave state.

Missouri was plagued with outlaws and raiders that had their beginnings even before the Civil War. The 1857 Dred Scott Decision helped to inflame the anti-slavery feelings in Missouri. During the Civil War, raiders and outlaws such as William Clarke Quantrill, Frank and Jesse James and the Cole Younger gangs terrorized Missouri. In the eyes of some these outlaws were heroes, but the law prevailed in the end.

Each new Gold Rush lured more people to Missouri on their way to make their fortune. There was a California Gold Rush in 1848; the Colorado Gold Rush in 1858 and the Klondike Gold Rush in the Yukon in 1896-1897. Many lost sons went to look for gold as well as whole families with only a child born in Missouri to show their passing through the state.

St. Joseph, Missouri was the starting point for the Pony Express. It promised delivery of the mail to Sacramento, California in eight to ten days. Although it was only in operation for eighteen months, these riders gained a glamorous spot in Missouri history.

Although there are extant census records for Missouri starting in 1830 many travelers and pioneering settlers were missed in the census years or only lived in the state between the census years. The purpose of this collection is to help the researcher pinpoint his ancestor between the census years.

All names appear as written on the records including the abbreviations of given names. The surnames appearing in the parentheses are included in the index. No attempt has been made to make corrections in spelling. Cemetery listings and mortality schedules include only persons born in 1840 or later.

In some instances it was necessary to use abbreviations. They are as follows:

m	Month	y -	Year
d	Day/Died	RD -	Recorded Date
b	Born	CLK -	Clerk
D	Date	GR -	Grantor
GE	Grantee	IN -	Instrument
P	Page	I -	Issue
R	Range	C -	Court Cases
AP	Application	Dis -	Dismissed
MOC	Missouri Connection	SUS -	Suspended
TWP	Township	APP -	Appraiser
A	Age	St -	Martial Status
BP	Birth Place	RES -	Residence
OC	Occupation	ADM/AD -	Admission
MD	Marriage Date	MG -	Minister
CMTS	Comments	SVC -	Service
DP	Place of Death	PMD	Place Married
PO -	Post Office	TE -	Executed
ID	Issue Date	AN	Accession No.
POC	Previous Occupation	POL	Politics

Good luck in finding your ancestors within these pages.

TABLE OF CONTENTS

	Page

ANDREW COUNTY

Testimonials, Nichols Santorium, 1935	37
Democratic County Committee, 1936-1938	199
Officers of the Bar Association, 1919-1920	215

ATCHISON COUNTY

Souvenir of School District No 4 Lincoln Township, Fall Term, 1896.	1
Democratic County Committee, 1936-1938	200
Obituary of John Gaunce, Aug. 31, 1917	200

BARRY COUNTY

Heads of Household, 1840	24
Antioch Church Cemetery	123
Democratic County Committee, 1936-1938	201
Obituary of Frances Jewell Patton	203

BUCHANAN COUNTY

Marriage Records, 1840-1841	3
Death Register, 1883-1893	63
Business Owners, Agency, 1893, R. G. Dunn	124
Land Patents, 1846	145
Pensioners List, 1883	188

CLARK COUNTY

Business Owners, Acasto, 1893, R. G. Dunn	122
Democratic Committee, 1936-1938	204
Luray, Business Owners, R. G. Dunn Directory, 1893	205
Land Patents, 1841-1849	206
Officers of the Bar Association, 1919-1920	215

CLAY COUNTY

Business Owners, Acme, 1893, R. G. Dunn	123

Officers of the Bar Association, 1919-1920   215

HOLT COUNTY

Old Settlers Atlas, 1877	37
Democratic County Committee, 1936-1938	212
Officers of the Bar Association, 1919-1920	216

HOWARD COUNTY

Heads of Household, 1840 Census	139
Attendees of the Schoenhal Family Reunion, Shattuck, OK, *"Northwest Oklahoman,"* Aug. 21, 2003	203
Democratic County Committee, 1936-1938	213

JACKSON COUNTY

Obituary of Thelka Lamind Wooden	104
Obituary of Francis P. Reddington	194
Obituary of Alpha May Seimears Thurman	202

JOHNSON COUNTY

Marriage Records, 1840-1849	27
Officers of the Bar Association, 1919-1920	215

LAWRENCE COUNTY

Johnson vs. Johnson, Feb. Term, 1896	1
Land Patents, 1861-1899	104

LINN COUNTY

Veterans Census, 1890	185
Land Patents, 1845, Fayette Land Office	126

NODAWAY COUNTY

Souvenir High Prairie School, Dist. 40. Lincoln Township, 1919	2
Pensioners List, 1883	194

PIKE COUNTY

Business Owners, Aberdeen, 1893, R. G. Dunn	123

ST. LOUIS COUNTY

Marriages, 1840	103
Declarations of Intent	
113	
Business Owners, Afton, 1893, R. G. Dunn	123
Probate Listings, 1881	124
Marriage Notice, *"Fort Worth, TX Democrat"*	129
Death Records, 1901	165
Obituary of Mrs. Virginia Smith	
193	
Employees of the Driver's License Department, Branch Office, St. Louis, 1837-1838	213
Graduates Soldan High School, June, 1916	215

SHELBY COUNTY

Surnames in Will Book A, 1845-1869, and Book A, 1845-1845	2
Democratic County Committee, 1936-1938	214

MISCELLANEOUS MISSOURIANA

Missourians buried in Lamar Co., TX	1
Missouri Veterans, 1893 Nebraska Census	
5	
Miscellaneous Railroad Information	122
Missourians in the 1867-1869 Montague County, Texas Voters List	
126	
Missourians in the 1867-1869 Hood County, Texas Voters List	
126	
Missouri Songwriters and Lyricists	129

Lawrence County, Missouri, Circuit Court, February term, 1896.
   Oliver P. Johnson, Sr. Plaintiff, against William P. Johnson, Defendant. Comes now the plaintiff, Oliver P. Johnson, Senior, and says that on August 30, A.D., 1895, he was entitled to the following described real estate situate in Lawrence County, Missouri, viz. The west half of the south west quarter of the northeast quarter; and the south half of the north west quarter, all in section twenty seven: and the southeast quarter of the north twenty nine of range twenty five; containing two hundred and twenty acres, more or less, and afterward, while the plaintiff was so entitled to the possession thereof, on September 1, 1896, the defendant, William P. Johnson, entered into the said premises and detains the possetion thereof from the plaintiff, to his damage one hundred dollars: the rents and profits of the said premises are of the monthly value of thirty dollars; Plaintiff asks judgement for the possessin of the said premises and for him damages and rents and profits aforesaid, and for all proper relief. Signed Henry Baumback, Attorney of Plaintiff. State of Missouri in the Lawrence County Circuit Court February Term 1896, Oliver P. Johnson Sr. Plaintiff vs. William P. Johnson Defendant. Comes now the defendant William P. Johnson and for his answer to plaintiffs petition denies each and every allegation set fourth therein. Signed Landrum Crooks, Atty for Defendant. Source: Oliver P.Johnson vs Wm. P. Johnson NO 7840, Filed Jan. 11 1896, C. E. Silverwood, circuit clerk. Copy of original.

Missourians buried in Lamar County, Texas
   Ellis, William Norton, b. 4 Mar. 1839, d. 22 Aug. 1912, buried in Northeast section of Blossom Cemetery, Pvt., Co. D, 9th Missouri Cavalry.
   Crain, W. T., b. Not Known, d. 2 Nov. 1894, buried in Prairie Ridge Cemetery, Co. D, 3rd Missouri Cavalry.
   Herron, William McAdoo, b. 13 Jan. 1843, d. 7 Sep. 1922, buried in Southwest section of Providence Cemetery, 2nd Lt., Quantrill's Partisan Rangers, Missouri.

Souvenir of School District No 4 Lincoln Township, Atchison Co, Missouri. Fall Term, 1896.
   N. M. Piester, Teacher-Directors-J W. Berry, Clerk. Thos. Dewhurst, President. George Brand.
   Students: Pearl VanGundy, Fred VanGundy, Bryson VAnGundy, Sallie VanGundy, Thomas McKnight, Maggie McKnight, Scott McKnight, Mary McKnight, Samuel Brand, Ezra Brand, Lena Brand, Lota Ddewhurst, Lincoln Dewhurst, Earl Bewhurst, Ella Cox, Alice Cox, George Berry, Inez Rouse, Georgia Piester, Earl Mumford, Mary Hamilton, Calist Hurst, Pearl Stevens, Grace Stevens, Oscar Teague, Orley Teague, Hilma Lowquist, Bennie McIntosh.

Souvenir High Prairie School, Dist. 40. Lincoln Twp., Nodaway County, MO 1919

Miss Anna Grace O'Brien, Teacher C.E. Graham, Clerk Directors E.N. Vansickle, J.H. Barnes C. J. Jennings

Students: Arcelle Vansickle, Thressa Jennings, Everett Barnes, Roy Baker, Lola Graves, Louese Calfee, Raymond Atherton, Ray Horn, Matt Thomas, Alfreda Castillo, Ellsworth Horn, Fern Calfee, Vernel Horn, Dorothy Jennings, Pansy Baker, Della Calfee, Wilma Vansickle, Lora Tudder, Nora Horn, Jim Andy Browning, Emory Hindle, Glenn Daugherty, Leroy Wilson, Lamont Wilson, Mary Baker, Edward Horn, Dollie Thomas, Fletcher Sheets, Olin Barnes, Trenie Belle Thomas, Velma Bowman, Glenn Castillo, Charlotte Gipe, Myrene Castillo, Dorothy Ennen, Geraldine Baker, Leo Barnes, Monroe Bowman, Richard Mires, Elverda Horn, Clarence Calfee, Iris Horn, Theron Reece, Lillia Gipe.

Shelby County, Missouri, Surnames in Will Book A, 1845-1869, Recorders Office and Book A, 1845-1845, Probate Office

Aduddle, Allison, Anderson, Andrew, Arnett, Author, Babb, Bailey, Baldwin, Balle,. Balthrope, Barker, Barr, Bartup, Belch, Belden, Bell, Berry, Bethards, Billings, Bishop, Blackburn, Blakey, Blatten, Blizzard, Bookee, Booker, Bowers, Bowling, Bradley, Brady, Brigham, Brinkerhoff, Brooks, Brown, Buckner, Buford, Buzzard, Caldwell, Calhoun, Campbell, Canall, Capp, Carothers, Carr, Carrico, Carroll, Cartright, Carver, Chadick, Chapman, Chester, Church, Clark, Clemens, Clements. Clemmons, Coard, Corckerille, Coleman, Collier, Connor, Coon, Cord, Cossett, Cotton, Cox, Craig, Creed, Crow, Crutcher, Davis, Dawson, Day, DeHaven, Dick, Dickerson, Dill, Dillon, Dimmitt, Dines, Dores, Douglass, Dryden, Dugeon, Duncan, Dungeon, Dunn, Durbin, Dwyer, Dye, Eakle, Earnest, Easley, Eaton, Edgar, Elgin, Elligood, Elliott, Ennis, Eskridge, Estel, Etling, Evans, Ferguson, Findling, Finn, Finney, Firman, Fletcher, Foley, Ford, Foreman, Forester, Forman, Forsythe, Foster, Fowler, Fox, Fuller, Gamble, Garnett, Gartrell, Geigkey, Gentry, Gibbons, Gidney, Giesy, Gillespie, Gillis, Gilman, Givan, Glasscock, Glessner, Golay, Goodhue, Gordon, Graham, Grant, Gray, Green, Greene, Gregory, Griffith, Grout, Grove, Gunby, Haffner, Hagar, Hagarman, Haines, Hale, Hall, Halls, Hamerick, Hardy, Haskins, Haskings, Hastings, Hawkins, Heckard, Heckart, Heiterich, Henry, Herdon, Hewitt, Hickman, Hilcher, Hilton, Hirst, Holliday, Hollyman, Holmes, Hoofer, Hope, Horn, Hottman, Howe, Hughes, Hurlebaus, Hyde, Irwin, Irving, Jackson, Jefferson, Jessup, Jett, Johns, Johnson, Jones, Keal, Keegan, Keil, Kelton, Kennedy, Kinchloe, King, Kneppepper, Knight, Kronough, Kyle, Lafon, Lair, Lane, Langdon, Lanshaw, Larman, Latham, Latimer, Lear, Leflet, Lillie, Link, Little, Looney, Louthan, Lyle, Maddox, Madkins. Mahan, Malone, Mansfield, Manuel, Marks, Marmaduke, Martin, Mason, Matkins, Melson, Milam, Millerm Minor, Moffett, Montieth, Moore,

Morgan, Morton, Moss, Muldrow, Murry, McAfee, McCroskey, McDonald, McElroy, McGee, McGlothin, McKinney, McLain, McMurry, McPike, Naylor, Neel, Newcomb, Nichols, Nicol, Nowlin, Oakley, Olmstead, Owen, Pagett, Parker, Parr, Parrish. Parsons, Payne, Payton, Peake, Peoples, Pepper, Perry, Philliber, Phillips, Pickett, Pilcher, Pollard, Pondney, Porter, Potts, Proctor, Ragsdale, Reamy, Rector, Redman, Reeside, Reid, Reynolds, Rhodes, Ricardo, Rice, Richards, Riggets, Riggs, Right, Robb, Roberts, Robinson, Rodes, Rogers, Rookwood, Rosencraft, Rust, Rutter, Sage Sanders, Saunders, Savage, Sayre, Schmidt, Schneider, Scoville, Seaver, Selsor, Semer, Sharp, Shaw, Sheetz, Shelton, Sherman, Sherry, Shirley, Shrout, Shubert, Shuffit, Shumaker, Sibley, Sigler, Simple, Slayback, Small, Smith, Snell, Speace, Speed, Springle, Stalcup, Starret, Stewart, Stone, Stover, Strachan, Strode, Sturgis, Styles, Swearingen, Tarbell, Taylor, Thomas, Thorn, Tingle, Tittle, Tobin, Todd, Triplett, Trumpeter, Tufts, Turner, Turpin, Vaihinger, Vanderen, Vanmetre, Vanlandingham, Vanskoike, Vaughn, Vawter, Vick, Wade, Wagner, Wailes, Walker, Wallace, Wartz, Watson, Weise, Welch, Werts, West, Wheeler, White, Whiter, Whitow, Whitney, Wiggins, Williams, Williamson, Willis, Willy, Wilson, Winger, Winger, Witherbee, Witherspoon, Woldran, Wolfe, Wolfer, Wood, Woodman, Woolfolk, Wyatt, Yarnell, Young.

<u>Buchanan County, Missouri, Marriage Records, 1840-1841</u>
Aaron Johnson and Manuvry Fulton, (MD) Jan. 9, 1840
John B. Smith and Emily Thorp, (MD) Jan. 19, 1840
Wesley Hunter and Elizabeth Parker, (MD) Jan. 26, 1840
William Stuart and Eliza Jane Day, (MD) Feb. 6, 1840
Henry Patterson and Sindarella Cobb, (MD) Feb. 27, 1840
William Allen and Albina Jane Foster, (MD) Nov. 5, 1840
John Barnett and Nancy Brown, (MD) Jan. 23, 1840
George F. McKarle and Elizabeth B. Hoarl, (MD) Feb. 6, 1840
William McUmber and Nancy Wixam, (MD) Feb. 9, 1840
William M. Edwards and Polly R. Richison, (MD) Feb. 18, 1840
George Maffley and Mary Lemon, (MD) Feb. 27, 1840
William A. Price and Elizabeth Earls, (MD) Mar. 1, 1840
Robert H. Russell and Mary M. Crowley, (MD) Mar. 4, 1840
Abjiah ????? and Mary Jane Jackson, (MD) Mar. 5, 1840
Stephen K. Waymire and Mahala Elvira Gillmore, (MD) Mar. 5, 1840
Samuel Paul and Elmina Mitchel, (MD) Mar. 6, 1840
Orgo Castle and Constania Sollars, (MD) Mar. 8, 1840
James Russel and Susan Gann, (MD) Mar. 22, 1840
John Lincon nd Rachel Catching, (MD) Mar. 23, 1840
Barten Lee and Mary Harris, (MD) Apr. 2, 1840
James Davison and Elizabeth Ferguson, (MD) Apr. 6, 1840
John Frakes and Buley Sampson, (MD) Apr. 7, 1840
David Johnson and Araminta Thorp, (MD) Apr. 9, 1840

Benjamin Hanson Dixon and Charlotte Aurelina Wilcox, (MD) Jun. 30, 1840
John Elison and Perlina Curl, (MD) Jul. 1, 1840
John Henry and Susan McQueen, (MD) Jul. 5, 1840
Alexander H. Dunning and Sarah Ann Rector, (MD) Aug. 2, 1840
John Gartner and Sarak Ogle, (MD) Aug. 6, 1840
John St. John and Elizabeth Kithne, (MD) Aug. 23, 1840
Oliver P. Lucas and Mary Elizabeth Hargrove, (MD) Aug. 25, 1840
Green B. Taylor and Martha Finch, (MD) Aug. 26, 1840
James McMahon and Lydia Witt, (MD) Oct. 8, 1840
Joseph Hall and Elizabeth Cogdill, (MD) Sep. 3, 1840
Jeremiah McKown and Lucinda Roberts, (MD) Sep. 6, 1840
John Clasby and Sarah Ellison, (MD) Sep. 16, 1840
Noah Curtis and Lucinda Wilkerson, (MD) Sep. 17, 1840
Peter Bledsoe and Elizabeth Drake, (MD) Oct. 8, 1840
Muscilus Munkers and Elizabeth Boilston, (MD) Aug. 13, 1840
Benjamin Boilston and Polly Cunningham, (MD) May 31, 1840
Woodson Marrion and Elsie Davison, (MD) Nov. 6, 1840
Paschal Hany and Matilda Hungaford, (MD) Oct. 14, 1840
Benjamin Berkett and Anne Huntsucker, (MD) Oct. 15, 1840
Allen Miller and Lydia Ann Bradbury, (MD) Oct. 18, 1840
Peter Velmons and Kiziah Watkins, (MD) Oct. 20, 1840
Peter Master and Mary Kirk, (MD) Oct. 30, 1840
Amos F. Owens and Elizabeth Ashley, (MD) Nov. 5, 1840
Peasant Perkins and Martha Ann Pearson, (MD) Nov. 8, 1840
John P. Smith and Ellen Henderson, (MD) Nov. 22, 1840
William K. Richardson and Rebecca Brown, (MD) Nov. 26, 1840
Anderson Neal and Elizabeth Gibson, (MD) Dec. 8, 1840
Willis W. Neely and Jane Knapp, (MD) Dec. 8, 1840
Peter Kirk and Charity Travis, (MD) Dec. 17, 1840
William Scott and Charlotte Sellers, (MD) Dec. 17, 1840
Moses Morris and Mary M. Scott, (MD) Dec. 21, 1840
Thomas Strikelin and Hannah Penny, (MD) Dec. 24, 1840
Edmond Lane and Lucily O'Banon, (MD) Dec. 26, 1840
Edwin Ritemew and Mary Stanly, (MD) Dec. 30, 1840
John Groom and Polly Hadrick, (MD) Dec. 30, 1840
Harry Baum and Margaret Wilberton, (MD) Jan. 3, 1841
James F. Hamilton and Louisa Bell, (MD) Jan. 17, 1841
Isaac W. Gann and Abby Ann Poorter, (MD) Jan. 17, 1841
Roert Fitzhugh and Ann Grooms, (MD) Jan. 19, 1841
William Earixson and Delany Fitzhugh, (MD) Jan. 20, 1841
John Whitsell and Sarah Mufler, (MD) Jan. 3, 1841
Lawrence McKown and Deliana Morgan, (MD) Jan. 28, 1841
Wiley C. Hartman and Barbara Ann McKorle, (MD) Feb. 4, 1841
S. Palmon and Elizabeth Rousey, (MD) Feb. 14, 1841
Samuel Murphy and Amelia Tyler, (MD) Feb. 18, 1841

William H. Guthery and Malisa Aton, (MD) Feb. 23, 1841
Jacob Boyer and Hannah Kelser, (MD) Mar. 7, 1841
John Horne and Melissa Jane Bragg, (MD) Mar. 11, 1841
Thomas Austin and Louisa Blevins, (MD) Apr. 7, 1841
Thompson Burnan and Miram Morton, (MD) Apr. 13, 1841
Robert E. Doherty and Mary Ann Devoress, (MD) Apr. 15, 1841
Hugh R. Smith and Maria C. Davidson, (MD) Apr. 22, 1841
William Stokes and Mahaly Thourouman, (MD) May 6, 1841
John McKown and Rebecca Blakely, (MD) May 6, 1841
Thomas Duke and Eliza Pitman, (MD) May 18, 1841
Samuel McCaully and Louisa Maxwell, (MD) May 23, 1841
James Hudspeth and Elender Elliott, (MD) Jun. 1, 1841
Benja. Hartwell and Mary C. Hayes, (MD) Jun. 10, 1841
Joseph Lousingmont and Sarah Roaderick, (MD) Jun. 26, 1841
William Matheny and Polly Lilly, (MD) Jul. 1, 1841
Samuel Singleton and Rachel Cromwell, (MD) Jul. 1, 1841
Joshua Skinner and Elizabeth Mootry, (MD) Jul. 15, 1841
John Harrington and Mareda Blevins, (MD) Jul. 18, 1841
John H. Markwood and Elenor Hyde, (MD) Jul. 22, 1841
Bryan Linville and Elizabeth Day, (MD) Aug. 26, 1841
Barthlomew Hawley and Agatha Adams, (MD) Sep. 12, 1841
Robert Guinn and Malinda Allen, (MD) Sep. 12, 1841
Edward Clark and Olivia Brown, (MD) Sep. 26, 1841
Moses Jeffers and Sarah N. Buckland, (MD) Sep. 30, 1841
Clark Stephenson and Martha Persely, (MD) Sep. 30, 1841
William Combs and Nancy Vessar, (MD) Oct. 3, 1841
James Vance Bunting and Ursula Flanary, (MD) Oct. 19,1841
Archibald Adams and Sarah Margarett Witt, (MD) Oct. 28, 1841
John Enyart and Miriam Stephens, (MD) Oct. 29, 1841
John Bumbarger and Eveline Hangerford, (MD) Oct. 31, 1841
Elijah McCary and Nancy Jane Martin, (MD) Nov. 9, 1841
Henry Baker and Elizabeth Wilkerson, (MD) Nov. 26, 1841
Andrew Chambers and Mariah Boyer, (MD) Dec. 15, 1841
Joseph Norman and Phebe Ann Frakes, (MD) Dec. 21, 1841
Rural Lathrop and Melinday Johns, (MD) Dec. 21, 1841
Peter C. Templeton and Adaline McCain, (MD) Dec. 23, 1841
Nelson Rector and Sarah Emerick, (MD) Dec. 23, 1841
James Gauldin and Jemimah Allison, (MD) Dec. 23, 1841
Richard Sharp and Sarah Witt, (MD) Dec. 26, 1841

Missouri Veterans, 1893 Nebraska Census
Jas. A. Sims: (CEN) 1893 State Census, MO Veterans (MIL)
    1st MO Infantry, Co. M, (RES) Madrid, NE
Sanford Gartes: (CEN) 1893 State Census, MO Veterans (MIL)
    12th MO Infantry, Co. M, (RES) Rock Bluffs, NE
James F. Andrews: (CEN) 1893 State Census, MO Veterans (MIL)

11th MO Cavalry, Co. M, (RES) Lamar, NE
Oliver Baker: (CEN) 1893 State Census, MO Veterans (MIL)
12th MO Cavalry, Co. M, (RES) Oak, NE
John M. Crowfoot: (CEN) 1893 State Census, MO Veterans (MIL)
12th MO Cavalry, Co. M, (RES) Hebron, NE
James M. Smith: (CEN) 1893 State Census, MO Veterans (MIL)
12th MO Cavalry, Co. M, (RES) Blair, NE
Joseph Graff: (CEN) 1893 State Census, MO Veterans (MIL)
1st MO Cavalry, Co. M, (RES) Firth, NE
William S. Hampton: (CEN) 1893 State Census, MO Veterans (MIL)
2nd MO Cavalry, Co. M, (RES) Endicott, NE
Henry Jones: (CEN) 1893 State Census, MO Veterans (MIL)
2nd MO Cavalry, Co. M, (RES) Du Bois, NE
W. C. Lantis: (CEN) 1893 State Census, MO Veterans (MIL)
2nd MO Infantry, Co. M, (RES) Bloomington, NE
James Daniels: (CEN) 1893 State Census, MO Veterans (MIL)
4 Enrolled Mil, Co. M, (RES) Blair, NE
John F. Johnston: (CEN) 1893 State Census, MO Veterans (MIL)
7th MO Cavalry, Co. M, (RES) Wescott, NE
John Marshhall: (CEN) 1893 State Census, MO Veterans (MIL)
7th MO Cavalry, Co. M, (RES) Roseland, NE
John C. Palmer: (CEN) 1893 State Census, MO Veterans (MIL)
9th MO Cavalry, Co. M, (RES) Burchard, NE
J. W. White: (CEN) 1893 State Census, MO Veterans (MIL)
9th MO Cavalry, Co. M, (RES) Nelson, NE
M. Ittner: (CEN) 1893 State Census, MO Veterans (MIL)
National Guard, Co. M, (RES) Omaha, NE
A. G. Kingsbury: (CEN) 1893 State Census, MO Veterans (MIL)
1st MO Cavalry, Co. L. & B, (RES) Ponca, NE
Jacob H. Jacobs: (CEN) 1893 State Census, MO Veterans (MIL)
1st MO Infantry, Co. L, (RES) Weston, NE
Elias Spurgin: (CEN) 1893 State Census, MO Veterans (MIL)
9th MO Infantry, Co. L, (RES) Wallace, NE
J. P. Stewart: (CEN) 1893 State Census, MO Veterans (MIL)
69th MO Infantry, Co. L, (RES) Du Bois, NE
Henry Helvas: (CEN) 1893 State Census, MO Veterans (MIL)
1st MO Cavalry, Co. L, (RES) Gering, NE
C. D. King: (CEN) 1893 State Census, MO Veterans (MIL)
1st MO Cavalry, Co. L, (RES) Elmwood, NE
G. W. L. Mitchell: (CEN) 1893 State Census, MO Veterans (MIL)
2nd MO Artillery, Co. L, (RES) Arlington, NE
D. F. Canfield: (CEN) 1893 State Census, MO Veterans (MIL)
2nd MO Cavalry, Co. L, (RES) Rising City, NE
G. Sonnenschein: (CEN) 1893 State Census, MO Veterans (MIL)
4th MO Cavalry, Co. L, (RES) Stanton, NE
E. S. Whittenburg: (CEN) 1893 State Census, MO Veterans (MIL)

    6th MO Cavalry, Co. L, (RES) Beaver City, NE
Daniel Payton: (CEN) 1893 State Census, MO Veterans (MIL)
    6th MO S. M., Co. L, (RES) Beaver City, NE
H. F. Gagnebin: (CEN) 1893 State Census, MO Veterans (MIL)
    7th MO Cavalry, Co. L, (RES) Auburn, NE
D. L. Anderson: (CEN) 1893 State Census, MO Veterans (MIL)
    1st MO Infantry, Co. K, (RES) Ashland, NE
John Weeden: (CEN) 1893 State Census, MO Veterans (MIL)
    1st MO Infantry, Co. K, (RES) Bartley, NE
John F. Eilers: (CEN) 1893 State Census, MO Veterans (MIL)
    5th MO Infantry, Co. K, (RES) Sterling, NE
H. McShane: (CEN) 1893 State Census, MO Veterans (MIL)
    14th MO Infantry, Co. K, (RES) Lincoln, NE
N. W. Short: (CEN) 1893 State Census, MO Veterans (MIL)
    47th MO Infantry, Co. K, (RES) Gibbon, NE
D. N. Moore: (CEN) 1893 State Census, MO Veterans (MIL)
    1st Engineers, Co. K, (RES) Powell, NE
Geo. Pratt: (CEN) 1893 State Census, MO Veterans (MIL)
    10th MO Infantry, Co. K, (RES) David City, NE
Wm. H. Sullivan: (CEN) 1893 State Census, MO Veterans (MIL)
    11th MO Cavalry, Co. K, (RES) Omaha, NE
Adam Vesper: (CEN) 1893 State Census, MO Veterans (MIL)
    13th MO Cavalry, Co. K, (RES) Ord, NE
Watson Grossman: (CEN) 1893 State Census, MO Veterans (MIL)
    1st Light MO Artillery, Co. K, (RES) Angus, NE
Urbin Cachelin: (CEN) 1893 State Census, MO Veterans (MIL)
    1st MO Infantry, Co. K, (RES) DeSoto, NE
W. B. Wilson: (CEN) 1893 State Census, MO Veterans (MIL)
    20th MO Infantry, Co. K, (RES) Ragan, NE
John Little: (CEN) 1893 State Census, MO Veterans (MIL)
    3rd MO Infantry, Co. K, (RES) Hazard, NE
R. Elliott: (CEN) 1893 State Census, MO Veterans (MIL)
    48th MO Infantry, Co. K, (RES) Nemaha, NE
Albert Hanslerry: (CEN) 1893 State Census, MO Veterans (MIL)
    48th MO Infantry, Co. K, (RES) Tallin, NE
Oscar Scoville: (CEN) 1893 State Census, MO Veterans (MIL)
    48th MO Infantry, Co. K, (RES) Nemaha, NE
James Stephenson: (CEN) 1893 State Census, MO Veterans (MIL)
    48th MO Infantry, Co. K, (RES) Liberty, NE
James M. Truax: (CEN) 1893 State Census, MO Veterans (MIL)
    48th MO Infantry, Co. K, (RES) Taylor, NE
J. B. Pratt: (CEN) 1893 State Census, MO Veterans (MIL)
    4th MO Cavalry, Co. K, (RES) Julian, NE
J. S. Stevenson: (CEN) 1893 State Census, MO Veterans (MIL)
    4th MO Cavalry, Co. K, (RES) Nemaha, NE
F. M. Watson: (CEN) 1893 State Census, MO Veterans (MIL)

    4th MO Infantry, Co. K, (RES) Fullerton, NE
S. J. Cowperthwait: (CEN) 1893 State Census, MO Veterans (MIL)
    5th MO Cavalry, Co. K, (RES) Pawnee City, NE
John Hall: (CEN) 1893 State Census, MO Veterans (MIL)
    5th MO Cavalry, Co. K, (RES) Auburn, NE
Elias Hanna: (CEN) 1893 State Census, MO Veterans (MIL)
    5th MO Cavalry, Co. K, (RES) Tecumseh, NE
H. F. Zumbrun: (CEN) 1893 State Census, MO Veterans (MIL)
    6th MO Cavalry, Co. K, (RES) Nelson, NE
Stephen Rice: (CEN) 1893 State Census, MO Veterans (MIL)
    6th MO Infantry, Co. K, (RES) Davenport, NE
I. J. Ammerman: (CEN) 1893 State Census, MO Veterans (MIL)
    8th MO Cavalry, Co. K, (RES) So Sioux City, NE
Herman Hoins: (CEN) 1893 State Census, MO Veterans (MIL)
    9th MO Infantry, Co. K, (RES) Kiowa, NE
B. Lem: (CEN) 1893 State Census, MO Veterans (MIL)
    40th MO Infantry, Co. J, (RES) Cameo, NE
D. F. Fisher: (CEN) 1893 State Census, MO Veterans (MIL)
    1st Engineers, Co. I. & C, (RES) Fairfield, NE
John H. Day: (CEN) 1893 State Census, MO Veterans (MIL)
    4th MO Infantry, Co. I, (RES) Wood Lake, NE
L. A. Warner: (CEN) 1893 State Census, MO Veterans (MIL)
    11th MO Infantry, Co. I, (RES) Maple Creek, NE
Lewis B. Korns: (CEN) 1893 State Census, MO Veterans (MIL)
    18th MO Infantry, Co. I, (RES) Indianola, NE
T. S. Smith: (CEN) 1893 State Census, MO Veterans (MIL)
    23rd MO Infantry, Co. I, (RES) Amelia, NE
H. P. Smith: (CEN) 1893 State Census, MO Veterans (MIL)
    39th MO Infantry, Co. I, (RES) Sargent, NE
Josiah Gilliland: (CEN) 1893 State Census, MO Veterans (MIL)
    43rd MO Infantry, Co. I, (RES) South Auburn, NE
F. M. Lawe: (CEN) 1893 State Census, MO Veterans (MIL)
    43rd MO Infantry, Co. I, (RES) Palisade, NE
John S. Morgan: (CEN) 1893 State Census, MO Veterans (MIL)
    43rd MO Infantry, Co. I, (RES) Wilsonville, NE
W. S. Warner: (CEN) 1893 State Census, MO Veterans (MIL)
    11th MO Infantry, Co. I, (RES) Humphrey, NE
L. R. King: (CEN) 1893 State Census, MO Veterans (MIL)
    12th MO Cavalry, Co. I, (RES) Superior, NE
Ernst Kruse: (CEN) 1893 State Census, MO Veterans (MIL)
    12th MO Infantry, Co. I, (RES) Sidney, NE
Chas. H. Cormack: (CEN) 1893 State Census, MO Veterans (MIL)
    14th MO Cavalry, Co. I, (RES) Beaver City, NE
Julius Reid: (CEN) 1893 State Census, MO Veterans (MIL)
    15th MO Infantry, Co. I, (RES) Syracuse, NE
Charles Fitch: (CEN) 1893 State Census, MO Veterans (MIL)

   1st MO S. M., Co. I, (RES) Battle Creek, NE
J. S. Abernathy: (CEN) 1893 State Census, MO Veterans (MIL)
   21th MO Infantry, Co. I, (RES) Alma, NE
W. F. Bratcher: (CEN) 1893 State Census, MO Veterans (MIL)
   21th MO Infantry, Co. I, (RES) Harvard, NE
Israel Banks: (CEN) 1893 State Census, MO Veterans (MIL)
   26th MO Infantry, Co. I, (RES) Auburn, NE
 Howderm John W.: (CEN) 1893 State Census, MO Veterans (MIL)
   39th MO Infantry, Co. I, (RES) Albion, NE
J. L. Young: (CEN) 1893 State Census, MO Veterans (MIL)
   3rd MO Cavalry, Co. I, (RES) Tecumseh, NE
Abram Garber: (CEN) 1893 State Census, MO Veterans (MIL)
   3rd MO Infantry, Co. I, (RES) Guide Rock, NE
G. H. Anders: (CEN) 1893 State Census, MO Veterans (MIL)
   41th MO Infantry, Co. I, (RES) Pine Glen, NE
Adam Sliger: (CEN) 1893 State Census, MO Veterans (MIL)
   43th MO Infantry, Co. I, (RES) Nelson, NE
Charles York: (CEN) 1893 State Census, MO Veterans (MIL)
   43th MO Infantry, Co. I, (RES) Helvey, NE
J. M. Sims: (CEN) 1893 State Census, MO Veterans (MIL)
   43th MO Vol, Co. I, (RES) Ruskin, NE
C. Perreten: (CEN) 1893 State Census, MO Veterans (MIL)
   49th MO Infantry, Co. I, (RES) Rushville, NE
C. Martin Wilson: (CEN) 1893 State Census, MO Veterans (MIL)
   4th MO Cavalry, Co. I, (RES) Brady Island, NE
W. H. Orr: (CEN) 1893 State Census, MO Veterans (MIL)
   7th MO Cavalry, Co. I, (RES) Craig, NE
Lewis Rue: (CEN) 1893 State Census, MO Veterans (MIL)
   8th MO Zouaves, Co. I, (RES) Brock, NE
A. J. Henderson: (CEN) 1893 State Census, MO Veterans (MIL)
   9th MO Cavalry, Co. I, (RES) Grand Island, NE
Nathaniel Corbin: (CEN) 1893 State Census, MO Veterans (MIL)
   7th Cavalry, Co. I, (RES) Ayr, NE
Joseph Timmermeyer: (CEN) 1893 State Census, MO Veterans (MIL)
   9th MO Infantry, Co. I, (RES) Lincoln, NE
H. F. Keallper: (CEN) 1893 State Census, MO Veterans (MIL)
   1st MO Infantry, Co. H, (RES) McCook, NE
D. R. Johnson: (CEN) 1893 State Census, MO Veterans (MIL)
   3rd MO Infantry, Co. H, (RES) Tekamah, NE
August Moling: (CEN) 1893 State Census, MO Veterans (MIL)
   4th MO Infantry, Co. H, (RES) Jansen, NE
B. Reams: (CEN) 1893 State Census, MO Veterans (MIL)
   8th MO Infantry, Co. H, (RES) Franklin, NE
D. W. Bush: (CEN) 1893 State Census, MO Veterans (MIL)
   11th MO Infantry, Co. H, (RES) Bartley, NE
T. B. Moore: (CEN) 1893 State Census, MO Veterans (MIL)

14th MO Infantry, Co. H, (RES) Union, NE
Joseph Chasteen: (CEN) 1893 State Census, MO Veterans (MIL)
25th MO Infantry, Co. H, (RES) Decatur, NE
J. T. Dobbs: (CEN) 1893 State Census, MO Veterans (MIL)
33rd MO Infantry, Co. H, (RES) Hamilton, NE
Alfred Opelt: (CEN) 1893 State Census, MO Veterans (MIL)
33rd MO Infantry, Co. H, (RES) Brownville, NE
Sidney Shandy: (CEN) 1893 State Census, MO Veterans (MIL)
33rd MO Infantry, Co. H, (RES) Ruskin, NE
C. Wallover: (CEN) 1893 State Census, MO Veterans (MIL)
48th MO Infantry, Co. H, (RES) Oconto, NE
Chas. Thompson: (CEN) 1893 State Census, MO Veterans (MIL)
50th MO Infantry, Co. H, (RES) Bellwood, NE
I. M. Beck: (CEN) 1893 State Census, MO Veterans (MIL)
10th MO Infantry, Co. H, (RES) Wescott, NE
H. S. Smith: (CEN) 1893 State Census, MO Veterans (MIL)
10th MO Infantry, Co. H, (RES) St Paul, NE
D. P. Henry: (CEN) 1893 State Census, MO Veterans (MIL)
11th MO Infantry, Co. H, (RES) Tecumseh, NE
W. U. King: (CEN) 1893 State Census, MO Veterans (MIL)
12th MO Infantry, Co. H, (RES) Spring Ranch, NE
James White: (CEN) 1893 State Census, MO Veterans (MIL)
13th MO Cavalry, Co. H, (RES) Cedar Rapids, NE
W. H. Harrison: (CEN) 1893 State Census, MO Veterans (MIL)
15th MO Artillery, Co. H, (RES) Irvington, NE
John Harris: (CEN) 1893 State Census, MO Veterans (MIL)
1st MO Artillery, Co. H, (RES) Nelson, NE
J. B. Walker: (CEN) 1893 State Census, MO Veterans (MIL)
1st MO Cavalry, Co. H, (RES) Grant, NE
Griffey Vandike: (CEN) 1893 State Census, MO Veterans (MIL)
23th MO Infantry, Co. H, (RES) Huntley, NE
Geo. W. Frazier: (CEN) 1893 State Census, MO Veterans (MIL)
24th MO Infantry, Co. H, (RES) Fairmont, NE
Miles S. Weatherman: (CEN) 1893 State Census, MO Veterans (MIL)
25th MO Infantry, Co. H, (RES) Benkelman, NE
John Fiffer: (CEN) 1893 State Census, MO Veterans (MIL)
29th MO Infantry, Co. H, (RES) Lincoln, NE
Claus Voge: (CEN) 1893 State Census, MO Veterans (MIL)
29th MO Infantry, Co. H, (RES) Germantown, NE
Henry Lenger: (CEN) 1893 State Census, MO Veterans (MIL)
3rd MO Cavalry, Co. H, (RES) Fairbury, NE
T. F. Piersol: (CEN) 1893 State Census, MO Veterans (MIL)
3rd MO Cavalry, Co. H, (RES) La Platte, NE
George W. Swan: (CEN) 1893 State Census, MO Veterans (MIL)
3rd MO Infantry, Co. H, (RES) Alma, NE
S. H. Brown: (CEN) 1893 State Census, MO Veterans (MIL)

  40 & C, Co. H, (RES) Sartoria, NE
James Gray: (CEN) 1893 State Census, MO Veterans (MIL)
  6th MO Cavalry, Co. H, (RES) Champion, NE
R. D. Anderson: (CEN) 1893 State Census, MO Veterans (MIL)
  7th MO Cavalry, Co. H, (RES) De Witt, NE
William Butts: (CEN) 1893 State Census, MO Veterans (MIL)
  7th MO Cavalry, Co. H, (RES) Fremont, NE
Geo. W. Harvey: (CEN) 1893 State Census, MO Veterans (MIL)
  7th MO Cavalry, Co. H, (RES) Cedar Rapids, NE
Levi P. Roy: (CEN) 1893 State Census, MO Veterans (MIL)
  7th MO Cavalry, Co. H, (RES) O'Neill, NE
H. I. Shull: (CEN) 1893 State Census, MO Veterans (MIL)
  7th MO Cavalry, Co. H, (RES) Auburn, NE
J. A. Long: (CEN) 1893 State Census, MO Veterans (MIL)
  7th MO Infantry, Co. H, (RES) Douglas, NE
R. A. Long: (CEN) 1893 State Census, MO Veterans (MIL)
  7th MO Infantry, Co. H, (RES) Douglas, NE
D. H. Johnson: (CEN) 1893 State Census, MO Veterans (MIL)
  8th MO Infantry, Co. H, (RES) Central City, NE
W. H. Stout: (CEN) 1893 State Census, MO Veterans (MIL)
  th MO Infantry, Co. H, (RES) DeWitt, NE
Louie Schmidt: (CEN) 1893 State Census, MO Veterans (MIL)
  2nd MO Infantry, Co. G, (RES) Lincoln, NE
James Goodfellow: (CEN) 1893 State Census, MO Veterans (MIL)
  5th MO Infantry, Co. G, (RES) Cody, NE
C. T. Chaddock: (CEN) 1893 State Census, MO Veterans (MIL)
  6th MO Infantry, Co. G, (RES) Beatrice, NE
James Crawford: (CEN) 1893 State Census, MO Veterans (MIL)
  18th MO Infantry, Co. G, (RES) Kowanda, NE
A. J. Scott: (CEN) 1893 State Census, MO Veterans (MIL)
  27th MO Infantry, Co. G, (RES) Lebanon, NE
William Smith: (CEN) 1893 State Census, MO Veterans (MIL)
  33rd MO Infantry, Co. G, (RES) Filley, NE
Joel Wickham: (CEN) 1893 State Census, MO Veterans (MIL)
  43rd MO Infantry, Co. G, (RES) Wilber, NE
Michael Killean: (CEN) 1893 State Census, MO Veterans (MIL)
  10th MO Infantry, Co. G, (RES) Fairbury, NE
T. B. Johnson: (CEN) 1893 State Census, MO Veterans (MIL)
  11th MO Infantry, Co. G, (RES) Aurora, NE
J. H. Argabright: (CEN) 1893 State Census, MO Veterans (MIL)
  12th MO Cavalry, Co. G, (RES) Nemaha, NE
David Campbell: (CEN) 1893 State Census, MO Veterans (MIL)
  12th MO Cavalry, Co. G, (RES) Auburn, NE
Willis Webb: (CEN) 1893 State Census, MO Veterans (MIL)
  15th MO Cavalry, Co. G, (RES) Wymore, NE
J. A. Castile: (CEN) 1893 State Census, MO Veterans (MIL)

        1st MO Cavalry, Co. G, (RES) Orleans, NE
E. J. Smith: (CEN) 1893 State Census, MO Veterans (MIL)
        1st MO Cavalry, Co. G, (RES) Edgar, NE
John R. Wright: (CEN) 1893 State Census, MO Veterans (MIL)
        1st MO Cavalry, Co. G, (RES) St Edward, NE
Levi Clark: (CEN) 1893 State Census, MO Veterans (MIL)
        25th MO Vol, Co. G, (RES) Rushville, NE
B. Parker: (CEN) 1893 State Census, MO Veterans (MIL)
        29th MO Infantry, Co. G, (RES) Smartville, NE
James Ireland: (CEN) 1893 State Census, MO Veterans (MIL)
        2nd MO Cavalry, Co. G, (RES) Du Bois, NE
C. H. Bishop: (CEN) 1893 State Census, MO Veterans (MIL)
        32th MO Infantry, Co. G, (RES) Kearney, NE
John R. Worchley: (CEN) 1893 State Census, MO Veterans (MIL)
        38th MO Infantry, Co. G, (RES) North Platte, NE
Simon Long: (CEN) 1893 State Census, MO Veterans (MIL)
        3rd MO Cavalry, Co. G, (RES) Balir, NE
T. W. Johnson: (CEN) 1893 State Census, MO Veterans (MIL)
        42th MO Infantry, Co. G, (RES) Ord, NE
Jacob McAdam: (CEN) 1893 State Census, MO Veterans (MIL)
        43th MO Infantry, Co. G, (RES) Mullen, NE
I. M. Kingsolver: (CEN) 1893 State Census, MO Veterans (MIL)
        4th MO Cavalry, Co. G, (RES) Gresham, NE
Robert S. Frimple: (CEN) 1893 State Census, MO Veterans (MIL)
        51th MO Infantry, Co. G, (RES) Mullen, NE
W. J. Turner: (CEN) 1893 State Census, MO Veterans (MIL)
        5th MO Cavalry, Co. G, (RES) Red Cloud, NE
J. J. Rice: (CEN) 1893 State Census, MO Veterans (MIL)
        7th MO Cavalry, Co. G, (RES) Beatrice, NE
B. P. Munns: (CEN) 1893 State Census, MO Veterans (MIL)
        7th MO Infantry, Co. G, (RES) David City, NE
Wm. G. Ston: (CEN) 1893 State Census, MO Veterans (MIL)
        S Mth MO Cavalry, Co. G, (RES) Deweese, NE
C. W. Whitney: (CEN) 1893 State Census, MO Veterans (MIL)
        30th MO Infantry, Co. F. and C, (RES) Republican City, NE
Leonard Dinnell: (CEN) 1893 State Census, MO Veterans (MIL)
        3rd MO Infantry, Co. F, (RES) Galena, NE
N. A. Colman: (CEN) 1893 State Census, MO Veterans (MIL)
        6th MO Infantry, Co. F, (RES) London, NE
J. M. Wiggins: (CEN) 1893 State Census, MO Veterans (MIL)
        8th MO Infantry, Co. F, (RES) Gibbon, NE
John Harn: (CEN) 1893 State Census, MO Veterans (MIL)
        10th MO Infantry, Co. F, (RES) Tekamah, NE
J. Taylor: (CEN) 1893 State Census, MO Veterans (MIL)
        10th MO Infantry, Co. F, (RES) Chase, NE
Henry Tiaden: (CEN) 1893 State Census, MO Veterans (MIL)

11th MO Infantry, Co. F, (RES) Duncan, NE
James Rodgers: (CEN) 1893 State Census, MO Veterans (MIL)
12th MO Infantry, Co. F, (RES) Precept, NE
Robert Scott: (CEN) 1893 State Census, MO Veterans (MIL)
12th MO Infantry, Co. F, (RES) Precept, NE
H. D. Findley: (CEN) 1893 State Census, MO Veterans (MIL)
25th MO Infantry, Co. F, (RES) Imperial, NE
L. S. Flint: (CEN) 1893 State Census, MO Veterans (MIL)
43rd MO Infantry, Co. F, (RES) Hudson, NE
Christ Schoenthal: (CEN) 1893 State Census, MO Veterans (MIL)
1st Engineers, Co. F, (RES) Bennet, NE
Thos Keown: (CEN) 1893 State Census, MO Veterans (MIL)
12th MO Cavalry, Co. F, (RES) Hay Springs, NE
Jonathan B. Mattley: (CEN) 1893 State Census, MO Veterans (MIL)
12th MO Cavalry, Co. F, (RES) Burwell, NE
C. C. Scott: (CEN) 1893 State Census, MO Veterans (MIL)
12th MO Cavalry, Co. F, (RES) Oxford, NE
Marion Pennington: (CEN) 1893 State Census, MO Veterans (MIL)
13th MO Infantry, Co. F, (RES) Bertrand, NE
Benjamin Owen: (CEN) 1893 State Census, MO Veterans (MIL)
14th MO Cavalry, Co. F, (RES) Mason City, NE
J. W. Gennug: (CEN) 1893 State Census, MO Veterans (MIL)
14th MO Infantry, Co. F, (RES) Petersburg, NE
Fred Haseloh: (CEN) 1893 State Census, MO Veterans (MIL)
15th MO Infantry, Co. F, (RES) Harvard, NE
Henry Miller: (CEN) 1893 State Census, MO Veterans (MIL)
15th MO Infantry, Co. F, (RES) Wahoo, NE
David Potarf: (CEN) 1893 State Census, MO Veterans (MIL)
18th MO Infantry, Co. F, (RES) Angus, NE
W. P. Allen: (CEN) 1893 State Census, MO Veterans (MIL)
21th MO Infantry, Co. F, (RES) Homer, NE
William Scott: (CEN) 1893 State Census, MO Veterans (MIL)
21th MO Infantry, Co. F, (RES) Elba, NE
F. A. Whittemore: (CEN) 1893 State Census, MO Veterans (MIL)
21th MO Infantry, Co. F, (RES) Long Pine, NE
Elihu M. Raney: (CEN) 1893 State Census, MO Veterans (MIL)
25th MO Infantry, Co. F, (RES) Benkelman, NE
E. A. Fletcher: (CEN) 1893 State Census, MO Veterans (MIL)
2nd MO Cavalry, Co. F, (RES) Franklin, NE
Joseph Hampton: (CEN) 1893 State Census, MO Veterans (MIL)
2nd MO Cavalry, Co. F, (RES) Alma, NE
John W. Guyton: (CEN) 1893 State Census, MO Veterans (MIL)
31th MO Infantry, Co. F, (RES) Johnstown, NE
John Patterson: (CEN) 1893 State Census, MO Veterans (MIL)
3rd MO Cavalry, Co. F, (RES) Ayr, NE
C. W. Woff: (CEN) 1893 State Census, MO Veterans (MIL)

3rd MO Cavalry, Co. F, (RES) Burchard, NE
W. H. Hart: (CEN) 1893 State Census, MO Veterans (MIL)
3rd MO Infantry, Co. F, (RES) Alexandria, NE
I. P. Applegate: (CEN) 1893 State Census, MO Veterans (MIL)
43rd MO Infantry, Co. F, (RES) Ong, NE
James McGowan: (CEN) 1893 State Census, MO Veterans (MIL)
43th MO Infantry, Co. F, (RES) Surprise, NE
R. O. Terry: (CEN) 1893 State Census, MO Veterans (MIL)
43th MO Infantry, Co. F, (RES) Elsie, NE
William Spradling: (CEN) 1893 State Census, MO Veterans (MIL)
49th MO Infantry, Co. F, (RES) Auburn, NE
John L. Cox: (CEN) 1893 State Census, MO Veterans (MIL)
50th MO Infantry, Co. F, (RES) Cedar Rapids, NE
Benjamin F. Culp: (CEN) 1893 State Census, MO Veterans (MIL)
50th MO Infantry, Co. F, (RES) Pleasant Dale, NE
John S. Gearhard: (CEN) 1893 State Census, MO Veterans (MIL)
51th MO Infantry, Co. F, (RES) Blair, NE
Amos Spencer: (CEN) 1893 State Census, MO Veterans (MIL)
51th MO Infantry, Co. F, (RES) Spiker, NE
S. R. Gillaspie: (CEN) 1893 State Census, MO Veterans (MIL)
5th MO Cavalry, Co. F, (RES) Powell, NE
Manley J. Porter: (CEN) 1893 State Census, MO Veterans (MIL)
5th MO Cavalry, Co. F, (RES) Ansley, NE
Albert B. Trimble: (CEN) 1893 State Census, MO Veterans (MIL)
5th MO Cavalry, Co. F, (RES) Alma, NE
T. Chevront: (CEN) 1893 State Census, MO Veterans (MIL)
7th MO S. M., Co. F, (RES) Greenwood, NE
Lackey Devanney: (CEN) 1893 State Census, MO Veterans (MIL)
8th MO Infantry, Co. F, (RES) Bellwood, NE
Christopher Schroeder: (CEN) 1893 State Census, MO Veterans (MIL)
German Reg., Co. F, (RES) Kiowa, NE
W. A. Powell: (CEN) 1893 State Census, MO Veterans (MIL)
59th MO S. M., Co. F, (RES) Grafton, NE
Henry G. Rogers: (CEN) 1893 State Census, MO Veterans (MIL)
Missouri Guard, Co. F, (RES) Lebanon, NE
Chas. Smeed: (CEN) 1893 State Census, MO Veterans (MIL)
23rd MO Infantry, Co. E. and H, (RES) Lincoln, NE
A. H. Boehe: (CEN) 1893 State Census, MO Veterans (MIL)
2nd MO Infantry, Co. E, (RES) Omaha, NE
Fred Goemann: (CEN) 1893 State Census, MO Veterans (MIL)
5th MO Infantry, Co. E, (RES) Tecumseh, NE
Thomas Corr: (CEN) 1893 State Census, MO Veterans (MIL)
10th MO Infantry, Co. E, (RES) Staplehurst, NE
J. E. Wilson: (CEN) 1893 State Census, MO Veterans (MIL)
11th MO Infantry, Co. E, (RES) Indianola, NE
J. B. Grotts: (CEN) 1893 State Census, MO Veterans (MIL)

18th MO Infantry, Co. E, (RES) Diller, NE
W. H. Smith: (CEN) 1893 State Census, MO Veterans (MIL)
21st MO Infantry, Co. E, (RES) Indianola, NE
David Wertz: (CEN) 1893 State Census, MO Veterans (MIL)
38th MO Infantry, Co. E, (RES) Burwell, NE
Eli Smith: (CEN) 1893 State Census, MO Veterans (MIL)
39th MO Infantry, Co. E, (RES) Oxford, NE
Wm. Hughes: (CEN) 1893 State Census, MO Veterans (MIL)
1st Engineers, Co. E, (RES) Beatrice, NE
Wm. E. V. B. Moore: (CEN) 1893 State Census, MO Veterans (MIL)
18th MO Infantry, Co. E, (RES) Odessa, NE
James W. Pharris: (CEN) 1893 State Census, MO Veterans (MIL)
18th MO Infantry, Co. E, (RES) Superior, NE
Geo. W. Nelson: (CEN) 1893 State Census, MO Veterans (MIL)
1st MO Cavalry, Co. E, (RES) David City, NE
Jesse Elam: (CEN) 1893 State Census, MO Veterans (MIL)
1st S. S, Co. E, (RES) Blaineville, NE
David Oldfather: (CEN) 1893 State Census, MO Veterans (MIL)
21th MO Infantry, Co. E, (RES) Lexington, NE
John G. Daniels: (CEN) 1893 State Census, MO Veterans (MIL)
23th MO Infantry, Co. E, (RES) Adaton, NE
William Low: (CEN) 1893 State Census, MO Veterans (MIL)
23th MO Infantry, Co. E, (RES) Norfolk, NE
James Salmon: (CEN) 1893 State Census, MO Veterans (MIL)
23th MO Infantry, Co. E, (RES) Ragan, NE
W. H. Lewis: (CEN) 1893 State Census, MO Veterans (MIL)
25th MO Infantry, Co. E, (RES) Omaha, NE
Thomas Birmingham: (CEN) 1893 State Census, MO Veterans (MIL)
33th MO Infantry, Co. E, (RES) Hubbell, NE
A. S. Hurley: (CEN) 1893 State Census, MO Veterans (MIL)
42th MO Infantry, Co. E, (RES) Kearney, NE
W. G. Welden: (CEN) 1893 State Census, MO Veterans (MIL)
43th MO Infantry, Co. E, (RES) Lexington, NE
Geo. Engleman: (CEN) 1893 State Census, MO Veterans (MIL)
45th MO Infantry, Co. E, (RES) Wood River, NE
Fred Vete: (CEN) 1893 State Census, MO Veterans (MIL)
49th MO Infantry, Co. E, (RES) Fairbury, NE
Bencel Karel: (CEN) 1893 State Census, MO Veterans (MIL)
4th MO Infantry, Co. E, (RES) Ravenna, NE
Jacob Hoye: (CEN) 1893 State Census, MO Veterans (MIL)
50th MO Cavalry, Co. E, (RES) Edgar, NE
Charles Shurts: (CEN) 1893 State Census, MO Veterans (MIL)
5th MO S. M., Co. E, (RES) Brownville, NE
J. C. Gaddis: (CEN) 1893 State Census, MO Veterans (MIL)
6th MO Infantry, Co. E, (RES) Orleans, NE
Albert Armstrong: (CEN) 1893 State Census, MO Veterans (MIL)

7th MO Cavalry, Co. E, (RES) Syracuse, NE
William A. Patterson: (CEN) 1893 State Census, MO Veterans (MIL)
7th MO Cavalry, Co. E, (RES) Platte Centre, NE
J. F. Pointer: (CEN) 1893 State Census, MO Veterans (MIL)
7th MO Cavalry, Co. E, (RES) Palmer, NE
John Wameke: (CEN) 1893 State Census, MO Veterans (MIL)
1st MO Infantry, Co. D, (RES) Cramer, NE
William Dimmell: (CEN) 1893 State Census, MO Veterans (MIL)
5th MO Infantry, Co. D, (RES) Catharine, NE
John Hansberry: (CEN) 1893 State Census, MO Veterans (MIL)
5th MO Infantry, Co. D, (RES) Blue Springs, NE
H. D. King: (CEN) 1893 State Census, MO Veterans (MIL)
5th MO Infantry, Co. D, (RES) Peru, NE
J. H. Hungate: (CEN) 1893 State Census, MO Veterans (MIL)
11th MO Infantry, Co. D, (RES) Omaha, NE
Patrick O'Hara: (CEN) 1893 State Census, MO Veterans (MIL)
12th MO Infantry, Co. D, (RES) Alliston, NE
C. W. Bline: (CEN) 1893 State Census, MO Veterans (MIL)
21st MO Infantry, Co. D, (RES) La Platte, NE
W. Sweeten: (CEN) 1893 State Census, MO Veterans (MIL)
23rd MO Infantry, Co. D, (RES) Omaha, NE
Fred Wey: (CEN) 1893 State Census, MO Veterans (MIL)
25th MO Infantry, Co. D, (RES) Omaha, NE
Nathaniel Zink: (CEN) 1893 State Census, MO Veterans (MIL)
35th MO Infantry, Co. D, (RES) Stuart, NE
E. Haney: (CEN) 1893 State Census, MO Veterans (MIL)
39th MO Infantry, Co. D, (RES) Omaha, NE
James L. Underwood: (CEN) 1893 State Census, MO Veterans (MIL)
44th MO Infantry, Co. D, (RES) Alliance, NE
Walker Jones: (CEN) 1893 State Census, MO Veterans (MIL)
60th MO Infantry, Co. D, (RES) Union, NE
Herman Tebbins: (CEN) 1893 State Census, MO Veterans (MIL)
1st Engineers, Co. D, (RES) Omaha, NE
W. T. McKnight: (CEN) 1893 State Census, MO Veterans (MIL)
11th MO Infantry, Co. D, (RES) Grafton, NE
A. C. Howerton: (CEN) 1893 State Census, MO Veterans (MIL)
1st MO Cavalry, Co. D, (RES) Miller, NE
S. J. McClure: (CEN) 1893 State Census, MO Veterans (MIL)
1st MO Cavalry, Co. D, (RES) Madrid, NE
Hugh Aird: (CEN) 1893 State Census, MO Veterans (MIL)
1st MO Infantry, Co. D, (RES) Nebraska City, NE
Thos H. Doyle: (CEN) 1893 State Census, MO Veterans (MIL)
1st MO Infantry, Co. D, (RES) Omaha, NE
John Westerhoff: (CEN) 1893 State Census, MO Veterans (MIL)
2 S. M, Co. D, (RES) Germantown, NE
E. Triplett: (CEN) 1893 State Census, MO Veterans (MIL)

27th MO Cavalry, Co. D, (RES) Cook, NE
Samuel J. Atkinson: (CEN) 1893 State Census, MO Veterans (MIL)
2nd MO Cavalry, Co. D, (RES) Fairmont, NE
G. W. Kelrey: (CEN) 1893 State Census, MO Veterans (MIL)
2nd MO Cavalry, Co. D, (RES) Litchfield, NE
Sanford Hill: (CEN) 1893 State Census, MO Veterans (MIL)
35th MO Infantry, Co. D, (RES) Bodarc, NE
C. T. Daniels: (CEN) 1893 State Census, MO Veterans (MIL)
3rd MO Cavalry, Co. D, (RES) Ansley, NE
J. W. Gladwish: (CEN) 1893 State Census, MO Veterans (MIL)
3rd MO Infantry, Co. D, (RES) Seward, NE
T. W. Kreinheder: (CEN) 1893 State Census, MO Veterans (MIL)
3rd MO Infantry, Co. D, (RES) Hastings, NE
John W. Rice: (CEN) 1893 State Census, MO Veterans (MIL)
42th MO Infantry, Co. D, (RES) Ord, NE
Jesse Brown: (CEN) 1893 State Census, MO Veterans (MIL)
43th MO Infantry, Co. D, (RES) Hebron, NE
John W. Hixon: (CEN) 1893 State Census, MO Veterans (MIL)
43th MO Infantry, Co. D, (RES) Crawford, NE
M. M. Staples: (CEN) 1893 State Census, MO Veterans (MIL)
4th MO Calvary, Co. D, (RES) Table Rock, NE
Geo. Hodkins: (CEN) 1893 State Census, MO Veterans (MIL)
5 M. S. M, Co. D, (RES) Nemaha, NE
E. M. Baker: (CEN) 1893 State Census, MO Veterans (MIL)
5th MO Cavalry, Co. D, (RES) Auburn, NE
Amos R. Bradley: (CEN) 1893 State Census, MO Veterans (MIL)
5th MO Cavalry, Co. D, (RES) Alma, NE
Henry C. Carman: (CEN) 1893 State Census, MO Veterans (MIL)
5th MO Cavalry, Co. D, (RES) Cook, NE
F. H. D. Hunt: (CEN) 1893 State Census, MO Veterans (MIL)
5th MO Cavalry, Co. D, (RES) St. Dervin, NE
Geo. W. Neil: (CEN) 1893 State Census, MO Veterans (MIL)
5th MO Cavalry, Co. D, (RES) Nemaha, NE
Wm. C. Pavey: (CEN) 1893 State Census, MO Veterans (MIL)
5th MO Cavalry, Co. D, (RES) Red Cloud, NE
John F. Wolf: (CEN) 1893 State Census, MO Veterans (MIL)
5th MO Cavalry, Co. D, (RES) Wilson, NE
J. M. Bondurant: (CEN) 1893 State Census, MO Veterans (MIL)
5th MO Infantry, Co. D, (RES) Norfolk, NE
E. J. Randall: (CEN) 1893 State Census, MO Veterans (MIL)
5th MO Infantry, Co. D, (RES) Fairfield, NE
W. J. Farris: (CEN) 1893 State Census, MO Veterans (MIL)
6th MO Infantry, Co. D, (RES) Albion, NE
Geo. W. Kelly: (CEN) 1893 State Census, MO Veterans (MIL)
8th MO Infantry, Co. D, (RES) Tryon, NE
L. S. Hayden: (CEN) 1893 State Census, MO Veterans (MIL)

    9th MO Cavalry, Co. D, (RES) Indianola, NE
Theodore Moser: (CEN) 1893 State Census, MO Veterans (MIL)
    th MO Infantry, Co. D, (RES) Madison, NE
N. Roberts: (CEN) 1893 State Census, MO Veterans (MIL)
    2nd MO Infantry, Co. C, (RES) Liberty, NE
B. B. Case: (CEN) 1893 State Census, MO Veterans (MIL)
    3rd MO Infantry, Co. C, (RES) Holdrege, NE
D. H. Mayne: (CEN) 1893 State Census, MO Veterans (MIL)
    7th MO Infantry, Co. C, (RES) Omaha, NE
W. S. Hamilton: (CEN) 1893 State Census, MO Veterans (MIL)
    21st MO Infantry, Co. C, (RES) McCook, NE
G. C. Hopkins: (CEN) 1893 State Census, MO Veterans (MIL)
    35th MO Infantry, Co. C, (RES) Omaha, NE
J. W. Dans: (CEN) 1893 State Census, MO Veterans (MIL)
    42nd MO Infantry, Co. C, (RES) Curtis, NE
Chas. Roberts: (CEN) 1893 State Census, MO Veterans (MIL)
    42nd MO Infantry, Co. C, (RES) College View, NE
James Smithurst: (CEN) 1893 State Census, MO Veterans (MIL)
    43rd MO Infantry, Co. C, (RES) Odell, NE
R. A. Maloney: (CEN) 1893 State Census, MO Veterans (MIL)
    1st Engineers, Co. C, (RES) Madison, NE
Robt Statton: (CEN) 1893 State Census, MO Veterans (MIL)
    10th MO Infantry, Co. C, (RES) Kearney, NE
V. Bunchelberger: (CEN) 1893 State Census, MO Veterans (MIL)
    11th MO Cavalry, Co. C, (RES) Omaha, NE
J. M. Parker: (CEN) 1893 State Census, MO Veterans (MIL)
    12th MO Cavalry, Co. C, (RES) South Omaha, NE
J. C. Johnson: (CEN) 1893 State Census, MO Veterans (MIL)
    13th MO Cavalry, Co. C, (RES) Chappell, NE
W. H. Jones: (CEN) 1893 State Census, MO Veterans (MIL)
    1st Engineer, Co. C, (RES) Morse Bluff, NE
W. S. Peery: (CEN) 1893 State Census, MO Veterans (MIL)
    1st MO Cavalry, Co. C, (RES) Glenrock, NE
Leo Braun: (CEN) 1893 State Census, MO Veterans (MIL)
    1st MO Infantry, Co. C, (RES) Battle Creek, NE
J. A. Rogers: (CEN) 1893 State Census, MO Veterans (MIL)
    2 M. S. Mth MO Vol, Co. C, (RES) Nelson, NE
C. A. St John: (CEN) 1893 State Census, MO Veterans (MIL)
    20th MO Infantry, Co. C, (RES) Dorch, NE
O. J. Steele: (CEN) 1893 State Census, MO Veterans (MIL)
    211th MO Infantry, Co. C, (RES) Stoddard, NE
Elijah Archer: (CEN) 1893 State Census, MO Veterans (MIL)
    29th MO Infantry, Co. C, (RES) Geneva, NE
Henry Laup: (CEN) 1893 State Census, MO Veterans (MIL)
    2nd MO Artillery, Co. C, (RES) Upland, NE
Jackson Winn: (CEN) 1893 State Census, MO Veterans (MIL)

    2nd MO S. M., Co. C, (RES) Arapahoe, NE
John Wilson: (CEN) 1893 State Census, MO Veterans (MIL)
    30th MO Infantry, Co. C, (RES) Clarks, NE
W. H. Lorance: (CEN) 1893 State Census, MO Veterans (MIL)
    35th MO Vol, Co. C, (RES) Auburn, NE
S. A. Wright: (CEN) 1893 State Census, MO Veterans (MIL)
    43th MO Infantry, Co. C, (RES) St Edward, NE
T. F. Heironymus: (CEN) 1893 State Census, MO Veterans (MIL)
    45th MO Infantry, Co. C, (RES) Hebron, NE
Henry Massman: (CEN) 1893 State Census, MO Veterans (MIL)
    49th MO Infantry, Co. C, (RES) Battle Creek, NE
Edwin M. Bryant: (CEN) 1893 State Census, MO Veterans (MIL)
    4th MO Cavalry, Co. C, (RES) Fairbury, NE
E. J. Gilliand: (CEN) 1893 State Census, MO Veterans (MIL)
    56 Milli, Co. C, (RES) Auburn, NE
D. Holsten: (CEN) 1893 State Census, MO Veterans (MIL)
    5th MO Cavalry, Co. C, (RES) Scribner, NE
John W. Horn: (CEN) 1893 State Census, MO Veterans (MIL)
    5th MO Cavalry, Co. C, (RES) Brock, NE
S. Patten: (CEN) 1893 State Census, MO Veterans (MIL)
    5th MO Infantry, Co. C, (RES) Nebraska City, NE
Geo. M. Parks: (CEN) 1893 State Census, MO Veterans (MIL)
    68th MO Infantry, Co. C, (RES) Beatrice, NE
Thomas Winchester: (CEN) 1893 State Census, MO Veterans (MIL)
    79th MO Cavalry, Co. C, (RES) Max, NE
S. B. Loughbridge: (CEN) 1893 State Census, MO Veterans (MIL)
    7th MO Cavalry, Co. C, (RES) Lincoln, NE
Christopher Vesper: (CEN) 1893 State Census, MO Veterans (MIL)
    7th MO Cavalry, Co. C, (RES) Ord, NE
Orien McColery: (CEN) 1893 State Census, MO Veterans (MIL)
    8th MO Infantry, Co. C, (RES) Madison, NE
J. B. Benson: (CEN) 1893 State Census, MO Veterans (MIL)
    8th MO S. M., Co. C, (RES) Elwood, NE
C. W. Tullis: (CEN) 1893 State Census, MO Veterans (MIL)
    7th MO Cavalry, Co. C, (RES) Mineola, NE
A. S. Peirce: (CEN) 1893 State Census, MO Veterans (MIL)
    7th MO Infantry, Co. C, (RES) Hastings, NE
J. M. Skiles: (CEN) 1893 State Census, MO Veterans (MIL)
    Co. C, (RES) Holdrege, NE
Leonard Stuckert: (CEN) 1893 State Census, MO Veterans (MIL)
    1st MO Infantry, Co. B, (RES) Mason City, NE
J. L. McGer: (CEN) 1893 State Census, MO Veterans (MIL)
    3rd MO Infantry, Co. B, (RES) Beatrice, NE
Otto Walkenhaust: (CEN) 1893 State Census, MO Veterans (MIL)
    10th MO Infantry, Co. B, (RES) Alexandria, NE
T. W. Baird: (CEN) 1893 State Census, MO Veterans (MIL)

21st MO Infantry, Co. B, (RES) Steel City, NE
M. D. Bush: (CEN) 1893 State Census, MO Veterans (MIL)
35th MO Infantry, Co. B, (RES) Bower, NE
Reuben Dutcher: (CEN) 1893 State Census, MO Veterans (MIL)
43rd MO Infantry, Co. B, (RES) Kent, NE
Geo. W. Dewitt: (CEN) 1893 State Census, MO Veterans (MIL)
69th MO Infantry, Co. B, (RES) Sweetwater, NE
C. C. Boster: (CEN) 1893 State Census, MO Veterans (MIL)
1st Engineers, Co. B, (RES) Wayne, NE
Tom H. Leach: (CEN) 1893 State Census, MO Veterans (MIL)
10th MO Cavalry, Co. B, (RES) Plattsmouth, NE
Hiram L. Sweeney: (CEN) 1893 State Census, MO Veterans (MIL)
10th MO Infantry, Co. B, (RES) Champion, NE
W. H. Woods: (CEN) 1893 State Census, MO Veterans (MIL)
10th MO Infantry, Co. B, (RES) Ft Calhoun, NE
Calwin McGums: (CEN) 1893 State Census, MO Veterans (MIL)
11th MO Cavalry, Co. B, (RES) Blue Springs, NE
Wm. Pittman: (CEN) 1893 State Census, MO Veterans (MIL)
11th MO Cavalry, Co. B, (RES) North Platte, NE
R. A. Turner: (CEN) 1893 State Census, MO Veterans (MIL)
11th MO Cavalry, Co. B, (RES) Red Cloud, NE
J. C. Berwick: (CEN) 1893 State Census, MO Veterans (MIL)
11th MO Infantry, Co. B, (RES) Kearney, NE
Duncan McCall: (CEN) 1893 State Census, MO Veterans (MIL)
11th MO Infantry, Co. B, (RES) Republican Cy, NE
J. W. Wilson: (CEN) 1893 State Census, MO Veterans (MIL)
11th MO Infantry, Co. B, (RES) Kearney, NE
Franklin M. Betteys: (CEN) 1893 State Census, MO Veterans (MIL)
12th MO Cavalry, Co. B, (RES) Hastings, NE
W. H. Goddard: (CEN) 1893 State Census, MO Veterans (MIL)
13th MO Cavalry, Co. B, (RES) Imperial, NE
H. Hl Shapers: (CEN) 1893 State Census, MO Veterans (MIL)
13th MO Infantry, Co. B, (RES) Nebraska City, NE
S. G. Scarlet: (CEN) 1893 State Census, MO Veterans (MIL)
13th MO Vol, Co. B, (RES) Harbine, NE
Gottleib Neumister: (CEN) 1893 State Census, MO Veterans (MIL)
14th MO Infantry, Co. B, (RES) Avoca, NE
Edward Clair: (CEN) 1893 State Census, MO Veterans (MIL)
18th MO Infantry, Co. B, (RES) Fullerton, NE
D. Jones: (CEN) 1893 State Census, MO Veterans (MIL)
1st Engineer, Co. B, (RES) Cozad, NE
T. Luninghohner: (CEN) 1893 State Census, MO Veterans (MIL)
1st MO Artillery, Co. B, (RES) Admah, NE
James Bainter: (CEN) 1893 State Census, MO Veterans (MIL)
1st MO Cavalry, Co. B, (RES) Spring Ranch, NE
J. M. Kitchel: (CEN) 1893 State Census, MO Veterans (MIL)

  1st MO Cavalry, Co. B, (RES) Ragan, NE
J. A. Smith: (CEN) 1893 State Census, MO Veterans (MIL)
  1st MO Cavalry, Co. B, (RES) Beatrice, NE
W. W. Weaver: (CEN) 1893 State Census, MO Veterans (MIL)
  1st MO Cavalry, Co. B, (RES) Burchard, NE
Jacob A. Wolfe: (CEN) 1893 State Census, MO Veterans (MIL)
  1st MO Infantry, Co. B, (RES) North Bend, NE
N. G. Keoun: (CEN) 1893 State Census, MO Veterans (MIL)
  21th MO Infantry, Co. B, (RES) Ord, NE
A. J. Constance: (CEN) 1893 State Census, MO Veterans (MIL)
  23th MO Infantry, Co. B, (RES) Arcadia, NE
B. F. Leslie: (CEN) 1893 State Census, MO Veterans (MIL)
  23th MO Infantry, Co. B, (RES) Nemaha, NE
Marshall Tolle: (CEN) 1893 State Census, MO Veterans (MIL)
  23th MO Infantry, Co. B, (RES) Fairfield, NE
Chas. Zimmerman: (CEN) 1893 State Census, MO Veterans (MIL)
  29th MO Infantry, Co. B, (RES) Henderson, NE
James Williams: (CEN) 1893 State Census, MO Veterans (MIL)
  33th MO Infantry, Co. B, (RES) Hyannis, NE
John Finch: (CEN) 1893 State Census, MO Veterans (MIL)
  35th MO Infantry, Co. B, (RES) York, NE
Barney Jones: (CEN) 1893 State Census, MO Veterans (MIL)
  35th MO Infantry, Co. B, (RES) Inez, NE
Charles H. Betts: (CEN) 1893 State Census, MO Veterans (MIL)
  3rd MO Cavalry, Co. B, (RES) Valentine, NE
M. G. Merrell: (CEN) 1893 State Census, MO Veterans (MIL)
  3rd MO Cavalry, Co. B, (RES) Tekamah, NE
Dennis Gaughan: (CEN) 1893 State Census, MO Veterans (MIL)
  4th MO Cavalry, Co. B, (RES) Omaha, NE
Daniel Johnson: (CEN) 1893 State Census, MO Veterans (MIL)
  4th MO Cavalry, Co. B, (RES) Pleasanton, NE
C. G. Lutz: (CEN) 1893 State Census, MO Veterans (MIL)
  4th MO Cavalry, Co. B, (RES) Papillion, NE
Adolph Ruschick: (CEN) 1893 State Census, MO Veterans (MIL)
  4th MO S. M., Co. B, (RES) McCook, NE
David H. Morton: (CEN) 1893 State Census, MO Veterans (MIL)
  5th MO Cavalry, Co. B, (RES) Nemaha, NE
Adolph Hilpert: (CEN) 1893 State Census, MO Veterans (MIL)
  5th MO Infantry, Co. B, (RES) Phillips, NE
Joseph N. Allen: (CEN) 1893 State Census, MO Veterans (MIL)
  6th MO S. M., Co. B, (RES) Mt Clare, NE
J. L. Frakes: (CEN) 1893 State Census, MO Veterans (MIL)
  9th MO Infantry, Co. B, (RES) Cornell, NE
Joshua Tate: (CEN) 1893 State Census, MO Veterans (MIL)
  Mo State Militia, Co. B, (RES) Nora, NE
W. F. Hutton: (CEN) 1893 State Census, MO Veterans (MIL)

S M, Co. B, (RES) Glenrock, NE
Geo. Currie: (CEN) 1893 State Census, MO Veterans (MIL)
, Co. Â, (RES) Hoag, NE
Levi F. Perkins: (CEN) 1893 State Census, MO Veterans (MIL)
Co. A, (RES) Omaha, NE
James Rodgers: (CEN) 1893 State Census, MO Veterans (MIL)
1st MO Infantry, Co. A, (RES) Stamford, NE
Wm. Murphy: (CEN) 1893 State Census, MO Veterans (MIL)
2nd MO Infantry, Co. A, (RES) Lebanon, NE
Charles E. Sutton: (CEN) 1893 State Census, MO Veterans (MIL)
2nd MO Infantry, Co. A, (RES) Roten, NE
W. M. Snyder: (CEN) 1893 State Census, MO Veterans (MIL)
10th MO Infantry, Co. A, (RES) Tecumseh, NE
B. T. Garrison: (CEN) 1893 State Census, MO Veterans (MIL)
12th MO Infantry, Co. A, (RES) Cambridge, NE
Henry Lottridge: (CEN) 1893 State Census, MO Veterans (MIL)
18th MO Infantry, Co. A, (RES) Hershey, NE
John Ledoras: (CEN) 1893 State Census, MO Veterans (MIL)
31st MO Infantry, Co. A, (RES) Brownville, NE
W. A. Bain: (CEN) 1893 State Census, MO Veterans (MIL)
44th MO Infantry, Co. A, (RES) Elk Creek, NE
E. F. Teele: (CEN) 1893 State Census, MO Veterans (MIL)
1st Engineers, Co. A, (RES) Fremont, NE
John Earsom: (CEN) 1893 State Census, MO Veterans (MIL)
1st MO Prov. Militia, Co. A, (RES) Bloomington, NE
Ashley Peters: (CEN) 1893 State Census, MO Veterans (MIL)
11th MO Cavalry, Co. A, (RES) North Platte, NE
John M. McCord: (CEN) 1893 State Census, MO Veterans (MIL)
13th MO Cavalry, Co. A, (RES) Red Cloud, NE
W. F. McAdams: (CEN) 1893 State Census, MO Veterans (MIL)
143th MO Infantry, Co. A, (RES) Davenport, NE
J. R. Larimer: (CEN) 1893 State Census, MO Veterans (MIL)
14th MO Infantry, Co. A, (RES) Kearney, NE
J. D. Hamilton: (CEN) 1893 State Census, MO Veterans (MIL)
18th MO Infantry, Co. A, (RES) Geneva, NE
Charles Howard: (CEN) 1893 State Census, MO Veterans (MIL)
1st Eng, Co. A, (RES) Clarks, NE
Edward Wiedeberg: (CEN) 1893 State Census, MO Veterans (MIL)
1st MO Artillery, Co. A, (RES) Weeping Wtr, NE
John L. Pace: (CEN) 1893 State Census, MO Veterans (MIL)
1st MO Cavalry, Co. A, (RES) Lincoln, NE
Aug Steinbuck: (CEN) 1893 State Census, MO Veterans (MIL)
1st MO Infantry, Co. A, (RES) Glenville, NE
A. J. B. Fairbain: (CEN) 1893 State Census, MO Veterans (MIL)
2 State Troops, Co. A, (RES) Rockville, NE
J. Farley: (CEN) 1893 State Census, MO Veterans (MIL)

  23th MO Infantry, Co. A, (RES) Nebraska City, NE
James H. Gyles: (CEN) 1893 State Census, MO Veterans (MIL)
  25th MO Artillery, Co. A, (RES) Quick, NE
Samuel M. Bassett: (CEN) 1893 State Census, MO Veterans (MIL)
  26th MO Infantry, Co. A, (RES) Blair, NE
Thomas M. Roberts: (CEN) 1893 State Census, MO Veterans (MIL)
  26th MO Infantry, Co. A, (RES) Tekamah, NE
A. J. Gabell: (CEN) 1893 State Census, MO Veterans (MIL)
  27th MO S. M., Co. A, (RES) Mullen, NE
S. Clark Cooney: (CEN) 1893 State Census, MO Veterans (MIL)
  2nd MO Cavalry, Co. A, (RES) Fullerton, NE
L. A. Sprague: (CEN) 1893 State Census, MO Veterans (MIL)
  2nd MO Infantry, Co. A, (RES) Huntley, NE
E. S. Shelton: (CEN) 1893 State Census, MO Veterans (MIL)
  2nd MO S. M., Co. A, (RES) Brownville, NE
D. R. Bradford: (CEN) 1893 State Census, MO Veterans (MIL)
  35th MO Infantry, Co. A, (RES) Blue Springs, NE
H. Panghorn: (CEN) 1893 State Census, MO Veterans (MIL)
  39th MO Infantry, Co. A, (RES) Beatrice, NE
Willard B. Stockton: (CEN) 1893 State Census, MO Veterans (MIL)
  39th MO Infantry, Co. A, (RES) Maxwell, NE
G. B. Bevridge: (CEN) 1893 State Census, MO Veterans (MIL)
  3rd MO Cavalry, Co. A, (RES) Auburn, NE
F. S. Morris: (CEN) 1893 State Census, MO Veterans (MIL)
  3rd MO Cavalry, Co. A, (RES) Sargent, NE
Frank Derman: (CEN) 1893 State Census, MO Veterans (MIL)
  3rd MO Infantry, Co. A, (RES) Delta, NE
Seth Raymond: (CEN) 1893 State Census, MO Veterans (MIL)
  3rd MO Infantry, Co. A, (RES) Gering, NE
J. B. Rice: (CEN) 1893 State Census, MO Veterans (MIL)
  40th MO Infantry, Co. A, (RES) Davenport, NE
Chas. P. Schwer: (CEN) 1893 State Census, MO Veterans (MIL)
  41th MO Infantry, Co. A, (RES) Hebron, NE
Patrick Cline: (CEN) 1893 State Census, MO Veterans (MIL)
  50th MO Infantry, Co. A, (RES) Louisville, NE
Isaac M. Temple: (CEN) 1893 State Census, MO Veterans (MIL)
  51th MO Infantry, Co. A, (RES) St Edward, NE
Washington Fulton: (CEN) 1893 State Census, MO Veterans (MIL)
  52th MO Cavalry, Co. A, (RES) Upland, NE
Wm. Stevenson: (CEN) 1893 State Census, MO Veterans (MIL)
  5th MO Cavalry, Co. A, (RES) Auburn, NE
J. E. Flint: (CEN) 1893 State Census, MO Veterans (MIL)
  62th MO Infantry, Co. A, (RES) Bellevue, NE
B. B. Fitzgerald: (CEN) 1893 State Census, MO Veterans (MIL)
  6th MO Cavalry, Co. A, (RES) Jordan, NE
Benjamin Wilson: (CEN) 1893 State Census, MO Veterans (MIL)

   6th MO Infantry, Co. A, (RES) Doniphan, NE
J. P. Chaney: (CEN) 1893 State Census, MO Veterans (MIL)
   81th MO Cavalry, Co. A, (RES) Holbrook, NE
H. Schnackenberg: (CEN) 1893 State Census, MO Veterans (MIL)
   German Reg., Co. A, (RES) Kiowa, NE
George W. Wright: (CEN) 1893 State Census, MO Veterans (MIL)
   th MO Infantry, Co. A, (RES) Whitman, NE
William Peugh: (CEN) 1893 State Census, MO Veterans (MIL)
   1st MO Cavalry, (RES) Benkelman, NE
Thomas Young: (CEN) 1893 State Census, MO Veterans (MIL)
   1st MO S. M., (RES) Norfolk, NE
John W. Perry: (CEN) 1893 State Census, MO Veterans (MIL)
   26th MO Infantry, (RES) Ord, NE
Marvin Trote: (CEN) 1893 State Census, MO Veterans (MIL)
   27th MO Infrantry, (RES) Kearney, NE
C. A. Thieman: (CEN) 1893 State Census, MO Veterans (MIL)
   2nd MO Artillery, (RES) Omaha, NE
George M. Kearns: (CEN) 1893 State Census, MO Veterans (MIL)
   2nd MO Battery, (RES) Loup City, NE
Fritz Wirth: (CEN) 1893 State Census, MO Veterans (MIL)
   2nd MO Med. Staff, (RES) Omaha, NE
John Wolf: (CEN) 1893 State Census, MO Veterans (MIL)
   43rd MO Infantry, (RES) Kilmer, NE
Calloway Underwood: (CEN) 1893 State Census, MO Veterans (MIL)
   6th MO Cavalry, (RES) Carpenter, NE
Edwin Soule: (CEN) 1893 State Census, MO Veterans (MIL)
   7th MO Calavry, (RES) Pickrell, NE
Swan Swanson: (CEN) 1893 State Census, MO Veterans (MIL)
   8th Engineer, (RES) York, NE
Isaac Soule: (CEN) 1893 State Census, MO Veterans (MIL)
   8th MO Calavry, (RES) Wahoo, NE
M. Pruitt: (CEN) 1893 State Census, MO Veterans (MIL)
   National Guard, (RES) Omaha, NE
J. L. Reed: (CEN) 1893 State Census, MO Veterans (MIL)
   MO Squadron, (RES) Scotia, NE
S. Oeus: (CEN) 1893 State Census, MO Veterans (MIL)
   State Militia, (RES) Pine Glen, NE

Barry County, Missouri, Heads of Household, 1840 Census
Sugar Creek Township

Levi Arnold, James Bring, Reece Butler, Hugh Carrol, Andrew Carson, H. W. Cathon, Martin Cornelinson, John Curenton, Elias Ferguson, Phebe M. George, Lewis Goodwin, Abram Hamilton, William Howard, Thomas Keet, Willis Lane, Milles Lee, Joshua Leonard, Samuel Logan, Littleberry Mason, Henry McCary, Mack McMurbick, Joseph Morrison, Martha Parker, Isaac Percey, Gilbert Riggle, G. W. Riley, George Stevens,

Absalom Thompson, James Washburn, J. H. Young, J. W. Barber, William Blye, John Burton, John Carsner, W. C. Childers, C. J. Corder, Robert Eubank, Hardon Evans, J. H. Glover, J. T. Haddock, Zacanah Haddock, N. W. Kelly, Elizabeth Kirkpatrick, John Lang, J. G. Lock, J. J. Lock, Richard Lock, Josiah McCary, Isaac Newton, J. H. Pettit, John Reeves, Alexander Roach, J. S. Short, W. L. Short, Benjamin Smith, H. A. Spencer, Samuel Stanbery, Jesse Stein, Philip Stevens, Thomas Stockton, T. H. Trouch, Frederick Dorrell.

Mount Pleasant Township

William Abel, John Anderson, Payton Anderson, Thompson Anderson, Hiram Bays, Calmus Becket, Daniel Blye. Jesse Day, Joseph Doty, Jesse Gallaway, William Hilton, Sarah Hudson, John Jackson, John W. Kerr, H. L. Link, Patrick Lynch, Joseph McCan, George Myers, Bennet Nally, Joseph Schooling, W. Schooling, Polly Shock, Charles Thomas, Bryant Trent, Reuben Vermillon, James M. Williams, Aaron Winters, Joshua Woods, Asa Wormington, Benjamin Baker, Thomas Bennet, Hamilton Bonsey, Ezekiel Boyd, William Boyd, Abbertus Bright, Samuel Carlton, William Carry, C. G. Cowan, John Davis, Caswell England, Jeremiah Evans, Boswell Heeks, L. Inlow, Sampson Looney, G. W. McCabe, Martin Nelson, Uriah Posey, Abraham Sankey, Israel Schoolcraft, Henry Stinnet, James Stone, Martin Stone, William Stone, George Swanson, Elijah Tedd, H. Tucker, Margaret Webb, Nancy Williams, Robert Anderson, Jonathan Balad, J. W. Bibb, J. W. Briston, Edward Brown, William Brown, Charles Carter, S. J. Davison, Sarah Dicks, A. B. Fly, E. E. Ferguson, Elisha Fly, J. Fly, G. B. Gupton, John Hunels, Willard Jennings, E. G. Lartor, G. Lartor, John Montgomery, Wm, Montgomery, John Petersen, W. Pogue, Uriah Riddle, S. Rigney, T. Rogers, Henry Smith, John Stackey, Joshua Stackey, W. Stanley, Robert Wood, Munroe Batton, B. S. Briney, William Brown, William Clemens, William Clifton, John Dunham, Nathan H. Etheridge, Benjamin Hamilton, William Herdford, J. F. Herrel, J. J. Herrel, Jackson Howerton, Matthew Hubbard, Isaac King, Abel Lee, Elijah Lingo, John Logan, D. R. McClure, John McClure, A. McLaughling, Elias Oldham, Moses Pendigraft. Jeremiah Pennock, J. M. Rissey. James Skelton, John Waggoner, Jesse Warren, William Woodard, James Woodard, John Arnold, T. Burnet, Thomas Carroll, Randolph Carter, John Coneleson, Robert W. Crawford, Henry Cunningham, Moses Curtel, J. Davis, G. B. Easly, Charles Haddock, William Haddock, Jacob Hickam, James Hogan, Charles Hudder, Jesse King, Johnson King, John Lonkum, Shepard Masters, Clark McDonald, Hunt Meeks, John Meeks, Juddeth Meeks, Leroy Mullins, Juemiah Parish, Isaac Price, John Roller, F. D. Stevenson, M. Wornehuson

Spring River Township

N. Adams, Matthew Alburt, Hugh Black, W. A. Black, Abel Burton, William Carr, Robert Dagan, C. Gunn, George Hankins, John Hankins, Samuel Higgins, E. Hillhouse, S. Hillhouse, ??? McGreen, Caleb Nois, L. R. Peteel, Daniel Ray, V. Ragan, A. H. Sampson, Mick Sears, James

Shaw, Zaddack Tedwell, A. A. Young, Mary Adams, Aaron V. Allen, Benjamin Allen, Whart Anderson, A. W. Browning, David Browning, Joel Cotton, Gil Gibson, James E. Higdon, John Johnson, G. Lee, Matthew Lowder, H. H. McHall, George McRight, H. G. McWatt, Levian MCWatt, S. C. McWatt, John Miller, Elijah Neece, Jesse Newton, John Pharris, Samuel Pharris, J. M. Pharris, P. M. Pharris, H. H. Reece, Joseh Rinkel, B. Rogers, E. White, J. M. White, Jeptha White, John Wicks, A. Baugh, Benjamin Brown, Sarah Capps, John Casteel, George Duff, Robert Elkins, Peter Fishburn, David E. Gibson, James Gibson, G. H. Fishburn, John Gullit, Thomas Hamilton, Jacob Hashaw, Willian Henson, G. W. Hill, Henry Husly, William Jennings, Daniel Lee, Jacob Lee, Robert Lee, T. W. Marshall, Alfred Morre, Baldwin Parsons, Robert Patton, David Roark, Luke Ruchman, William StevensonW. L. Taylor, Z. Toney, Richard Watts. Jesse Zachary. J. W. Allen, Asberry Baily, William Basker, Charles Berry, John Hagerty, Philip Hash, John Hask, A. H. Henderson, Randolph Hennoe, David Hergan, J. K. Hords, Robert Jennings, John Lucas, Leland Mathus, M. Maybury, Harim Mullins, William Owen, John Patrick, James Radell, Jacob Spangler, R. Taylor, G. R. Terry, G. W. Thompson, Wm. Tolner, Franklin Truitt, G. White, John Williams, Oliver Woods, Sampson Wright, Wm. Bryant, John Chambers, William Connel, George Davidson, Jesse H. Duncan, Daniel Fuller, Rebecca Funk, J. A. Gutherie, J. Harris, James Hayworth, Lee Hickman, Jacob Lebaw, J. E. Martin, Benjamin St. Hall, Jude McGaher, Pleasant McGaher, R. C. McGeher, William Orr, S. H. Solaver, Ash Pennington, Gorkin Pennington, Simon Pennington, John Solaver, John Taylor, N. L. Taylor, Samuel Williams, Jessde Williamson, R. P. Anderson, John Baines, John Colly, William Compher, John C. Price, Susanah Rocheson, James Downing, Jacob Fisher, Robert Gillock, Henry Green, Henry Harper, John Huntly, John Mayhan, G. M. Messick, William Pharris, L. Siler, Horace Strong, Edward Stubblefield, G. Wing, Levi Walters, Allen Williams, William Wright,Thomas Berry, James Bird, O. R. Clark, Charles Day, David Duncan, Hiram Duncan, John Duncan, Moses Duncan, James Free, William Freeman, Alexander Gray, B. Gray, Thomas Green, Robert Hawkins, William Hodtons, Andrew Keingrey, Moses Green, Jesse McDaniel, A. J. Moyres, Isabell Patton, G. W. Resseloe, Randolph Rhodes, Lewis Richard, Anthony Ruly, Randolph Scott, E. Strait, P. M. Swatzen, W. Swingfee, J. J. Thompson, David Victor, J. C. Winlow, Richard Boswell, L. Bowles, W. Bryant, W. Carter, James Cherry, H. Cunningham, J. H. Ellis, Edw. Fowler, Reubin Freeland, Samuel Hendott, G. H. Hick, Jones R. James, Joseph Longmyre, Roland McRensey, Henry Owens, Edward Warnington, James Webber, S. H. Whapple, Russel Williams, G. H. Willock, Jacob Wills, Elizabeth Winters, W. H. Wood.

Smith Township

Anderson Alderson, L. Beardon, Walker Beashers, Benjamin Bowls, Absalom Collins, A. Cooper, Britton Finley, Sarah Gaither, Thomas Gaither, W. W. Gaither.

Johnson County, Missouri Marriages, 1840-1849
Charles C. Marcum and Sarah Ann Andrews, (MD) Jan. 9, 1840
James A. Roach and Elizabeth Brown, (MD) Jan. 16, 1840
Daniel Adams and Susan McCrary, (MD) Jan. 28, 1840
G. W. Renick and Carharine Simmerman, (MD) Feb. 6, 1840
Watson P. Forbes and Elizabeth Strange, (MD) Feb. 12, 1840
Andrew Neal and Martha Forbes, (MD) Feb. 13, 1840
James J. Tuggle and Lucy Bernet, (MD) Mar. 15, 1840
Samuel Graham and Margaret Hobson, (MD) Mar. 26, 1840
John J. Young and Susan K. Shackleford, (MD) Mar. 29, 1840
James Oldham and Martha Lowry, (MD) Apr. 5, 1840
Daniel W. Scraggs and Francis Ann Write, (MD) Apr. 16, 1840
Samuel M. Hays and Mary Ann Cockrile, (MD) May 4, 1840
Josiah B. Davis and Priscilla D. Bowman, (MD) Jun. 11, 1840
Hezekiah Brown and Joannah Douglas, (MD) Jun. 18, 1840
Joseph Hall and Mary Grisham, (MD) Jun. 25, 1840
James Antine and Leny West, (MD) Jul. 9, 1840
William Whitsett and Elizabeth E. Thompson, (MD) Jul. 14, 1840
Roger B. Snelling and Elizabeth S. Huff, (MD) Jul. 23, 1840
Michael Baker and Juliann Major, (MD) Aug. 23, 1840
Thomas Patterson and Rody Stephens, (MD) Sep. 13, 1840
John Fine and Martha Wisely, (MD) Sep. 17, 1840
Jeremiah V. Cockrell and Louisa Mays, (MD) Oct. 1, 1840
Benjamin Harrison and Elizabeth L.A. Wingfield, (MD) Oct. 1, 1840
Simon Hudson and Celia C. Mary, (MD) Oct. 6, 1840
David Aberson and Louisa Coy, (MD) Oct. 15, 1840
William Wolford and Caroline Lapsley, (MD) Oct. 15, 1840
Benjamin P. Franklin and Letha Jane Horn, (MD) Oct. 29, 1840
William White and Paralie Eliza Thaggs, (MD) Oct. 29, 1840
Lester E. Cocke and Mary Hannah, (MD) Nov. 8, 1840
John Ailer and Nancy J. Doke, (MD) Nov. 10, 1840
William Masterson and Eliza Violet, (MD) Nov. 19, 1840
Jesse Cox and Nancy Keeny, (MD) Dec. 6, 1840
Presley Jordan and Ecunder Wingfield, (MD) Dec. 17, 1840
John Mock and Eliza Thornton, (MD) Dec. 24, 1840
Abel Gilliland and Katherina Stuart, (MD) Jan. 7, 1841
James D. Black and Mrs. Nancy Cockeral, (MD) Jan. 12, 1841
Joseph Windsor and Deborah Masterson, (MD) Jan. 21, 1841
Hiram Warren and Frances Marshall, (MD) Jan. 28, 1841
James Chamberlain and Sarah R. Barton, (MD) Feb. 3, 1841
James M. Fisher and Mary Fine, (MD) Feb. 4, 1841
John Mcspadden and Margarett E. Sterling, (MD) Feb. 8, 1841
David Reed and Elizabeth Jane Baker, (MD) Feb. 18, 1841
John Catrel and Cintha Harrison, (MD) Feb. 21, 1841
Thomas F. Parker and Joannah Logan, (MD) Feb. 21, 1841

Willis Vilet and Saryan Windsor, (MD) Feb. 21, 1841
Henry Hinckle and Sary Emon, (MD) Feb. 24, 1841
Samuel E. Thompson and Eliza McCurdy, (MD) Mar. 1, 1841
James Sterling and Elizabeth Chamberlain, (MD) Mar. 4, 1841
Daniel Harrison and Ann McMahan, (MD) Mar. 7, 1841
William E. Weekley and ???? Skaggs, (MD) Mar. 14, 1841
Isaac Granger and Margaret Thornton, (MD) Mar. 18, 1841
Thomas Himple and Elizabeth Majors, (MD) Mar. 18, 1841
John Price and Jane Marshall, (MD) Mar. 18, 1841
Newton Chapman and Rebecca Craig, (MD) Mar. 25, 1841
Moses Fergerson and Rebecca Ann Simmerman, (MD) Mar. 25, 1841
Joseph P. Rice and Sarah Whitsett, (MD) Apr. 18, 1841
Joseph Longacre and Mary Paul, (MD) Apr. 22, 1841
William Davis and Emeline Mays, (MD) Apr. 29, 1841
William E. Cock and Francis Windsor, (MD) May 30, 1841
David Longacre and Delilah Majors, (MD) Jun. 10, 1841
Benjamin Turner and Mildred S. Pemberton, (MD) Jun. 10, 1841
James Marshall and Ann Price, (MD) Jul. 1, 1841
Martin Adams and Sarah Grainger, (MD) Jul. 15, 1841
Henry D. Edwards and Margaret Smelsor, (MD) Jul. 15, 1841
Martin Hackler and Sarah Hackler, (MD) Jul. 22, 1841
Jacob Epbright and Mary A. Smelsor, (MD) Aug. 5, 1841
John L. King and Elizabeth Barton, (MD) Aug. 19, 1841
Edward Good and Sarah C. North, (MD) Aug. 22, 1841
Robert Tapscott and Martha Simpson, (MD) Sep. 9, 1841
Oliver S. Maxwell and Margaret E. Oglesby, (MD) Sep. 23, 1841
James Cunnerman and Rebecca Furgeson, (MD) Oct. 3, 1841
Cyrus Lapsley and Elizabeth Brockman, (MD) Oct. 7, 1841
George Green and Mary Marr, (MD) Oct. 21, 1841
Samuel P. Kimsey and Cinthia Ann H. Wood, (MD) Oct. 25, 1841
William Woodruff and Jane Colburn, (MD) Oct. 31, 1841
James P. Booker and Mariah Warren, (MD) Nov. 7, 1841
Pleasant Carmichael and Catharine Jane Stirling, (MD) Nov. 11, 1841
Peter Huntsman and Clarky Ann Cowley, (MD) Dec. 21, 1841
Robert Maxwell and Louisa Ann Tibbs, (MD) Dec. 23, 1841
Benjamin W. Boisseau and Sybil Ann Duncan, (MD) Jan. 6, 1842
Jesse Dickson and Emily Marr, (MD) Jan. 7, 1842
Andrew Longacre and Belinda Simcocke, (MD) Jan. 20, 1842
Daniel Marr and Katharine Reed, (MD) Jan. 27, 1842
George P. Angell and Mary Ann Foster, (MD) Jan. 30, 1842
William McMahan and Rachel C. Stockton, (MD) Feb. 13, 1842
Archibald G. Baird and Sarah M. Ferguson, (MD) Feb. 15, 1842
William Molan and Matilda Warren, (MD) Mar. 6, 1842
Finis E. King and Sarah A. Wear, (MD) Mar. 7, 1842
William J. Hardin and Rebecca Smith, (MD) Mar. 10, 1842
Daniel Blevins and Elizabeth Blevins, (MD) Mar. 20, 1842

Henry Shaffner and Martha Lunday, (MD) Apr. 3, 1842
James P. Martin and Nancy A. Brown, (MD) Apr. 14, 1842
William Herndon and Amandaville Chatham, (MD) May 5, 1842
Isaac A. Hanna and Sarah Ann Coke, (MD) May 8, 1842
Isaac Meadows and Rhoda Warren, (MD) May 24, 1842
C. S. Fleming and Synthy Thompson, (MD) May 30, 1842
Alexander McFarland and Elizabeth Vanosdel, (MD) Jun. 3, 1842
James Davenport and Francis Jane Rader, (MD) Jun. 10, 1842
James B. Huff and Eunice T. Thistle, (MD) Jun. 16, 1842
James T. S. McCormick and Caroline Walford, (MD) Jul. 7, 1842
William D. Pinkston and Lucy Pemberton, (MD) Jul. 26, 1842
Soloman Cox and Dinah C. Cox, (MD) Aug. 4, 1842
Samuel S. Cox and Harriett Cox, (MD) Aug. 4, 1842
James H. Gilleland and Nancy Livengood, (MD) Aug. 23, 1842
Robert D. King and Lucinda Wear, (MD) Aug. 30, 1842
Pleasant Early and Susan Francis, (MD) Sep. 8, 1842
William A. Stevens and Margaret West, (MD) Sep. 11, 1842
Elijah Anderson and Polly Oliphant, (MD) Sep. 15, 1842
Fabius M. Butler and Lucy A. Pleasants, (MD) Oct. 2, 1842
John McCrumb and Mary Davis, (MD) Oct. 10, 1842
Daniel Douglas and Sarah Woodland, (MD) Oct. 20, 1842
John Egan and Sarah Burnett, (MD) Oct. 25, 1842
William B. Hobson and Delia Granger, (MD) Nov. 3, 1842
Hampton Quimby and Mary Jane Bradley, (MD) Nov. 20, 1842
James Ross and Tabitha Dunaway, (MD) Nov. 20, 1842
Washington Criger and Nancy Fitzgerald, (MD) Nov. 24, 1842
David Gloyd and Jane H. Duncan, (MD) Nov. 24, 1842
William Criger and Sarah West, (MD) Dec. 6, 1842
Jefferson Walker and Rebecca Roberts, (MD) Dec. 14, 1842
Hiram F. Cavitt and Martha J. Wade, (MD) Dec. 18, 1842
James C. Lapsley and Nancy Adams, (MD) Jan. 1, 1843
William H. Johnson and Minerva Gresham, (MD) Jan. 1, 1843
Isaac W. Brockman and Veliorada Buff, (MD) Jan. 24, 1843
Horatio Edwards and Elizabeth Dillingham, (MD) Jan. 24, 1843
Joseph F. Nelson and Nancy A. Leonard, (MD) Jan. 26, 1843
Elias Majors and Anna Hincle, (MD) Feb. 6, 1843
David J. Murry and Eveline Bradley, (MD) Feb. 9, 1843
Stewart Pipkin and Mary Warren, (MD) Feb. 9, 1843
William Glenn and Charlotte Hays, (MD) Feb. 23, 1843
James Townsley and Sarah Houston, (MD) Mar. 13, 1843
Joseph Francis and Mary C. Early, (MD) Mar. 15, 1843
Andrew M. Rader and Isabella A. McFarland, (MD) Mar. 15, 1843
Pollard Goings and Emily Marshall, (MD) Mar. 23, 1843
Joseph Walker Henderson and Sena Ann Luvena Houx, (MD)
    Mar. 23, 1843
Abner C. Houchins and Martha E. Martin, (MD) Mar. 23, 1843

Edward Schrines and Emily Jane Houx, (MD) Mar. 23, 1843
Samuel L. Hunt and Rutha D. Johnson, (MD) Mar. 23, 1843
William F. Alexander and Upina Smith, (MD) Mar. 24, 1843
William Brandon and Sina Swift, (MD) Apr. 9, 1843
William C. Farley and Martha Grainger, (MD) Apr. 9, 1843
William Parker and Jane Cornett, (MD) Apr. 19, 1843
Joseph Wade and Mary Tunblen, (MD) Apr. 19, 1843
Mumford Smith and Phebe Lurena Hornsby, (MD) Apr. 20, 1843
Henry B. Mays and Susan McMinn, (MD) May 16, 1843
Joseph Epright and MarthaÂ Chamberlain, (MD) May 17, 1843
Joseph Upright and Martha Chamberlain, (MD) May 17, 1843
Martin P. Allison and Rachel Odel, (MD) Jun. 8, 1843
John W. Smith and Elizabeth Davidson, (MD) Jun. 8, 1843
Houston Rawlings and Jemima Hornbuckle, (MD) Jun. 11, 1843
Lucilius Knight and Permelia Bradley, (MD) Jun. 13, 1843
Dennis Hubbard and Minn Rader, (MD) Jun. 17, 1843
Richard C. Combs and Sinthia M. Snelling, (MD) Jun. 29, 1843
George Fickas and Martha Wainscott, (MD) Jun. 29, 1843
Henry Ratts and Betsey Beck, (MD) Jul. 9, 1843
Riley Blevins and Matilda McCrary, (MD) Jul. 13, 1843
Samuel Castle and Catharine Ferguson, (MD) Jul. 18, 1843
Joseph Howard and Amanda Simcocks, (MD) Jul. 30, 1843
Isaac N. Bradshaw and Francis B. Combs, (MD) Aug. 22, 1843
Peter Campbell and Mary Cox, (MD) Aug. 30, 1843
Robert D. Means and Juliet G. Cooper, (MD) Aug. 31, 1843
Samuel Davis and Leannah Masterson, (MD) Sep. 21, 1843
James C. Herndon and Sarah Foster, (MD) Sep. 24, 1843
Solomon Kimsey and Mary A. Dillingham, (MD) Oct. 17, 1843
Joseph Buff and Elizabeth Carter, (MD) Oct. 22, 1843
Hugh E. Wear and Sarah Thompson, (MD) Oct. 26, 1843
James M. Foster and Mary E. Boyles, (MD) Dec. 10, 1843
John Ray Boumer and Hily Ann Thornton, (MD) Dec. 14, 1843
Taylor Sterling and Hannah Ann Jackson, (MD) Dec. 14, 1843
John B. Mays and Martha Ann Gillum, (MD) Dec. 21, 1843
Benjamin F. Hays and Jane Howel, (MD) Dec. 21, 1843
Felix Oliphant and Rebecca Williams, (MD) Dec. 28, 1843
William Hopper and Mary Cobb, (MD) Jan. 4, 1844
John Wede and Missouri Kimsey, (MD) Jan. 4, 1844
Jacob Saum and Susan C. Furguson, (MD) Jan. 14, 1844
George W. Himes and Elmira M. Foster, (MD) Jan. 25, 1844
Presley E. Gordon and Margaret Jane Edwards, (MD) Jan. 30, 1844
Levi Fickas and Katharine Marr, (MD) Feb. 1, 1844
William H. Anderson and Mary Aladeah Davis, (MD) Feb. 4, 1844
Thomas Divers and Nancy Goeshan, (MD) Feb. 8, 1844
Josiah Agen and Martha Ann Harrison, (MD) Feb. 11, 1844
Findley E. Barnett and Evenlainea Rankin, (MD) Feb. 22, 1844

James S. Corder and Rebecca Wood, (MD) Feb. 22, 1844
John Slaterwrite and Sarah Ann Redford, (MD) Mar. 3, 1844
Washington Howard and Hannah Cockrell, (MD) Mar. 10, 1844
Jacob A. Browning and Elizabeth E. Combs, (MD) Mar. 21, 1844
John Bones and Squickla Carpenter, (MD) Mar. 26, 1844
John Bowes and Sarah Ann Redford, (MD) Mar. 26, 1844
Hardin Wooten and Catharine Hicks, (MD) Mar. 28, 1844
William J. Duglass and Mary A. Thompson, (MD) Apr. 2, 1844
William S. Wilcoxen and Lucinda Ramsey, (MD) Apr. 4, 1844
Thompson H. Foster and Susannah A. Walker, (MD) Apr. 14, 1844
Richard M. Miller and Polly Hornsby, (MD) Apr. 18, 1844
Thomas J. Ammerson and Liddy R. Dunaway, (MD) May 16, 1844
William Perman and Elizabeth Hazlip, (MD) May 26, 1844
James Martin and Eldora Cooper, (MD) Jun. 6, 1844
Richard M. King and Elizabeth J. Stewart, (MD) Jun. 7, 1844
William Reef and Margaret Gils, (MD) Jun. 12, 1844
Walker P. Redford and Ann Hiatt, (MD) Aug. 6, 1844
Harris Samuel J. and Catharine M. Cully, (MD) Aug. 13, 1844
Wesley H. Duncan and Margaret Duncan, (MD) Aug. 15, 1844
Thomas Majors and Polly Epman, (MD) Aug. 15, 1844
Joseph Gibson and Arzala Smith, (MD) Aug. 22, 1844
Samuel Hackler and Martha Ann Smith, (MD) Sep. 5, 1844
Martin Read and Margaret Hill, (MD) Sep. 12, 1844
William Miller and Margaret Alexander, (MD) Oct. 5, 1844
Hugh Agen and Margaret C. Harrison, (MD) Oct. 17, 1844
John F. Webster and Lutila Morgan, (MD) Dec. 5, 1844
M.P. Amsbary and Mary A. Bradley, (MD) Dec. 24, 1844
Audonus S. Thornton and Mary Ann Thistle, (MD) Dec. 24, 1844
William B. Moody and Mary E. Rench, (MD) Dec. 26, 1844
John Patton and Martha E. Sanders, (MD) Dec. 31, 1844
Ephraim D. Harris and Martha E. Smith, (MD) Jan. 1, 1845
Andrew A. Johnson and Caroline Cunningham, (MD) Jan. 2, 1845
Orren E. Synde and Eliza Johnson, (MD) Jan. 2, 1845
Isaac Wiley and Rachel Bradley, (MD) Jan. 5, 1845
James Fitzpatrick and Elizabeth P. Mcluney, (MD) Jan. 15, 1845
German Burnett and Sarah Jane Bradley, (MD) Jan. 16, 1845
William Knight and Nancy E. Bradley, (MD) Mar. 5, 1845
Franklin Goodwin and Elizabeth Enlow, (MD) Mar. 13, 1845
John F. Henshaw and Susan M. Adams, (MD) Apr. 3, 1845
Joseph Alexander and Elizabeth Jane Simmerman, (MD) Apr. 10, 1845
Henry Lowry and Elizabeth Harrison, (MD) Apr. 10, 1845
Thomas T. Foster and Temperance McAlester, (MD) Apr. 11, 1845
Samuel Crimbert and Mary West, (MD) May 20, 1845
William Paul and Adelade Longacre, (MD) Jun. 8, 1845
James H. Harris and Sarah Jane Arterberry, (MD) Jun. 10, 1845
Abner Wood and Mary R. Dalton, (MD) Jun. 17, 1845

John Alexander and Rebecca Davis, (MD) Jul. 24, 1845
Peter S. Baker and Virginia S. Craig, (MD) Aug. 25, 1845
John Gest and Lucy Ann Tyler, (MD) Aug. 25, 1845
Benjamin Longacre and Mary C. Graves, (MD) Aug. 25, 1845
George J. McFarland and Louisa Jane Whitsett, (MD) Sep. 3, 1845
John Burton and Mary McFarland, (MD) Sep. 4, 1845
John W. Barksdol and Julia Thornton, (MD) Sep. 18, 1845
Nathan Bradley and Susan Jones, (MD) Sep. 25, 1845
Samuel McMahan and Joannah Thompson, (MD) Sep. 25, 1845
Elias Far and Rebecca Prithohett, (MD) Oct. 23, 1845
Joseph L. Gant and Sarah Elizabeth Bradley, (MD) Oct. 30, 1845
Moses G. Mullins and Kessiah McFarland, (MD) Nov. 26, 1845
Elexander Porter and Adaline Phillips, (MD) Dec. 18, 1845
Young E. W. Berry and Jane Warnick, (MD) Dec. 31, 1845
Louis Hornbuckle and Malinda Walker, (MD) Jan. 1, 1846
John Ousley and Susan Enlow, (MD) Jan. 8, 1846
Seiver A. Lynde and Manerva J. Jones, (MD) Jan. 22, 1846
John Jackson Longacre and Ruth Longacre, (MD) Feb. 10, 1846
Samuel McFarland and Molly Ann Simpson, (MD) Feb. 12, 1846
Aron V. Fergason and Eliza Emmons, (MD) Feb. 13, 1846
Carrol Reece and Charlotte Smith, (MD) Feb. 15, 1846
Robert M. Gragg and Catharine Cook, (MD) Feb. 25, 1846
Lynn B. Gorden and Cassander Fulkerson, (MD) Feb. 26, 1846
Jesse L. Lee and Harriet Tandy, (MD) Feb. 26, 1846
Thomas James and Elizabeth Hodge, (MD) Mar. 12, 1846
Jacob Yankee and Nancy Hays, (MD) Apr. 2, 1846
John Brockman and Adaline Gresham, (MD) Apr. 9, 1846
William Gant and Elizabeth Jane Fine, (MD) Apr. 16, 1846
Andrew V. Davidson and Sofronia Tomlin, (MD) Apr. 19, 1846
Calvin Share and Sarah Davis, (MD) Apr. 26, 1846
Lewis G. Aldredge and Tonday Crocker, (MD) May 26, 1846
Peter H. Duncan and Julianne Stumpff, (MD) Jun. 4, 1846
William H. Smith and Elizabeth Fergason, (MD) Jun. 7, 1846
George W. McMahan and Hannah Cockrill, (MD) Jun. 21, 1846
Thomas Graden and Mary E. Marr, (MD) Jun. 21, 1846
Lucullus Hornbuckle and Susan Ann Durall, (MD) Jul. 5, 1846
John C. Sparks and Sarah M. Crable, (MD) Jul. 9, 1846
Sidney J. Brooks and Martha J. Hobson, (MD) Jul. 28, 1846
Shackley Adams and Katharine Parman, (MD) Aug. 2, 1846
Benjamin F. Dalton and Martha Thaxton, (MD) Aug. 5, 1846
J.C. Anderson and Julia Ann McClarsey, (MD) Aug. 6, 1846
Kesiah Smith and Francis N. Hackney, (MD) Aug. 12, 1846
James M. How and Amanda L. Simmer, (MD) Aug. 26, 1846
Nathaniel Nickels and Sarah J. Fine, (MD) Aug. 30, 1846
William Davis and Jane Miller, (MD) Sep. 6, 1846
Sidney Scott and Martha M. Jackson, (MD) Sep. 9, 1846

Samuel Hale and Pheby C. Cluck, (MD) Sep. 24, 1846
David W. Reed and Mary H. Lea, (MD) Sep. 29, 1846
Peter A. Hall and Mariah T. Cockrell, (MD) Oct. 4, 1846
John Ulan and Ann Vitello, (MD) Oct. 4, 1846
George Fickas and Katharine Wainscott, (MD) Oct. 25, 1846
William C. Duncan and Mary Jane Stumpff, (MD) Oct. 30, 1846
Marcus A. Turner and Amelia Thistle, (MD) Nov. 12, 1846
Benjamin F. McCluney and Mary E. Roberts, (MD) Nov. 24, 1846
Lot Watts and Maryanne H. Stockton, (MD) Nov. 24, 1846
John T. Kindrick and Mary Ousley, (MD) Nov. 25, 1846
Drucilla Anderson and Ambrous D. Brooks, (MD) Dec. 10, 1846
Nathaniel D. Thornton and Sarah Ellen Hornbuckle, (MD) Dec. 10, 1846
Levi Dennis and Levina Tyler, (MD) Dec. 23, 1846
Josiah Allen and Nancy Grissom, (MD) Jan. 4, 1847
Louis M. McCoy and Katharine Odell, (MD) Jan. 15, 1847
Annsted Milner and Sarah H. Graham, (MD) Jan. 28, 1847
Erasmus D. Walice and Delia A. Wear, (MD) Feb. 4, 1847
Littleberry Strang and Lorenda Ferguson, (MD) Feb. 4, 1847
James S. Bales and Eliza Edwards, (MD) Feb. 7, 1847
Phimers L. Fulton and Margaret M. Beard, (MD) Feb. 7, 1847
Elias M. Walker and Mary Cornett, (MD) Feb. 11, 1847
William Dunaway and Elizabeth Demasters, (MD) Feb. 14, 1847
Franklin White and Eliza Masterson, (MD) Mar. 3, 1847
William W. Murray and Margaret A. Rice, (MD) Mar. 4, 1847
Thomas Grainger and Polly Adams, (MD) Mar. 21, 1847
Jehu Stone and Nancy Laneir, (MD) Mar. 25, 1847
Jesse Nelson and Lucretia Fox, (MD) Apr. 1, 1847
David Grover and Hannah V. Brown, (MD) Apr. 3, 1847
Samuel Starr and Margaret Auston, (MD) Apr. 7, 1847
Willy Reece and Jones Simmerson, (MD) Apr. 18, 1847
Robert M. Gladden and Lydia J. Ervin, (MD) Apr. 22, 1847
Mariah Barnet and Jessie Grice, (MD) May 6, 1847
Gabriel Bradley and Mary Shuff, (MD) May 16, 1847
John Kelley and Lucy Harmon, (MD) May 27, 1847
Thomas J. Jones and Mary J. Hodges, (MD) Jun. 14, 1847
James Tyler and Elizabeth Anderson, (MD) Jun. 30, 1847
Washington Radford and Deborah Shacelford, (MD) Jun. 30, 1847
Michael Houx and Harriett McFarland, (MD) Jul. 27, 1847
William Offitt and Amanda Windsor, (MD) Jul. 28, 1847
Thomas Tapscott and Elizabeth Utt, (MD) Jul. 28, 1847
Eveline Longacre and Helery Simcock, (MD) Aug. 27, 1847
William Harrison and Elizabeth Bradley, (MD) Sep. 16, 1847
JamesÂ Ralbeson and Mary Coy, (MD) Sep. 16, 1847
Robert Warrick and Amanda Oglesby, (MD) Oct. 1, 1847
Philip Chapman and Cyntha White, (MD) Oct. 13, 1847
Benjamin Thornton and Caroline Jones, (MD) Oct. 27, 1847

Robert L. England and Elizabeth Whitsett, (MD) Oct. 28, 1847
John Keeny and Narcissa Thompson, (MD) Nov. 11, 1847
John Davis and Sarah Jane Coulbern, (MD) Nov. 17, 1847
William Ellis and Sarahan More, (MD) Nov. 21, 1847
Benjamin F. Dobyns and Margaret Morrow, (MD) Dec. 1, 1847
Isaac Ragan and Parmelia Brown, (MD) Dec. 9, 1847
Silas Baxter and Sarah Guyun, (MD) Dec. 13, 1847
Aaron M. Murphy and Malvina McCoy, (MD) Dec. 15, 1847
Thomas Kerr and Katharine Matthews, (MD) Dec. 20, 1847
James M. Shepherd and Andelila Chatham, (MD) Dec. 22, 1847
Richard McMahan and Amanda Hall, (MD) Dec. 22, 1847
John Marr and Susan King, (MD) Dec. 23, 1847
Isaac Brockman and Malinda Motsinger, (MD) Dec. 29, 1847
Richard Marshall and Emaline Warren, (MD) Dec. 30, 1847
William Perdee and Sarah Pemberton, (MD) Jan. 6, 1848
John Jackson and Nancy Anderson, (MD) Jan. 12, 1848
Henry Butts and Polly Hitchens, (MD) Jan. 21, 1848
Thomas R. Odell and Sarah Huff, (MD) Jan. 30, 1848
Leander H. Creasman and Elizabeth Ann Harrass, (MD) Feb. 3, 1848
George F. Herndon and Elizabeth F. Foster, (MD) Feb. 9, 1848
John Reece and Orlena Janes Mayse, (MD) Feb. 13, 1848
Jacob Crammer and Sarah Hubbard, (MD) Feb. 20, 1848
Robert Matthews and Nancy Ann Davidson, (MD) Feb. 27, 1848
James Green and Martha E. Dudley, (MD) Mar. 2, 1848
Upton Stewart and Jane Milner, (MD) Mar. 14, 1848
John Wiley and Eliza Jane Wilson, (MD) Mar. 16, 1848
James Anderson and Sarah Star, (MD) Mar. 25, 1848
Polly Epright and George Harris, (MD) Mar. 28, 1848
John Cesterson and Sara Elizabeth Conway, (MD) Apr. 13, 1848
Robert L. Thompson and Elizabeth McMahan, (MD) Apr. 13, 1848
Andrew Kirkpatrick and Jane Adams, (MD) Apr. 23, 1848
Hezakiah Brown and Hulda Houston, (MD) May 11, 1848
Alexander Fox and Jane Prine, (MD) May 18, 1848
John L. Trap and Caroline M. Stockton, (MD) May 18, 1848
Jeremiah Crowley and Agnes Skidmore, (MD) May 28, 1848
Jesse B. Thompson and Julia M. Divers, (MD) Jun. 5, 1848
William F. Collins and Francis E. Harris, (MD) Jun. 8, 1848
Sidney Vernon Job and Mary Elizabeth Hall, (MD) Jun. 8, 1848
James Pruett and Myram Hubbard, (MD) Jun. 8, 1848
James M. Paul and Elizabeth Rhea, (MD) Jun. 9, 1848
John Brown and Martha E. Tyler, (MD) Jun. 15, 1848
John D. Miller and Mrs. Jane Teeter, (MD) Jun. 21, 1848
Cilas Wright Fitzgerell and Agnes West, (MD) Jun. 22, 1848
Margaret Jane Frost and Hardin T. Jones, (MD) Jun. 23, 1848
Robert D. Means and Susan E. Tindall, (MD) Jul. 5, 1848
Anthony Helms and Susan E. Howard, (MD) Jul. 11, 1848

John Anderson and Elizabeth Hannah, (MD) Jul. 13, 1848
Simon Taylor and Martha Austen, (MD) Jul. 13, 1848
Samuel Henry Prigmore and Nancy Jane Marr, (MD) Jul. 20, 1848
James C. Lapsley and Emely Steward, (MD) Jul. 25, 1848
David B. Warren and Jemima Snelling, (MD) Jul. 25, 1848
Benjamin L. Graham and Susan Savage, (MD) Aug. 7, 1848
William S. Foster and Miranda Jane Jones, (MD) Aug. 17, 1848
Robert Rhea and Louisa Hopper, (MD) Aug. 17, 1848
Reuben Vaughn and Anna Linch, (MD) Aug. 20, 1848
William Ashley and Malvina Box, (MD) Sep. 6, 1848
Sarah Ann Cully and Jefferson G. Harris, (MD) Sep. 10, 1848
Thompson Foster and Francis Brown, (MD) Sep. 21, 1848
John Conrad Bryant and Sarah Ann Shaffer, (MD) Sep. 21, 1848
William B. Compton and Martha A. Harris, (MD) Sep. 21, 1848
Jacob Taggart and Sarah Lanier, (MD) Sep. 21, 1848
James Brown and Theresa Divers, (MD) Sep. 24, 1848
Jesse Harrison and Martha Farley, (MD) Oct. 6, 1848
Archibald G. Beard and Susan Anderson, (MD) Oct. 8, 1848
Samuel Chamberlain and Margaret Jackson, (MD) Oct. 8, 1848
David Morrow and Sally Brewer, (MD) Oct. 12, 1848
Thomas H. Foster and Sarah L. Brown, (MD) Oct. 12, 1848
Washington Bradley and Sereny Simmons, (MD) Oct. 16, 1848
Milam B. Coats and Elizabeth M. Egbert, (MD) Oct. 18, 1848
Jeremiah Harris and Rachel Collins, (MD) Oct. 18, 1848
John B. Siple and Julia Ann White, (MD) Oct. 19, 1848
James S. Grant and Verlinda Rice, (MD) Nov. 2, 1848
Zachariah Anderson and Susan Jane Gilkerson, (MD) Nov. 7, 1848
James H. Erwin and Nancy Stewart, (MD) Nov. 9, 1848
Lee Dennis and Caroline Young, (MD) Nov. 16, 1848
Charles C. Orre and Deborah Hayes, (MD) Nov. 16, 1848
William Stephenson and Margaret Warren, (MD) Nov. 19, 1848
Andrew J. Radford and Margaret E. Harrison, (MD) Dec. 6, 1848
Edward C. Carew and Mary Coal, (MD) Dec. 9, 1848
Thornton T. Harrison and Salina Harrison, (MD) Dec. 13, 1848
John J. Odean and Mary Ann Thompson, (MD) Dec. 13, 1848
Andrew Horn and Eliza Powell, (MD) Dec. 18, 1848
William Campbell and Synthia Adam, (MD) Dec. 19, 1848
Henry Sanders and Mahaley Jennings, (MD) Dec. 19, 1848
Isaac Kimsey and Margaret Adams, (MD) Dec. 28, 1848
Pierce W. Melton and Viana Crumpton, (MD) Dec. 28, 1848
Joseph G. Reynolds and Elizabeth Murri, (MD) Jan. 7, 1849
James Goodin and Martha Marshall, (MD) Jan. 9, 1849
William Tucker and Amanda Brazzil, (MD) Jan. 11, 1849
Thomas Evans and Nancy Reece, (MD) Jan. 14, 1849
William R. Cully and Mary Brown, (MD) Jan. 16, 1849
Woodson Revis and Sarah Jennings, (MD) Feb. 8, 1849

James Fox and Sarah Strange, (MD) Mar. 1, 1849
Jacob Fickas and Elizabeth Adams, (MD) Mar. 3, 1849
George Green and Mary A. Adams, (MD) Mar. 4, 1849
William Windsor and Elizabeth Horn, (MD) Mar. 15, 1849
William Harrison and Lucinda Vanosdel, (MD) Mar. 23, 1849
William Miller and Julia Emmons, (MD) Mar. 25, 1849
Samuel Kerly and Tabitha Cockrill, (MD) Mar. 26, 1849
James Kinder and Mary Jane Claunch, (MD) Apr. 2, 1849
John Combs and Ann Brener, (MD) Apr. 3, 1849
David Brick and Mary Kerby, (MD) May 8, 1849
David Parsons and Elizabeth Tebbs, (MD) May 14, 1849
Alexander Mars and Nancy Jane Walker, (MD) Jun. 13, 1849
John Hinckle and Mary Jane Majors, (MD) Jul. 8, 1849
Hiram Key and Abigal Adams, (MD) Jul. 23, 1849
William Rollins and Margaret Riddle, (MD) Jul. 27, 1849
Charles Silliman and Phoebe Ann Thaxton, (MD) Aug. 30, 1849
John Baker and Margaret Potts, (MD) Oct. 21, 1849
John Donham and Mary Douglass, (MD) Oct. 25, 1849
William Perry and Mary Garret, (MD) Oct. 25, 1849
Bowlin Coats and Lucinda Warren, (MD) Nov. 7, 1849
Thomas Houts and Fetna Thornton, (MD) Nov. 11, 1849
David Saunders and Vsinna McMahan, (MD) Nov. 11, 1849
Marion Frost and Martha Homer, (MD) Nov. 25, 1849
Andrew Longacre and Mary Shumate, (MD) Nov. 25, 1849
John Box and Nancy Potts, (MD) Dec. 4, 1849
Leonard Cloyd and Elizabeth Goen, (MD) Dec. 5, 1849
James Bailey and Eliza Bradley, (MD) Dec. 10, 1849
William Shannon and Arabella Neal, (MD) Dec. 13, 1849
James Shackleford and Margaret Eagen, (MD) Dec. 16, 1849
W. Pemberton and Mrs. W. Davis, (MD) Dec. 17, 1849
Nathaniel Fisher and Martha Marshall, (MD) Dec. 18, 1849
Thomas Windsor and Malinda Gilmore, (MD) Dec. 18, 1849
Hezekiah Brown and Betsy Donham, (MD) Dec. 22, 1849
Thomas Jennings and Elizabeth Bradley, (MD) Dec. 23, 1849
John B. Harris and Sarah Cockrell, (MD) Dec. 27, 1849
James Richey and Elizabeth Martin, (MD) May 13, 1849
James Hunsucker and Arena Dunaway, (MD) May 31, 1849
Hiram Henderson and Elizabeth Henderson, (MD) Jun. 13, 1849
Benjamin Stone and Nancy Ousley, (MD) Jun. 14, 1849
David Eseman and Elizabeth Majors, (MD) Jun. 24, 1849
John Marr and Mary Marshall, (MD) Jul. 8, 1849
Levin Grainger and Angaletta Conner, (MD) Jul. 22, 1849
Z.W. Taylor and Mariah Reed, (MD) Aug. 2, 1849
Sanford Purtle and Rachel Blevins, (MD) Aug. 9, 1849
Francisa M. Ramsey and Mary Marr, (MD) Aug. 29, 1849
George Bradley and Elizabeth Bradley, (MD) Sep. 9, 1849

John Pain and Polly Barnett, (MD) Sep. 13, 1849
Ansalem Hargrave and Mary Gallaher, (MD) Oct. 9, 1849
James Fitzgerald and Hannah Cockrell, (MD) Oct. 11, 1849
Green Stephens and Nancy Compton, (MD) Oct. 11, 1849
Pendeleton Edwards and Margaret Dillingham, (MD) Oct. 14, 1849
Fountain Nailor and Jane Hanna, (MD) Oct. 18, 1849

Holt County, Missouri, Old Settlers Atlas, 1877,
Richard Acton, James L. Allen, Judge George Anderson, Joseph Anselment, Uriah Blair, J. W. Bridgemon, Judge Richard Collison, J. H. C. Curtis, Henry A. Dankers, W. W. Davenport, Joseph Dodds, Levi Dodge, Fountin Donan, T. C. Dungan, Captain W. W. Frazer, William A. Gardner, George W. Gaskill, John Glenn, Dr. A. Goslin, V. L. Graham, Jacob Groesbeck, Calvin M. Guilliams, William Hoblitzell, John H. Hogrefe, Dr. J. L. Johnstun, William Kaucher, Adam Klippel, Daniel Kunkel, F. Libby, James Limbird, Henry C. Long, T. W. McCoy, Daniel McDonald, R. D. Markland, Horace Martin, Dr. B. Meek, Andrew Meyer, George Meyer, S. W. Morrison, Fred Myers, Dr. J. Noel, Levi Oren, W. H. Poynter, Henry Roselius, E. Rozell, R. H. Russell, John Schrantz, Christian Shults, Henry Shutts, George P. Skeels, M. M. Smith, John W. Stokes, W. F. Taylor, Dr. John M. Tracy, E. Van Buskirk, Daniel Van Wormer, F. W. Walter, E. F. Weller, S. R. Young, Daniel Zook

Andrew County, Missouri, Testimonials Nichols Cancer Santorium, Savanah, 1935

Nebraska

Name	Residence
Mrs. M. E. Adams	Peru
Mr. C. L. Adelung	Amherst
Mr. W. J. Adkisson	Farnam
Mrs. Louise Albers	Falls City
Mr. E. E. Allen	Freedom
Mr. J. R. Ammon	Hammond
James Amos	Fairbury
Mr. A. P. Andersen	Ruskin
Davi A. Anderson	Prague
Mr. J. A. Anderson	Wahoo
Mrs. L. C. Anderson	Marquette
Milton Anderson	Stromsburg
Mr. Per Anderson	Taylor
Victor Anderson	Bladen
Mrs. Wilhelmina Anderson	Holdrege
Fred E. Andrews	Mullen
Mrs. L. O. Andrews	Oxford
Thomas Andrews	Haigler
Mrs. G. Anfinson	Hartington

Laurent Anville	Peru
Jesse Applebee	Beatrice
John Arkfeld	Norfolk
Mrs. J. W. Arney	Silver Creek
Mr. G. W. Arthurs	Kearney
David Asche	Huntley
John Y. Askins	Lincoln
Mr. I. J. Ault	Holmesville
Leon H. Ayle	Sidney
Mr. J. B. Bailey	Naper
Mrs. John Bajeck	Plattsmouth
Byron Baker	Weeping Water
Mr. E. H. Baker	Grand Island
Mr. W. G. Baker	McCook
Mr. W. N. Ballard	Wood Lake
John Banks	Chappell
Mrs. William C. Bantz	Auburnl
Mr. E. F. Barfoot	Kimball
Mrs. Charles Bargstadt	Douglas
Mr. W. S. Barker	Tekamah
Mr. J. M. Barnett	Wymore
Ewing Barrett	Harrisburg
Mr. W. L. Barrett	Weeping Water
Mrs. Amanda Barry	Curtis
Alvin B. Bartlett	Murray
Arthur M. Bartlett	Chadron
Mrs. Joe Bartsch	Nebraska City
Mr. J. M. Bass	Thedford
John S. Bateman	Beatrice
Mr. Dud Bates	Riverview
Mr. G. C. Battin	lma
Mr. R. R. Beach	Mitchell
Mr. H. E. Beadle	Kearney
Herman Beccard	Eagle
Mrs. A. B. Becker	Falls City
Frank Becker	Stapleton
Mrs. Fritz Beerbohn	Wisner
Mrs. Catharine Beery	Farnam
Edward Beery	Farnam
Mrs. Jennie C. Beeson	Morrill
Mrs. Caroline Beethe	Elk Creek
Henry J. Beethe	Elk Creek
Mrs. Henry J. Beethe	Elk Creek
Mrs. A. G. Behlers	Wisner
Miss Bertha Behling	Westpoint
Mr. H. Behrends	Lodgepole

John F. Bell	Harrison
Mr. W. E. Bell	Nebraska City
Mrs. Jake Benda	Wymore
Mrs. J. M. Bennett	Clearware
Walter Bennett	Belgrade
Mr. J. E. Benson	Ong
Mr. J. M. Berkey	Davenport
Bob Bernard	Parks
Albert Best	Morrill
Mr. C. R. Best	Moorfield
Mrs. L. E. Bevins	Cedar Rapids
Mr. J. E. Bible	Cambridge
Mr. Aurelius Bierce	Ogallala
Herman Biere	Dunbar
Mr. H. D. Bingham	Omaha
Mr. A. I. Bird	Alvo
Mrs. Fanny M. Blaisdell	Belvidere
Mrs. William Blaise	Grand Island
Mrs. E. C. Blakeslee	Imperial
Mr. G. H. Blevins	Stapleton
Mrs. J. R. Blevins	Brownlee
John H. Block, Jr.	Hooper
Martin G. Block	Gothenburg
Mr. J. R. Blomenkamp	Hastings
Lloyd Bloxham	Arnold
Mrs. Lulu Bloxham	Arnold
Mrs. S. J. Blumer	Ashton
Mrs. A. W. Bohling	Alma
Mrs. William Bolts	Alma
Frank J. Bonsack	Shelton
Mrs. J. T. Bonta	Arnold
Mrs. Armeda Booth	Springview
Mr. W. R. Borin	Indianola
Frank Bors	Wilber
William Borwege	Bladen
William Boss	Elwood
Mr. G. Bowland	Wymore
Mrs. E. J. Boyd	Ainsworth
William Brahmsteadt	York
Joseph Bramblette	Stratton
Miss Agnes Brand	Madison
Mrs. Fred Brandt	Beatrice
Mrs. Mamie Brandt	Hershey
Mrs. Sarah J. Bratton	Palisade
Carl Bredemeier, Jr.	DuBois
Mrs. R. D. Breeden	Ansley

Owen Brennen	Holbrook
Mr. W. H. Brestel	Morrfield
Mr. S. C. Brogan	Keystone
Walter R. Brolliar	Wilbur
Mr. E. J. Bronson	Lincoln
Mrs. J. C. Brouhard	Hendley
Claude L. Brown	Curtis
Henry C. Brown	Fremont
Mrs. John Brown	Inavale
Mrs. T. E. Brown	Whitney
Mr. W. S. Brown	Sumner
Henry Broz	Wilber
Jacob Bruns	Lodgepole
William Brunz	Oxford
George W. Bryant	Haigler
Mr. C. W. Bucknell	Elmwood
Theo. A. Buhrman	Libory
Mr. P. L. Bumgardner	Ericson
Mrs. M. Burch	Lincoln
Mrs. Ed. Bures	Geneva
August Burk	Dalton
Miss Frances V. Burkhard	Grand Island
Mrs. J. W. Burns	Verdon
John F. Byrne	Wolbach
Mr. P. J. Byrne	Wolbach
Mr. T. J. Cahill	South Sioux City
Clyde S. Calkins	Wood River
Mrs. Amos Cappen	Weeping Water
Mrs. S. C. Carlson	Bertrand
Mrs. Florence Carlsten	Oakland
Mr. L. L. Carpenter	Milford
Mrs. P. R. Carpenter	Bassett
Mr. R. B. Carpenter	Sutherland
Mrs. Alma Carr	Wakefield
Edward Carr	Indianola
Mrs. J. A. Carr	Eddyville
Mr. J. H. Carroll	Valentine
Dale T. Carse	Palisade
Mrs. Pearl Carter	Lincoln
Mrs. Dora D. Carver	North Platte
John W. Carver	Hay Springs
Mr. H. D. Caspers	Auburn
Mrs. Laura A. Cast	Cambridge
Michael Caveny	Wood River
Mr. F. O. Chadwick	Cotesfield
Boose Chalupa	Chadron

Ross Chapman	Bayard
Mr. T. E. Chase	Benkelman
Mrs. A. B. Chatterton	York
Mrs. O. E. Cheyney	Clearwater
Mrs. Ethel Christensen	St. Paul
Mrs. Albert Churchill	Geneva
Mrs. Jacob T. Claussen	Fairbury
Mr. C. A. Clark	Broadwater
Everett J. Clark	Diller
Mrs. W. C. Clark	Boelus
Rev. T. H. Clarke	Aurora
Mrs. Claus Clausen, Jr.	Boelus
William D. Claussen	O'Neill
Mr. J. C. Claybaugh	Seneca
Mr. A. H. Cleal	Long Pine
Mr. H. O. Clegg	Haigler
Mr. W. H. Cline	Oxford
Mrs. L. R. Clouse	O'Neill
Mr. G. S. Coe	Alma
Mrs. O. C. Coe	Wauneta
Mrs. John Cohagan	Polk
Mrs. W. E. Coke	Kearney
Mr. M. V. Cole	Peru
Mr. W. H. Cole	Beatrice
Earl A. S. Collins	Beaver City
Mrs. Reine Comstock	Miller
Mr. C. A. Conant	South Sioux City
Miss Carrie Cook	Edgar
Mrs. S. B. Cook	Cook
Mrs. Lulia Coons	Mullen
Mr. W. T. Coons	York
Mrs. Clara Cooper	Oshkosh
George F. Corson	Blair
Roy Coulter	Auburn
Mrs. G. C. Courtright	North Platte
William N. Covell	Homer
Guy Cowan	Oxford
Eli Cox	Berwyn
Mrs. Lavinia Cox	Cedar Rapids
Charles Craig	Morrill
George E. Cramer	Indianola
Mr. Sant Crawford	Orleans
Mrs. M. W. Crews	Shubert
Mrs. Beryl Peck Crile	Sterling
Mr. L. P. Crittinden	Beatrice
Mrs. Ella Croissant	Riverdale

Mrs. E. A. Crosby	Sutherland
Mr. P. F. Crosby	Blair
Mr. G. A. Cumro	Wymore
Mrs. C. C. Cunningham	Kennard
Mrs. E. W. Cuplin	Ainsworth
Mrs. William Cunningham	Auburn
John S. Curry	Stockville
Frank W. Daddow	Rockville
Peter Dahlsten	Ericson
Mr. W. H. Daugherty	David City
Mrs. Hiram Davey	Scottsbluff
Edwin O. Davis	Omaha
George H. Davis	Sidney
Mr. J. C. Davis	Burr
Mr. R. M. Davis	South Beand
Mr. T. L. Davis	Davenport
Mr. H. M. Dayton	Alma
Mrs. W. A. Deal	Callaway
Mr. A. C. Deaver	Stamford
Mr. A. Delano	Fairbury
Mr. G. H. Delano	Fairbury
Mr. I. N. Dempey	North Platte
Mrs. J. W. Depriest	North Platte
Emil Derler	Overton
Dennis Lee Devall	Shelton
Fred Devish	Mason City
John S. DeWalt	Chadron
Mrs. F. E. Dick	Maywood
Math Diederick	Humphrey
William Dingwell	Burchard
George E. Ditloff	Bradshaw
William Dittbrenner	Auburn
Harry Dively	Burr
Miss Mary Dively	Unadilla
Mrs. Earl N. Dixon	Haigler
Christ Dohmen	Lindsay
Peter W. Dooley	Greeley
Mrs. Matt Dority	Cedar Rapids
Mr. W. W. Dorothy	Fullerton
Mr. C. H. Dorsch	Tecumseh
Francis Doud	Halsey
Mr. F. A. Dove	Wood Lake
Mr. M. V. Doyle	South Omaha
Mrs. Louise Downing	Omaha
Mrs. Mary Dredge	Harrison
Mrs. Fred Droescher	Chadron

Mr. S. G. Dulany	McCook
Mr. J. W. Dunaway	Overton
Mrs. V. L. Duncan	Nebraska City
Mr. R. A. Dunn	Ponca
Mr. W. W. Dye	Comstock
Mrs. Lily Dykes	Rushville
Mr. C. H. Eatinger	Thedford
Mr. L. H. Ebbeka	Geneva
Mr. R. H. Edgington	Steele City
Alfred Edwards	McCook
Mrs. Carrie Edwards	Brownville
Mr. C. W. Edwards	Ruskin
John Edwards	Meadow Grove
Mr. G. D. Eells	Brady
Mr. W. D. Eggleston	Naponee
Mr. M. Ehmen	Sterling
Mr. C. Eichelberger	Shickley
Mrs. Clara Eickmeier	Kearney
Earl Eickmeier	Kearney
Mr. C. A. Eiker	Ogalla
Mr. B. V. Ellis	Stamford
Ross Ellis	Red Cloud
Mr. A. J. Ellison	Diller
Mr. W. D. Elmore	Humbolt
Mrs. Curtis H. Elshire	Valentine
Oscar Eman	Oxford
Mrs. George Emerson	Eddyville
Mr. O. W. Emick	Palisade
Mr. A. I. Engleman	Litchfield
Jacob D. Engleman	Litchfield
Adolph A. Englert	Lodgepole
Mrs. Mary A. Ensley	Holbrook
Charles Erickson	Omaha
Mrs. Erick H. Erickson	Lincoln
Henry Erickson	Mead
Fred Ernst	Rulo
Arthur Escher	Edison
Mrs. Mary Escher	Beaver City
Mrs. R. B. Eshom	North Platte
Mrs. A. J. Evans	Hershey
Miss Nora Eveland	Elmwood
Mrs. Herman Falke	Creighton
Mrs. Ernest Farrignton	Chadron
Mrs. Henry Fass	Auburn
Eon Faulhaber	Thedford
George Feather	Bayard

Mr. J. C. Feeney	Brady
William R. Fees	Sumner
Mrs. Rose Feicht	Brownlee
Mrs. Charles Feilings	Madison
Mr. O. H. Feldman	Fremont
Mr. J. N. Fostermaker	Davenport
Mrs. Anna Filmer	Oconto
Ernest F. Filter	Bloomfield
Mrs. W. F. Finnegan	Grafton
August Fintel	Deshler
Mrs. R. E. Fishcer	Kimball
Mrs. C. M. Fisher	Arnold
Mr. F. D. Fitch	Atlanta
Mr. J. H. Fitch	Hershey
Herbert L. Fitzgerald	McCook
Mrs. John Fix	Kramer
Mrs. A. E. Flock	Maywood
Mr. M. E. Flock	Maywood
Mr. W. T. Forbes	Crawford
Mr. E. E. Ford	Genoa
Grove Fosket	Hemingford
Mr. J. R. Fowkes	Belvidere
Mr. J. W. Foy	Blair
Mrs. H. H. Franzen, Sr.	Gothenburg
Mrs. W. H. Frazell	Grand Island
John M. Frear	Republic City
Mrs. Flora Freeman	Omaha
Miss Gertie R. Freeman	Craig
Joseph Freeouf, Sr.	Wilbur
Mrs. R. E. French	McCook
John J. Friedricksen	Bloomfield
William Friesman	Grand Island
Harry Frink	Tilden
Mr. A. A. Fritz	Naponee
Mrs. A. A. Fritz	Naponee
Mrs. John Fritz	Crete
Mrs. Sophia Fritz	Elgin
Joh Fromong	Fairbury
Mrs. George Froschheiser	Lincoln
Mr. C. W. Fruit	Keystone
Raymond Funkhouser, Jr.	Beatrice
Charles F. Gage	Franklin
Mt. F. L. Galbreath	Crawford
Mrs. Robert Gale	York
Peter Gammel	Milford
Willaim Gardner	Fontanelle

Mrs. Nellie Garman	Cambridge
Mr. J. H. Garrett	Mullen
Robert Garrett	White
Mr. W. J. Garrett	Steele City
Grant Gaston	Gordon
Mrs. James Gault	Lincoln
Mr. J. C. Gear	Fairbury
Mr. C. M. Gebhard	Falls City
Mr. E. J. Gebhard	Verdon
Mrs. Foyd George	Superior
Mrs. Walter Gerard	Fairbury
George T. Gerdes	Humbolt
Ricke Gerdes	Benkelman
Miss Sadie Gilchrist	Hastings
Mr. J. A. Gilkeson	Sutherland
Humphrey M. Gill	Stuart
William A. Gill	Stuart
Mr. C. E. Gilmore	Fairbury
Mr. E. S. Gilmore	Lincoln
Mrs. Alice Ginder	Omaha
Mrs. Minnie Glampe	Clearwater
Raymond Glather	Humbolt
Mr. R. R. Glover	Alliance
Mrs. Henry Goeking	Gilead
Matt Goergen	Ponca
Frank Goetzen	Paxton
Miss Bess Goff	Omaha
Mrs. C. H. Goldfish	Greeley
John Good	Elmere
Mrs. Viola Good	Curtis
Mrs. T. W. Goodwin, Sr.	Hastings
Mrs. Grant Goolsby	Verdon
Herman Gosda	Grand Island
Mr. N. L. Gould	Humboldt
John Graff	Gresham
Hesse Graham, Sr.	Albion
Mrs. Lynn Graham	Ashby
Mr. R. E. Graner	Omaha
Charles A. Grannis	Holbrook
Sheriman Grant	Sumner
George W. Graves	Peru
Mr. N. E. Graves	Tilden
Charles L. Green	Ponca
Mr. J. M. Griffiths	Verdon
George Grim	Chambers
Mrs. George Grim	Chambers

Frank Grimes	Utica
Mrs. B. Gonewold	Gothenburg
Mr. W. W. E. Grossnicklaus	Loup City
Ernest G. Grossoehme	Peru
Ernst F. Gruber	Falls City
Mrs. Lucile Grupe	Agate
Gus Gunderson	Elm Creek
Mrs. Thomas J. Gunsolly	Sioux City
Phineas Gurnsey	Scottsbluff
Mr. G. Guntherless	Maxwell
Victor Gylfe	Oakland
Mrs. William Haffner	Omaha
Frank G. Hagemeir	Pickrell
Mrs. Mary Hajek	Maywood
Mrs. C. W. Hall	Hastings
David M. Hall	Bloomfield
Mr. J. H. Halterman	Salem
Mrs. M. A. Halterman	Verdon
Mrs. Anton Hamernik	Clarkson
Lloyd L. Hamilton	Thedford
Mrs. T. P. Hamilton	Thedford
Lewis Hammer	Sumner
Mr. M. Hanawald	Bridgeport
Mrs. Wilbur Hanchette	York
Mr. A. J. Hanika	Shubert
Mr. Ed Hankins	Hay Springs
Mr C. A. Hanners	McCook
Mrs. Nels P. Hansen	Plainview
Henry Hanson	Holstein
John Hanson	Benedict
Mrs. J. M. Hanssen	Grand Island
Mrs. Ella Harbaugh	Dalton
Fred Hardt, Sr.	Bayard
Andrew Hardy	Diller
Mr. J. Harkins	Burchard
Mr. T. W. Harland	Beatrice
Clarence Hamer	Weeping Water
Albert Hamers	Gilead
Mr. J. C. Harnish	O'Neill
Harry Harper	Benkelman
Mrs. Lydia E. Harris	Neleigh
Mr. V. D. Harris	Lincoln
Mr. E. M. Harrison	North Platte
James Warren Hartley	Chester
Fred Hartung	Dubois
Mrs. Sam Harvey	Stapleton

Herman Hass	Wisner
Mr. F. E. Haswell	Tekamah
Mr. C. C. haught	Ord
Fred Haussler	Holbrook
Mrs. George Hayden	Ruskin
Lewis Hayden	Maywood
Mr. F. M. Hayes	Arthur
Mrs. D. M. Headley	Burwell
Mrs. Ellen Heald	Orafino
Mrs. E. S. Heath	Hastings
Mrs. John Heesch	Phillips
Mrs. H. L. Hefty	Lincoln
Lorenz Heiden	Waco
Mr. A. F. Heier	Lincoln
Rev. A. W. Heimes	Grand Island
Mrs. Herman Heinemann	Wisner
Henry Heinen	Martel
Mrs. Fred T. Heinken	Grand Island
Mrs. Gilbert Henline	Lincoln
Ernest Hennecke	Beatrice
Mr. B. G. Henry	Callaway
Mrs. John T. Hentges	Lincoln
Mrs. H. A. Hermsmeyer	Johnstown
Mrs. Dave Hershberger	Milford
Mr. R. E. Hickenbottom	Callaway
Mrs. R. E. Hickenbottom	Callaway
Mr. H. F. Higgins	Auburn
Mrs. J. M. Higgins	Lincoln
Mrs. O. E. Higley	Benkelman
George M. Hill	Imperial
Mr. D. A. Hunkle	Cambridge
Mr. O. O. Hodges	Holdrege
Henry Hohmann	Grand Island
Mrs. Harry L. Hohnbaum	Friend
Alfred Holm	Loomis
Mr. W. O. Holverson	Beaver City
Mrs. Emma Holz	Ewing
William Homolka	Wilber
Mr. D. B. Hooten	Holmesville
Mrs. Dell Hoschouer	Maywood
Charlie A. Houghton	Blair
Mrs. Clarence Hoy	Fullerton
Hugh Hudson	Crawford
Mr. J. A. Hudson	Gering
William Huebner	Horace
Mr. L. R. Huelle	Newman Grove

Mr. H. L. Huff	Hastings
Mrs. Annie Huffman	Beatrice
Mrs. S. J. Huffman	York
Edwin Hughes	Strang
James A. Hughes	Crawford
Mr. C. G. Hultman	Wausa
Mrs. H. H. Human	Lincoln
Mrs. F. L. Humpal	David City
William F. Humphreys	Franklin
Mr. D. Hunter	Republican City
Mr. W. L. Hunter, Sr.	Benkelman
William Hupp	Ewing
Miss Cordelia E. Ingraham	Broken Bow
Mrs. J. H. Isbell	Hastinga
John H. Itzen	Gilead
Mrs. H. H. Itzen	Gilead
Mr. A. C. Jackson	Wymore
Mrs. Lena Jacobs	Wahoo
Mr. W. A. Jacobs	Rushville
Mr. W. D. Jacobs	Ashland
Mrs. John Jacobson	Newman Grove
Martin Janecek	Wilbur
Mr. K. G. Jannsen	Steele City
Louis Janssen	Franklin
Mr. C. J. Janzen	Henderson
Mr. W. W. Jefferson	Lincoln
Chris C. Jensen	Conzad
Mrs. Hannah Jensen	Bloomington
Mr. N. Jensen	Boelus
Mrs. Matt Jetter	Kearney
Andrew J. Jez	Clarks
Mrs. Lena L. Jewett	Springview
Mrs. August W. Johnson	Brady
Miss Betty Jane Johnson	Arnold
Charles Johnson	Conzad
Mr. E. A. Johnson	Laurel
Ed Johnson	Ericson
Mrs. E. E. Johnson	St. Paul
Mr. F. H. Johnson	Lincoln
Mrs. George W. Johnson	Eli
Mr. L. A. Johnson	Edward
Louis Johnson	Ericson
Mr. M. H. Johnson	Oxford
Peter A. Johnson	Doniphan
Mr. T. M. Johnson	Gandy
Mrs. Warren Johnson	Horace

Mr. A. S. Johnston	York
Mrs. James R. Jones	Auburn
Mrs. J. R. Jones	Plattsmouth
Albert Jorgensen	Winside
Roy Jorgensen	Paxton
Mrs. Anna Joura	Swanton
August Juedes	Deshler
Theodore Juedes	Gurley
Ed Jungek	Blue Hill
Mrs. Mary Kadlec	Crete
Mr. J. E. Kahny	Pierce
Mrs. F. J. Kalina	Friend
Mr. F. Kanzelmeyer	Alma
John J. Karpisek	Wilbur
William Kassebaum	Hebron
Fred Katz	DeWitt
Sherman Kauffman	Auburn
Mrs. J. D. Kaufman	Newman Grove
Henry Kautz	Culbertson
Ed Kearney	Elm Creek
Eugene Kearns	Rushville
Peter Kearns	Rushville
Ray Keating	Greeley
Thomas Keating	Fremont
Mr. S. M. Keenan	Thedford
Mrs. John Keech	Ainsworth
Mrs. L. F. Kellogg	McCook
Mr. M. L. Kennedy	David City
Mr. L. Kern	Bayard
Mr. P. R. Kerrigan	Greeley
John Kieffe	Hastings
Mrs. W. F. King	Hemingford
Mr. T. A. Kinnan	Oakdale
Mrs. Ernest Kirby	Ord
Mr. P. C. Kirkpatrick	Sidney
Mr. J. H. Kisling	Litchfield
Nick Klein	Steinauer
Albert Klimek	Ord
William Klunder	Amherst
Gerald Knowles	Norfolk
Mrs. Elmer Knutson	Wilsonville
John Koch	Eustis
John Kohler	Otoe
Frank F. Kolar	Loup City
Mrs. Frank F. Kolar	Loup City
Mrs. E. T. Kopietz	Hastinigs

Mrs. J. B. Korell	Culbertson
John Kostal, Sr.	Wilber
Mrs. William Kottich	Falls City
Frank Kratocvil	Friend
Rev. B. O. Krocker	Jansen
Henry Kroeger	Pleasanton
Mr. J. O. Krohn	Neligh
Henry Krueger, Jr.	Pierce
Louis Krutsinger	Parks
Mrs. William Kumm	Bazile Mills
Harry Kuster	Wellfleet
Charles Kutsch	Sumner
William W. Lambie	Fairfield
Henry Lamm	Libory
Arthur Lammers	Litchfield
Mrs. Louie Land	Auburn
Herman W. Landwehr	Dunbar
Mrs. D. S. Lang	York
Mr. J. L. Langdon	Gretna
Charles Lange	Whitney
John D. Lange	Weeping Water
Mrs. D. B. Lantz	Tecumseh
Mr. A. O. Larson	Hooper
Carl Larson	Clarks
Mrs. Ephraim Larson	Gothenburg
Mrs. E. M. Laughlin	Wayne
Frank Lawson	Ansley
Mr. M. L. Lechliter	Auburn
Mr. E. O. Leep	Comstock
Mr. J. Walter Legg	Lincoln
Mr. W. S. Leon	North Platte
Mrs. Richard C. Lemburg	Boelus
Mr. B. F. Leslie	Auburn
Ellis Lester	Franklin
Mrs. Nellie J. Lewis	Miller
Mr. W. H. Libby	Long Pine
Mrs. Hugo Lichte	Chadron
Chris S. Lichti	Shickley
Mrs. William Liermann	Amelia
Albert Liesner	Pierce
Mr. E. H. Lillie	Fremont
Mrs. Rose Linabery	Valentine
Mrs. A. W. Line	Broken Bow
Miss Lorna Lipker	Davenport
John D. Lipponcott	Hasting
Mrs. Edw. L. Lippold	Auburn

Mr. F. F. Liska	Hay Springs
Mr. J. Lockhart	Aurora
Mr. H. S. Lockwood	Valentine
Mrs. Mary M. Lodl	Schuyler
Jurgen Loeding	Bloomfield
William Lohmann	Grand Island
Mrs. Luther Long	York
Mrs. J. R. Longfellow	Broken Bow
Mrs. E. L. Loock	Diller
Mr. P. A. Loveless	Richland
Charles S. Loving	Omaha
Mr. C. L. Low	Norfolk
William Ludwig	Beemer
Louis H. Lueders	Deshler
Charles Lugenbeel	Williams
Edgar Lukefahr	Greely
Mrs. Elmer Lumkin	Palisade
Mrs. Lawrence Lund	Cushing
Mr. A. E. Lundberg	Creighton
Mrs. J. W. Lyon	Brock
Mr. C. Engle Macumber	Ellsworth
George Macumber	Chadron
Mr. F. I. Magee	Chester
Mrs. Floremce MaGill	Ainsworth
Mrs. William Mahlman	Hallam
Mr. B. B. Main	Belgrade
Mrs. James Malack	Indianola
Mrs. Mabel Markey	Wellfleet
Mr. H. C. Marks	Ord
Mr. A. M. Markey	Omaha
Mr. D. C. Martin	Scribner
Mr. H. L. Martin	Hickman
Mr. T. C. Martin	Fremont
Edward J. Mashek	Wilbur
Mr. J. F. Mason	Litchfield
Mr. H. J. Mattison	Ponca
Mrs. E. N. Mattson	Ceresco
Mrs. C. A. Mau	Sutton
August May	Bennet
Charles E. Mayhew	Mullen
Albert Mead	Superior
Mrs. Minnie Meenen	Fairbury
Mr. C. W. Meier	Dubois
Thad E. Mendenhall	Fairbury
Mr. Leslie Menking	Elsie
Mrs. Herman H. Meyer	Davenport

Mr. A. H. Meyer	Burwell
Mr. J. H. Meyer	Auburn
Mr. W. C. Meyer	Maywood
Mr. S. L. Meyers	Hendley
Mrs. Anna Michels	Fairbury
Mrs. George Miksch	Red Cloud
Mrs. George A. Millar	North Bend
August H. Miller	Litchfield
Bert Miller	Elm Creek
Mrs. C. A. Miller	Lincoln
Henry Miller	Chadron
Mr. J. E. Miller	Lincoln
Mrs. J. J. Miller	Hardy
Levi Miller	Benkelman
Mr. M. H. Miller	Kimball
Mrs. M. J. Miller	Grand Island
Mr. R. E. Miller	Wilsonville
Mrs. Will L. Miller	Lyons
Mrs. F. P. Mills	Gordon
Mr. D. C. Milne	Creighton
Mr. J. A. Milne	Creighton
Thomas Minor	Eddyville
Mrs. Stella Mintle	Scottsbluff
Alex Mitchell	Weeping Water
Mr. R. E. Mitchell	Inavale
Mrs. Henry Moers	McCook
Mrs. William Mong	Oshkosh
Mr. H. L. Monroe	Ainsworth
John A. Monroe	Thompson
Mr. J. C. Morgan	Omaha
Mrs. M. O. Moritz	Stella
Guy L. Morris	Belvidere
Oscar Morris	Hay Springs
Mr. G. P. Morrow	Plainview
Mrs. George P. Morrow	Plainview
Mr. W. F. Morrow	Cozad
Mrs. Harrison Morse	St. Paul
Mr. N. O. Mortensen	Dennebrog
Ward Mosher	Goirdon
Floyd Mosley	Gothenburg
Grant Mosley	Ong
Mr. J. W. Mosley	Eustis
Mr. H. Moyer	Danbury
Mrs. August Mueller	Clearwater
Mr. C. A. Mues	Arapahoe
James Muir	Republican City

Mr. J. F. Mundhenke	Milford
Mrs. Clara Goodall Murray	Franklin
Mrs. Mary Murray	Falls City
Charles Myers	Alliance
Mrs. G. S. Myers	McCook
Mr. H. Myers	Beatrice
Rev. F. J. McCaffree	Scottsbluff
Mr. W. J. McCart (sic)	Alliance
Mr. E. E. McCartney	Elm Creek
Mrs. R. G. McClanahan	Kimball
Roy McCloud	Ewing
Mrs. F. W. McComb	Wilsonville
Mr. A. McConnaughey	Peru
William McCord	Bladen
Mr. J. L. McCorkle	Benkelman
Walter McCracken	Blair
Mr. P. E. McEntee	Eddyville
Mrs. Sarah McFadden	Sidney
Mrs. John McFarland	Reynolds
Mrs. O. W. McHenry	Gering
Mrs. W. A. McIntosh	Sargent
John C. McKay	Nebraska City
Mr. C. L. McKenney	Auburn
Mr. A. P. McKillip	Hayes Center
Mrs. A. P. McKillip	Hayes Center
William McKune	Lewellen
Mr. A. C. McLain	Crawford
Mr. T. J. McLoyghlin	Lincoln
Millard C. McNair	Bladen
Bernard McNally	Ulysses
Mrs. Katie McNealy	Franklin
Mr. J. E. McQuiston	Republican City
Mrs. C. V. McRae	Bayard
James McWhorter	Foster
Mrs. William Nealeigh	Trenton
Mrs. Arthur Nelson	Hardy
Enon Nelson	Big Spring
Gustave Nelson	St. Edward
Care of George B. Nelson	
Mrs. Minnie E. Nelson	St. Edward
Mr. N. A. Nelson	Ong
Mr. N. E. Nelson	Minden
Mrs. Peter Nelson	McCook
Mrs. R. C. Nelson	Ord
Mr. R. W. Nelson	Lincoln
Mrs. Roy E. Nelson	Leigh

Edwin R. Nesmith	McCook
James Neville	York
Mrs. V. J. Newman	Hastings
Benjamin L. Nicholas	Mason City
Sam B. Nichols	Nebraska City
Mrs. P. W. Nickel	Elmwood
Mrs. J. F. Nickman	Pleasanton
Mrs. Andrew Nicol	Lincoln
William Nieman	Barnston
William Noerenberg	North Loup
Mrs. Anna Nolte	Fairbury
Charlie Nordin	Gothenburg
Mr. M. F. Norton	O'Neill
Peter Nunn	Alexandria
Mr. D. L. Nutt	Papillion
Mrs. Ella Nutter	Wymore
Mr. M. O'Connor	Benkelman
Mrs. S. J. O'Connor	Elsie
Mrs. George Ohlmann	Crookston
Mr. H. E. Oliver, Sr.	Shelton
Arthur Olsen	Flowerfield
Mr. F. H. Olson	Holdrege
Dick Oltmans	Filley
James Opocensky	South Omaha
Mrs. N. H. Osberg	Lyons
James Opocensky	South Omaha
Mrs. N. J. Osberg	Lyons
Mrs. William Osterman	Kilgore
William Otte	Litchfield
Paul Ottens	Avoca
Mr. W. A. Overman	Hayes Center
Mr. W. L. Oviatt	Virginia
Mr. C. A. Owen	Burchard
Lewis B. Paget	Inavale
Mrs. Carrie Palmerton	Cambridge
Mrs. Gus Panas	Dalton
Miss Estella Pancake	Riverview
Michael Parker	Rushville
Mr. C. G. Parks	Seward
George Parris	Lincoln
William Parsons	Omaha
Mr. D. L. Patterson	Wakefield
George W. Paul	Alvo
Mrs. W. H. Paul	Stella
Mr. S. M. Paulson	Genoa
Joseph Pavelka	Crete

Mrs. H. A. Payzant	Schuyler
Edward Peatling	Omaha
Adolph Peeka	Crete
Mrs. Marie W. Peirce	Kearney
Mrs. J. C. Penney	Auburn
Charles F. Perry	Oxford
Mrs. H. Peters	Glenvil
Mrs. Fred T. Peters	Bloomfield
Marquard Petersen	Alliance
William Petersen	Winside
Mr. C. H. Peterson	Wausa
Mrs. Glenn Peterson	Omaha
Niels P. Peterson	Gordon
Otto Peterson	Sparks
Theodore Peterson	Stromsburg
Mrs. Lovica Pethoud	Beatrice
Mrs. Agnes T. Pettijohn	O'Neill
James Pettipiece	Crawford
Mrs. George Petri	Bayard
Mr. O. E. Petrick	Ravenna
Mr. A. S. Phelps	Orleans
Adolph Pieper	Waco
Mrs. Adolph Pieper	Waco
Adolph Pieschke	Chester
Mr. E. S. Pinegar	Omahah
Charlie Piper	Maywood
Mr. J. M. Plank	Minden
Mr. P. E. Pocock	Ord
Mrs. Steve Pojar	Wisner
Mr. G. W. Pool	Omaha
Luther Pope	Grand Island
Mr. E. J. Powers	Taylor
Brice Prater	Falls City
Mrs. O. C. Prill	Ianavale
Mr. D. F. Prime	Arapahoe
Mark Prime	Arapahoe
Mrs. R. W. Putbrese	Callaway
Charles Quartz	Loup City
Mr. W. H. Quinn	Oxford
Cecil Radcliffe	Stuart
Mr. Heye Rademacher	Johnson
Henry Rafert	Osmond
Mr. J. R. Ragland	Elgin
Mr. G. C. Railsback	Peru
Will Rasmussen	Wolbach
John Rathbun	Omaha

Mr. I. F. Ratzlaff	Jansen
James Ray	Benkleman
Thomas B. Rea	Omaha
Mrs. John Readle	Ord
Mrs. Fred Reckling	Princeton
Carl T. Rector	Weeping Water
Mrs. J. A. Rediger	Milford
Philip R. Reece	Ashland
Mr. J. C. Peeve	Nelson
Ernest F. Reher	Grand Island
Mr. R. R. Reinmuth	Dalton
Mr. T. H. Retherford	Martel
Mrs. T. H. Retherford	Martel
Mr. Eber Richards	Elm Creek
George A. Richards	Kearney
Mrs. Ella Ricker	Bladen
George Rickers	Bloomfield
Charles L. Rider	Nemaha
Mr. G. P. Rief	Crawford
Mr. W. F. Ring	Lincoln
Mrs. E. E. Roberts	Crawford
James J. Rodgers	Lincoln
Mr. T. S. Rodgers	Cozad
Rev. Charles Rodgers	Lincoln
Mrs. Charles Root	Hemingford
Mr. A. W. Rose	Blair
Mrs. A. W. Rose	Blair
Mrs. Westhannah Rosenberger	Fairbury
Gus Rosentreader	Ansley
Mrs. Bernard Rotter	Geneva
Mrs. Annettie Rounds	Auburn
Mrs. C. C. Rowell	Comstock
Mrs. Retta M. Rowland	Cairo
Frank C. Royer	Dalton
Mr. A. A. Rudd	Sidney
Mrs. Myrtle Rudd	Maxwell
Mrs. May Ruhs	Hildreth
Harry B. Rumbeck	Miller
Jacob Rummel	Sioux City
Mr. J. J. Runestad	Newman Grove
August Runge	Columbus
Richard Runge	Litchfield
Mrs. Mae Runolfson	Bassett
Mrs. H. C. Ruppert	Quick
Mrs. Lloyd Rupport	McCook
Mrs. J. H. Russell	Kimball

Mrs. Nancy J. Rust	Franklin
Mrs. D. M. Rutherford	Maywood
Mr. E. F. Rutherford	Hamlet
Mrs. J. E. Ryan	Stockville
Mrs. Paul Ryan	Bushnell
Martin Saali	Peru
Mr. H. J. Sack	Springfield
Mrs. Irving St. John	Charleston
Mr. C. F. Salisbury	Neligh
Mr. W. B. Salisbury	North Platte
Charles Sanders	Wellfleet
Mrs. Loretta Sasse	Orleans
Mrs. Henry Sassen	Grand Island
Adolph Sateren	Pilger
Mrs. Ida Sattley	Red Cloud
Earl Saunders	Oshkosh
Mrs. Otto Schellenberg	Scribner
Mrs. Ida E. Schilling	Stanton
Mr. J. E. Schindler	Grand Island
Mrs. Fred Schirkofsky	Grand Island
Ed Schleif	Superior
Fred Schleis	Wilber
Mrs. Fred Schleufer	Deshler
Mrs. Charles Schmale	Campbell
Jake Schmidt	Leigh
Mrs. Ludia Schmidt	Hebron
Mrs. Charles Schober	Verdon
Mrs. Freed A. Schoettger	Burton
Mr. J. M. Schoonover	David City
Mrs. J. M. Schoonover	David City
Henry Schriner	Riverton
Arnold Schulz	Humboldt
August Schulze	Benkleman
Mrs. Louisa Schulzkump	Westpoint
Frank A. Schwenke	Martell
Mrs. Emma M. Schwensen	Belgrade
August Schwichtenberg	Pierce
Mr. C. E. Scott	Alma
James P. Scott	Culbertson
Mrs. William A. Scott	Omaha
Mrs. Laura Scriven	Hamlet
McKinley Scriven	Hamlet
Mr. A. M. Dearle	Plattsmouth
Walter Sears	Rushville
Mrs. John Sebold	Boelus
Harvey Sechker	Wilcox

Paul Seiders	Octavavia
Mr. O. R. Selders	Winside
August Senn	Sumner
Albert Senseney	Wood River
Mr. F. J. Sevcik	St. Paul
Mr. B. F. Seyster	Fairbury
Mrs. George Shadley	Sumner
John Henry Shaffner	Thedford
Mrs. W. N. Sharp	Grand Island
Mr. T. M. Sheaff	Fullerton
Mrs. Mary J. Shermer	Plainview
Mr. J. V. Shestak	Wilber
Mrs. W. C. Shoemaker	Cumro
Mr. G. M. Shrdtridge	Golead
Mr. G. A. Shostrom	Gothenburg
Mrs. Nick Shriner	Thedford
Mr. H. A. Shrock	Anselmo
Mrs. J. O. Shroyer	Humboldt
Mr. E. E. Shuck	Lincoln
Mr. D. C. Shull	Cortland
Mr. S. J. Sillasen	Paxton
Mr. J. M. Silver	Superior
Mr. G. C. Simmerman	Bassett
Mr. J. N. Simmons	Auburn
Mr. F. S. Simpson	Blair
Mr. Leslie Simpson	Holdredge
Mr. C. W. Skeels	Republican City
Mr. C. Emil Skeen	Brownsville
Mrs. Ford Skeen	Auburn
Mr. A. W. Skidmore	Brule
Mr. J. T. Slonecker	Edison
Archie O. Smith	South Sioux City
Mr. C. M. Smith	Cushing
Mrs. D. E. Smith	Lincoln
Mr. G. D. Smith	Lisco
Mrs. G. W. Smith	Crawford
Mr. H. E. Smith	Cambridge
Mrs. J. F. Smith	Eustis
Kile Smith	Chadron
Mr. L. D. Smith	Craighton
Mike L. Smith	Elm Creek
Nelson Smith	Loup City
Mrs. W. B. Smith	Auburn
Lewis K. Snider	Maywood
Mr. F. C. Snyder	Nemaha
Mrs. O. H. Sollenberger	Fairbury

Andrew C. Sorenssen	Kearney
John Sothan	Beatrice
Mr. L. S. Soucie	Upland
Mrs. S. H. Spellman	Roca
Mrs. Margaret Spoering	Wisner
Kermit Squibb	Marsland
Mrs. F. W. Stabenow	Scribner
Miss Margaret Stadfeld	Wilsonville
Martin Stafford	Grand Island
Mrs. Harvey Stahl	Ansley
Mrs. A. E. Stanley	Loomis
Theodore Starkjohan	Plattsmouth
Mrs. L. L. Steele	Fullerton
Mrs. Carrie Steeves	Panama
Mr. J. T. Steffes	Humphrey
Mrs. Mary Steinkruger	Upland
Mr. J. H. Stephens	Fairfield
Richard Stephens	Chappell
Mr. J. A. Stern	Nelson
Mrs. E. W. Stewart	Alliance
Mr. A. R. Stickley	Cushing
Mr. B. J. Stindt	Pickrell
Mrs. John G. Stockdale	Bassett
Mr. W. E. Stokes	Auburn
John Stolzenburg	Beatrice
Mrs. H. O. Stone	Lyons
Harvey Stoops	Fullerton
Mrs. Sarah F. Story	Falls City
Mrs. William Strabel	Elmwood
Mrs. William Strandt	Kearney
Mrs. W. H. Stratton	Scottsbluff
Mrs. J. T. Strawn	Oak
Mrs. Herman Strumpler	Hebron
Fred Stucky	DuBois
Mr. W. H. Stull	St. Edward
Mrs. Alvin Stutzman	Milford
Harry F. Suehl	Winside
Mrs. George E. Sundell	Omaha
Mr. D. H. Sutherland	Wauneta
Mrs. Ellen Braden Sutton	Ord
Thomas Svanda	Table Rock
Charles Swanson	Sargent
Mrs. O. W. Swanson	Nora
Mr. C. B. Swartout	Omaha
Mrs. Mike Sweeney	Lindsay
Mr. C. N. Sweett	Ainsworth

Mr. F. F. Tart	Gering
Mr. F. E. Taylor	Indianola
Mr. H. T. Taylor	Norfolk
Mrs. Minnie E. Taylor	Riverton
Mrs. Masry M.Terrell	Trenton
Mrs. Ernestine Therens	Scribner
Mrs. C. E. Thomas	Mitchell
Mrs. Fred Thomas	Grand Island
Mrs. George Thomazin	Genoa
Mr. R. G. Thompson	Tecumseh
Mrs. Thomas F. Thomsen	Maxwell
Ralph E. Thull	Omaha
Mr. W. F. Thurnagle	Big Spring
Micael Tighe	Omaha
Mrs. S. J. Tilden	Minature
Mr. C. J. Tilton	Bloomfield
Mr. A. J. Tisthammer	Albion
George Tiaden	Wymere
Mrs. J. S. Torey	Ewing
Mrs. Lottie Townsend	Glenvil
Mr. B. D. Tracy	Henderson
Mr. E. N. Tracy	Cedar Bluffs
Mrs. C. J. Treat	Seneca
George Trew	Sumner
Marvin A. Trew	Ansley
Mrs. Marvin Triggs	Allen
Mrs. Eva Trimble	Kearney
Mrs. W. F. Triplett	Miller
Mr. G. A. Trollope	Orleans
Frank Trullinger	Clarks
Mrs. Tom Truscott	Sterling
Ernest O. Turner	Omaha
Mrs. R. A. Turner	Fullerton
Mr. V. D. Turner	Lincoln
Mr. N. J. Tuttle	Maywood
Mr. E. L. Twist	Arnold
Joseph Tyser	Wilbur
Byron Ufford	Alliance
Mr. J. B. Ufford	Alliance
Israel Ulmer	Dawson
Mrs. W. A. Umland	Beatrice
James Vacik	Lodgepole
Mr. Vaclav Valenta	Wilbur
Mrs. Donald Van Orman	Hardy
Mr. D.R. Van Orman	Hardy
Mrs. J. G. Van Schooten	Princeton

Mrs. John Vant	Greenwood
Mrs. Emery Van Vleet	Danbury
Gottlob Veigel	Falls City
Mrs. Blanche Vernoy	Ewing
Mr. J. P. Viersen	Maywood
Everett Vise	Cambridge
Mr. J. W. Vogt	Broken Bow
Walter Vohs	Burr
Henry Von Lindern	Bruning
Louis Vortman	Carleton
Frank Vosika	Lodgepole
Fred Voss	Cairo
Frank Waggoner	Loup City
William Waggoner	Republican City
Mr. J. B. Wait	Seward
Mr. W. R. Waite	Arcadia
Mr. H. Walden	Belmont
William Walden	Belmont
Mr. L. Walgren	Hay Springs
Charles Walker	Maywood
Thomas F. Walker	Alexandria
Mr. E. J. Wallace	Eddyville
Mr. G. M. Wallace	Orleans
Mr. Louis Walters	Hemingford
Mrs. C. H. Warren	Cambridge
Mrs. L. A. Warner	Norfolk
David Wanmer	Fairfield
Mr. C. H. Watkinson	Eddyville
Mrs. Hattie Watkinson	Sumner
Ed Watmore	Fairmont
William Watmore	Geneva
Albert W. Weaver	Stella
Joe Wegrzyn	Ord
Mr. A. H. Weichel	Elmwood
Mr. D. O. Welch	South Sioux City
Roy Welsh	Seward
Edward A. Wenzl	Burchard
Mrs. Thomas Werner	Humphrey
Frank West	Nemaha
Mrs. Julia H. West	Stockville
Mr. T. F. West	Maywood
Mr. W. F. West	Republican City
Mrs. W. S. West	Lincoln
Mr. R. L. Westapher	Omaha
Mrs. Al Wetzel	Westpoint
Mrs. Mary Wheeler	Orleans

Mrs. J. M. White	Lyman
Charles Whitesel	Miller
Mrs. Clara A. Whitsell	Hamlet
Mrs. George Wick	Bassett
Daniel W. Widaman	Merna
Mrs. Artur Wigren	Lyons
Mr. E. B. Wilbur	South Sioux City
Henry Wilcott	Sutherland
Mrs. Fred Wilkens	Pender
Mrs. L. T. Wilkinson	Ansley
George Wilks	Wolbach
Mr. D. L. Williams	Burwell
Jess B. Williams	Franklin
Mr. L. Willman	Sprague
Mrs. Annetta Wilson	Lincoln
Mrs. Lillian M. Wilson	Lincoln
Mr. J. C. Wilson	Lemoyne
John T. Wilson	Chadron
Mr. J. E. Winfrey	Stella
Julius Winter	Pierce
Henry Wohlers	Avoca
Robert J. Wolf	Hastings
Mr. H. T. Woodgate	Maxwell
Mr. E. H. Woolrdige	McCook
Mr. H. L. Wookman	Auburn
Mr. C. E. Wright	Wayne
Fred H. Yant	Crete
Mr. W. S. Yates	Franklin
John C. Yoesel	Falls City
Mr. L. Yost	McCook
Mr. C. G. Youngquist	Holdredge
Allen Zehr	Kearney
Mrs. G. G. Zehr	Stockham
Mrs. Charles J. Zimmerman	Falls City

Nevada

Name	City
Mr. A. W. Jones	McGill
Stephen V. Mills	Wells
Mr. L. H. Rathfon	Halleck
William O. Spane	Ruth
Waldo M. Wilson	Ely

Buchanan County, Missouri Death Register, 1883-1893
Caroline Ladage: (A) 2M 1 day, (BP) St. Joseph, (D) Dec. 18, 1883, (CMTS) Cause of death whooping cough
Dora Eliz Wilson: (A) 1Y 1M 4D, (BP) MO, (D) Oct. 15, 1891, (CMTS)

Cause of death whooping cough
Stella Ladd: (A) 2Y 1M 11D, (BP) MO, (D) Aug. 16, 1889, (CMTS)
Cause of death whooping cough
Daisy Raschy: (A) 1Y 3M, (BP) MO, (D) Jun. 8, 1884, (CMTS)
Cause of death whooping cough Mr.
Arnold L. Chokcee: (A) 2Y 4M, (BP) MO, (D) May 3, 1890, (CMTS)
Cause of death whooping cough
Horeuse Gregory: (A) 5M 15D, (BP) MO, (D) Jan. 31, 1892, (CMTS)
Cause of death whooping cough
William M. Withren: (A) 1Y 6M 24D, (BP) MO, (D) Jun. 13, 1890, (CMTS) Cause of death whooping cough
Dola D. Griffith: (A) 2Y 2M 12D, (BP) MO, (D) Aug. 13, 1884, (CMTS)
Cause of death whooping cough
Homer Lee Finley: (A) 1Y 5M 14D, (BP) MO, (D) Nov. 17, 1883, (CMTS) Cause of death whooping cough
Joseph Warren: (A) 54Y, (D) Oct. 6, 1889, (CMTS)
Cause of death Valvular trouble of heart
Margaret Rainey: (A) 11Y 1M 22D, (BP) OH, (D) Sep. 13, 1890, (CMTS)
Cause of death Valvular insufficiency of heart
Johannah Peahle: (A) 73Y, (Status) Widow, (BP) Germany, (D) Feb. 23, 1893, (CMTS) Cause of death Valvular heart disease
Minnie Robinson: (A) 47Y 8M 29D, (Status) Married, (BP) OH, (D) Nov. 23, 1890, (CMTS) Cause of death Valvular disease of heart
Lizzie Blake: (A) 38Y, (Status) Married, (BP), (D) Mar. 29, 1884, (CMTS) Cause of death Uterine Firbord
Benjamin Seidel: (A) 45Y, (Status) Married, (BP) Pennsylvania, (D) Oct. 13, 1892, (CMTS) Cause of death Uremia
Charles Stephan: (A) 68Y, (Status) Widower, (BP) Austria, (D) Mar. 25, 1893, (CMTS) Cause of death Uremia
Joseph Farrell: (A) 52Y, (Status) Married, (BP) KS, (D) Jul. 31, 1892, (CMTS) Cause of death Uranial convulsions
Grove Roberts: (A) 4Y, (BP) MO, (D) May 7, 1893, (CMTS)
Cause of death Unknown
Wilhemina Bauer: (A) 3M 9D, (BP) MO, (D) Mar. 11, 1891, (CMTS)
Cause of death Unknown
Sydnia Frakes: (A) 8Y 2M 26D, (BP) MO, (D) Feb. 24, 1885, (CMTS)
Cause of death Uncertain
Mrs. James Dysart: (A) 47Y, (Status) Married, (BP) MO, (D) Sep. 3, 1890, (CMTS) Cause of death Ulceration of stomach
Susan Randall Adams: (A) 56Y 1M 9D, (Status) Married, (BP) NY, (D) Jun. 26, 1889, (CMTS) Cause of death Ulcer of stomach
Charles Wood: (A) 27Y, (Status) Married, (BP) KY, (D) May 16, 1890, (CMTS) Cause of death Typhus fever
James M.Cris: (A) 11Y, (BP) MO, (D) Dec. 16, 1889, (CMTS)
Cause of death Typho-malarial fever
Zora Zengbranner: (A) 8Y 4M, (BP) MO, (D) Oct. 17, 1889, (CMTS)

Cause of death Typhomalaria
Morris A. Smith: (A) 45Y 4M 16D, (Status) Married, (BP) KY, (D)
Apr. 14, 1884, (CMTS) Cause of death Typhoid-Malaria
Margaret Gordon: (A) 67Y 10M 11D, (Status) Married, (BP) VA, (D)
Dec. 11, 1892, (CMTS) Cause of death Typhoid pneumonia
John A. Carpenter: (A) 30Y, (Status) Married, (BP) MO, (D)
Oct. 28, 1884, (CMTS) Cause of death Typhoid Pneumonia
Mrs. Elizabeth Duncan: (A) 47Y 4M 2D, (Status) Married, (BP) England,
(D) Feb. 4, 1891, (CMTS) Cause of death Typhoid pneumonia
Alex Servis: (A) 21Y, (BP) IL, (D) Apr. 19, 1891, (CMTS)
Cause of death Typhoid pneumonia
Anna Ladage: (A) 3D, (BP) MO, (D) Jan. 13, 1885, (CMTS)
Cause of death Typhoid pneumonia
Bert McCartin: (A) 25Y, (Status) Married, (BP) IL, (D) Mar. 23, 1889,
(CMTS) Cause of death Typhoid pneumonia
Manliff Tooter: (A) 72Y, (Status) Married, (BP) NC, (D) Feb. 5, 1884,
(CMTS) Cause of death Typhoid pneumonia
Louis Vinyard: (A) 62Y, (BP) KY, (D) Nov. 14, 1884, (CMTS)
Cause of death Typhoid Pneumonia
Samuel Whitmyer: (A) 59Y 23D, (Status) Widower, (BP) Pennsylvania,
(D) Oct. 29, 1892, (CMTS) Cause of death Typhoid malarial fever
Bernice Smith: (A) 26Y, (Status) Married, (BP) MO, (D) Apr. 17, 1893,
(CMTS) Cause of death Typhoid fever
James Russell: (A) 16Y 1M 10D, (BP) IL, (D) Nov. 12, 1889, (CMTS)
Cause of death Typhoid fever
Mary Wilson: (A) 21Y, (D) Nov. 7, 1889, (CMTS)
Cause of death Typhoid fever
William H. Patrick: (A) 20Y 11M 20D, (BP) NE, (D) Nov. 13, 1890,
(CMTS) Cause of death Typhoid fever
Winston D. Judson: (A) 18Y, (BP) NY, (D) Nov. 20, 1892, (CMTS)
Cause of death Typhoid fever
S. O'Connell: (A) 25Y 2M 27D, (BP) Holland, (D) Nov. 5, 1883,
(CMTS) Cause of death Typhoid fever
William Wetherall: (A) 32Y, (Status) Married, (BP) WV, (D)
Oct. 7, 1890, (CMTS) Cause of death Typhoid fever
John Kappen: (A) 30Y, (D) Oct. 5, 1889, (CMTS)
Cause of death Typhoid fever
Jacob Muhliman: (A) 57Y, (Status) Widower, (BP) Switzerland, (D)
Sep. 21, 1889, (CMTS) Cause of death Typhoid fever
Ann Bridget Sheridan: (A) 76Y, (Status) Widow, (BP) Ireland, (D)
Sep. 14, 1889, (CMTS) Cause of death Typhoid fever
Thomas M. Moorby: (A) 41Y 3M 17D, (Status) Married, (BP) VT, (D)
Sep. 26, 1884, (CMTS) Cause of death Typhoid fever
M. F. Jones: (A) 33Y, (Status) Married, (BP) MO, (D) Sep. 26, 1889,
(CMTS) Cause of death Typhoid fever
George Reinert: (A) 42Y, (Status) Married, (BP) Germany, (D)

Sep. 22, 1889, (CMTS) Cause of death Typhoid fever
Fritz Hindley: (A) 2Y 11M, (BP) MO, (D) Sep. 2, 1889, (CMTS)
   Cause of death Typhoid fever
Charles Wamsley: (A) 31Y, (BP) MO, (D) Sep. 17, 1890, (CMTS)
   Cause of death Typhoid fever
Emilie L. Dankens: (A) 25Y 7M 11D, (Status) Married, (BP) MO, (D)
   Aug. 19, 1890, (CMTS) Cause of death Typhoid fever
Frank Gross Berger: (A) 7M, (BP), (D) Aug. 29, 1888, (CMTS)
   Cause of death Typhoid fever
Fredrick Linisby: (A) 19Y 7M 3D, (BP) KS, (D) Aug. 26, 1889, (CMTS)
   Cause of death Typhoid fever
Mary Hayes: (A) 13Y 27D, (BP) MO, (D) Aug. 24, 1892, (CMTS)
   Cause of death Typhoid fever
Peter Kerrigan: (A) 60Y 8M 16D, (Status) Married, (BP) Ireland, (D)
   Jul. 16, 1889, (CMTS) Cause of death Typhoid fever
Gertrude Spangler: (A) 14Y 8M 6D, (BP) MO, (D) May 24, 1893,
   (CMTS) Cause of death Typhoid fever
David C. Lyon: (A) 38Y, (Status) Married, (BP) NY, (D) Apr. 10, 1890,
   (CMTS) Cause of death Typhoid fever
Eldridge Burns: (A) 24Y, (Status) Married, (BP) MO, (D) Apr. 4, 1893,
   (CMTS) Cause of death Typhoid fever
Estella Cobb: (A) 11Y 1M 3D, (BP) MO, (D) Mar. 30, 1890, (CMTS)
   Cause of death Typhoid fever
Annie Gibson: (A) 19Y, (BP) MO, (D) Feb. 27, 1890, (CMTS)
   Cause of death Typhoid fever
F. G. Newdorff: (A) 6Y 6M, (BP) MO, (D) Feb. 20, 1892, (CMTS)
   Cause of death Typhoid fever
Jennie C. Mann: (A) 25Y 7M 4D, (Status) Married, (BP) MA, (D)
   Jan. 30, 1893, (CMTS) Cause of death Typhoid fever
Maggie N. Dunn: (A) 23Y, (BP), (D) Oct. 20, 1889, (CMTS)
   Cause of death Typhoid fever
Prewett Allen: (A) 25Y, (BP) MO, (D) Jan. 18, 1890, (CMTS)
   Cause of death Typhoid fever
Martha Lewis: (A), (BP) VA, (D) Aug. 25, 1884, (CMTS)
   Cause of death Typhoid fever
Willie Bergom: (A) 14Y 11M 11D, (BP) MO, (D) Dec. 2, 1883,
   (CMTS) Cause of death Typhoid fever
Louisa Atheline Sifro: (A) 48Y, (Status) Married, (BP) MO, (D)
   Nov. 24, 1884, (CMTS) Cause of death Typhoid fever
Hattie Brown: (A) 13Y 9D, (BP) MO, (D) Oct. 18, 1892, (CMTS)
   Cause of death Typhoid fever
Noah Wright: (A) 39Y 11M, (Status) Married, (BP) MO, (D)
   Oct. 18, 1884, (CMTS) Cause of death Typhoid fever
Annie Cox: (A) 24Y 11M 9D, (BP) MO, (D) Oct. 8, 1884, (CMTS)
   Cause of death Typhoid fever
William Alvey Smith: (A) 18Y 11M 12D, (BP) MO, (D) Sep. 12, 1889,

(CMTS) Cause of death Typhoid fever
Lizzie Bolen: (A) 6Y, (BP) MO, (D) Nov. 1, 1891, (CMTS)
  Cause of death Typhoid fever
Ayen C. King: (A) 19Y 1 day, (BP) Barbados, (D) Sep. 27, 1889, (CMTS)
  Cause of death Typhoid
George W. Bond: (A) 27Y 5M 12D, (BP) OH, (D) Aug. 1, 1889, (CMTS)
  Cause of death Typhoid
Lulu Chaney: (A) 6Y 5M 1 day, (BP) Wyoming Terr, (D) May 9, 1884,
  (CMTS) Cause of death Typhoid
Agnes C. Rupert: (A) 20Y 7M 7D, (BP) VA, (D) Jun. 5, 1891, (CMTS)
  Cause of death Typho malarial fever
John Richert: (A) 42Y 8D, (Status) Married, (BP) Germany, (D)
  May 3, 1890, (CMTS) Cause of death Typho malarial fever
Clarence William Hicks: (A) 1Y 2M 2D, (BP), (D) Aug. 7, 1889, (CMTS)
  Cause of death Typho malarial fever
Jerry Hawkins: (A) 34Y, (BP) MO, (D) Mar. 22, 1890, (CMTS)
  Cause of death Tumor of the brain
Alvin Dennis Carter: (A) 11Y 6M 15D, (BP) KS, (D) Sep. 25, 1889,
  (CMTS) Cause of death Tubular meningitis
Lizzie McKinney: (A) 30Y, (Status) Married, (BP) MO, (D)
  Mar. 22, 1891, (CMTS) Cause of death Tuberculosis
George H. Bush: (A) 43Y, (Status) Married, (BP), (D) Aug. 2, 1891,
  (CMTS) Cause of death Tuberculosis
Albert Haher: (A) 48Y, (BP) Germany, (D) Jan. 29, 1892, (CMTS)
  Cause of death Tuberculosis
Nickolas Grurshaier: (A) 1Y 2M 10D, (D) Apr. 19, 1893, (CMTS)
  Cause of death Tuberculosis
Carrie Hauley: (A) 24Y 3M 19D, (Status) Married, (BP) WI, (D)
  Apr. 13, 1891, (CMTS) Cause of death Tuberculosis
Hattie Vanhouger: (A) 12Y, (BP) MO, (D) May 3, 1890, (CMTS)
  Cause of death Tuberculosis
Howard R. Conroe: (A) 2Y 4M 20D, (BP) KS, (D) May 31, 1890,
  (CMTS) Cause of death Tubercular meningitis
Hannah Jane Matlock: (A) 42Y, (Status) Married, (D) Sep. 20, 1884,
  (CMTS) Cause of death Typho Malaria
James Rowley Johnson: (A) 5M 8D, (BP) MO, (D) Jul. 25, 1889, (CMTS)
  Cause of death Thrush
Annie Bowman: (A) 19Y, (BP) MO, (D) Nov. 11, 1884, (CMTS)
  Cause of death Typho-malarial fever
Whitney R. Bromley: (A) 1M 9D, (BP) MO, (D) Jan. 17, 1892, (CMTS)
  Cause of death Synovitis
Eldora Cobb: (A) 1Y 11M 9D, (BP) MO, (D) Feb. 24, 1890, (CMTS)
  Cause of death Synochel fever
Francis Willett: (A) 35Y, (BP) MO, (D) Jun. 15, 1892, (CMTS)
  Cause of death Surgery to remove abdominal tumor
Hermine Schmidt: (A) 1Y 9M 7D, (BP) Germany, (D) Jul. 23, 1890,

(CMTS) Cause of death Summer complaint
William Beasley: (A) 60Y, (Status) Married, (BP), (D) Mar. 11, 1889, (CMTS) Cause of death Struck by locomotive
James Moris: (BP) Germany, (D) Nov. 7, 1889, (CMTS) Cause of death Strangulation-suicide
Oscar E. Corner: (A) 6M, (BP) MO, (D) Oct. 18, 1883, (CMTS) Cause of death Strangulation
Fannie Ella Myers: (A) 27Y 6M, (Status) Married, (BP) MO, (D) Nov. 13, 1884, (CMTS) Cause of death Strangulated hernia
Martha Ambrose: (A) 27Y, (Status) Married, (BP) England, (D) Oct. 10, 1889, (CMTS) Cause of death Starvation and alcohol abuse
John Ruffing: (A) 50Y, (Status) Married, (D) Sep. 23, 1889, (CMTS) Cause of death Stab in the heart-suicide
Mary A. Nedarf: (A) 58Y 11M 4D, (Status) Widow, (BP) France, (D) Jan. 6, 1891, (CMTS) Cause of death Spinal trouble
Edward O'Brian: (A) 4D, (BP) MO, (D) Aug. 14, 1890, (CMTS) Cause of death Spinal meningitis
Elvina Schmidt: (A) 1Y 6M 10D, (BP) MO, (D) May 19, 1885, (CMTS) Cause of death Spinal meningitis
Ethel Kelly: (A) 11M 1 day, (BP) MO, (D) Jul. 11, 1884, (CMTS) Cause of death Spinal meningitis
George Weekly Johnson: (A) 1Y 5M, (BP) MO, (D) Mar. 4, 1886, (CMTS) Cause of death Spinal meningitis
George B. Maupin: (A) 11Y 6M 30D, (BP) MO, (D) Mar. 30, 1886, (CMTS) Cause of death Spinal meningitis
Frank Stuart Butler: (A) 7D, (BP) MO, (D) Oct. 5, 1892, (CMTS) Cause of death Spasms
Hulda Viola Hickman: (A) 1M 13D, (BP) MO, (D) May 6, 1892, (CMTS) Cause of death Spasms
Eugene Combs: (A) 5M, (BP) MO, (D) Feb. 2, 1891, (CMTS) Cause of death Spasms
E.M. Riddle, Jr.: (A) 4D, (BP), (D) Sep. 24, 1889, (CMTS) Cause of death Spasms
Margaret Sherman: (A) 63Y, (Status) Widow, (BP) KY, (D) Nov. 29, 1883, (CMTS) Cause of death Softening of the brain
Mary E. F. Cacey: (A) 36Y 11M 15D, (Status) Married, (BP) MO, (D) May 28, 1885, (CMTS) Cause of death Smallpox
John Richard Cacey: (A) 5Y 8M 3D, (BP) MO, (D) May 26, 1885, (CMTS) Cause of death Smallpox
Annie Goring: (A) 23Y, (Status) Married, (BP) MO, (D) May 23, 1885, (CMTS) Cause of death Smallpox
Fora Beck Cacey: (A) 8Y 2D, (BP) MO, (D) May 25, 1885, (CMTS) Cause of death Smallpox
Louis Edward Webber: (A) 27Y 3M 5D, (Status) Married, (BP) MO, (D) May 2, 1889, (CMTS) Cause of death Skull fracture-Concussion

Fritz Bergman: (A) 52Y, (BP) Germany, (D) Aug. 5, 1889, (CMTS)
    Cause of death Skull fracture
Miss Krepper: (A) 18Y, (BP) MO, (D) Feb. 10, 1893, (CMTS)
    Cause of death Shock from surgical operation
William Allison: (A) 88Y 2M 29D, (Status) Married, (BP) KY, (D)
    Apr. 1, 1891, (CMTS) Cause of death Senility
Squire Doyle: (A) 39Y, (Status) Married, (BP) MO, (D) Oct. 5, 1889,
    (CMTS) Cause of death Scrofula
Hanna Senwoode: (A) 1M 15D, (BP), (D) Oct. 8, 1884, (CMTS)
    Cause of death Scrofula
Cici May Billings: (A) 14M, (BP) MO, (D) Mar. 21, 1892, (CMTS)
    Cause of death Scarlet fevr
Lucy Tibbeth: (A) 7Y, (BP) MO, (D) Nov. 21, 1891, (CMTS)
    Cause of death Scarlet fever
Johnny Marsee: (A) 4Y, (BP), (D) Jun. 17, 1890, (CMTS)
    Cause of death Scarlet fever
Mary McDonald: (A) 1Y 7M, (BP) MO, (D) May 24, 1890, (CMTS)
    Cause of death Scarlet fever
Alice Pruice: (A) 5Y 9M, (BP) MO, (D) Apr. 24, 1893, (CMTS)
    Cause of death Scarlet fever
James R. Jeffers: (A) 1Y, (BP) MO, (D) Apr. 18, 1893, (CMTS)
    Cause of death Scarlet fever
Hazel Danty: (A) 4Y 3M 14D, (BP) MO, (D) Feb. 24, 1893, (CMTS)
    Cause of death Scarlet fever
Dora Elizabeth McDaniel: (A) 4Y 9M 1D, (BP) SD, (D) Mar. 28, 1892,
    (CMTS) Cause of death Scarlet fever
Oliver Buskirk: (A) 2Y 4M, (BP) KS, (D) Dec. 22, 1883, (CMTS) Cause
    of death Scarlet fever
Roy Snell: (A) 3Y 9M, (BP) MO, (D) Mar. 27, 1893, (CMTS)
    Cause of death Scarlatina maligna
Dorothy Davis: (A) 4Y 2M 21D, (BP) MO, (D) Jan. 15, 1892, (CMTS)
    Cause of death Scarlatina
Adda Coffman: (A) 16Y, (BP), (D) Mar. 10, 1893, (CMTS)
    Cause of death Scarlatina
Lillian Grist: (A) 1Y 8M, (BP), (D) Oct. 6, 1889, (CMTS)
    Cause of death Scalding
Mary Dalse Ogden: (A) 39Y 1M 21D, (BP), (D) Apr. 11, 1884, (CMTS)
    Cause of death Rupture of heart
Charles MBrown: (A) 31Y, (BP) MO, (D) May 20, 1890, (CMTS)
    Cause of death Rupture of bladder
Fritz Watson: (A) 11Y 6M, (BP) MO, (D) Jun. 15, 1885, (CMTS)
    Cause of death Rheumatism
Mary Hagar: (A) 48Y 2M 6D, (Status) Married, (BP) MO, (D)
    May 28, 1887, (CMTS) Cause of death Rheumatism
Alice Adams: (A) 4Y 5M 3D, (BP) MO, (D) Feb. 4, 1890, (CMTS)
    Cause of death Remittent fever

William Wesley Corpine: (A) 33Y 2M 1 day, (BP) OH, (D) Oct. 14, 1891, (CMTS) Cause of death Remittent fever

Annie E. Bevins: (A) 6Y 5M 13D, (BP) MO, (D) May 8, 1890, (CMTS) Cause of death Relapsing fever

George B. Imel: (A) 24Y 11M 25D, (BP) Pennsylvania, (D) Aug. 20, 1889, (CMTS) Cause of death Railroad Accident

J. C. Haskins: (A) 33Y, (Status) Married, (BP) IN, (D) Aug. 9, 1889, (CMTS) Cause of death R.R. Collision

Nettie Arstip: (A) 23Y, (BP) MO, (D) Mar. 27, 1893, (CMTS) Cause of death Pulmonary tuberculosis

Rosina Cleghorn: (A) 29Y, (Status) Married, (BP) England, (D) Dec. 3, 1889, (CMTS) Cause of death Pulmonary phthisis

Mary Dublin: (A) 50Y, (Status) Widow, (BP) Germany, (D) Nov. 22, 1889, (CMTS) Cause of death Pulmonary phthisis

John Henry Hartshorn: (A) 7Y 6M 5D, (BP) MO, (D) Nov. 13, 1889, (CMTS) Cause of death Pulmonary phthisis

Mattie Sherman: (A) 18Y, (BP) MO, (D) Mar. 24, 1893, (CMTS) Cause of death Pulmonary hemorahage

Howard Allen Meder: (A) 20Y 7M, (BP) MO, (D) Mar. 13, 1893, (CMTS) Cause of death Pulmonary disease

Edward R. Barry: (A) 32Y, (D) Feb. 24, 1890, (CMTS) Cause of death Pulmonary consumption

Florence May Anderson: (A) 20Y, (BP) IL, (D) Oct. 22, 1883, (CMTS) Cause of death Pulmonary consumption

Martha Garton: (A) 23Y, (BP) MO, (D) Jun. 13, 1890, (CMTS) Cause of death Pulmonary consumption

Lula Irwin: (A) 5Y, (BP) KS, (D) Mar. 20, 1890, (CMTS) Cause of death Pulmonary consumption

Susan M. Hedenburg: (A) 86Y 1 day, (Status) Widow, (BP) NY, (D) Nov. 7, 1889, (CMTS) Cause of death Pulmonary congestion

John Durkin: (A) 30Y, (BP), (D) Sep. 15, 1884, (CMTS) Cause of death Pulmonary congestion

C. R. Wisher: (A) 2M, (BP) MO, (D) Jul. 18, 1884, (CMTS) Cause of death Pulmonary congestion

Lizzie Emma Rordee: (A) 2M 5D, (BP) MO, (D) Mar. 5, 1889, (CMTS) Cause of death Pulmonary congestion

Alfred Hawks: (A) 1D, (BP) MO, (D) Aug. 23, 1890, (CMTS) Cause of death Pulmonary congestion

William G. Woodruff: (A) 29Y 18D, (BP) IN, (D) Apr. 3, 1893, (CMTS) Cause of death Pulmonary

Edna M. Waldron: (A) 29Y, (Status) Married, (BP) MI, (D) Jul. 27, 1892, (CMTS) Cause of death Puerperal fever

Mrs. Elenora Tucker: (A) 31Y 3M, (Status) Married, (BP) Germany, (D) Jan. 8, 1891, (CMTS) Cause of death Puerpeal peritonitis

Hamella Gellett: (A) 37Y 11M, (Status) Married, (BP) IN, (D) Sep. 10, 1891, (CMTS) Cause of death Puerpal convulsions

George Collar: (A) 65Y 10M 27D, (Status) Married, (BP) OH, (D) Oct. 5, 1890, (CMTS) Cause of death Progressive muscular atrophy

Mary Ann Blake: (A) 77Y 11M 21D, (Status) Married, (BP) Pennsylvania, (D) Sep. 22, 1892, (CMTS) Cause of death Progressive general paralysis

Myrtle Withrow: (A) 8D, (BP) MO, (D) Jun. 28, 1888, (CMTS) Cause of death Premature labor

Thomas Kenyon: (A) 16D, (BP) MO, (D) Jan. 10, 1891, (CMTS) Cause of death Premature birth

Samuel Willman: (A) 7 hours, (BP) MO, (D) Apr. 24, 1884, (CMTS) Cause of death Premature birth

Mary Edwards: (A) 21Y, (Status) Married, (BP) MO, (D) Oct. 2, 1889, (CMTS) Cause of death Poison-Suicide

Jessie Butts: (A) 6M, (BP) MO, (D) Oct. 22, 1883, (CMTS) Cause of death Poisoning by Accident

Coleman R. Wilson: (A) 27Y, (BP) IN, (D) Sep. 25, 1889, (CMTS) Cause of death Poisoning

Herman Schnitz: (A) 3Y 6M 23D, (BP) MO, (D) Jun. 14, 1890, (CMTS) Cause of death Poisoned by gasoline

Laura M. Montgomery: (A) 3Y 4D, (BP) MO, (D) Oct. 20, 1890, (CMTS) Cause of death Pneumonia infantile

George Rogers: (A) 9Y 6M, (BP) MO, (D) Feb. 10, 1890, (CMTS) Cause of death Pneumonia & meningitis

John Cross: (A) 51Y 1M 26D, (Status) Married, (BP) England, (D) Apr. 14, 1890, (CMTS) Cause of death Pneumonia

Stella Clark: (A) 7Y, (BP) MO, (D) Apr. 24, 1886, (CMTS) Cause of death Pneumonia

Ann Smith: (A) 64Y, (Status) Married, (BP) England, (D) Dec. 7, 1883, (CMTS) Cause of death Pneumonia

George W. Dunne: (A) 40Y, (Status) Married, (BP) NC, (D) Dec. 20, 1889, (CMTS) Cause of death Pneumonia

Ford Goring: (A) 3M, (BP) St. Joseph, (D) Dec. 14, 1883, (CMTS) Cause of death Pneumonia

Lillie Hinton: (A) 27Y, (BP) IL, (D) Dec. 16, 1889, (CMTS) Cause of death Pneumonia

James Ormand Farnsworth: (A) 3Y, (BP) MO, (D) Dec. 30, 1889, (CMTS) Cause of death Pneumonia

Peter J. O'Riley: (A) 48Y 11M 9D, (BP) Ireland, (D) Dec. 29, 1891, (CMTS) Cause of death Pneumonia

John Hayes: (A) 71Y 4M, (Status) Widower, (BP) CT, (D) Nov. 11, 1883, (CMTS) Cause of death Pneumonia

Gertrude M. Wright: (A) 21Y 5M 19D, (Status) Widow, (BP) IL, (D) Oct. 10, 1890, (CMTS) Cause of death Pneumonia

Hannah Oberg: (A) 50 years, (Status) Widow, (BP) American, (D) Oct. 7, 1883, (CMTS) Cause of death Pneumonia

Jacob B. Louse: (A) 69Y 4M 20D, (Status) Married, (BP) PA, (D)
   Oct. 23, 1892, (CMTS) Cause of death Pneumonia
Stella Parman: (A) 1Y 11M 14D, (BP) MO, (D) Oct. 26, 1883,
   (CMTS) Cause of death Pneumonia
Josephine B. Kraush: (A) 56Y 2M 21D, (Status) Widow, (BP) PA, (D)
   Sep. 2, 1889, (CMTS) Cause of death Pneumonia
Ella Agnes Vaughn: (A) 5M 2D, (BP) MO, (D) Jul. 4, 1885, (CMTS)
   Cause of death Pneumonia
Martin Kennedy: (A) 60Y, (BP) Ireland, (D) Jul. 18, 1890, (CMTS)
   Cause of death Pneumonia
Anderson A. Quarles: (A) 1Y 5D, (BP) MO, (D) Jun. 24, 1885, (CMTS)
   Cause of death Pneumonia
Richard Allen Minor: (A) 19Y 4M 18D, (BP) MO, (D) May 18, 1889,
   (CMTS) Cause of death Pneumonia
Bartie Marshaffer: (A) 5M, (BP) MO, (D) May 1, 1893, (CMTS)
   Cause of death Pneumonia
Mrs. June Goading: (A) 66Y, (BP) KY, (D) May 2, 1893, (CMTS)
   Cause of death Pneumonia
John W. Montgomery: (A) 38Y 6M 16D, (Status) Married, (BP) OH, (D)
   Apr. 10, 1891, (CMTS) Cause of death Pneumonia
Janet King: (A) 40Y 9M, (Status) Married, (BP) Barbados, (D)
   Apr. 14, 1891, (CMTS) Cause of death Pneumonia
John Self: (A) 2Y 2M, (BP) MO, (D) Apr. 2, 1890, (CMTS)
   Cause of death Pneumonia
Edith Campbell: (A) 5M, (BP) MO, (D) Apr. 11, 1891, (CMTS)
   Cause of death Pneumonia
Grace Edwards: (A) 1Y 1M 20D, (BP) MO, (D) Apr. 12, 1893, (CMTS)
   Cause of death Pneumonia
Annie E. McIntyre: (A) 22Y 5M 18D, (BP) IL, (D) Apr. 24, 1893,
   (CMTS) Cause of death Pneumonia
Johanna Coffey: (A) 56Y, (Status) Widow, (BP) Ireland, (D)
   Mar. 16, 1884, (CMTS) Cause of death Pneumonia
Emily Cartzenderfer: (A) 37Y, (Status) Widow, (BP) IN, (D)
   Mar. 30, 1890, (CMTS) Cause of death Pneumonia
Stella Glenn: (A) 32Y, (Status) Married, (D) Mar. 14, 1893, (CMTS)
   Cause of death Pneumonia
Benjamin Mills: (A) 15M 16D, (D) Mar. 4, 1890, (CMTS) Cause of death
   Pneumonia
Morgan Miller: (A) 37Y, (BP) MO, (D) Mar. 12, 1890, (CMTS)
   Cause of death Pneumonia
Gwendoline Reed: (A) 1Y 3M 9D, (BP) MO, (D) Mar. 27, 1892, (CMTS)
   Cause of death Pneumonia
Frederick Wm. Koch: (A) 76Y 10M 4D, (Status) Married, (BP) Germany,
   (D) Feb. 6, 1890, (CMTS) Cause of death Pneumonia
Susan Hicks: (A) 35Y, (Status) Married, (BP), (D) Feb. 16, 1893, (CMTS)
   Cause of death Pneumonia

E. O. Dell: (A) 1Y 4M, (BP) KS, (D) Feb. 4, 1886, (CMTS) Cause of
Death Pneumonia

W. H. Wilson: (A) 24Y, (D) Feb. 6, 1890, (CMTS) Cause of death
Pneumonia

Beulah Jones: (A) 4Y 3M 14D, (BP) MO, (D) Feb. 17, 1891, (CMTS)
Cause of death Pneumonia

Roy Gregory: (A) 3Y 1M, (BP) KS, (D) Feb. 4, 1892, (CMTS)
Cause of death Pneumonia

Roy Davis: (A) 2Y 9M 21D, (BP) MO, (D) Feb. 1, 1892, (CMTS)
Cause of death Pneumonia

Dora F. Hetherington: (A) 1Y 2M 28D, (BP) MO, (D) Feb. 21, 1893,
(CMTS) Cause of death Pneumonia

Sarah Billips: (A) 63Y 1M 9D, (Status) Widow, (BP) MO, (D)
Jan.,-1890, (CMTS) Cause of death Pneumonia

James M. Blakely: (A) 43Y, (Status) Married, (BP) MO, (D)
Jan. 25, 1890, (CMTS) Cause of death Pneumonia

Pearlie Jones: (A) 3Y 6M, (BP) St. Joseph, (D) Jan. 20, 1884, (CMTS)
Cause of death Pneumonia

Charles H. Smith: (A) 23Y 11M 15D, (BP) NY, (D) Jan. 12, 1890,
(CMTS) Cause of death Pneumonia

Pearlie Bevins: (A) 1Y 3M 26D, (D) Jan. 24, 1890, (CMTS)
Cause of death Pneumonia

Edward W. Hatfield: (A) 1M 7D, (BP) MO, (D) Jan. 29, 1891, (CMTS)
Cause of death Pneumonia

Claud Hetherington: (A) 2Y 9M 14D, (BP) MO, (D) Jan. 21, 1893,
(CMTS) Cause of death Pneumonia

Rodney Hall: (A) 2Y 8M 4D, (BP) MO, (D) Jan. 29, 1893, (CMTS)
Cause of death Pneumonia

Bridget Benchel: (A) 67Y, (Status) Widow, (BP) Germany, (D)
Dec. 31, 1889, (CMTS) Cause of death Pneumonia

Gameh B. Devorse: (A) 22Y, (BP) MO, (D) Mar. 28, 1890, (CMTS)
Cause of death Pneumonia

Elise M. Worles: (A) 3M 11D, (BP) MO, (D) Dec. 16, 1883,
(CMTS) Cause of death Pneumonia

Nancy C. Allison: (A) 44Y 11M 12D, (Status) Married, (BP) MO, (D)
Jan. 7, 1884, (CMTS) Cause of death Pneumonia

Burnette Kerns: (A), (BP) KY, (D) May 4, 1884, (CMTS) Cause of death
Pneumonia

Sarah Teresa Cunningham: (A) 64Y 3M 2D, (Status) Married, (BP) KY,
(D) Jan. 6, 1891, (CMTS) Cause of death Pneumonia

Orlando Knapp: (A) 54Y, (Status) Widower, (BP) IL, (D) Jan. 18, 1890,
(CMTS) Cause of death Pneumonia

James Hancock: (A) 24Y, (BP) KS, (D) Apr. 12, 1890, (CMTS)
Cause of death Pneumonia

Mamie Ella Kane: (A) 5Y 10M 19D, (BP) MO, (D) Jan. 12, 1891,
(CMTS) Cause of death Pneumonia

Joseph Nash: (A) 82Y, (Status) Married, (BP) MO, (D) Jan. 1, 1885,
(CMTS) Cause of death Pneumonia
Thomas Young: (A) 74Y, (BP) Ireland, (D) Dec. 28, 1889, (CMTS)
Cause of death Pneumonia
John Barnett: (A) 8M 10D, (BP) Buchanan Co., (D) Dec. 15, 1883,
(CMTS) Cause of death Pneumonia
Esther Pearl Deppen: (A) 11M 23D, (BP) MO, (D) Dec. 5, 1890, (CMTS)
Cause of death Pneumonia
William Layfatte: (A), (Status) Married, (BP) NC, (D) Apr. 22, 1884,
(CMTS) Cause of death Pneumonia
Adale May Burce: (A) 3M 24D, (BP), (D) Apr. 5, 1885, (CMTS)
Cause of death Pneumonia
Jesse Welsh: (A) 6M 1 day, (BP) MO, (D) Mar. 10, 1884, (CMTS)
Cause of death Pneumonia
William Derrin: (A) 56Y, (Status) Widower, (BP) KY, (D) Feb. 23, 1884,
(CMTS) Cause of death Pneumonia
Sarah Duval: (A) 68Y 3M, (Status) Widow, (BP) KY, (D) Feb. 23, 1884,
(CMTS) Cause of death Pneumonia
Mary Van Hoosier: (A) 11M 4D, (BP) MO, (D) Aug. 20, 1886, (CMTS)
Cause of death Pneumonia
M. J. Hacknell: (A) 38Y 10M, (Status) Widow, (BP) NY, (D)
Jan. 24, 1890, (CMTS) Cause of death Pleuro-pneumonia
Mattie Lane: (A) 3Y, (BP) MO, (D) Dec. 15, 1885, (CMTS)
Cause of death Pleuro pneumonia
Barney B. Crouch: (A) 23Y, (BP) IL, (D) Jul. 20, 1889, (CMTS)
Cause of death Pistol shot
Charles Friend: (A) 46Y, (BP) England, (D) Apr. 7, 1889, (CMTS)
Cause of death Pistol shot
William Sneed: (A) 35Y, (Status) Married, (D) Apr. 12, 1893, (CMTS)
Cause of death Pistol shot
Rachel Gates: (A) 76Y, (BP), (D) Oct. 20, 1889, (CMTS)
Cause of death Physical exhaustion
Mary Roedde: (A) 35Y 11M, (Status) Married, (BP) WV, (D)
Aug. 13, 1889, (CMTS) Cause of death Phthisis-internal
hemmorhage
Charles Dibble: (A) 59Y 6M 5D, (BP) Germany, (D) Dec. 27, 1890,
(CMTS) Cause of death Phthisis pulmonari
John D. Cole: (A) 32Y, (BP) VA, (D) Dec. 25, 1893, (CMTS)
Cause of death Phthisis pulmonari
Thomas Kinkide: (A) 6Y 5M 17D, (BP) OH, (D) Nov. 23, 1884, (CMTS)
Cause of death Phthisis pulmonari
Millie Younger: (A) 32Y, (Status) Married, (BP) VA, (D) Sep. 25, 1889,
(CMTS) Cause of death Phthisis pulmonari
Euphratis Powell: (A) 24Y 6M 7D, (Status) Married, (BP) IA, (D)
Jul. 11, 1892, (CMTS) Cause of death Phthisis pulmonari
Jennie Crae: (A) 25Y, (Status) Married, (BP) MO, (D) May 29, 1890,

(CMTS) Cause of death Phthisis pulmonari
Sophia Weaver: (A) 19Y 1M 6D, (Status) Married, (BP) MO, (D) May 18 9 3, (CMTS) Cause of death Phthisis pulmonari
Mary M. Morton: (A) 70Y, (Status) Widow, (BP) KY, (D) Apr. 8, 1884, (CMTS) Cause of death Phthisis pulmonari
Mrs. E. A. Donelan: (A) 54Y, (Status) Married, (BP), (D) Apr. 23, 1890, (CMTS) Cause of death Phthisis pulmonari
James R. Murray: (A) 20Y, (BP) MO, (D) Apr. 30, 1892, (CMTS) Cause of death Phthisis pulmonari
Ed Ling: (A) 21Y, (BP) IL, (D) Apr. 10, 1893, (CMTS) Cause of death Phthisis pulmonari
Margaret Lucinda Orr: (A) 24Y 4M, (Status) Married, (BP) IA, (D) Mar. 8, 1889, (CMTS) Cause of death Phthisis pulmonari
Henry Wright: (A) 38Y, (Status) Married, (D) Mar. 8, 1892, (CMTS) Cause of death Phthisis pulmonari
Mrs. Francis Adams: (A) 34Y 11M, (Status) Married, (BP) NC, (D) Mar. 7, 1893, (CMTS) Cause of death Phthisis pulmonari
John M. Curtis: (A) 58Y, (BP), (D) Mar. 12, 1884, (CMTS) Cause of death Phthisis pulmonari
Betsy L. Lord: (A) 73Y 1M 9D, (Status) Widow, (BP) NY, (D) Feb. 23, 1891, (CMTS) Cause of death Phthisis pulmonari
James Crook: (A) 42Y, (BP), (D) Feb. 28, 1884, (CMTS) Cause of death Phthisis pulmonari
L. N. Ransome: (A) 21Y 10M 25D, (Status) Married, (BP) MO, (D) Jan. 6, 1884, (CMTS) Cause of death Phthisis pulmonari
Annie Baxter Newton: (A) 43Y 10D, (Status) Married, (BP) MO, (D) Jan. 7, 1884, (CMTS) Cause of death Phthisis Pulmonari
Henrietta Scott: (A) 20Y 4D, (Status) Married, (BP) MO, (D) Jan. 28, 1885, (CMTS) Cause of death Phthisis pulmonari
Lula Jones: (A) 20Y 3M 6D, (BP) MO, (D) Jan. 1, 1890, (CMTS) Cause of death Phthisis pulmonari
Eliza Bruce: (A) 25Y, (BP) MO, (D) Jan. 15, 1890, (CMTS) Cause of death Phthisis pulmonari
Antoine Rose: (A) 25Y, (BP) MO, (D) Jan. 25, 1890, (CMTS) Cause of death Phthisis pulmonari
Mattie Hoover: (A) 18Y 10M 23D, (BP) MO, (D) Feb. 4, 1885, (CMTS) Cause of death Phthisis Pulmonari
Ethel Ainge: (A) 8M 17D, (BP) MO, (D) Feb. 8, 1890, (CMTS) Cause of death Phthisis pulmonari
Herman Fiecker: (A) 80Y, (BP) Germany, (D) May 12, 1893, (CMTS) Cause of death Phthisis pulmonari
Melina Words: (A) 18Y 1M 13D, (Status) Married, (BP) MO, (D) Feb. 11, 1884, (CMTS) Cause of death Phthisis pulmonari
E. K. Thomas: (A) 1Y 26D, (BP) MO, (D) Jan. 17, 1885, (CMTS) Cause of death Phthisis pulmonari
Katherine Gardner: (A) 65Y 11M 8D, (Status) Married, (BP) KY, (D)

Oct. 26, 1884, (CMTS) Cause of death Phthisis pulmonari
Amanda E. Coates: (A) 26Y 11M 2D, (Status) Married, (BP) VA, (D)
 Feb. 2, 1884, (CMTS) Cause of death Phthisis Pulmonari
Zecharia Page: (A) 26Y, (Status) Married, (BP) MO, (D) Dec. 1, 1883,
 (CMTS) Cause of death Phthisis
Mary Jane Rice: (A) 29Y, (Status) Married, (BP) OH, (D) Nov. 26, 1889,
 (CMTS) Cause of death Phthisis
Matilda Earhart: (A) 60Y, (BP) VA, (D) Nov. 3, 1889, (CMTS)
 Cause of death Phthisis
Laura Dawson: (A) 35Y, (BP) MO, (D) Apr. 5, 1890, (CMTS)
 Cause of death Phthisis
John Carroll: (A) 37Y, (BP) OH, (D) Mar. 25, 1890, (CMTS)
 Cause of death Phthisis
David Bisbee: (A) 41Y, (BP) MO, (D) Feb. 8, 1890, (CMTS)
 Cause of death Phthisis
James Elliston: (A) 46Y, (BP), (D) Jan. 2, 1890, (CMTS)
 Cause of death Phthisis
Jacob Loudon: (A) 24Y, (BP) MO, (D) Jan. 20, 1890, (CMTS)
 Cause of death Phthisis
Wm. Harry Teagadon: (A) 1M 24D, (BP) MO, (D) Feb. 17, 1890,
 (CMTS) Cause of death Phrenitis
Robert Spurgeon: (A) 1Y 2M, (BP) MO, (D) Mar. 13, 1893, (CMTS)
 Cause of death Pertussis
Sarah Keling: (A) 42 urs, (Status) Married, (BP) MO, (D) Jan. 31, 1890,
 (CMTS) Cause of death Peritonitis
Goldie Pugh: (A) 27Y, (Status) Married, (BP) MO, (D) Dec. 3, 1892,
 (CMTS) Cause of death Peritonitis
Mariah H. Jones: (A) 61Y, (Status) Widow, (BP) Born at sea, (D)
 Oct. 7, 1889, (CMTS) Cause of death Peritonitis
Susan B. Sherwood: (A) 81Y 3M 17D, (Status) Married, (BP) VT, (D)
 Aug. 7, 1891, (CMTS) Cause of death Peritonitis
P. Mulkins: (A) 9Y, (BP), (D) Jul. 28, 1892, (CMTS) Cause of death
 Peritonitis
Mary Eliza Williams: (A) 18Y, (BP), (D) May 21, 1889, (CMTS) Cause
 of death Peritonitis
Mary Ann Lawless: (A) 36Y 28D, (Status) Marrried, (BP) Pennsylvania,
 (D) Mar. 8, 1884, (CMTS) Cause of death Peritonitis
William J. Kennedy: (A) 37Y, (BP) MO, (D) Feb. 14, 1890, (CMTS)
 Cause of death Peritonitis
Emma Newman: (A) 23Y, (Status) Married, (BP) MO, (D) Jan. 17, 1892,
 (CMTS) Cause of death Peritonitis
Almeda Wamsley: (A) 61Y 9M 12D, (Status) Widow, (BP) VA, (D)
 Sep. 15, 1889, (CMTS) Cause of death Peritonitis
Nannie Thomas: (A) 24Y, (Status) Married, (BP) MO, (D) Feb. 24, 1892,
 (CMTS) Cause of death Peritonitis
Mrs. Henry Brann: (A) 40Y, (Status) Married, (BP) IL, (D) Feb. 15, 1884,

(CMTS) Cause of death Peritonitis
Robert D. Moore: (A) 38Y, (BP) MO, (D) Jul. 28, 1890, (CMTS) Cause of death Peritonitis
Alex Stewart: (A) 61Y 4M 2D, (Status) Married, (BP) Scotland, (D) Mar. 2, 1892, (CMTS) Cause of death Pericarditis
Emily Pearson: (A) 30Y, (BP) England, (D) Mar. 23, 1890, (CMTS) Cause of death Pericarditis
Mary Mergawaski: (A) 26Y, (Status) Married, (BP) West Prussia, (D) Oct. 10, 1889, (CMTS) Cause of death Peoepal fever
Malinda Mitchell: (A) 55Y, (Status) Married, (BP) MO, (D) Mar. 28, 1890, (CMTS) Cause of death Pelvic abcess
Frederke Schadt: (A) 50Y 9M 13D, (Status) Married, (BP) Germany, (D) Apr. 18, 1890, (CMTS) Cause of death Paralysis of the heart
Sarah E. Russell: (A) 45Y 3M 15D, (BP) NC, (D) Mar. 16, 1885, (CMTS) Cause of death Paralysis of the heart
Catherine M. Fitzgerald: (A) 37Y 2M, (Status) Married, (BP) Ireland, (D) Sep. 16, 1889, (CMTS) Cause of death Paralysis of heart
Ella Manerva Holmes: (A) 24Y, (Status) Married, (BP), (D) Jun. 17, 1889, (CMTS) Cause of death Paralysis of heart
Fredrick Barhendt: (A) 72Y, (Status) Married, (BP), (D) Sep. 15, 1889, (CMTS) Cause of death Paralysis of heart
William Joseph Phillips: (A) 76Y 5M, (Status) Married, (BP) MO, (D) Jan. 16, 1892, (CMTS) Cause of death Paralysis of face
Hester Hensenger: (A) 67Y, (Status) Widower, (BP), (D) Sep. 25, 1889, (CMTS) Cause of death Paralysis of brain
Martha Jane Cully: (A) 9Y 7M 3D, (BP) MO, (D) Oct. 10, 1884, (CMTS) Cause of death Paralysis of the heart
Hannah Hyde: (A) 70Y 5M 20D, (Status) Widow, (BP) Pennsylvania, (D) Dec. 15, 1883, (CMTS) Cause of death Paralysis
Marista Marshall: (A) 26Y 3M 20D, (BP) MO, (D) Apr. 26, 1893, (CMTS) Cause of death Paralysis
James Rodman: (A), (Status) Married, (BP) American, (D) Aug. 14, 1883, (CMTS) Cause of death Paralysis
Worthy Brown: (A) 38Y 5M 3D, (BP) MO, (D) Apr. 15, 1884, (CMTS) Cause of death Paralysis
Joab Shultz: (A) 81Y, (Status) Married, (BP) VA, (D) Apr. 20, 1893, (CMTS) Cause of death Paralysis
Lotta P. Mott: (A) 18Y, (BP) MO, (D) Feb. 12, 1891, (CMTS) Cause of death Palpitation heart
G.W. McCrary: (A) 57Y, (Status) Married, (BP) IN, (D) Jun. 23, 1890, (CMTS) Cause of death Overdose of opium
Edward M. Theis: (A) 25Y, (Status) Married, (BP) Germany, (D) Jun. 2, 1890, (CMTS) Cause of death Overdose of morphine
Ford Pfleiderer: (A) 78Y, (Status) Married, (BP), (D) Aug. 24, 1889, (CMTS) Cause of death Overdose of medicine
Sarah Ellen Petam: (A) 37Y 7M 3D, (Status) Married, (BP) IN, (D)

Oct. 5, 1889, (CMTS) Cause of death Overdose of laudanum
Mary Wright: (A) 28Y 7M 14D, (BP) IL, (D) Feb. 9, 1892, (CMTS)
   Cause of death Ovarian tumor
Joseph Francis: (A) 65Y 4M 14D, (Status) Married, (BP) England, (D)
   Jun. 29, 1892, (CMTS) Cause of death Osteo sarcoma
Sibbie O'Keefe: (A) 29Y, (Status) Married, (BP) MO, (D) Mar. 18, 1893,
   (CMTS) Cause of death Organic disease of heart
George H. Cloud: (A), (Status) Married, (BP) IN, (D) May 1, 1893,
   (CMTS) Cause of death Opium narcosis
Sarah K. White: (A) 74Y 11M 22D, (Status) Widow, (BP) NY, (D)
   Jan. 27, 1890, (CMTS) Cause of death Old age-Bronchitis
Nancy Dunning: (A) 80Y 12D, (BP) IN, (D) Aug. 5, 1884, (CMTS) Cause
   of death Old age
Thomas Heaps: (A) 71Y 7M 15D, (Status) Married, (BP) England, (D)
   Nov. 14, 1891, (CMTS) Cause of death Old age
Sylvia Gray: (A) 84Y, (Status) Married, (BP) MO, (D) Oct. 18, 1889,
   (CMTS) Cause of death Old age
Nancy Galloway: (A) 87Y, (BP) KY, (D) Apr. 24, 1893, (CMTS) Cause \
   of death Old age
David M. Hickok: (A) 86Y 9M, (Status) Widower, (BP) VT, (D)
   Mar. 11, 1892, (CMTS) Cause of death Old age
Thomas Kirkman: (A) 87Y 1M 10D, (Status) Married, (BP) NC, (D)
   Sep. 15, 1889, (CMTS) Cause of death Old age
Sallie Dunlap: (A) 66Y, (Status) Married, (BP) KY, (D) Sep. 8, 1884,
   (CMTS) Cause of death Old age
Sarah M. Tibbs: (A) 33Y 3M 1 day, (Status) Married, (BP) IN, (D)
   Dec. 12, 1891, (CMTS) Cause of death Obstruction of bowels
Herbert A. Walker: (A) 40Y 4M 28D, (Status) Married, (BP) NY, (D)
   Aug. 20, 1890, (CMTS) Cause of death Nervous frustration & low
   fever
Jeremiah Oswald Mann: (A) 6Y 1M 24D, (BP) IA, (D) Jun. 13, 1890,
   (CMTS) Cause of death Nephritis
Martin Meister: (A) 45Y, (Status) Married, (BP) Switzerland, (D)
   Jun. 2, 1890, (CMTS) Cause of death Morphine poison
Carl T. Stiffons: (A) 65Y, (BP) Germany, (D) Jan. 27, 1891, (CMTS)
   Cause of death Morphine
Mary Knapp: (A) 34Y, (Status) Married, (BP) Bavaria, (D) Nov. 30, 1889,
   (CMTS) Cause of death Mitral infsufficiency
Mella B. Reeves: (A) 21Y 10M 5D, (BP) IA, (D) May 2, 1893, (CMTS)
   Cause of death Miscarriage
William H. Dysart: (A) 49Y, (Status) Married, (BP) KY, (D) Apr., 1893,
   (CMTS) Cause of death Meningitis
Ira Myrtle Tetrick: (A) 1Y 4M, (BP) MO, (D) Dec. 10, 1890, (CMTS)\
   Cause of death Meningitis
John Begly: (A) 1Y 14D, (BP) MO, (D) Jul. 3, 1891, (CMTS) Cause of
   death Meningitis

Arthur Juton: (A) 6Y 19D, (BP) MO, (D) May 20, 1891, (CMTS) Cause of death Meningitis

Emma Givens: (A) 13Y, (BP) MO, (D) Apr. 25, 1884, (CMTS) Cause of death Meningitis

Dora Knotts: (A) 24Y, (BP) IA, (D) Apr. 24, 1890, (CMTS) Cause of death Meningitis

Bernice Stewart: (A) 2Y, (BP) MO, (D) Apr. 4, 1893, (CMTS) Cause of death Meningitis

John T. Hackett: (A) 7M 22D, (BP) MO, (D) Feb. 2, 1890, (CMTS) Cause of death Meningitis

Beny J. Thomas: (A) 2Y 1M 28D, (BP) MO, (D) Jun. 12, 1884, (CMTS) Cause of death Meningitis

Wilford Thomas: (A) 6M 19D, (BP) MO, (D) Feb. 5, 1886, (CMTS) Cause of death Meningitis

Elmer Mesant: (A) 1Y 6M 2D, (BP) CT, (D) Dec. 17, 1883, (CMTS) Cause of death Meningitis

Fannie Magill: (A) 2Y, (BP), (D) Dec. 5, 1890, (CMTS) Cause of death Membranous croup

Joseph Engelman: (A) 6Y 9M, (BP) St. Joseph, (D) Nov. 7, 1889, (CMTS) Cause of death Membranous croup

Joseph Chandler: (A) 7Y, (BP) MO, (D) Nov. 23, 1889, (CMTS) Cause of death Membranous croup

Mamie Maxwell: (A) 5Y 9M, (BP) KS, (D) Mar. 21, 1886, (CMTS) Cause of death Membranous croup

Frank Allen Wuhl: (A) 6Y 4D, (BP) MO, (D) Nov. 10, 1890, (CMTS) Cause of death Membranous croup

William H. Wendt: (A) 1Y 21D, (BP) MO, (D) Dec. 22, 1884, (CMTS) Cause of death Membranous croup

Frederick Vondenbouchy: (A) 2Y 11M 17D, (BP) MO, (D) Dec. 22, 1884, (CMTS) Cause of death Membranous croup

Daisy Cass: (A) 9M, (BP), (D) Oct. 19, 1889, (CMTS) Cause of death Membranous croup

Willie Houseman: (A) 1Y 2M, (BP), (D) Feb. 27, 1885, (CMTS) Cause of death Membranous croup

Sallie Dunlap: (A) 62Y, (Status) Married, (BP) NC, (D) Feb. 18, 1892, (CMTS) Cause of death Melancholia following La Grippe

Lily Lerner: (A) 18Y, (BP) MO, (D) Sep. 23, 1889, (CMTS) Cause of death Melancholia

Joseph Louis Tate: (A) 3Y 7M 15D, (BP) MO, (D) Jun. 28, 1888, (CMTS) Cause of death Measles

Bertha Annie Osborne: (A) 2Y 5M 24D, (BP) MO, (D) Apr. 28, 1890, (CMTS) Cause of death Measles

Glee Legrand: (A) 1Y 1M 3D, (BP) KS, (D) Apr. 7, 1887, (CMTS) Cause of death Measles

Zora Sedford: (BP) MO, (D) Apr. 17, 1892, (CMTS) Cause of death Marasmus

James E. Long: (A) 48Y 1M 27D, (Status) Married, (BP) MO, (D) Nov. 3, 1884, (CMTS) Cause of death Marasmus

D. D. Jones: (A) 1Y 1M, (BP) Buchanan Co., (D) Dec. 12, 1883, (CMTS) Cause of death Marasmus

G. W. Duncan: (A) 1Y 4M, (BP) MO, (D) Aug. 5, 1887, (CMTS) Cause of death Marasmus

Frank A. Nero: (A) 28Y, (BP) Sweden, (D) Jul. 30, 1890, (CMTS) Cause of death Maniacal exhaustion

Dennis Mahaney: (A) 28Y, (Status) Married, (BP) OH, (D) Oct. 30, 1889, (CMTS) Cause of death Maniacal exhaustion

J. E. Wallace: (BP) MO, (D) Aug. 22, 1886, (CMTS) Cause of death Malformation

Willis Edward Raymond: (A) 2Y 9M 15D, (BP) MO, (D) Oct. 20, 1889, (CMTS) Cause of death Malerious croup

Henry Hemphill: (A) 13Y 3M 9D, (BP) MO, (D) May 29, 1889, (CMTS) Cause of death Malerial typhoid

Estella May Lord: (A) 5Y 11M, (BP) MO, (D) Mar. 14, 1890, (CMTS) Cause of death Malarial remittent fever

John Wm. Arthur Hazzard: (A) 1M 16D, (BP) MO, (D) Jun. 8, 1890, (CMTS) Cause of death Malarial remittent fever

Charles Hunt: (A) 36Y 2M 11D, (Status) Married, (BP) NY, (D) Jun. 16, 1890, (CMTS) Cause of death Malarial fever

John W. Sliney: (A) 28Y, (BP) IL, (D) Apr. 6, 1893, (CMTS) Cause of death Malarial fever

Elvina Dix: (A) 66Y 4M, (Status) Married, (BP) KY, (D) Jan. 9, 1885, (CMTS) Cause of death Malarial fever

M. J. Suswell: (A) 44Y, (D) Feb. 13, 1885, (CMTS) Cause of death Malarial fever

Gracie Riley: (A) 1Y 10M, (BP) MO, (D) Nov. 19, 1889, (CMTS) Cause of death Laryngitis-croup

Minnie E. Russell: (A) 24Y, (Status) Married, (BP) KS, (D) Mar. 31, 1892, (CMTS) Cause of death Laryngitis

Julia Hall: (A) 24Y, (Status) Married, (BP) IL, (D) Jan. 7, 1891, (CMTS) Cause of death Laryngitis

Kate Thompson: (A) 8Y 6M, (BP) MO, (D) Oct. 25, 1889, (CMTS) Cause of death Laryngitis

Wade Thompson: (A) 3M 1 day, (BP) MO, (D) Sep. 7, 1889, (CMTS) Cause of death Laryngitis

Josiah R. White: (A) 74Y, (Status) Widower, (BP) VA, (D) Dec. 30, 1891, (CMTS) Cause of death La Grippe

Lucy Burris: (A) 50Y, (BP) MO, (D) Feb. 10, 1890, (CMTS) Cause of death La Grippe

Sarah E.C. Floyd: (A) 73Y 4D, (Status) Widow, (BP) NH, (D) Jan. 23, 1892, (CMTS) Cause of death La Grippe

Minnie C. Fleming: (A) 32Y 26D, (Status) Married, (BP) IL, (D) Jan. 10, 1892, (CMTS) Cause of death La Grippe

Della Mae Lawless: (A) 1Y 27D, (BP) MO, Jan. 5, 1892, (CMTS) Cause of death La Grippe
Anna McGuire: (A) 88Y 3M, (Status) Widow, (BP) WV, Feb. 4, 1890, (CMTS) Cause of death La Grippe
Solomon Long: (A) 73Y, (Status) Married, (BP) TN, (D) Dec. 26, 1892, (CMTS) Cause of death La Grippe
James Adams: (A) 20Y, (BP) MO, (D) Feb. 24, 1890, (CMTS) Cause of death La Grippe
Eppie Le Campbell: (A) 3M, (BP) MO, (D) Feb. 3, 1890, (CMTS) Cause of death La Grippe
Rachel Riley: (A) 21D, (BP) MO, (D) Dec. 30, 1891, (CMTS) Cause of death Jaundice
Mabel Iden: (A), (D) Jan. 27, 1890, (CMTS) Cause of death Jaundice
William Harrie: (A) 50Y, (BP) MO, (D) Feb. 8, 1889, (CMTS) Cause of death Intoxication- Exposure
John Lee Bailey: (A) 13Y, (BP) MO, (D) Mar. 9, 1893, (CMTS) Cause of death Intestinal obstruction
William Abbit: (A) 84Y 3M 4D, (Status) Widower, (BP) KY, (D) Nov. 20, 1883, (CMTS) Cause of death Intestinal hephritis
Henry Parnell: (A) 44Y, (Status) Married, (BP) England, (D) Jan. 31, 1890, (CMTS) Cause of death Intestinal grippe
Carrie A. Burk: (A) 51Y 9M 1 day, (Status) Married, (BP) MD, (D) Aug. 6, 1889, (CMTS) Cause of death Intestinal catarrh
Martha Richardson: (A) 80Y, (Status) Widow, (D) Jan. 7, 1893, (CMTS) Cause of death Internal injuries
Jesse Newberry: (A) 6Y 2M 14D, (BP) MO, (D) Aug. 19, 1889, (CMTS) Cause of death Intermittent fever
Arthur Pennington: (A) 1Y 20D, (BP) MO, (D) Oct. 28, 1884, (CMTS) Cause of death Intermittent fever
William P. Morrison: (A) 84Y 7M 15D, (Status) Widower, (BP) OH, (D) Nov. 17, 1891, (CMTS) Cause of death Intermittent catarrh
Clinton J. Francisco: (A) 70Y 5M 20D, (Status) Married, (D) Apr. 28, 1890, (CMTS) Cause of death Insufficiency of third valve of heart
John Jones: (A) 38Y, (Status) Married, (BP) MO, (D) Jun. 3, 1889, (CMTS) Cause of death Injuries from bank falling on him
Josephine Jones: (A) 53Y, (Status) Married, (BP) MO, (D) Mar. 9, 1890, (CMTS) Cause of death Influenza
Mary Donnelly: (A) 70Y, (Status) Widow, (BP) Ireland, (D) Jan. 12, 1890, (CMTS) Cause of death Influenza
Frank Lee Hite: (A) 26Y 11M 2D, (BP) MO, (D) Jan. 26, 1884, (CMTS) Cause of death Inflammatory rhumatism
Myrtle Stella Christy: (A) 2Y 7M 20D, (BP), (D) Jul. 21, 1884, (CMTS) Cause of death Inflammatory diarrhea
Grace Petrie: (A) 16Y 5M 19D, (BP) IL, (D) Jul. 9, 1888, (CMTS) Cause of death Inflammation of the heart

Raymond Murphy: (A) 4M 15D, (BP) MO, (D) Sep. 17, 1891, (CMTS)
    Cause of death Inflammation of the brain
Ollie Zirkle: (A) 2Y 9M 5D, (BP) MO, (D) Jun. 30, 1888, (CMTS)
    Cause of death Inflammation of the bowels
Bernice May Hopkins: (A) 1Y 5M, (BP) MO, (D) Nov. 19, 1890, (CMTS)
    Cause of death Inflammation of stomach & bowels
Ernst Mang: (A) 4M, (BP) MO, (D) Jan. 22, 1892, (CMTS)
    Cause of death Inflammation of lungs
Oscar Vaughn: (A) 11M 3D, (BP) MO, (D) Jan. 15, 1892, (CMTS)
    Cause of death Inflammation of lungs
Muryal Brancleave: (A) 80Y 4M 10D, (Status) Married, (BP) KY, (D)
    Apr. 23, 1889, (CMTS) Cause of death Inflammation of kidneys
Bertha Zeigler: (A) 7Y 11M, (BP) MO, (D) Aug. 31, 1892, (CMTS)
    Cause of death Inflammation of brain
William Doherty: (A) 1Y 6M 3D, (BP) MO, (D) Feb. 23, 1891, (CMTS)
    Cause of death Inflammation of bowel
Mildred Overton: (A) 1Y 11M 29D, (BP) MO, (D) Nov. 10, 1884,
    (CMTS) Cause of death Inflammation croup
Helen Payue: (A) 2M, (BP) MO, (D) Apr. 25, 1893, (CMTS)
    Cause of death Infantile pneumonia
Alford Hartsoch: (A) 8M 28D, (BP) MO, (D) Jun. 28, 1889, (CMTS)
    Cause of death Infantile diarrhea
Armisted Hickman: (A) 68Y, (BP), (D) Apr. 26, 1893, (CMTS)
    Cause of death Indigestion-paralysis
Ottie Shoforer: (A) 2M, (BP) MO, (D) Nov. 24, 1891, (CMTS)
    Cause of death Inanition from indigestion
Della May Keland: (A) 1M 21D, (BP) MO, (D) Sep. 27, 1884, (CMTS)
    Cause of death Inanition
John Uhl: (A) 42Y, (Status) Married, (BP) Germany, (D) Dec. 21, 1889,
    (CMTS) Cause of death Inanition
William Alyea: (A) 8D, (BP) MO, (D) Sep. 8, 1891, (CMTS)
    Cause of death Inanition
Rose Baker: (A) 3M, (BP) MO, (D) Jul. 13, 1890, (CMTS)
    Cause of death Inanition
Mary Francis: (A) 14D, (BP) MO, (D) Feb. 21, 1890, (CMTS)
    Cause of death Inanition
Rose May Stanley: (A) 4D, (BP) MO, (D) Apr. 17, 1889, (CMTS)
    Cause of death Inanition
Jennie M. McClain: (A) 7M 10D, (BP) MO, (D) Apr. 5, 1892, (CMTS)
    Cause of death Inanition
Frank Goinns: (A) 39Y 7M 8D, (Status) Married, (BP) LA, (D)
    Dec. 30, 1886, (CMTS) Cause of death Hydrothorax
Robert Steele: (A) 43Y, (Status) Married, (BP) KY, (D)
    Apr. 2, 1893, (CMTS) Cause of death Hydro periocardium
William Jutton: (A) 1M 17D, (BP) St. Joseph, (D) Jan. 17, 1884, (CMTS)
    Cause of death Hereditary syphilis

E. James Carter: (A) 49Y 5M, (Status) Married, (BP) TN, (D)
 Jan. 22, 1885, (CMTS) Cause of death Hepattis
Sam J. Pyles: (A) 63Y 8M 7D, (Status) Married, (BP) MO, (D)
 Mar. 17, 1890, (CMTS) Cause of death Hepatitis
Sarah Jane Neal: (A) 38Y, (Status) Married, (BP) IN, (D) Mar. 29, 1891,
 (CMTS) Cause of death Hemorrhage
Annie Eliza Smith: (A) 36Y, (Status) Married, (BP) MO, (D)
 Oct. 29, 1883, (CMTS) Cause of death Hemorhage of the bowels
John Taylor: (A) 67Y 2M 14D, (Status) Married, (BP) Pennsylvania, (D)
 Nov. 3, 1883, (CMTS) Cause of death hemorhage of the bowels
John Wonderlick: (A) 50Y 3M 20D, (BP) Germany, (D) Nov. 2, 1883,
 (CMTS) Cause of death Hemorhage of the bowels
Ada Lewis: (A) 1M 7D, (BP) MO, (D) May 27, 1890, (CMTS)
 Cause of death Hemmorhage of the brain
Barbara Kell: (A) 54Y, (Status) Married, (D) Apr. 29, 1893, (CMTS)
 Cause of death Hemmorhage
Betty Edmonds: (A), (BP) KY, (D) Mar. 19, 1884, (CMTS)
 Cause of death Hemmorhage
James S. Downing: (A) 3D, (BP) Crawford Twp, (D) Mar. 11, 1884,
 (CMTS) Cause of death Hemmorhage
Nancy Jane Fiddler: (A) 36 years, (Status) Married, (BP) MO, (D)
 Sep. 12, 1883, (CMTS) Cause of death Hemmorhage
Johanna Cadde: (A) 30Y, (BP), (D) Mar. 20, 1893, (CMTS)
 Cause of death Heart trouble
Derrissa Bradway: (A) 68Y, (Status) Widow, (BP) OH, (D)
 Aug. 13, 1890, (CMTS) Cause of death Heart failure from age
William Dengler: (A) 3Y 2M 6D, (BP) MO, (D) Apr. 3, 1893, (CMTS)
 Cause of death Heart failure
Henry Bergman: (A) 48Y, (BP) Germany, (D) Feb. 6, 1891, (CMTS)
 Cause of death Heart failure
Peter Brill: (A) 41Y, (BP) MO, (D) Feb. 2, 1893, (CMTS)
 Cause of death Heart failure
John Delaney: (A) 87Y, (Status) Married, (BP) Ireland, (D) Apr. 15, 1890,
 (CMTS) Cause of death Heart failure
Jane Wood: (A) 56Y, (Status) Married, (BP) KY, (D) Feb. 28, 1891,
 (CMTS) Cause of death Heart failure
Ouly Poior: (A) 56Y 6M 20D, (Status) Married, (BP) SC, (D) Jul. 8, 1889,
 (CMTS) Cause of death Heart disease- rheumatism
Mary Ann Goss: (A) 81Y, (Status) Widow, (BP), (D) Mar. 22, 1885,
 (CMTS) Cause of death Heart disease
Elizabeth Arnold: (A) 60Y, (Status) Widow, (BP) MO, (D) Nov. 8, 1889,
 (CMTS) Cause of death Heart disease
Cecilia Wilmuth: (A) 46Y, (Status) Widow, (BP) French, (D)
 Nov. 13, 1883, (CMTS) Cause of death Heart disease
William E. Hosea: (A) 46Y 11M 21D, (Status) Widower, (BP) DE, (D)
 Apr. 17, 1893, (CMTS) Cause of death Heart disease

Frank Zeman: (A) 30Y, (BP) Bohemia, (D) Mar. 21, 1893, (CMTS)
   Cause of death Heart disease
Francis Nadean: (A) 73Y, (Status) Widower, (BP) Canada, (D)
   Sep. 13, 1889, (CMTS) Cause of death Heart disease
Arthur Kelly: (A) 71Y 8M 16D, (Status) Married, (BP) TN, (D)
   Feb. 14, 1885, (CMTS) Cause of death Heart disease
Carrie Adams: (A) 17Y 13D, (BP) MO, (D) Sep. 17, 1884, (CMTS)
   Cause of death Heart disease
Susan Cole: (A) 67Y, (Status) Widow, (BP), (D) Jul. 24, 1884, (CMTS)
   Cause of death Heart disease
T. Johnson: (A) 37Y, (BP), (D) Apr. 20, 1884, (CMTS)
   Cause of death Heart Disease
J. C. Cauley: (A) 32Y, (Status) Married, (BP) MO, (D) Aug. 25, 1889,
   (CMTS) Cause of death He hung himself with A. rope
William J. Taylor: (A) 31Y, (Status) Married, (BP) MO, (D)
   Dec. 28, 1884, (CMTS) Cause of death Gunshot wound to
   abdomen
Nelilia Hundley: (A) 81Y 7M 1 day, (Status) Widow, (D) Jun. 21, 1892,
   (CMTS) Cause of death General progressive paresis
Solomon A. White: (A) 57Y 8M 26D, (Status) Married, (BP) TN, (D)
   Aug. 25, 1884, (CMTS) Cause of death General paralysis
Mary Withers: (A), (BP) MO, (D) Feb. 18, 1890, (CMTS)
   Cause of death General exhaustion
Claude Walkendorfer: (A) 71Y 2M 10D, (Status) Widower, (BP)
   Germany, (D) Mar. 27, 1884, (CMTS) Cause of death General
   dropsy
James A. Cabineso: (A) 68Y, (Status) Widower, (BP) VA, (D)
   Jul. 23, 1884, (CMTS) Cause of death General debility
Phillip Doyle: (A) 80Y, (BP), (D) Dec. 18 8 9, (CMTS)
   Cause of death General debility
Sarah Wright: (A) 73Y, (Status) Widow, (BP), (D) Oct. 22, 1889, (CMTS)
   Cause of death General debility
Hannah Williams: (A) 72Y, (D) Mar. 31, 1884, (CMTS)
   Cause of death General debility
Samuel Butsher: (A) 70Y 9M, (Status) Widower, (BP) VA, (D)
   Jan. 3, 1890, (CMTS) Cause of death General debility
George Andrews: (A) 83Y, (Status) Widower, (BP) Scotland, (D)
   Jan. 31, 1890, (CMTS) Cause of death General debility
Nancy Hughes: (A) 72Y 2M, (Status) Widow, (BP) KY, (D) Jan. 3, 1890,
   (CMTS) Cause of death General debility
Edmund W. Cone: (A) 47Y, (Status) Married, (BP) VT, (D) Jun. 19, 1890,
   (CMTS) Cause of death General of the insane
Mason J. Hurst: (A) 1Y 3M 18D, (BP) MO, (D) Sep. 17, 1892, (CMTS)
   Cause of death Gastronitis
Charles James Christian: (A) 1Y 6M 10D, (BP) MO, (D) Oct. 27, 1891,
   (CMTS) Cause of death Gastro enteritis

Leslie Hunter: (A) 4M 2D, (BP) KS, (D) Oct. 1, 1892, (CMTS)
   Cause of death Gastro enteritis
Bessie Cargill: (A) 2Y 5M 2D, (BP) MO, (D) Jul. 11, 1892, (CMTS)
   Cause of death Gastro enteritis
Lizzie Talent: (A), (BP) MO, (D) May 7, 1890, (CMTS)
   Cause of death Gastro enteritis
Mary F. Bishop: (A) 2Y 11M 23D, (BP) MO, (D) Mar. 19, 1892, (CMTS)
   Cause of death Gastro enteritis
Ethal Perkins: (A) 12Y, (BP) MO, (D) Feb. 21, 1890, (CMTS)
   Cause of death Gastro enteritis
Lizzie Van Hozer: (A) 12Y, (BP) MO, (D) Aug. 13, 1891, (CMTS)
   Cause of death Gastro enteritis
Willie Dittemore: (A) 7M, (BP) MO, (D) Oct. 2, 1891, (CMTS)
   Cause of death Gastro enteritis
Emma McMinus: (A) 47Y, (Status) Married, (D) Nov. 9, 1889, (CMTS)
   Cause of death Gastric ulcer
Charles Ricks: (A) 60Y, (Status) Married, (BP) Germany, (D)
   Mar. 2, 1890, (CMTS) Cause of death Gangrene of the lungs
Jimmy Harvey: (A) 120Y, (Status) Widow, (BP) KY, (D) Apr. 6, 1890,
   CMTS) Cause of death Gangrene of foot
Abram C. Martain: (A) 67Y 9M, (Status) Widower, (BP) MO, (D)
   Sep. 19, 1889, (CMTS) Cause of death From A. fall
Andrew Jackson Auth: (A) 64Y, (Status) Widower, (BP) KY, (D)
   Dec. 20, 1889, (CMTS) Cause of death Fractured spinal column
Nancy Arnold: (A) 64Y 1M 28D, (BP) NC, (D) Aug. 28, 1884, (CMTS)
   Cause of death Flux
Lorin Beck: (A) 11Y, (BP) MO, (D) May 6, 1889, (CMTS)
   Cause of death fight paralyzed the heart
Jacob Kline: (A) 11Y 3M, (BP) MO, (D) Apr. 24, 1884, (CMTS)
   Cause of death Fifteen inches of something
John L. Hamilton: (A) 64Y, (BP) MD, (D) Aug. 2, 1889, (CMTS)
   Cause of death Fever followed by heart attack
Nancy Anne Dittemore: (A) 42Y, (Status) Widow, (BP), (D)
   Mar. 15, 1885, (CMTS) Cause of death fever
Betty Clark: (A) 23Y, (Status) Married, (BP) MS, (D) Oct. 20, 1884,
   (CMTS) Cause of death fever
Henry Garlon: (A) 20Y 11M 24D, (Status) Married, (BP), (D)
   Mar. 16, 1885, (CMTS) Cause of death fell on pitchfork, near heart
Fred Behrginan: (A) 45Y, (Status) Widower, (BP) Germany, (D)
   Aug. 5, 1889, (CMTS) Cause of death Fell down stairs
Josie Southerland: (A) 63Y, (Status) Married, (BP) IA, (D) May 18, 1893,
   (CMTS)   Cause of death Fatty heart
Harriet N. Cox: (A) 60Y, (Status) Married, (BP) NH, (D) Dec. 16, 1889,
   (CMTS) Cause of death Fatty degeneration of liver
Osker Totten: (A) 16Y 2M, (BP) MO, (D) Sep. 7, 1889, (CMTS)
   Cause of death Fatty degeneration of heart

Henry T. Small: (A) 41Y, (BP) MO, (D) Jan. 28, 1890, (CMTS)
Cause of death Exhaustion from mental illness
John D. Richards: (A) 45Y, (Status) Married, (BP) KY, (D) Jul. 4, 1890,
(CMTS) Cause of death Exhaustion from maniacal exertion
Margaret J. Alexander: (A) 41Y, (BP) MO, (D) Jul. 7, 1890, (CMTS)
Cause of death Exhaustion from maniacal exertion
J. R. M. Hurly: (A) 67Y, (BP) IN, (D) Jan. 30, 1890, (CMTS)
Cause of death Exhaustion from chronic insanity
Kate Dameron: (A) 35Y, (Status) Married, (BP) MO, (D) Dec. 4, 1889,
(CMTS) Cause of death Exhaustion from acute mania
Rhoda Moore: (A) 40Y, (Status) Married, (BP), (D) May 12, 1890,
(CMTS) Cause of death Exhaustion from acute mania
George Stup: (A) 70Y, (Status) Widower, (BP) England, (D)
Mar. 12, 1891, (CMTS) Cause of death Exhaustion
Louvena Lantz: (A) 26Y, (BP) MO, (D) Jul. 6, 1890, (CMTS)
Cause of death Exhaustion
Mrs. R. C. Humm: (A) 24Y, (D) Feb. 2, 1893, (CMTS) Cause of death
Erysipelas of brain
George Moore: (A) 21Y 7M, (BP) MO, (D) Nov. 4, 1890, (CMTS)
Cause of death Erysipelas & blood poison
Jessie Watson: (A) 17D, (BP), (D) Mar. 9, 1885, (CMTS)
Cause of death Erysipelas
William O'Brian: (A) 37Y, (BP) MO, (D) Jan. 14, 1890, (CMTS)
Cause of death Erysipelas
Ambrose Wenda: (A) 20Y 4M 11D, (BP) Germany, (D) Nov. 5, 1883,
(CMTS) Cause of death Erysipelas
Elizabeth Lyons: (A) 1 year, (BP) MO, (D) Sep. 1, 1883, (CMTS)
Cause of death Erysipelas
Perry Hardon: (A) 60Y 10M 3D, (Status) Married, (BP) IN, (D)
Jun. 4, 1885, (CMTS) Cause of death Erysipelas
George Bentley: (A) 25Y, (BP) NY, (D) Jul. 5, 1890, (CMTS)
Cause of death Epilepsy
Mary Barnett: (A) 7Y, (BP) MO, (D) Jun. 4, 1889, (CMTS)
Cause of death Epilepsy
E. V. Reel: (A) 41Y, (Status) Married, (BP), (D) May 2, 1890, (CMTS)
Cause of death Epilepsy
Harry Buzzard: (A) 24Y, (BP) MO, (D) Mar. 5, 1893, (CMTS)
Cause of death Epilepsy
Elkanah W. Ruth: (A) 28Y, (BP) MO, (D) Feb. 11, 1890, (CMTS)
Cause of death Epilepsy
Leroy Hall: (A) 9M, (BP) KS, (D) Jul. 28, 1890, (CMTS)
Cause of death Entro colitis
Ivy Stein: (A) 1Y 21D, (BP) MO, (D) Jul. 28, 1890, (CMTS)
Cause of death Entro colitis
Grace Jeanette Grimes: (A) 1Y 6M 24D, (BP) IL, (D) Jul. 7, 1889,
(CMTS) Cause of death Entero colitis

John H. Eppner: (A) 1Y 8M 2D, (BP) MO, (D) Jun. 16, 1890, (CMTS)
  Cause of death Entero colitis
Lucy May Bowland: (A) 9M, (D) Sep. 18, 1884, (CMTS)
  Cause of death Entero colitis
James Hickman: (A) 7M 11D, (BP) MO, (D) Jul. 3, 1891, (CMTS)
  Cause of death Entero colitis
William Hickman: (A) 7M 18D, (BP) MO, (D) Jul. 15, 1891, (CMTS)
  Cause of death Entero colitis
Mamie Shultz: (A) 5M, (BP) MO, (D) Oct. 19, 1891, (CMTS)
  Cause of death Enteritis
Carl Hindley: (A) 6M 15D, (BP) MO, (D) Jul. 19, 1884, (CMTS)
  Cause of death Enteritis
Wilford N. Kingston: (A) 11M 22D, (BP) MO, (D) Aug. 14, 1889,
  (CMTS) Cause of death Enteritis
John W. Miller: (A) 42Y, (Status) Married, (BP) OH, (D) Aug. 11, 1889,
  (CMTS) Cause of death Enseme poisioning
Sarah M. Carlson: (A) 31Y 10M 27D, (Status) Married, (D) Jul. 21, 1884,
  (CMTS) Cause of death Eclampsia
Marjarte Ann Smith: (A) 33Y 4M 17D, (Status) Married, (BP) KS, (D)
  Mar. 2, 1891, (CMTS) Cause of death Eclampsia
Randel Zodock: (A) 60Y 1M, (Status) Married, (BP) NY, (D)
  Aug. 1, 1889, (CMTS) Cause of death Dysentery-inflammation of
  bowels
Jeff Fowler: (A) 1Y 11D, (BP) MO, (D) Oct. 17, 1883, (CMTS)
  Cause of death Dysentery
Emma Slaink: (A) 5M 16D, (BP) MO, (D) Sep. 20, 1889, (CMTS)
  Cause of death Dysentery
Peter A. Keller: (A) 11M 17D, (BP) MO, (D) Jul. 5, 1884, (CMTS)
  Cause of death Dysentery
P. P. E. Rumpff: (A) 2Y 10M 19D, (BP) MO, (D) Jul. 23, 1884, (CMTS)
  Cause of death Dysentery
Erma Sloidk: (A) 5M 16D, (BP), (D) Sep. 20, 1889, (CMTS) Cause of
  death Dysentery
Blanch Hubbard: (A) 10M 8D, (BP) MO, (D) Oct. 2, 1883, (CMTS)
  Cause of death Dysentery
Caleb Carper: (A) 68Y, (Status) Married, (BP) VA, (D) Aug. 3, 1884,
  (CMTS) Cause of death Dysentery
Jesse Alvis Lemon: (A) 1Y 20D, (BP), (D) Aug. 9, 1889, (CMTS)
  Cause of death Dysentery
Effie T. Vincent: (A) 1Y 6M 18D, (BP) MO, (D) Jan. 2, 1890, (CMTS)
  Cause of death Dysentery
A. D. Jurness: (A) 1Y 4M 3D, (BP) MO, (D) Sep. 22, 1886, (CMTS)
  Cause of death Dysentery
Gustave Henske: (A) 37Y 8M, (BP) Germany, (D) Jun. 8, 1889, (CMTS)
  Cause of death Drowned
James Washington: (A) 16Y, (BP) MO, (D) Jul. 8, 1889, (CMTS)

Cause of death Drowned
John A. Iden: (A) 40Y, (Status) Widower, (BP), (D) Aug. 5, 1889,
   (CMTS) Cause of death Drowned
Frankie Hays: (A) 6Y, (BP), (D) Jul. 30, 1889, (CMTS)
   Cause of death Drownded in MO River
William Arthur Duncan: (A) 2Y, (BP) MO, (D) Jan. 19, 1891, (CMTS)
   Cause of death Dropsy of the heart
Mrs. Keller: (A) 45Y, (Status) Married, (BP), (D) Nov. 26, 1889, (CMTS)
   Cause of death Dropsy
Elizabeth Crum: (A) 67Y 11M 25D, (Status) Married, (BP) MO, (D)
   Jan. 24, 1890, (CMTS) Cause of death Dropsy
Eliza Dorsey: (A) 39Y, (Status) Married, (BP) KY, (D) Jan. 25, 1893,
   (CMTS) Cause of death Dropsy
E. S. White: (A) 50Y, (Status) Married, (BP) NC, (D) May 3, 1891,
   (CMTS) Cause of death Dropsy
Joseph Woods: (A) 1Y 3M 17D, (BP) MO, (D) Jun. 28, 1884, (CMTS)
   Cause of death Dropsey
Lucy A. James: (A) 29Y 11M 3D, (Status) Married, (BP) MO, (D)
   Nov. 3, 1883, (CMTS) Cause of death Dropsey
Mollie Roberts: (A) 29Y, (Status) Married, (BP) MO, (D) Jun. 12, 1890,
   (CMTS) Cause of death Double pneumonia
Lilas Woodson: (A) 16Y 6M 10D, (BP) MO, (D) Dec. 29, 1891, (CMTS)
   Cause of death Double pneumonia
Joseph Frakes: (A) 78Y, (Status) Married, (BP) KY, (D) Nov. 3, 1891,
   (CMTS) Cause of death Double pneumonia
Elizabeth J. Brumley: (A) 74Y, (Status) Widow, (BP) KY, (D)
   Jan. 11, 1892, (CMTS) Cause of death Double pneumonia
Margaret Judah: (A) 80Y, (Status) Widow, (BP) KY, (D) Jan. 17, 1892,
   (CMTS) Cause of death Double pneumonia
Josie Gates: (A) 30Y, (Status) Married, (D) Feb. 3, 1889, (CMTS)
   Cause of death Dose of digitalis & chloral hydrate
Mary A. Turner: (A) 66Y, (Status) Widow, (BP) TN, (D) Jun. 30, 1884,
   (CMTS) Cause of death Diseased liver
Ann Elizabeth Clutter: (A) 77Y 8M 1 day, (Status) Widow, (BP) WV, (D)
   Oct. 23, 1889, (CMTS) Cause of death Disease of the heart
Carrie Martha Efner: (A) 3Y 3M 11D, (BP) KS, (D) Dec. 9, 1889,
   (CMTS) Cause of death Diptheria-croup
Hazel Scales: (A) 4Y, (D) Dec. 27, 1890, (CMTS) Cause of death
   Diptheria croup
Sallie Shrader: (A) 6Y 3M 3D, (BP) MO, (D) Nov. 13, 1889, (CMTS)
   Cause of death Diptheria
William Kane: (A) 2Y, (BP) IA, (D) Dec. 27, 1884, (CMTS)
   Cause of death Diptheria
Worth Kilder: (A) 5Y 4M 21D, (BP) IA, (D) Dec. 24, 1889, (CMTS)
   Cause of death Diptheria
Letha Brumbeck: (A) 10M, (BP) MO, (D) Dec. 9, 1889, (CMTS)

Cause of death Diptheria
Roy Casteel: (A) 2Y 14D, (BP) MO, (D) Dec. 7, 1891, (CMTS)
    Cause of death Diptheria
Rose Bombeck: (A) 50 years, (Status) Widow, (BP) MO, (D) Oct. 7, 1883,
    (CMTS) Cause of death Diptheria
George R. Nolan: (A) 4Y 8M, (BP) MO, (D) Oct. 25, 1890, (CMTS)
    Cause of death Diptheria
C. Stewart: (A) 7Y 3M, (BP) MO, (D) Sep. 27, 1890, (CMTS)
    Cause of death Diptheria
Alvin Scott: (A) 8Y, (BP) KS, (D) Sep. 10, 1891, (CMTS)
    Cause of death Diptheria
Rose Ida Schmidt: (A) 12Y, (BP) MO, (D) Jul. 31, 1891, (CMTS) Cause
    of death Diptheria
Benjamin H. Lasee: (A) 2Y 6M 5D, (BP) NE, (D) Mar. 19, 1891, (CMTS)
    Cause of death Diptheria
M. E. McCabe: (A) 12Y 1M, (BP), (D) Jan. 14, 1885, (CMTS)
    Cause of death Diptheria
M. G. Mannan: (A) 11Y, (BP) MO, (D) Jan. 11, 1885, (CMTS)
    Cause of death Diptheria
Anton Lorens: (A) 5Y 9M, (BP) MO, (D) Jan. 12, 1889, (CMTS)
    Cause of death Diptheria
Vena Esther Robinson: (A) 1Y 7M 18D, (BP) MO, (D) Nov. 30, 1884,
    (CMTS) Cause of death Diptheria
Walter Call: (A) 2Y 7M 15D, (BP) MO, (D) May 14, 1885, (CMTS)
    Cause of death Diptheria
Nancy Alice Wells: (A) 3Y, (BP), (D) Nov. 11, 1886, (CMTS)
    Cause of death Diptheria
Austin Cobb: (A) 10M 10D, (BP) MO, (D) Mar. 7, 1884, (CMTS)
    Cause of death Diptheria
Mamie Combs: (A) 1Y 1M 11D, (D) Oct. 11, 1884, (CMTS)
    Cause of death Diptheria
Ben M. Kennedy: (A) 2Y 1M, (BP) MO, (D) Jan. 7, 1890, (CMTS)
    Cause of death Diptheria
Manda Ethel McCauly: (A) 1Y 5M, (BP) MO, (D) Jan. 1, 1890, (CMTS)
    Cause of death Diptheria
Hattie D. Ferrell: (A) 3Y 3M 15D, (BP) MO, (D) Oct. 20, 1884, (CMTS)
    Cause of death Diptheria
Benjamin Duncan: (A) 7Y 2M 17D, (BP) MO, (D) Oct. 17, 1883, (CMTS)
    Cause of death Diptheria
Myrta Lykins: (A) 4 years, (BP) MO, (D) Aug. 17, 1883, (CMTS)
    Cause of death Diptheria
Mary Ann Mollett: (A) 62Y 9M 4D, (Status) Widow, (BP) Switzerland,
    (D) May 29, 1890, (CMTS) Cause of death Dilated heart chorea
Edward Jordan: (A) 75Y, (BP) NC, (D) Aug. 23, 1884, (CMTS)
    Cause of death Diarrhea
Annie Benson: (A) 2Y, (BP) KS, (D) Jul. 12, 1890, (CMTS)

Cause of death Diarrhea
Delia Clifton: (A) 11M, (BP) MO, (D) Jul. 25, 1890, (CMTS)
 Cause of death Diarrhea
Nellie Williams: (A) 5M, (BP) MO, (D) May 6, 1893, (CMTS)
 Cause of death Diarrhea
Mart Ann Lawport: (A) 63Y 5M 3D, (BP) England, (D) Jan. 10, 1891,
 (CMTS) Cause of death Diabetes
Cora Witt: (A) 13Y, (BP) MO, (D) Dec. 31, 1885, (CMTS)
 Cause of death Diabetes
Bartholomew Schuler: (A) 52Y, (Status) Married, (BP) Germany, (D)
 May 23, 1884, (CMTS) Cause of death Delerium tremons
William Glenn: (A) 30Y, (BP) MO, (D) Mar. 13, 1890, (CMTS)
 Cause of death Degeneration
Mrs. R. C. Sterrett: (A) 84Y 3M, (Status) Widow, (BP) PA, (D)
 Feb. 16, 1884, (CMTS) Cause of death Debility
William Burnett: (A) 74Y 7M, (Status) Married, (BP) TN, (D)
 Nov. 11, 1884, (CMTS) Cause of death Debility
Mary Gay Kingsburry: (A) 68Y 9M 29D, (Status) Married, (BP) NY, (D)
 May 16, 1889, (CMTS) Cause of death Cystic tumor on left ovary
Henry Weaver: (A) 85Y, (Status) Married, (D) Jun. 14, 1889, (CMTS)
 Cause of death Crushed under brick wall
Eugene Early: (A) 15Y 7M 13D, (BP) MO, (D) Mar. 24, 1889, (CMTS)
 Cause of death Croupous bronchitis
Mary Ann McSpeen: (A) 2Y, (BP) Ireland, (D) Nov. 5, 1883, (CMTS)
 Cause of death Croup
Anna Thomas: (A) 4M 5D, (BP) MO, (D) Nov. 9, 1883, (CMTS)
 Cause of death Croup
Herman Eibett: (A) 3Y 4M 15D, (BP), (D) Oct. 29, 1889, (CMTS)
 Cause of death Cramp
Mamie L. Esherton: (A) 1Y 4M 4D, (BP) KS, (D) Jul. 3, 1890, (CMTS)
 Cause of death Corrosive poisoning
Minnie Elizabeth Parker: (A) 5Y 6M 7D, (BP) KS, (D) Oct. 3, 1889,
 (CMTS) Cause of death Convulsions
Frank E. Linnvillle: (A) 3M 21D, (BP) MO, (D) Sep. 6, 1884, (CMTS)
 Cause of death Convulsions
Minnie Harris: (A) 11M, (BP), (D) Sep. 4, 1889, (CMTS)
 Cause of death Convulsions
Pansy Lee Clutter: (A) 49D, (BP) MO, (D) Sep. 25, 1889, (CMTS)
 Cause of death Convulsions
Leola Tanner: (A) 1Y 1M 17D, (BP) MO, (D) Aug. 5, 1890, (CMTS)
 Cause of death Convulsions
Edna Richardson: (A) 1M 7D, (BP) MO, (D) Mar. 23, 1889, (CMTS)
 Cause of death Convulsions
Martha D. Selectman: (A) 58Y, (Status) Widow, (BP) KY, (D)
 Nov. 1, 1891, (CMTS) Cause of death Consumption of the bowels
James A. Hull: (A) 32Y 7M 4D, (Status) Married, (BP) IL, (D)

Oct. 19, 1883, (CMTS) Cause of death Consumption of lungs
Jake B. Finch: (A) 30Y 2M 25D, (BP), (D) Mar. 18, 1885, (CMTS)
 Cause of death Consumption
Andrew Lashaway: (A) 58Y, (Status) Married, (BP) France, (D)
 Dec. 23, 1883, (CMTS) Cause of death Consumption
Peter Hanson: (A) 31Y, (Status) Married, (BP) Germany, (D)
 Dec. 2, 1889, (CMTS) Cause of death Consumption
Dan Wilson: (A) 22Y, (BP) MO, (D) Dec. 2, 1889, (CMTS)
 Cause of death Consumption
Susan Northrup: (A) 25Y, (Status) Widow, (BP) MO, (D) Oct. 27, 1889,
 (CMTS) Cause of death Consumption
Elizabeth Alexander: (A) 36Y, (Status) Widow, (BP) KY, (D)
 Oct. 6, 1890, (CMTS) Cause of death Consumption
Cora Stafford: (A) 27Y, (Status) Married, (BP) MO, (D) Oct. 23, 1889,
 (CMTS) Cause of death Consumption
Ed. C. Ripley: (A) 34Y, (Status) Married, (D) Jul. 22, 1886, (CMTS)
 Cause of death Consumption
Henry Matzoff: (A), (Status) Married, (BP), (D) Jul. 8, 1889, (CMTS)
 Cause of death Consumption
Margaret M. Johnson: (A) 36Y, (BP) MI, (D) Jul. 27, 1890, (CMTS)
 Cause of death Consumption
Edwin McDonald: (A) 29Y 4M 12D, (BP) Pennsylvania, (D)
 Jul. 11, 1892, (CMTS) Cause of death Consumption
Ellen Mahaney: (A) 27Y 7M 14D, (Status) Widow, (D) May 19, 1890,
 (CMTS) Cause of death Consumption
Clara Gillespie: (A), (Status) Married, (D) Apr. 15, 1893, (CMTS)
 Cause of death Consumption
John Schmitte: (A) 62Y, (Status) Widower, (BP) Germany, (D)
 Mar. 12, 1893, (CMTS) Cause of death Consumption
Linda Gardner: (A) 21Y 8M 12D, (Status) Married, (BP) IA, (D)
 Mar. 19, 1890, (CMTS) Cause of death Consumption
E. E. Crowle: (A) 49Y 11M, (Status) Married, (BP) IA, (D) Mar. 1, 1890,
 (CMTS) Cause of death Consumption
Charlotte E. Vaughn: (A) 27Y 1M 7D, (BP), (D) Mar. 6, 1885, (CMTS)
 Cause of death Consumption
Lydia Thompson: (A) 36Y, (Status) Married, (BP) MO, (D) Feb. 17, 1890,
 (CMTS) Cause of death Consumption
Elizabeth Shirley: (A) 58Y, (BP) KY, (D) Feb. 23, 1890, (CMTS)
 Cause of death Consumption
Alexander Green: (A) 24Y, (BP) MO, (D) Feb. 2, 1891, (CMTS)
 Cause of death Consumption
W. O. McDonald: (A) 30Y 9M 27D, (BP) PA, (D) Feb. 2, 1891, (CMTS)
 Cause of death Consumption
Flora L. Blount: (A) 29Y 8M, (Status) Married, (BP) MO, (D)
 Jan. 2, 1884, (CMTS) Cause of death Consumption
Elizabeth Kiene: (A) 36Y, (BP) England, (D) Jan. 11, 1884, (CMTS)

Cause of death Consumption
Aaron S. Balm: (A) 23Y, (BP), (D) Jan. 29, 1890, (CMTS)
Cause of death Consumption
Carciannis Cianciola: (A) 23Y 3M, (BP) Italy, (D) Jan. 12, 1893, (CMTS)
Cause of death Consumption
Martha Hill: (A) 32Y 5M 5 dys, (Status) Married, (BP) MO, (D)
    Dec. 7, 1890, (CMTS) Cause of death Consumption
Ellen Grover: (A) 29Y 1M, (Status) Married, (BP) MO, (D)
    May 29, 1885, (CMTS) Cause of death Consumption
Paul Kessler: (A) 41Y 1M 6D, (BP) MO, (D) Nov. 17, 1890, (CMTS)
    Cause of death Consumption
Emma Jane Wadsworth: (A) 17Y 7M 21D, (BP) MO, (D) Apr. 15, 1891,
    (CMTS) Cause of death Consumption
Benjamin Franklin Jones: (A) 15Y 11M 16D, (BP) MO, (D) Jul. 26, 1891,
    (CMTS) Cause of death Consumption
Laura Lee King: (A) 26Y 10M 15D, (BP) MO, (D) Feb. 26, 1890,
    (CMTS) Cause of death Consumption
Sidney Ann Hale: (A) 29Y 4M 18D, (Status) Married, (BP) MO, (D)
    Aug. 16, 1884, (CMTS) Cause of death Consumption
J. C. Gordon: (A) 46Y 11M 20D, (Status) Married, (BP) NC, (D)
    Oct. 7, 1884, (CMTS) Cause of death Consumption
Sabrina Gordon: (A) 63Y 14M, (BP) KY, (D) May 3, 1884, (CMTS)
    Cause of death Consumption
William W. Clark: (A) 45Y 20D, (Status) Married, (BP) NY, (D)
    Apr. 25, 1884, (CMTS) Cause of death Consumption
Edna E. Riley: (A) 30Y 10M 10D, (Status) Married, (BP), (D)
    Mar. 27, 1885, (CMTS) Cause of death Consumption
Godfrey Rietzlaw: (A) 57Y, (Status) Married, (BP) Germany, (D)
    Mar. 28, 1893, (CMTS) Cause of death Consumption
Herman Heamelni: (A) 32Y, (BP), (D) Sep. 5, 1889, (CMTS)
    Cause of death Consumption
Fredrick Curtis: (A) 8M, (BP) MO, (D) Jan. 29, 1889, (CMTS)
    Cause of death Congeston of the lungs
Gerusha Knapp: (A) 52Y, (Status) Married, (BP) KY, (D) Jan. 18, 1890,
    (CMTS) Cause of death Congestive chill
Harry Willis: (A) 6Y, (BP) KS, (D) Jun. 23, 1885, (CMTS)
    Cause of death Congestive chill
Sarah J. Wilson: (A) 9Y 2M 10D, (D) Dec. 9, 1883, (CMTS)
    Cause of death congestion-chill
Emma Thomas: (A) 41Y, (Status) Married, (BP) MO, (D) Aug. 18, 1891,
    (CMTS) Cause of death Congestion, stomach and bowels
Maggie Spaulding: (A), (BP) MO, (D) Dec. 3, 1889, (CMTS)
    Cause of death Congestion pulmonary
Martha Mary Sestrup: (A) 8M 30D, (BP) MO, (D) May 12, 1893, (CMTS)
    Cause of death Congestion of the lungs
Mary Langdon: (A) 21Y, (D) Jan. 17, 1890, (CMTS)

Cause of death Congestion of the lungs
Arthur Gray: (A) 9 1/2D, (BP), (D) Aug. 28, 1889, (CMTS)
   Cause of death Congestion of the lungs
Liza Willis: (A) 60Y, (Status) Widow, (BP), (D) Apr. 6, 1889, (CMTS)
   Cause of death Congestion of the lungs
Evan Jordan: (A) 73Y 11M 7D, (BP) NC, (D) Jan. 23, 1886, (CMTS)
   Cause of death Congestion of the lungs
Adda Arnold: (A) 4M 20D, (BP) MO, (D) Aug. 2, 1883, (CMTS)
   Cause of death Congestion of the lungs
Caroline Deits: (A) 10M. 20D, (BP) MO, (D) Jul. 20, 1883, (CMTS)
   Cause of death Congestion of the lungs
Pearl Blaine Gacson: (A) 2M 5D, (BP) MO, (D) Dec. 31, 1884, (CMTS)
   Cause of death congestion of the lungs
Raymond Adams: (A) 1Y 6M, (BP) MO, (D) Aug. 26, 1883, (CMTS)
   Cause of death Congestion of the lungs
Joseph H. Igler: (A) 43Y 6M, (Status) Married, (BP) Prussia, (D)
   Sep. 28, 1889, (CMTS) Cause of death Congestion of the brain
Albert McDowell: (A) 17Y, (BP) MO, (D) Apr. 10, 1889, (CMTS)
   Cause of death Congestion of the brain
Mrs. Gus Fleming: (A) 27Y, (Status) Married, (BP) MO, (D)
   Feb. 11, 1885, (CMTS) Cause of death Congestion of the brain
Josiah Howard: (A) 39Y 6M, (BP), (D) Jan. 15, 1885, (CMTS)
   Cause of death Congestion of the brain
Rosa T. McPherson: (A), (BP) MO, (D) Nov. 25, 1889, (CMTS)
   Cause of death Congestion of stomach and bowel
Judge Patrick McIntyre: (A) 57Y 5M, (Status) Married, (BP) Ireland, (D)
   Sep. 29, 1890, (CMTS) Cause of death Congestion of stomach &
   bowels
Lucy Ann Deshon: (A) 20Y, (BP) MO, (D) Aug. 1884, (CMTS)
   Cause of death Congestion of lungs
Lee S. Gordon: (A) 2Y 6M, (BP) MO, (D) Sep. 30, 1890, (CMTS)
   Cause of death Congestion of lungs
Viola May Howard: (A) 4M 28D, (BP) MO, (D) Jun. 7, 1890, (CMTS)
   Cause of death Congestion of lungs
Infant Gartsby: (A) 11D, (BP) MO, (D) Apr. 12, 1891, (CMTS)
   Cause of death Congestion of lungs
Henry Miller: (A) 3Y 8M, (BP) MO, (D) Jan. 3, 1891, (CMTS)
   Cause of death Congestion of lungs
Clinton Allen: (A) 6M, (BP) MO, (D) Feb. 24, 1890, (CMTS)
   Cause of death Congestion of brain & cord
Thomas Smith: (A) 27Y, (BP), (D) Oct. 5, 1884, (CMTS)
   Cause of death Congestion of brain
Clifton McDye: (A) 9D, (BP) MO, (D) Aug. 13, 1889, (CMTS)
   Cause of death Congestion of brain
Helen F. Magress: (A) 1Y 2M 7D, (BP) MO, (D) Jun. 30, 1891, (CMTS)
   Cause of death Congestion of brain

William Krach: (A) 19Y, (BP) MO, (D) Apr. 13, 1890, (CMTS)
  Cause of death Congestion of brain
Sadie Wamington: (A) 4M 26D, (BP) MO, (D) Mar. 28, 1890, (CMTS)
  Cause of death Congestion of brain
Henry Bullard Mann: (A) 1Y 4M 22D, (BP) MO, (D) Jan. 3, 1893,
  (CMTS) Cause of death Congestion of brain
Thomas J. Bryant: (A) 62Y, (Status) Married, (BP) KY, (D) Jan. 21, 1893,
  (CMTS) Cause of death Congestion of bowels
Elizabeth Robinson: (A) 80Y 10M 22D, (Status) Widow, (BP) KY, (D)
  Mar. 7, 1886, (CMTS) Cause of death Congestion of bowels
Smith Stevens: (A) 40Y, (Status) Widower, (D) Jun. 23, 1889, (CMTS)
  Cause of death Congestion
Anna Francis Weuges: (A) 5Y 13D, (BP) MO, (D) Jul. 9, 1891, (CMTS)
  Cause of death Congestion
Thomas Culligan: (A) 61Y, (Status) Married, (BP) County Clare, Ireland,
  (D) Dec. 28, 1888, (CMTS) Cause of death Concussion of the
  brain
Almis Cauedy: (A), (Status) Married, (D) Apr. 27, 1893, (CMTS)
  Cause of death Concussion of the brain
Frank Callihan: (A) 32Y, (Status) Married, (BP) MO, (D) Sep. 14, 1889,
  (CMTS) Cause of death Concussion of brain from blow
Terry Rose: (A) 55Y 7M 3D, (Status) Married, (D) Sep. 10, 1889,
  (CMTS) Cause of death Concussion of brain
Bethenia Almond: (A) 72Y, (Status) Widow, (BP) MO, (D)
  Aug. 15, 1884, (CMTS) Cause of death Complications
Regina Hindley: (A) 23Y 2M 7D, (Status) Married, (BP) Germany, (D)
  May 28, 1884, (CMTS) Cause of death Complications
Maggie M. Wood: (A) 1Y 1M 9D, (BP) MO, (D) Jan. 22, 1884, (CMTS)
  Cause of death Combination
A. R. Foye: (A) 36Y, (Status) Married, (BP) OH, (D) Dec. 29, 1888,
  (CMTS) Cause of death Collision with A. train and streetcar
James Cameron Fisher: (A) 2Y 1M 17D, (BP) MO, (D) Jul. 29, 1884,
  (CMTS) Cause of death Colitis
Fredrick Jorgensen: (A) 7M 28D, (BP) MO, (D) Jul. 14, 1885, (CMTS)
  Cause of death Colitis
Rettie May Saunders: (A) 4M 18D, (BP) MO, (D) Jan. 27, 1885, (CMTS)
  Cause of death Colitis
James Gabbert: (A) 2Y 6M, (BP) MO, (D) Aug. 11, 1891, (CMTS)
  Cause of death Colitis
Elizabeth J. Regan: (A) 53Y 7M, (Status) Married, (BP) OH, (D)
  Jun. 30, 1889, (CMTS) Cause of death Colignatic diarrhea
Fannie R. Chase: (A) 46Y, (Status) Married, (BP) NH, (D) Oct. 1, 1889,
  (CMTS) Cause of death Cirrhosis of liver
Josephine Alders: (A) 28Y 6M 9D, (Status) Married, (BP) Germany, (D)
  Mar. 17, 1893, (CMTS) Cause of death Childbed fever
Fredrick Westphaling: (A) 71Y 10M 7D, (Status) Married, (BP) Germany,

(D) Jan. 19, 1890, (CMTS) Cause of death Chronic softening of the brain

James C. Pruitt: (A) 8Y, (D) Feb. 15, 1893, (CMTS) Cause of death Chronic rheumatism

Michael Hogan: (A) 56Y, (Status) Widower, (BP) Ireland, (D) Jan. 14, 1890, (CMTS) Cause of death Chronic phthisis pulmonari

Harvey L. Williams: (A) 73Y 4M 27D, (Status) Married, (BP) NH, (D) Aug. 9, 1889, (CMTS) Cause of death Chronic intestinal nephritis

John B. Allen: (A) 41Y, (Status) Married, (BP) MO, (D) Apr. 7, 1890, (CMTS) Cause of death Chronic insanity

William Henry Matthews: (A) 29Y, (Status) Married, (BP) KY, (D) Oct. 31, 1889, (CMTS) Cause of death Chronic hepatitis

John H. Hunt: (A) 43Y 7M, (Status) Married, (BP) KY, (D) Jun. 1, 1891, (CMTS) Cause of death Chronic hepatitis

Rosina Dicker: (A) 67Y, (BP) Germany, (D) Feb. 25, 1892, (CMTS) Cause of death Chronic hepatitis

Americus Vespucius Murphy: (A) 57Y 7M 15D, (Status) Married, (BP) KY, (D) Feb. 14, 1891, (CMTS) Cause of death Chronic gastritis

Daniel W. Cornish: (A) 66Y, (BP) Ireland, (D) Oct. 6, 1891, (CMTS) Cause of death Chronic gastritis

William O'Hara: (A) 49Y 7M 12D, (Status) Married, (BP) Ireland, (D) Dec. 24, 1889, (CMTS) Cause of death Chronic disease of spinal cord

Peter Kessler: (A) 35Y 3M 2D, (Status) Married, (BP) KY, (D) Jan. 13, 1885, (CMTS) Cause of death Chronic diarrhea

James Rekman: (A) 64Y 2D, (Status) Married, (BP) VA, (D) May 16, 1884, (CMTS) Cause of death Chronic congestion

Eddie Francis Stewart: (A) 10M 14D, (D) Apr. 9, 1890, (CMTS) Cause of death Chronic bronchitis

Sara Ford: (A) 76Y 6M, (Status) Widow, (BP) NY, (D) Feb. 21, 1890, (CMTS) Cause of death Chronic bronchitis

Mrs. E. J. Feland: (A) 67Y 3M 8D, (Status) Married, (BP) KY, (D) Feb. 14, 1886, (CMTS) Cause of death Chronic Bronchitis

Bridget Cannon: (A) 58Y, (Status) Married, (BP) Ireland, (D) Feb. 5, 1890, (CMTS) Cause of death Chronic Brights disease

Gwin Chicklaw: (A) 62Y, (Status) Married, (BP), (D) Feb. 12, 1892, (CMTS) Cause of death Chronci hepatitis

Emma Clay: (A) 9M 24D, (BP), (D) Sep. 10, 1884, (CMTS) Cause of death Cholera infantum

William C. Fisher: (A) 2Y 1M 1 day, (BP) MO, (D) Jul. 13, 1884, (CMTS) Cause of death Cholera infantum

Clarence Gant: (A) 2Y, (BP) MO, (D) Jul. 24, 1884, (CMTS) Cause of death Cholera infantum

Melina Melissa McBride: (A) 2Y 7M 14D, (BP) MO, (D) Jul. 11, 1889, (CMTS) Cause of death Cholera infantum

Hazel Kirke Richardson: (A) 3M 9D, (BP) MO, (D) Jul. 6, 1889, (CMTS)

Cause of death Cholera infantum
William Henry Marshall: (A) 5M, (BP) MO, (D) Jul. 26, 1889, (CMTS)
 Cause of death Cholera infantum
Henry Dunbar: (A) 6M 28D, (BP) MO, (D) Jul. 10, 1890, (CMTS)
 Cause of death Cholera infantum
James H. Powell: (A) 1Y 7D, (BP) MO, (D) Jul. 11, 1892, (CMTS)
 Cause of death Cholera infantum
Ethel Florence Rapp: (A) 7M 15D, (BP), (D) Jun. 8, 1889, (CMTS)
 Cause of death Cholera infantum
James Cassell: (A) 5M 1 day, (BP) MO, (D) Jun. 17, 1889, (CMTS)
 Cause of death Cholera infantum
Ray Mitchell: (A) 1Y 1M 1 day, (BP) MO, (D) Jun. 27, 1889, (CMTS)
 Cause of death Cholera infantum
Birdie May Brown: (A) 1Y 7M 3D, (BP) MO, (D) Jun. 3, 1890, (CMTS)
 Cause of death Cholera infantum
Bertha Alma Davidson: (A) 9M 23D, (D) May 29, 2889, (CMTS)
 Cause of death Cholera infantum
Lillie Mae Rodie: (A) 6Y 6M 6D, (BP) St. Joseph, (D) Feb. 26, 1884,
 (CMTS) Cause of death Cholera infantum
Charley C. Kirkman: (A) 11M, (BP) MO, (D) Jul. 30, 1886, (CMTS)
 Cause of death Cholera infantum
E. J. Smith: (A) 1Y 5M 27D, (BP) MO, (D) Jul. 9, 1887, (CMTS)
 Cause of death Cholera infantum
Millard Frakes: (A) 5M, (BP) MO, (D) Jul. 19, 1890, (CMTS)
 Cause of death Cholera infantum
John Frakes: (A) 5M, (BP) MO, (D) Jul. 19, 1890, (CMTS)
 Cause of death Cholera infantum
Lawrence August Wetteroth: (A) 9M 14D, (BP), (D) Sep. 4, 1889,
 (CMTS) Cause of death Cholera infantum
Herman O. Gleaves: (A) 7M 23D, (BP) MO, (D) Aug. 5, 1884, (CMTS)
 Cause of death Cholera infantum
Cerena Graves: (A) 39Y 12D, (Status) Married, (BP) MO, (D)
 Mar. 22, 1885, (CMTS) Cause of death Childbirth
Clara Barada: (A) 27Y 2M, (Status) Married, (BP) KS, (D) Mar. 29, 1890,
 (CMTS) Cause of death Childbed fever
Eliza Jane Carrity: (A) 40Y, (Status) Married, (BP) IN, (D) Aug. 1, 1884,
 (CMTS) Cause of death Childbed fever
Henry Ellinger: (A) 3Y, (BP) MO, (D) May 16, 1889, (CMTS)
 Cause of death Cerebro spinal meningitis
Maggie Nolan: (A) 15Y 9M, (BP) NE, (D) Jul. 6, 1889, (CMTS)
 Cause of death Cerebro spinal meningitis
J. Perry Cunningham: (A) 41Y 3M 22D, (Status) Married, (BP) KY, (D)
 Nov. 8, 1883, (CMTS) Cause of death Cerebro spinal meningitis
James Nash: (A) 27Y, (Status) Married, (BP) MO, (D) Jan. 1, 1886,
 (CMTS) Cause of death Cerebral meningitis
William Striblen: (A) 55Y 9M 25D, (Status) Married, (BP) Germany, (D)

Mar. 11, 1893, (CMTS) Cause of death Cerebral hemorrhage
August Edward Matzing: (A) 7M 13D, (BP) MO, (D) Nov. 28, 1891, (CMTS) Cause of death Cerebral convulsions
Luretta Jeris: (A) 6M 2D, (BP) MO, (D) Aug. 4, 1889, (CMTS) Cause of death Cerebral congestion
Fay Agnes Burke: (A) 5M 15D, (BP) MO, (D) Jun. 10, 1889, (CMTS) Cause of death Cerebral congestion
Samuel B. Green: (A) 40Y 5M 3D, (Status) Married, (BP) MO, (D) Jun. 26, 1890, (CMTS) Cause of death Cerebral apoplexy
Mary N. Works: (A) 75Y 7D, (Status) Widow, (BP) KY, (D) Jan. 21, 1892, (CMTS) Cause of death Cerebral apoplexy
Frank Bosley Campbell: (A) 32Y, (Status) Married, (BP) KY, (D) Jan. 7, 1891, (CMTS) Cause of death Cerebral apoplexy
William Luce: (A) 10Y, (BP), (D) Oct. 18, 1889, (CMTS) Cause of death Cerebral affection
Mildred Ethel Gray: (A) 1Y 1M 27D, (BP) MO, (D) Nov. 17, 1890, (CMTS) Cause of death Cerebral abcess
John G. Harrison: (A) 48Y 2M 27D, (Status) Married, (BP) IL, (D) Mar. 4, 1890, (CMTS) Cause of death Central hemorrhage of bowels
Julian H. Johnson: (A) 24Y 3M 2D, (BP), (D) Sep. 25, 1889, (CMTS) Cause of death Cattarrh & pneumonia
Frank Dennis: (A) 2Y 2M 14D, (BP) MO, (D) Apr. 18, 1890, (CMTS) Cause of death Catarrh pneumonia
Charles W. Smith: (A) 34Y 7M 24D, (Status) Married, (BP) KS, (D) Apr. 4, 1893, (CMTS) Cause of death Cardiac neuralgia
Fritz George Law: (A) 49Y, (BP) Germany, (D) Apr. 5, 1893, (CMTS) Cause of death Cardiac
Martha A. Williams: (A) 71Y 4M 13D, (Status) Married, (BP) MO, (D) Jan. 23, 1892, (CMTS) Cause of death Carcinoma of uterus
Lizzie Miller: (A) 2Y, (BP) MO, (D) Nov. 22, 1889, (CMTS) Cause of death Capillary pneumonia
Anna Maria Schneider: (A) 1Y 11M, (BP) MO, (D) Dec. 21, 1889, (CMTS) Cause of death Capillary bronchitis
Mamie Baddock: (A) 4M 20D, (BP) MO, (D) Dec. 31, 1891, (CMTS) Cause of death Capillary bronchitis
Albert F. Holly: (A) 2M 21D, (BP) MO, (D) Dec. 28, 1891, (CMTS) Cause of death Capillary bronchitis
Ethel May Harrison Doyle: (A) 9M 7D, (BP) MO, (D) Jun. 17, 1889, (CMTS) Cause of death Capillary bronchitis
Minnie May Russell: (A) 1Y 11M 3D, (BP) KS, (D) Jun. 23, 1889, (CMTS) Cause of death Capillary bronchitis
John Cline: (A) 5Y 3M, (BP) NE, (D) Apr. 28, 1889, (CMTS) Cause of death Capillary Bronchitis
Nettie Cline: (A) 3Y 3M 25D, (BP) MO, (D) Apr. 25, 1889, (CMTS) Cause of death Capillary bronchitis

Charles Arthur Hardy: (A) 3Y 3M 6D, (BP) MO, (D) Apr. 6, 1890,
    (CMTS) Cause of death Capillary bronchitis
Josie Pryor: (A) 1M 7D, (BP) MO, (D) Apr. 2, 1893, (CMTS)
    Cause of death Capillary bronchitis
Cecil Sherman: (A) 1Y 10M 29D, (BP) MO, (D) Feb. 1, 1892, (CMTS)
    Cause of death Capillary bronchitis
Cora Augusta Wilson: (A) 1Y 5M 3D, (BP) MO, (D) Feb. 14, 1892,
    (CMTS) Cause of death Capillary bronchitis
Alice Clark: (A) 11M, (BP) MO, (D) Feb. 18, 1890, (CMTS)
    Cause of death Capillary bronchitis
Rachel Strong: (A) 79Y, (Status) Married, (BP) PA, (D) May 17, 1884,
    (CMTS) Cause of death Capilary Bronchitis
Thomas C. Carrington: (A) 1Y 4M 29D, (BP) MO, (D) Oct. 8, 1884,
    (CMTS) Cause of death Cancrumotis
Mary Bailey Phillips: (A) 53Y 3M 19D, (Status) Widow, (BP) England,
    (D) Dec. 12, 1889, (CMTS) Cause of death Cancer of womb
Elizabeth Booth: (A) 71Y 9M, (BP) KY, (D) Feb. 16, 1890, (CMTS)
    Cause of death Cancer of the stomach
Charles Robert Hegan: (A) 51Y 1M 13D, (Status) Married, (BP)
    Germany, (D) Feb. 13, 1892, (CMTS) Cause of death Cancer of
    stomach
Michael O'Brian: (A) 60Y, (BP) Ireland, (D) Jul. 31, 1890, (CMTS)
    Cause of death Cancer of stomach
Thaddius Muller: (A) 65Y, (Status) Widower, (BP) Europe, (D)
    May 21, 1886, (CMTS) Cause of death Cancer of stomach
Paul Fisher: (A) 60Y, (Status) Widower, (BP), (D) Sep. 11, 1889, (CMTS)
    Cause of death Cancer in throat
Joseph Brady: (A) 48Y, (Status) Married, (BP) VA, (D) Dec. 29, 1889,
    (CMTS) Cause of death Cancer
Mary Acklum: (A) 55Y, (Status) Married, (BP) KY, (D) Nov. 10, 1892,
    (CMTS) Cause of death Cancer
James Runcie: (A) 55Y 9D, (Status) Married, (BP) Ireland, (D)
    May 12, 1889, (CMTS) Cause of death Cancer
Lucy Young: (A) 37Y 10M 15D, (BP) MO, (D) Apr. 1, 1889, (CMTS)
    Cause of death Cancer
Matilda Parks: (A) 40Y, (Status) Married, (BP) KY, (D) Aug. 20, 1889,
    (CMTS) Cause of death by falling from A. train in motion
Johnson Foster: (A) 59Y, (Status) Married, (D) Sep. 15, 1889, (CMTS)
    Cause of death Burned to death
Alice Pearl Topper: (A) 10M, (BP) MO, (D) Mar. 21, 1890, (CMTS)
    Cause of death Broncho pneumonia
Louis Miller: (A) 65Y, (Status) Married, (BP) Germany, (D)
    Feb. 13, 1890, (CMTS) Cause of death Broncho pneumonia
Alice Elwin Leneur: (A) 1Y, (BP) MO, (D) Apr. 6, 1890, (CMTS)
    Cause of death Bronchitis with convulsion
Eugene Troy: (A) 7Y, (BP) KS, (D) Dec. 16, 1889, (CMTS)

Cause of death Bronchitis and croup
Elizabeth Elder: (A) 65Y 21D, (BP) KY, (D) May 26, 1885, (CMTS) Cause of death Bronchitis
Amanda Viola Keaton: (A) 6M, (BP) MO, (D) Nov. 26, 1889, (CMTS) Cause of death Bronchitis
Bartholemew Klonski: (A) 59Y 12D, (Status) Married, (BP) Prussia, (D) Sep. 6, 1889, (CMTS) Cause of death Bronchitis
Clarence C. Churdhill: (A) 21Y, (D) Sep. 16, 1884, (CMTS) Cause of death Bronchitis
James H. Barnett: (A) 33Y 1M 8D, (Status) Married, (BP) MO, (D) Jul. 3, 1891, (CMTS) Cause of death Bronchitis
Kitty Washington: (A) 30Y, (BP) MO, (D) Apr. 2, 1893, (CMTS) Cause of death Bronchitis
David Ray Christie: (A) 6Y 15D, (BP) NE, (D) Mar. 22, 1884, (CMTS) Cause of death Bronchitis
Thomas W. Palmer: (A) 7M, (BP), (D) Mar. 16, 1884, (CMTS) Cause of death Bronchitis
Alvel Wooster: (A) 5Y, (BP) MA, (D) Mar. 27, 1884, (CMTS) Cause of death Bronchitis
Walter Wolfolk: (A) 31Y, (BP) TN, (D) Mar. 30, 1885, (CMTS) Cause of death Bronchitis
Zula Wilson: (A) 5Y, (BP) MO, (D) Mar. 12, 1890, (CMTS) Cause of death Bronchitis
Charles A. Stout: (A) 2Y 14M, (BP), (D) Feb. 8, 1891, (CMTS) Cause of death Bronchitis
Charles Smith: (A) 2Y 8M 16D, (BP) St. Joseph, (D) Jan. 27, 1887, (CMTS) Cause of death Bronchitis
Price Starks: (A) 1Y 7M, (BP) MO, (D) Jan. 25, 1891, (CMTS) Cause of death Bronchitis
Polly Jane West: (A) 71Y 26D, (Status) Widow, (BP) KY, (D) Mar. 14, 1886, (CMTS) Cause of death Bronchitis
Martha Ann Baker: (A) 83Y 6M 24D, (Status) Widow, (BP) NC, (D) Dec. 4, 1883, (CMTS) Cause of death Bronchitiis
Jesse Anderson: (A) 62Y, (Status) Married, (D) Nov. 10, 1889, (CMTS) Cause of death Bronchial pneumonia
James Gilmore: (A) 42Y 7M 20D, (Status) Widower, (BP) MO, (D) May 3, 1889, (CMTS) Cause of death Bronchial pneumonia
Mary E. Coylein: (A) 70Y 7M 19D, (BP) VT, (D) Mar. 31, 1884, (CMTS) Cause of death Bronchial catarrh
Elizabeth Russell: (A) 34Y, (Status) Married, (BP) Scotland, (D) Nov. 7, 1891, (CMTS) Cause of death Brights disease of kidneys
James F. Walker: (A) 71Y 11M 13D, (Status) Widower, (BP) NC, (D) Jul. 13, 1890, (CMTS) Cause of death Brights disease of kidneys
Mahlon Cain: (A) 55Y, (Status) Married, (BP) OH, (D) May 5, 1890, (CMTS) Cause of death Brights disease of kidneys
Jane Hickman: (A) 71Y, (Status) Widow, (BP) IN, (D) Sep. 13, 1891,

(CMTS) Cause of death Brights disease and heart failure
Henry J. Davis: (A) 62Y 3M, (Status) Married, (BP) WV, (D)
   Jul. 12, 1891, (CMTS) Cause of death Brights disease
Adolphus Duane: (A) 20Y 4M 13D, (BP) MO, (D) Jan. 17, 1891, (CMTS)
   Cause of death Brights disease
Martha Kelly: (A) 62Y 8M 3D, (Status) Widow, (BP), (D) Nov. 11, 1886,
   (CMTS) Cause of death Bright disease
Francis Basser: (A) 76Y, (Status) Married, (BP) France, (D)
   Nov. 12, 1893, (CMTS) Cause of death Brain softening
Mary Jane Jenkins: (A) 5M, (BP) MO, (D) Sep. 27, 1884, (CMTS)
   Cause of death Brain inflammation
William Norris: (A) 6Y, (BP) MO, (D) Dec. 30, 1885, (CMTS)
   Cause of death Brain fever
Dexter D. Frendh: (A) 9M 3D, (BP) MO, (D) Aug. 4, 1890, (CMTS)
   Cause of death Brain fever
Maud Hall: (A) 1Y 8M 5D, (BP) MO, (D) Aug. 14, 1890, (CMTS)
   Cause of death Brain fever
Chrissie E. Alley: (A) 24Y, (Status) Married, (BP) KS, (D) Aug. 8, 1884,
   (CMTS) Cause of death Bowel inflammation
A. A. Deatherage: (D) Aug. 25, 1884, (CMTS) Cause of death Bowel
   hemmorhage
Vance Morrow: (A) 60Y 5M 10D, (Status) Married, (BP) PA, (D)
   Jul. 3, 1884, (CMTS) Cause of death Bowel congestion
Elizabeth Smith: (A) 6Y 6M 4D, (BP), (D) Apr. 28, 1893, (CMTS)
   Cause of death Blood poisoning
Isaac Smith: (A) 35Y, (Status) Married, (BP) MO, (D) Aug. 2, 1889,
   (CMTS) Cause of death Blood poisoning
Oscar Saylor: (A) 38Y, (Status) Married, (BP) MO, (D) Jun. 22, 1890,
   (CMTS) Cause of death Basilor meningitis
Etta Knopp: (A) 24Y, (Status) Married, (BP) IL, (D) Jun. 26, 1889,
   (CMTS) Cause of death Asthma cardis
B. Weller: (A) 80Y, (Status) Married, (BP) Germany, (D) Oct. 31, 1891,
   (CMTS) Cause of death Asthma & pulmonary edema
Margaret Clark: (A) 66Y, (Status) Widow, (BP) NY, (D) Mar. 7, 1890,
   (CMTS) Cause of death Asthma & influenza
Simeon Warner: (A) 76Y 9M, (Status) Married, (BP) England, (D)
   May 9, 1891, (CMTS) Cause of death Asthma
M. E. Roents: (A) 59Y 3M, (Status) Married, (BP) Germany, (D)
   Aug. 14, 1889, (CMTS) Cause of death Asthma
Henry T. Calhoun: (A) 1 1/2M, (BP) MO, (D) Feb. 10, 1890, (CMTS)
   Cause of death Asphyxia, strangled
Amelia Ringer: (A) 55Y, (Status) Married, (BP) Germany, (D)
   Jan. 23, 1884, (CMTS) Cause of death Apoplexy of brain
James H. Rings: (A) 56Y, (Status) Married, (BP) KY, (D) Oct. 2, 1890,
   (CMTS) Cause of death Apoplexy
Loren Z. Rupp: (A) 70Y 8M, (Status) Widower, (BP) Germany, (D)

Feb. 14, 1890, (CMTS) Cause of death Apoplexy
Jacob Diddy: (A) 75Y 11M, (Status) Married, (BP) PA, (D) Aug. 18,1884, (CMTS) Cause of death Apoplexy
Susan Daniel: (A) 75Y 11M 23D, (Status) Widow, (BP) KY, (D) May 14, 1885, (CMTS) Cause of death Apoplexy
Woodford George: (A), (Status) Married, (BP) MO, (D) Oct. 5, 1884, (CMTS) Cause of death Apoplexy
Sarah A. Norris: (A) 50Y 11M 18D, (Status) Married, (BP) MO, (D) Aug. 15, 1884, (CMTS) Cause of death Apoplexy
John Calhoun: (A) 80Y 3M 7D, (Status) Married, (BP) PA, (D) Nov. 18, 1891, (CMTS) Cause of death Anemia
Jemima Hargrove: (A) 24Y 3M 15D, (Status) Married, (BP) MO, (D) Feb. 10, 1885, (CMTS) Cause of death Anemia
Clait Phillips: (A) 49Y, (Status) Married, (BP) MO, (D) Sep. 28, 1889, (CMTS) Cause of death Alcoholism and heart disease
Charles Gilman: (A) 30Y, (BP), (D) Sep. 15, 1884, (CMTS) Cause of death Alcoholism
James Fitzgerald: (Status) Widower, (BP) Ireland, (D) Feb. 23, 1890, (CMTS) Cause of death Acute yellow atrophy of liver
Daisy Conner: (A) 3 years 10M, (D) Oct. 8, 1883, (CMTS) Cause of death Acute tonsilitis
David Hardin: (A) 10Y, (BP) IN, (D) Jul. 20, 1890, (CMTS) Cause of death Acute rheumatism
Annie Brown: (A) 12Y, (BP) MO, (D) Apr. 9, 1890, (CMTS) Cause of death Acute pneumonia
Ellen Powers: (A) 7D, (BP) MO, (D) Mar. 28, 1893, (CMTS) Cause of death Acute pneumonia
Alvin B. Clark: (A) 25Y 2M 5D, (Status) Married, (BP) IA, (D) Aug. 24, 1889, (CMTS) Cause of death Acute peritonitis
Eliza Sewell: (A) 65Y, (Status) Widow, (D) Feb. 25, 1893, (CMTS) Cause of death Acute laryngitis
Clark Schneider: (A) 39Y 13D, (Status) Married, (BP) VA, (D) Mar. 27, 1893, (CMTS) Cause of death Acute inflammatory rheumatism
Isaac Bunting: (A) 2M 2D, (BP) MO, (D) Apr. 8, 1890, (CMTS) Cause of death Acute hydrocephalus
Bertha Mark: (A) 4M, (BP) MO, (D) Jul. 8, 1890, (CMTS) Cause of death Acute gastritis
Dottie Jones: (A) 2M 14D, (BP) MO, (D) Jul. 5, 1891, (CMTS) Cause of death Acute gastritis
Samuel Harry Gay: (A) 2Y 5M 11D, (BP) MO, (D) Aug. 3, 1889, (CMTS) Cause of death Acute encephalitis
Francis Mary Bloomer: (A) 11D, (BP) MO, (D) Aug. 9, 1889, (CMTS) Cause of death Acute congestion of lungs
Patrick Galvin: (A) 35Y, (Status) Widower, (D) Feb. 18, 1893, (CMTS) Cause of death Acute alcoholism

George Barnes: (A) 14Y 4D, (BP) MO, (D) Jan. 19, 1885, (CMTS) Cause of death Accidental shotgun wound
James Garth: (A) 26Y, (BP), (D) Jan. 10, 1891, (CMTS) Cause of death Accidental gunshot wound
Jane Hix: (A) 86Y 7M, (Status) Widow, (BP) NC, (D) Sep. 21, 1884, (CMTS) Cause of death Accidental fall
Mrs. C. Balter: (A) 61Y, (Status) Married, (BP) Germany, (D) Sep. 15, 1889, (CMTS) Cause of death Accidental fall
Joseph Weidner: (A) 28Y, (D) Apr. 13, 1893, (CMTS) Cause of death Accident
Rosa Brown: (A) 18Y 10M, (BP) KS, (D) Apr. 28, 1892, (CMTS) Cause of death Abortion-puerperal septicemia
Ellen DeClue: (A) 48Y 10M 3D, (Status) Married, (BP) Wales, (D) Mar. 22, 1884, (CMTS) Cause of death Abdominal dropsy
Sarah H. Bush: (A) 31Y, (Status) Married, (BP) MO, (D) May 9, 1884, (CMTS) Cause of death Abdominal dropsey
Martha A. King: (A) 59Y 7M 3D, (Status) Widow, (BP) KY, (D) Feb. 20, 1885, (CMTS) Cause of death Abdominal disease
A. M. Wilson: (A) 31Y, (Status) Married, (BP) MO, (D) Apr. 21, 1890, (CMTS) Cause of death Abcess of liver
John Reisberge: (A) 38Y, (BP) Sweden, (D) Sep. 13, 1889, (CMTS) Cause of death Abcess of liver
Andrew Cartha: (A), (Status) Married, (BP), (D) May 20, 1890, (CMTS) Cause of death Abcess of brain
Margaret Shulz: (A) 47Y 3M 14D, (Status) Married, (BP) Switzerland, (D) Oct. 21, 1890, (CMTS) Cause of death Abcess
T. J. Thomas: (A) 24Y 4M 1 day, (BP) MO, (D) Jun. 12, 1891
William Wilson: (A) 54Y 3M 7D, (Status) Widower, (BP) IN, (D) Apr. 5, 1885
Jane Highlane: (A) 55Y, (Status) Married, (BP) KY, (D) May 16, 1885
John Dougherty: (A) 2Y, (BP) MO, (D) Dec. 7 1 -189
Grover E. Roberts: (A) 4Y, (D) Apr. 28, 1893
Marie T. Rice: (A) 53Y, (Status) Widow, (BP) MA, (D) Apr. 1, 1891
Paul Sheridan: (A) 21Y, (BP) Ireland, (D) Mar. 14, 1891
Hendrach Felling: (A) 73Y, (Status) Married, (BP) Germany, (D) Dec. 24, 1891
Edna May Buchanan: (A) 1Y, (BP) MO, (D) Dec. 18, 1889
Joseph Kenyon: (A) 6D, (BP) MO, (D) Dec. 31, 1890
Lucinda L. Gage: (A) 50Y 8M 19D, (Status) Married, (BP) NY, (D) Oct. 18, 1884
Gilbert H. Rough: (A) 11M 8D, (BP) MO, (D) Oct. 17, 1889
Robert Brown: (A) 13D, (BP) MO, (D) Oct. 21 8 90
Ralph L. Powell: (A) 16Y 11M 14D, (BP) KS, (D) Oct. 29, 1890
Matilda Ann Walker: (A) 18 years, (BP) MO, (D) Oct. 18, 1883
John Dillon Hunt: (A) 4Y 8M 10D, (BP) MO, (D) Oct. 24, 1883
Agnes Louise Perry: (A) 4Y 14D, (BP) MO, (D) Sep. 5, 1891

Lula Vaugh: (A) 2Y 2M 11D, (BP) MO, (D) Aug. 29, 1884
Verah Vance: (A) 1Y 7M 8D, (BP) MO, (D) Jul. 28, 1884
Estell Maud Casteel: (A) 7Y 6M, (BP) MO, (D) Jun. 1, 1884
Eliza J. Brown: (A) 60Y, (Status) Widow, (BP), (D) May 14 1893
John B. Fitzpatrick: (A) 43Y, (Status) Married, (BP) WI, (D)
    May 11, 1893
Nellie Brady: (A) 6M 17D, (BP) MO, (D) May 7, 1884
Clarence A. Monaghan: (A) 5M, (BP) MO, (D) May 29, 1890
Hannah Ballenger: (A) 71Y, (BP), (D) Apr. 19, 1893
William Minton: (A) 48Y 4M 4D, (Status) Married, (BP) England,
    (D) Mar. 31, 1885
Lena Kusker: (A) 28Y, (Status) Married, (BP) Germany,
    (D) Mar. 17, 1893
Annie Lula Barber: (A), (BP) MO, (D) Mar. 29, 1892
Catherine Brand: (A) 41Y, (Status) Married, (BP) Ireland, (D)
    Feb. 8, 1884
Clara Lisette Neudorff: (A) 29Y 11M 18D, (Status) Married, (BP) IA,
    (D) Feb. 6, 1892
Warren M. Colgne: (A) 10M 18D, (BP) KS, (D) Feb. 24, 1891
Emma R. Ritter: (A) 31Y 4M 7D, (BP) MO, (D) Feb. 25, 1892
Margretha Stewart: (A) 9M, (BP) MO, (D) Feb. 28, 1892
John Stars: (A), (BP) Switzerland, (D) Feb. 12, 1892
Mrs. Mary Warburton: (A) 79Y 9M 12D, (Status) Widow, (BP) England,
    (D) Jan. 23, 1891
Mary Horeuse Mooney: (A) 31Y 3M 10D, (Status) Married, (BP) MO,
    (D) Jan. 12, 1892
Erastus S. Tate: (A) 36Y, (Status) Widower, (BP) VA, (D) Jan. 11, 1884
James M. Steinbaugh: (A) 33Y 7M 6D, (Status) Married, (BP) IN, (D)
    Feb. 19, 1891
John M. Jeffries: (A) 62Y 11D, (BP) IA, (D) Dec. 2, 1884
Maney Hamm: (A) 1Y 9M 8D, (BP) Rushville, (D) Sep. 24, 1887
Emma R. Jones: (A) 27Y 4M 22D, (Status) Married, (BP) MO,
    (D) Jul. 18, 1884
Susan Forkner: (A) 29Y, (Status) Married, (BP) MO, (D) Feb. 22, 1885
J. C. McSpadden: (A) 34Y, (Status) Married, (BP) MO, (D) Apr. 4, 1890
Joseph P. Brown: (A) 64Y 10M 12D, (Status) Married, (BP) ME, (D)
    Jul. 10, 1891
Catherine Bryant: (A) 66Y, (Status) Married, (BP) MO, (D) Jan. 20, 1885
Laura Combs: (A) 32Y 11M 5D, (Status) Married, (BP) KS, (D)
    Nov. 9, 1892
Margaret P. Waller: (A) 30Y 3M 16D, (Status) Married, (BP) MO, (D)
    May 10, 1893
Henry B. Sanders: (A) 70Y 11M 28D, (Status) Widower, (BP) VA, (D)
    Nov. 4, 1883
Lizzie Degan: (A) 2Y 8M 14D, (BP) VA, (D) Oct. 26, 1884
Annie Francis Galvin: (A) 9Y 1M 21D, (BP) MO, (D) Apr. 11, 1884

Sally M. Conn: (A) 37Y, (Status) Married, (BP) MO, (D) Feb. 29, 1884
Pearl Stafford: (A) 1Y 3M, (BP) MO, (D) Feb. 10, 1884
Hew J. Sprocke: (A) 1Y 4M 26D, (BP), (D) Jan. 15, 1885
Mrs. C. A. Welch: (A) 31Y 10M, (Status) Married, (BP), (D) Aug. 4, 1891
James Mullhollen: (A) 58Y, (Status) Married, (BP) Germany, (D) Jan. 22, 1884
Charles R.. Schirtzer: (A) 33Y, (BP) OH, (D) Jan. 31, 1890
A. Hoss: (A) 71Y, (BP), (D) Dec. 18 8 9
Vealin Minner: (A) 15Y, (D) Nov. 20, 1884
Liddie Fiddler: (A) 19Y, (Status) Married, (BP), (D) Apr. 10, 1885
Albert Pasternack: (A) 3Y, (D) Apr. 26, 1886
Henry Hyre: (A) 41Y 4M 3D, (D) Apr. 7, 1886
Mollie Courterey: (A) 4M 24D, (BP) MO, (D) Jan. 4, 1891

St. Louis County, Missouri Marriages, January, 1840
Henry Brinkmann and Mary C. Ralfs, (MD) Jan. 21, 1840
Joseph Bruns and Margaret A. Bralmann, (MD) Jan. 20, 1840
John Casper and Margaret Marcline, (MD) Jan. 18, 1840
Francois Castongn and Therese DesAutels, (MD) Jan. 21, 1840
John Davis and Elizabeth Barry, (MD) Jan. 15, 1840
Adam Deuschbauer and Catharine Borel, (MD) Jan. 1, 1840
John Fetlor and Mary Marg Conrod, (MD) Jan. 1, 1840
George Fr Frass and Anna M. Knoch, (MD) Jan. 12, 1840
Bernard T. Friemann and Ann C. Westerkamp, (MD) Jan. 28, 1840
Thomas Gahan and Elizabeth Murphy, (MD) Jan. 28, 1840
Henry Gerdemann and Katharine Sachtleben, (MD) Jan. 23, 1840
Frederich Gruen and Anna Catha Knecht, (MD) Jan. 8, 1840
John Heun and Dorothy Zwingmann, (MD) Jan. 30, 1840
Wilhelm Holsbach and Elizabeth Och, (MD) Jan. 7, 1840
Robert Keys and Nancy P. Rogers, (MD) Jan. 26, 1840
Dieterich Krening and Catharine Seekers, (MD) Jan. 18, 1840
John P. Lollar and Mary Whitset, (MD) Jan. 2, 1840
Michael McCaffrey and Ann Hussey, (MD) Jan. 12, 1840
Daniel Moore and Ellen Ayres, (MD) Jan. 21, 1840
John Adam Muller and Mary Blubach, (MD) Jan. 15, 1840
Carsten Octkis and Ann Lisette Bruning, (MD) Jan. 27, 1840
Joseph Opal and Eliza Allen, (MD) Jan. 27, 1840
Christoph Schiller and Elizabeth Korn, (MD) Jan. 2, 1840
Joseph Schumacher and Maria Magdal Eckart, (MD) Jan. 23, 1840
John Henry Sirunk and Dustokea Grevenstede, (MD) Jan. 22, 1840
Samuel Steel and Mrs. Catherine Williams, (MD) Jan. 0, 1840
Harrison C. W. Tyler and Laura D. Watson, (MD) Jan. 26, 1840
John W. Wieberg and Bernardina Schulte, (MD) Jan. 7, 1840
Stephen Young and Ann Fries, (MD) Jan. 27, 1840

Obituary of Thelka Laming Wooden, "*Leavenworth, KS Times,* "May 19, 1992

Thelka Lamind Wooden of Lee's Summit, Mo., A. homemaker, died Monday, May 18, 1992. She was 84. She was born Oct. 20, 1907, in Tonganoxie, the daughter of John Caulton and Daisy Poetsch Laming. She had been A. resident of the John Knox Village, Lee's Summit, for the past 15 years, moving there from Lawrence. Mrs. Wooden was A. 1929 graduate of Kansas University, where she was A. member of Kappa Kappa Gamma sorority. She married James C. Wooden on Jan. 2, 1934, in Tonganoxie. He died Dec. 21, 1965. Survivors include A. son, John C. Wooden, Lawrence; A. sister, Lenore Jenkins, Lee's Summit; and three grandchildren. Visitation will be from 6:30 to 8 p.m. today at the Quisenberry funeral Chapel. Tonganoxie. Burial will be in Hubbell Hill Cemetery.

Lawrence County, Missouri, Springfield Land Office, Land Patents, 1861-1899

John Ackerson: (ID) Jun. 11, 1895, (AN) MO6000.422
Sampson Adams: (ID) Dec. 20, 1881, (AN) MO5890.058
John W. Adcock: (ID) Nov. 23, 1891, (AN) MO5950.304
Polina E. Alexander: (ID) Feb. 5, 1872, (AN) MO5820.035
Thomas J. Alexander: (ID) Sep. 5, 1895, (AN) MO6010.156
William B. Allen: (ID) Oct. 10, 1866, (AN) MO3240.250
Lemuel W. Allen: (ID) Mar. 15, 1865, (AN) MO3230.348
Lemuel W. Allen: (ID) Mar. 1, 1867, (AN) MO3250.115
Lemuel W. Allen: (ID) Mar. 1, 1867, (AN) MO3250.281
James W. Allen: (ID) Mar. 10, 1873, (AN) MO5830.015
Lemuel W. Allen: (ID) Jul. 17, 1890, (AN) MO5930.186
James Allman: (ID) Oct. 21, 1891, (AN) MO5950.157
James Allman: (ID) Sep. 10, 1880, (AN) MO5880.424
John F. Anderson: (ID) Jul. 5, 1866, (AN) MO3240.121
Joseph Anderson: (ID) Jul. 5, 1866, (AN) MO3240.234
Leroy P. Anderson: (ID) Mar. 25, 1872, (AN) MO5820.066
John D. Arnhart: (ID) Mar. 23, 1889, (AN) MO5910.493
William H. Atkerson: (ID) Feb. 5, 1872, (AN) MO5820.046
Nathaniel Atkerson: (ID) Mar. 25, 1873, (AN) MO5830.014
Aaron A. Baxter: (ID) Aug. 25, 1871, (AN) MO5810.200
Isaac A. Beckett: (ID) Dec. 30, 1871, (AN) MO5810.416
Elias M. Bennett: (ID) Jul. 10, 1883, (AN) MO5890.456
Aaron H. Berry: (ID) Oct. 1, 1872, (AN) MO5820.232
Joseph F. Berry: (ID) Oct. 1, 1872, (AN) MO5820.183
James Birmingham: (ID) Jun. 23, 1888, (AN) MO5900.366
Charles Bogart: (ID) Oct. 1, 1861, (AN) MO5720.482
William N. Bottom: (ID) Sep. 10, 1861, (AN) MO5720.470
George F. Bowers: (ID) Jul. 1, 1871, (AN) MO5740.389

John J. Bowers: (ID) Jul. 1, 1871, (AN) MO5740.389
William H. Bowers: (ID) Jul. 1, 1871, (AN) MO5740.389
William Bowles: (ID) Mar. 15, 1877, (AN) MO5870.130
Dio C. Brashers: (ID) Nov. 15, 1871, (AN) MO5810.282
James A. Bridges: (ID) Oct. 21, 1891, (AN) MO5950.130
Samuel Bridges: (ID) Dec. 1, 1865, (AN) MO3230.443
John Brown: (ID) Jun. 1, 1868, (AN) MO3250.298
John Brown: (ID) Jul. 10, 1871, (AN) MO5810.151
William Brown: (ID) Apr. 10, 1874, (AN) MO5840.021
Elisha Browning: (ID) Mar. 27, 1861, (AN) MO5720.225
Elisha Browning: (ID) Sep. 7, 1867, (AN) MO5730.081
Elisha Browning: (ID) Mar. 1, 1867, (AN) MO3250.042
Samuel M. Brumback: (ID) Jan. 5, 1875, (AN) MO5840.319
Silas Burnett: (ID) Jun. 23, 1888, (AN) MO5900.470
William Burrow: (ID) Dec. 30, 1871, (AN) MO5810.439
Ignatius Cagle: (ID) Nov. 1, 1871, (AN) MO5810.279
Mahulda Cagle: (ID) Jul. 10, 1871, (AN) MO5810.114
David Cagle: (ID) Aug. 20, 1872, (AN) MO5750.184
Samuel Caldwell: (ID) Aug. 25, 1871, (AN) MO5810.192
Joseph Call: (ID) Feb. 1, 1873, (AN) MO5820.450
William L. Call: (ID) Apr. 22, 1889, (AN) MO5920.032
Andrew T. Call: (ID) Apr. 6, 1898, (AN) MO6030.205
George W. Campbell: (ID) Dec. 15, 1892, (AN) MO5980.304
Cornelius Canine: (ID) Jul. 20, 1869, (AN) MO5740.019
James H. Carnette: (ID) Nov. 25, 1870, (AN) MO5810.010
Amon Carr: (ID) Nov. 1, 1871, (AN) MO5810.262
William P. Carson: (ID) Mar. 13, 1895, (AN) MO6000.254
Elizabeth J. Carter: (ID) Apr. 18, 1891, (AN) MO5940.447
John D. Carter: (ID) Jun. 30, 1879, (AN) MO5880.135
Peter Carter: (ID) Aug. 15, 1888, (AN) MO5910.374
Robert Castiller: (ID) Dec. 1, 1869, (AN) MO5740.041
Francis M. Castley: (ID) Apr. 1, 1871, (AN) MO5740.326
James B. Chandler: (ID) Mar. 23, 1897, (AN) MO5800.130
Jefferson Clark: (ID) Aug. 25, 1871, (AN) MO5810.198
James M. Clark: (ID) Mar. 25, 1873, (AN) MO5830.016
Francis Clayton: (ID) Nov. 15, 1871, (AN) MO5810.293
David Coble: (ID) Jan. 25, 1878, (AN) MO5870.329
Thomas Cochran: (ID) Mar. 1, 1861, (AN) MO5720.297
David A. Cole: (ID) Aug. 25, 1871, (AN) MO5810.182
William C. Cole: (ID) Mar. 17, 1871, (AN) MO5740.367
John N. Cole: (ID) Jun. 30, 1879, (AN) MO5880.113
Green L. Colley: (ID) Jul. 10, 1871, (AN) MO5810.110
William H. Collins: (ID) Oct. 30, 1874, (AN) MO5840.250
Abner M. Collins: (ID) Mar. 25, 1872, (AN) MO5820.080
Henry Compton: (ID) Oct. 1, 1872, (AN) MO5820.230
Chesley P. Cook: (ID) Feb. 15, 1875, (AN) MO5850.019

John C. Costley: (ID) Mar. 20, 1873, (AN) MO5820.457
Louisa Costley: (ID) Mar. 20, 1873, (AN) MO5820.457
Cynthia A. Cox: (ID) Sep. 10, 1880, (AN) MO5880.389
Samuel H. Criteser: (ID) Sep. 25, 1894, (AN) MO6000.006
Charles R. Cummings: (ID) Mar. 1, 1867, (AN) MO3250.228
Charles R. Cummings: (ID) Feb. 1, 1873, (AN) MO5820.327
James W. Curtis: (ID) Mar. 25, 1872, (AN) MO5820.079
Andrew J. Davidson: (ID) Dec. 1, 1865, (AN) MO3230.430
Andrew J. Davidson: (ID) Jun. 15, 1866, (AN) MO3240.040
Andrew J. Davidson: (ID) Jun. 15, 1866, (AN) MO3240.041
Andrew J. Davidson: (ID) Jul. 5, 1866, (AN) MO3240.173
Andrew J. Davidson: (ID) Mar. 1, 1867, (AN) MO3250.216
Timothy W. Davis: (ID) Jun. 15, 1866, (AN) MO3240.026
Timothy W. Davis: (ID) Jun. 15, 1866, (AN) MO3240.027
Ephreigm Davis: (ID) Feb. 1, 1873, (AN) MO5820.422
Thomas B. Davis: (ID) Feb. 1, 1873, (AN) MO5820.423
Samuel Davis: (ID) Jul. 27, 1897, (AN) MO5800.149
Selima Derrick: (ID) Mar. 25, 1871, (AN) MO5810.013
Columbus Dillow: (ID) Oct. 23, 1895, (AN) MO6010.167
Amburs J. Doss: (ID) Sep. 25, 1894, (AN) MO6000.007
William Downey: (ID) Nov. 15, 1875, (AN) MO5750.383
Andrew J. Druen: (ID) Jul. 30, 1878, (AN) MO5870.401
Albert J. Dudley: (ID) Apr. 18, 1891, (AN) MO5940.468
George M. Dugger: (ID) Oct. 1, 1870, (AN) MO5740.177
William Duvault: (ID) Mar. 1, 1861, (AN) MO5720.305
Harvey Eastess: (ID) Jan. 10, 1876, (AN) MO5860.116
Joseph W. Ellis: (ID) Jul. 1, 1871, (AN) MO5740.427
Fred Erickson: (ID) Apr. 2, 1891, (AN) MO5780.452
Nathaniel Ethridge: (ID) Dec. 30, 1871, (AN) MO5810.456
Ernst G. Fellwock: (ID) Apr. 5, 1883, (AN) MO5890.411
Alexander Fellwock: (ID) Mar. 22, 1896, (AN) MO6010.469
Abraham Fetter: (ID) Sep. 12, 1888, (AN) MO5910.433
Jacob A. Flourney: (ID) Jun. 15, 1866, (AN) MO3240.097
Jacob A. Flourney: (ID) Jun. 15, 1866, (AN) MO3240.098
Jacob A. Flourney: (ID) Jun. 15, 1866, (AN) MO3240.099
Jacob A. Flourney: (ID) Jun. 15, 1866, (AN) MO3240.100
Jacob A. Flourney: (ID) Jun. 15, 1866, (AN) MO3240.101
Jacob A. Flourney: (ID) Jun. 15, 1866, (AN) MO3240.106
Jacob A. Flourney: (ID) Jun. 15, 1866, (AN) MO3240.108
Jacob A. Flourney: (ID) Jun. 15, 1866, (AN) MO3240.109
Jacob A. Flourney: (ID) Jun. 15, 1866, (AN) MO3240.110
Jacob A. Flourney: (ID) Jun. 15, 1866, (AN) MO3240.111
Jacob A. Flourney: (ID) Jul. 5, 1866, (AN) MO3240.115
Jacob A. Flournoy: (ID) Oct. 10, 1866, (AN) MO3240.284
Jacob A. Flournoy: (ID) Oct. 10, 1866, (AN) MO3240.285
Jacob A. Flournoy: (ID) Oct. 10, 1866, (AN) MO3240.286

Jacob A. Flournoy: (ID) Oct. 10, 1866, (AN) MO3240.287
Jacob A. Flournoy: (ID) Oct. 10, 1866, (AN) MO3240.288
Jacob A. Flournoy: (ID) Oct. 10, 1866, (AN) MO3240.244
Jacob A. Flournoy: (ID) Oct. 10, 1866, (AN) MO3240.245
Jacob A. Flournoy: (ID) Jun. 15, 1866, (AN) MO3240.085
Jacob A. Flournoy: (ID) Jun. 15, 1866, (AN) MO3240.086
Jacob A. Flournoy: (ID) Jun. 15, 1866, (AN) MO3240.088
Jacob A. Flournoy: (ID) Jun. 15, 1866, (AN) MO3240.089
Jacob A. Flournoy: (ID) Jun. 15, 1866, (AN) MO3240.091
Jacob A. Flournoy: (ID) Mar. 1, 1867, (AN) MO3250.004
James H. Foglesong: (ID) Apr. 23, 1889, (AN) MO5920.193
George L. Forlines: (ID) Mar. 10, 1862, (AN) MO5730.011
Monroe Fortner: (ID) Dec. 15, 1892, (AN) MO5980.339
Abram P. Fraiser: (ID) Aug. 25, 1871, (AN) MO5810.194
Reason Friend: (ID) Aug. 20, 1872, (AN) MO5750.186
Thomas Fullbright: (ID) Jul. 10, 1871, (AN) MO5810.152
William H. Gardner: (ID) Sep. 10, 1880, (AN) MO5880.391
William D. Garrison: (ID) Jun. 15, 1866, (AN) MO3240.037
Henry H. Gaw: (ID) Dec. 30, 1871, (AN) MO5810.422
John L. George: (ID) Aug. 25, 1871, (AN) MO5810.189
James W. Gholston: (ID) Sep. 5, 1895, (AN) MO6010.157
Sarah J. Gilbert: (ID) Feb. 1, 1873, (AN) MO5820.405
Sylvanus O. Goodrich: (ID) Nov. 25, 1871, (AN) MO5810.358
Sylvanus O. Goodrich: (ID) Mar. 20, 1871, (AN) MO3270.297
Thomas Graham: (ID) Dec. 20, 1875, (AN) MO5860.034
Edwin H. Green: (ID) Jan. 14, 1899, (AN) MO1150.398
Edwin H. Greer: (ID) Jul. 5, 1866, (AN) MO3240.131
John W. Griffith: (ID) Nov. 10, 1875, (AN) MO5850.431
John F. Griffith: (ID) Nov. 1, 1873, (AN) MO5830.350
William B. Grissom: (ID) Jul. 20, 1869, (AN) MO5740.020
Jesse M. Gum: (ID) Jan. 4, 1898, (AN) MO6030.074
John J. Gunter: (ID) Oct. 5, 1875, (AN) MO5850.340
James A. Hammer: (ID) Jun. 15, 1866, (AN) MO3240.038
R. G. Hankins: (ID) Nov. 15, 1871, (AN) MO5810.281
George N. Hannah: (ID) Jun. 30, 1879, (AN) MO5880.081
James R. Harden: (ID) Nov. 25, 1871, (AN) MO5810.359
Cairrel C. Harden: (ID) Jun. 25, 1885, (AN) MO5770.163
John S. Hargrove: (ID) Mar. 10, 1870, (AN) MO5740.084
Polina E. Hargrove: (ID) Feb. 5, 1872, (AN) MO5820.035
George W. Harris: (ID) Mar. 6, 1896, (AN) MO6010.419
Cyrus W. Hatfield: (ID) Mar. 1, 1868, (AN) MO5730.249
Dan Heaton: (ID) Mar. 1, 1867, (AN) MO3250.128
Julia A. Hewlett: (ID) Nov. 25, 1870, (AN) MO5810.009
Thomas J. Hewlett: (ID) Nov. 25, 1870, (AN) MO5810.009
James P. Hewlett: (ID) Jul. 5, 1866, (AN) MO3240.176
Thomas J. Hewlett: (ID) Mar. 1, 1867, (AN) MO3250.022

James P. Hewlett: (ID) Oct. 1, 1872, (AN) MO5820.190
John M. Hewlett: (ID) Aug. 20, 1872, (AN) MO5750.180
Mary M. Hewlett: (ID) Oct. 1, 1872, (AN) MO5820.190
John R. Hillhouse: (ID) Jun. 1, 1866, (AN) MO3230.497
Elijah B. Hillhouse: (ID) Mar. 1, 1867, (AN) MO3250.117
Elijah B. Hillhouse: (ID) Mar. 1, 1867, (AN) MO3250.118
James D. Hillhouse: (ID) Mar. 1, 1867, (AN) MO3250.127
William R. Hillhouse: (ID) Aug. 1, 1871, (AN) MO5810.158
Elijah B. Hillhouse: (ID) Feb. 1, 1873, (AN) MO5820.294
Thomas H. Holland: (ID) Jun. 10, 1873, (AN) MO5830.197
Rachel S. Holmes: (ID) Jul. 17, 1890, (AN) MO5930.207
Eli W. Hood: (ID) Oct. 25, 1893, (AN) MO5990.311
John A. Hood: (ID) Oct. 1, 1872, (AN) MO5820.145
Peter M. Hood: (ID) Aug. 10, 1888, (AN) MO5910.260
Lorenzo D. Hooker: (ID) Oct. 1, 1872, (AN) MO5820.177
James M. Hoover: (ID) Jul. 1, 1874, (AN) MO5840.038
William Hopkins: (ID) Jul. 30, 1878, (AN) MO5870.410
William F. Hundley: (ID) Jul. 10, 1871, (AN) MO5810.115
Daniel Hunt: (ID) Mar. 1, 1861, (AN) MO5720.272
Andrew Huston: (ID) Nov. 20, 1899, (AN) MO6060.404
Joseph L. Irby: (ID) Mar. 1, 1861, (AN) MO5720.304
Eastin Irby: (ID) Feb. 1, 1873, (AN) MO5820.432
James P. Isbell: (ID) Nov. 25, 1870, (AN) MO5810.011
Richard Jay: (ID) Jan. 10, 1876, (AN) MO5860.060
Joseph Wade Jeffries: (ID) Apr. 23, 1889, (AN) MO5920.158
Mary A. Jeffries: (ID) Apr. 23, 1889, (AN) MO5920.158
Achille Jemison: (ID) Dec. 30, 1871, (AN) MO5810.415
John P. Johnson: (ID) Dec. 30, 1871, (AN) MO5810.459
Loney Johnson: (ID) Oct. 1, 1872, (AN) MO5820.187
Elisha B. Johnson: (ID) Mar. 6, 1896, (AN) MO6010.418
Moses Jones: (ID) Dec. 30, 1871, (AN) MO5810.417
Saul C. Jones: (ID) Feb. 5, 1872, (AN) MO5820.025
Alexander B. Jones: (ID) Jul. 30, 1875, (AN) MO5850.225
Joseph Jones: (ID) Aug. 1, 1877, (AN) MO5870.236
Jesse E. Jones: (ID) Apr. 26, 1893, (AN) MO5990.105
James Jones: (ID) Aug. 14, 1894, (AN) MO5990.464
Bartley B. Kimmons: (ID) Jun. 15, 1863, (AN) MO5730.056
Granville P. Kirby: (ID) Mar. 17, 1892, (AN) MO5970.099
George W. Kirby: (ID) Aug. 24, 1897, (AN) MO6020.471
David Lambert: (ID) Dec. 30, 1871, (AN) MO5820.002
Albert P. Lee: (ID) Dec. 9, 1892, (AN) MO5790.260
James T. Lemaster: (ID) Mar. 15, 1887, (AN) MO5520.465
Jacob W. Lemaster: (ID) Sep. 5, 1895, (AN) MO6010.151
Daniel Lester: (ID) Feb. 5, 1872, (AN) MO5820.026
George Long: (ID) Mar. 27, 1861, (AN) MO5720.215
Epaminondas Lusk: (ID) Nov. 15, 1871, (AN) MO5810.289

Samuel M. Mayhew: (ID) Nov. 1, 1873, (AN) MO5830.332
James McCloud: (ID) Mar. 10, 1873, (AN) MO5830.091
William J. McClure: (ID) Jan. 11, 1892, (AN) MO5950.449
Sarah J. McCormack: (ID) Aug. 25, 1871, (AN) MO5810.181
William McCormack: (ID) Aug. 25, 1871, (AN) MO5810.181
Harvy T. McCune: (ID) Mar. 10, 1870, (AN) MO5740.060
Russell B. McFall: (ID) Nov. 30, 1894, (AN) MO6000.120
Pleasant F. McKinley: (ID) Nov. 25, 1870, (AN) MO5810.004
Samuel N. McKinley: (ID) Nov. 25, 1870, (AN) MO5810.001
Samuel N. McKinley: (ID) Mar. 27, 1861, (AN) MO5720.267
Pleasant F. McKinley: (ID) Jul. 5, 1866, (AN) MO3240.139
Paul McKinley: (ID) Sep. 10, 1880, (AN) MO5880.390
Benjamin F. McNeal: (ID) Dec. 20, 1881, (AN) MO5890.103
James Meek: (ID) Jul. 5, 1866, (AN) MO3240.140
John Messick: (ID) Apr. 2, 1891, (AN) MO5780.442
Charles F. Messick: (ID) Mar. 17, 1892, (AN) MO5790.057
William A. Miller: (ID) Feb. 15, 1875, (AN) MO5850.036
Abram O. Miller: (ID) Feb. 20, 1891, (AN) MO5940.245
Thomas Miner: (ID) Jul. 5, 1866, (AN) MO3240.235
Philip P. Misemer: (ID) Feb. 17, 1890, (AN) MO5920.368
Benjamin Morris: (ID) Nov. 1, 1866, (AN) MO3240.503
William W. Morris: (ID) Oct. 1, 1872, (AN) MO5820.138
Benjamin Morris: (ID) Feb. 5, 1872, (AN) MO5820.055
James W. Morris: (ID) Nov. 1, 1873, (AN) MO5830.290
John Morriss: (ID) Aug. 1, 1871, (AN) MO5810.176
Cornelius Mosby: (ID) Mar. 7, 1892, (AN) MO5970.017
Nathan P. Murphy: (ID) Mar. 1, 1867, (AN) MO3250.242
Mitchell Murrell: (ID) Mar. 10, 1873, (AN) MO5830.153
Linville M. Mynatt: (ID) Mar. 31, 1892, (AN) MO5970.357
Harrison Neece: (ID) Mar. 25, 1871, (AN) MO5810.012
Simon P. Newman: (ID) Dec. 30, 1871, (AN) MO5810.425
Simon P. Newman: (ID) Mar. 1, 1867, (AN) MO3250.119
Russell B. Nicholas: (ID) Nov. 25, 1871, (AN) MO5810.355
John Nicholas: (ID) Feb. 1, 1894, (AN) MO5990.394
William P. Norman: (ID) Jun. 15, 1866, (AN) MO3240.028
Alvin D. Norris: (ID) Feb. 1, 1873, (AN) MO5820.245
Isaac Owens: (ID) Oct. 17, 1892, (AN) MO5980.024
John B. Paris: (ID) Jun. 13, 1899, (AN) MO6060.315
John W. Parker: (ID) Nov. 25, 1870, (AN) MO5810.003
McClellan Patten: (ID) Jul. 9, 1895, (AN) MO6010.087
Thomas Patterson: (ID) Jun. 10, 1873, (AN) MO5830.204
John W. Pendleton: (ID) Nov. 25, 1870, (AN) MO5810.008
John Pendleton: (ID) Jun. 15, 1866, (AN) MO3240.077
John Pendleton: (ID) Oct. 1, 1872, (AN) MO5820.188
Nathan C. Pendleton: (ID) Feb. 5, 1872, (AN) MO5820.024
Ignaz Pfitzner: (ID) Feb. 26, 1890, (AN) MO5780.299

Mary Phariss: (ID) Dec. 1, 1865, (AN) MO3230.444
Abzada Phillips: (ID) Nov. 25, 1870, (AN) MO5810.007
Sidney Pilkerton: (ID) Jan. 12, 1895, (AN) MO6000.234
Nancy Pirtle: (ID) Aug. 23, 1876, (AN) MO5860.356
John W. Pitts: (ID) Mar. 20, 1886, (AN) MO5900.322
John W. Plummer: (ID) Apr. 3, 1896, (AN) MO6010.387
John R. Poindexter: (ID) Apr. 18, 1891, (AN) MO5940.415
Reuben Poland: (ID) Mar. 1, 1867, (AN) MO3250.006
Mary A. Prichett: (ID) Sep. 10, 1861, (AN) MO5720.467
Andrew J. Pruitt: (ID) Dec. 30, 1871, (AN) MO5810.423
Egbert H. Pruitt: (ID) Dec. 30, 1871, (AN) MO5810.421
Egbert H. Pruitt: (ID) Dec. 1, 1865, (AN) MO3230.431
Newton Putnam: (ID) Jul. 5, 1866, (AN) MO3240.175
Newton Putnam: (ID) Aug. 25, 1871, (AN) MO5810.197
William W. Ramsey: (ID) Jul. 5, 1866, (AN) MO3240.146
Daniel Ray: (ID) Nov. 20, 1872, (AN) MO5750.199
John F. Ray: (ID) Dec. 3, 1892, (AN) MO5980.204
Timothy Regan: (ID) Oct. 10, 1866, (AN) MO3240.284
Timothy Regan: (ID) Oct. 10, 1866, (AN) MO3240.285
Timothy Regan: (ID) Oct. 10, 1866, (AN) MO3240.286
Timothy Regan: (ID) Oct. 10, 1866, (AN) MO3240.287
Timothy Regan: (ID) Oct. 10, 1866, (AN) MO3240.288
Timothy Regan: (ID) Oct. 10, 1866, (AN) MO3240.244
Timothy Regan: (ID) Oct. 10, 1866, (AN) MO3240.245
Timothy Regan: (ID) Jun. 15, 1866, (AN) MO3240.085
Timothy Regan: (ID) Jun. 15, 1866, (AN) MO3240.086
Timothy Regan: (ID) Jun. 15, 1866, (AN) MO3240.088
Timothy Regan: (ID) Jun. 15, 1866, (AN) MO3240.089
Timothy Regan: (ID) Jun. 15, 1866, (AN) MO3240.091
Timothy Regan: (ID) Jun. 15, 1866, (AN) MO3240.097
Timothy Regan: (ID) Jun. 15, 1866, (AN) MO3240.098
Timothy Regan: (ID) Jun. 15, 1866, (AN) MO3240.099
Timothy Regan: (ID) Jun. 15, 1866, (AN) MO3240.100
Timothy Regan: (ID) Jun. 15, 1866, (AN) MO3240.101
Timothy Regan: (ID) Jun. 15, 1866, (AN) MO3240.106
Timothy Regan: (ID) Jun. 15, 1866, (AN) MO3240.108
Timothy Regan: (ID) Jun. 15, 1866, (AN) MO3240.109
Timothy Regan: (ID) Jun. 15, 1866, (AN) MO3240.110
Timothy Regan: (ID) Jun. 15, 1866, (AN) MO3240.111
Timothy Regan: (ID) Jul. 5, 1866, (AN) MO3240.115
Timothy Regan: (ID) Mar. 1, 1867, (AN) MO3250.004
John S. Richmond: (ID) Mar. 30, 1882, (AN) MO5760.039
Thomas Rickman: (ID) Jul. 1, 1861, (AN) MO5720.387
James E. Roberson: (ID) Feb. 20, 1891, (AN) MO5940.244
Thomas J. Roberts: (ID) Oct. 1, 1872, (AN) MO5820.157
William W. Robertson: (ID) Mar. 25, 1872, (AN) MO5820.100

Francis M. Ruark: (ID) Feb. 15, 1875, (AN) MO5850.035
Elmer G. Ruark: (ID) Feb. 21, 1893, (AN) MO5980.482
Doctor T. Russell: (ID) Sep. 10, 1880, (AN) MO5750.480
Isaiah H. Russell: (ID) Sep. 5, 1895, (AN) MO6010.158
Jared Ryker: (ID) Nov. 25, 1870, (AN) MO5810.002
Jacob A. Ryker: (ID) Mar. 27, 1861, (AN) MO5720.214
Jared S. Ryker: (ID) Mar. 10, 1873, (AN) MO5830.123
Bradford Samuels: (ID) Jun. 23, 1888, (AN) MO5900.478
Moses M. Sanders: (ID) Nov. 23, 1891, (AN) MO5950.323
Cornelius Seburn: (ID) Oct. 1, 1872, (AN) MO5820.231
Jacob Seigal: (ID) Feb. 17, 1890, (AN) MO5920.279
Alvis Sheppard: (ID) Jun. 25, 1885, (AN) MO5770.162
Reuben Shipman: (ID) Nov. 1, 1875, (AN) MO5850.445
Elias W. Shirley: (ID) Mar. 27, 1861, (AN) MO5720.258
Robert Shults: (ID) Jan. 15, 1872, (AN) MO5740.473
Andrew J. Slankard: (ID) Oct. 1, 1872, (AN) MO5820.167
John T. Smith: (ID) Oct. 10, 1866, (AN) MO3240.284
John T. Smith: (ID) Oct. 10, 1866, (AN) MO3240.285
John T. Smith: (ID) Oct. 10, 1866, (AN) MO3240.286
John T. Smith: (ID) Oct. 10, 1866, (AN) MO3240.287
John T. Smith: (ID) Oct. 10, 1866, (AN) MO3240.288
John T. Smith: (ID) Oct. 10, 1866, (AN) MO3240.244
John T. Smith: (ID) Oct. 10, 1866, (AN) MO3240.245
Abraham Smith: (ID) Nov. 25, 1870, (AN) MO5810.006
John T. Smith: (ID) Jun. 15, 1866, (AN) MO3240.085
John T. Smith: (ID) Jun. 15, 1866, (AN) MO3240.086
John T. Smith: (ID) Jun. 15, 1866, (AN) MO3240.088
John T. Smith: (ID) Jun. 15, 1866, (AN) MO3240.089
John T. Smith: (ID) Jun. 15, 1866, (AN) MO3240.091
John T. Smith: (ID) Jun. 15, 1866, (AN) MO3240.097
John T. Smith: (ID) Jun. 15, 1866, (AN) MO3240.098
John T. Smith: (ID) Jun. 15, 1866, (AN) MO3240.099
John T. Smith: (ID) Jun. 15, 1866, (AN) MO3240.100
John T. Smith: (ID) Jun. 15, 1866, (AN) MO3240.101
John T. Smith: (ID) Jun. 15, 1866, (AN) MO3240.106
John T. Smith: (ID) Jun. 15, 1866, (AN) MO3240.108
John T. Smith: (ID) Jun. 15, 1866, (AN) MO3240.109
John T. Smith: (ID) Jun. 15, 1866, (AN) MO3240.110
John T. Smith: (ID) Jun. 15, 1866, (AN) MO3240.111
John T. Smith: (ID) Jul. 5, 1866, (AN) MO3240.115
John T. Smith: (ID) Mar. 1, 1867, (AN) MO3250.004
John Smith: (ID) Mar. 25, 1876, (AN) MO5860.222
Thomas E. Smith: (ID) Apr. 14, 1894, (AN) MO5990.460
Elender Speakman: (ID) Mar. 10, 1873, (AN) MO5830.119
Matthias Speers: (ID) Jan. 14, 1899, (AN) MO1150.397
John J. Spilman: (ID) Jun. 23, 1888, (AN) MO5900.460

Joseph R. Still: (ID) Mar. 10, 1862, (AN) MO5730.005
Joseph R. Still: (ID) Mar. 1, 1867, (AN) MO3250.116
Thomas Stockton: (ID) Nov. 6, 1893, (AN) MO5990.314
Hillery M. Stokes: (ID) Feb. 1, 1873, (AN) MO5820.388
R L. Stone: (ID) Mar. 10, 1870, (AN) MO5740.140
Eppy Sullivan: (ID) Dec. 30, 1871, (AN) MO5810.406
Hiram P. Sullivan: (ID) Nov. 23, 1891, (AN) MO5950.342
Joseph Sullivan: (ID) Aug. 25, 1871, (AN) MO5810.190
William C. Sullivan: (ID) Aug. 25, 1871, (AN) MO5810.183
Thomas Swearingen: (ID) Aug. 20, 1872, (AN) MO5750.157
Francis H. Taney: (ID) Sep. 10, 1880, (AN) MO5880.412
Aaron P. Terrel: (ID) Mar. 25, 1873, (AN) MO5830.021
Joshua Thomas: (ID) Aug. 20, 1873, (AN) MO5830.230
Henry P. Till: (ID) Mar. 27, 1861, (AN) MO5720.136
Perry Town: (ID) Jun. 23, 1888, (AN) MO5900.469
John A. Turner: (ID) Sep. 14, 1896, (AN) MO6020.009
John H. Van Dyke: (ID) Jan. 9, 1886, (AN) MO5900.263
Mary S. Van Dyke: (ID) Jan. 9, 1886, (AN) MO5900.263
Rawley Vandergrif: (ID) Apr. 18, 1891, (AN) MO5940.410
Alvies Vandergrif: (ID) Aug. 10, 1888, (AN) MO5910.227
John Vermillion: (ID) Dec. 30, 1871, (AN) MO5810.457
Narcissa C. Wadkins: (ID) Mar. 17, 1892, (AN) MO5970.079
Willburn H. Waid: (ID) Oct. 1, 1872, (AN) MO5820.164
Hiram Waller: (ID) Jul. 5, 1866, (AN) MO3240.236
Asa Ware: (ID) Feb. 20, 1891, (AN) MO5940.205
John Y Weatherspoon: (ID) Apr. 23, 1889, (AN) MO5920.140
George W. Welsh: (ID) Nov. 12, 1894, (AN) MO6000.015
Isaac West: (ID) Jun. 26, 1871, (AN) MO5810.101
Sarah J. West: (ID) Jun. 23, 1888, (AN) MO5900.476
Thomas R. Whaley: (ID) Mar. 1, 1867, (AN) MO3250.114
William B. Whann: (ID) Mar. 25, 1871, (AN) MO5810.014
Jacob B. Wheat: (ID) Dec. 1, 1865, (AN) MO3230.404
Joseph R. Wheat: (ID) Apr. 9, 1892, (AN) MO5790.179
Benjamin Wheeler: (ID) Mar. 10, 1873, (AN) MO5830.144
James M. White: (ID) Nov. 1, 1866, (AN) MO3240.47
James H. Whitley: (ID) Jun. 23, 1888, (AN) MO5900.430
John W. Whitley: (ID) Jun. 23, 1888, (AN) MO5900.431
Jason L. Wight: (ID) Dec. 30, 1871, (AN) MO5820.001
Richard S. Wilks: (ID) Oct. 1, 1872, (AN) MO5820.165
William R. Wilks: (ID) Mar. 25, 1872, (AN) MO5820.087
James Willhite: (ID) Mar. 10, 1873, (AN) MO5830.147
Isham H. Williams: (ID) Jul. 10, 1871, (AN) MO5810.155
James M. Williams: (ID) Jan. 15, 1872, (AN) MO5750.006
John W. Wise: (ID) Jun. 26, 1871, (AN) MO5810.069
Nancy Wishon: (ID) Dec. 30, 1871, (AN) MO5810.430
Nancy Wishon: (ID) Jul. 1, 1861, (AN) MO5720.362

Andrew Withers: (ID) Jul. 1, 1871, (AN) MO5740.466
Andrew Withers: (ID) Aug. 20, 1872, (AN) MO5750.125
Samuel D. Withers: (ID) Feb. 1, 1873, (AN) MO5820.235
Wiley P. Woodruff: (ID) Dec. 15, 1892, (AN) MO5980.355
Sarah A. Woods: (ID) Nov. 25, 1879, (AN) MO5880.365
John B. Woods: (ID) Mar. 27, 1861, (AN) MO5720.238
John B. Woods: (ID) Mar. 27, 1861, (AN) MO5720.239
Thomas Woods: (ID) Jul. 9, 1895, (AN) MO6010.102
George Woolever: (ID) Dec. 1, 1876, (AN) MO5860.423
Nancy J. Wooley: (ID) Jul. 10, 1871, (AN) MO5810.123
Isaac Young: (ID) Nov. 30, 1894, (AN) MO6000.146
William H. Younger: (ID) Jul. 20, 1869, (AN) MO5730.293

St. Louis County, Missouri, U. S. District Count, Declarations of Intent
Aaron Seligsohn: (DI) Sep. 27, 1890 (A) 27 Y, (B) 1863, (BP) Russian Poland
Alexander Brodzinski: (DI) Dec. 16, 1890 (A) 23 Y, (B) 1867, (BP) Russia
Andreas Boenceke: (DI) Dec. 29, 1890 (A) 31 Y, (B) 1859, (BP) Germany
Andreas Zarzenrsky: (DI) Dec. 1, 1890 (A) 37 Y, (B) 1853, (BP) Germany
Anton Friska: (DI) Dec. 1, 1890 (A) 29 Y, (B) 1861, (BP) Bohemia
Antonio Bafunno: (DI) Dec. 5, 1890 (A) 39 Y, (B) 1851, (BP) Italy
August Mengersen: (DI) Dec. 1, 1890 (A) 35 Y, (B) 1855, (BP) Germany
August Pokrefke: (DI) Dec. 1, 1890 (A) 35 Y, (B) 1855, (BP) Germany
Bernard Haverkamp: (DI) Oct. 28, 1890 (A) 33 Y, (B) 1857, (BP) Germany
Christian Kreinkamp: (DI) Dec. 1, 1890 (A) 36 Y, (B) 1854, (BP) Germany
Edward Mars: (DI) Dec. 1, 1890 (A) 38 Y, (B) 1852, (BP) Switzerland
Frank Weigend: (DI) Dec. 1, 1890 (A) 45 Y, (B) 1845, (BP) Austria
Fred Schindler: (DI) Sep. 19, 1890 (A) 34 Y, (B) 1856, (BP) Germany
George Bueter: (DI) Dec. 1, 1890 (A) 41 Y, (B) 1849, (BP) Germany
George Sebastian: (DI) Oct. 6, 1890 (A) 41 Y, (B) 1849, (BP) Germany
Heinrick Hettmenn*: (DI) Dec. 1, 1890 (A) 61 Y, (B) 1829, (BP) Germany
Henry Kettmenn: (DI) Dec. 1, 1890 (A) 61 Y, (B) 1829, (BP) Germany
Henry Koenig: (DI) Oct. 6, 1890 (A) 41 Y, (B) 1849, (BP) Germany
Henry Kuenker: (DI) Dec. 1, 1890 (A) 32 Y, (B) 1858, (BP) Germany
Henry Schiess: (DI) April. 2, 1890 (A) 38 Y, (B) 1852, (BP) Germany
Henry Volz: (DI) Oct. 6, 1890 (A) 34 Y, (B) 1856, (BP) Germany
Henry W. Brueseke: (DI) Dec. 1, 1890 (A) 29 Y, (B) 1861, (BP) Germany
Herman S. Graber: (DI) Oct. 2, 1890 (A) 23 Y, (B) 1867, (BP) Switzerland
Hermann Hulfemeyer: (DI) Oct. 6, 1890 (A) 39 Y, (B) 1851, (BP) Germany
Hermann Tassemeyer: (DI) Oct. 6, 1890 (A) 40 Y, (B) 1850, (BP)

Germany
Hermann Willen: (DI) Oct. 6, 1890 (A) 26 Y, (B) 1864, (BP) Germany
James Carlin: (DI) Dec. 1, 1890 (A) 28 Y, (B) 1862, (BP) Ireland
John Albalt: (DI) Oct. 21, 1890 (A) 50 Y, (B) 1840, (BP) Germany
John Luethge: (DI) Oct. 6, 1890 (A) 38 Y, (B) 1852, (BP) Germany
John Mahan: (DI) Sep. 22, 1890 (A) 29 Y, (B) 1861, (BP) Ireland
Joseph Pelinski: (DI) Dec. 1, 1890 (A) 30 Y, (B) 1860, (BP) Germany
Lawrence McNally: (DI) Dec. 1, 1890 (A) 26 Y, (B) 1864, (BP) Ireland
Michael Casserly: (DI) Sep. 22, 1890 (A) 33 Y, (B) 1857, (BP) Ireland
Michael Sebastian: (DI) Oct. 6, 1890 (A) 38 Y, (B) 1852, (BP) Germany
Nicholas Scher: (DI) Dec. 1, 1890 (A) 36 Y, (B) 1854, (BP) Germany
Ola Johnson: (DI) Oct. 13, 1890 (A) 48 Y, (B) 1842, (BP) Sweden
Paul DuBois: (DI) Nov. 17, 1890 (A) 28 Y, (B) 1862, (BP) Switzerland
Peter Stanton: (DI) Sep. 17, 1890 (A) 34 Y, (B) 1856, (BP) Ireland
Philip G. Johnston: (DI) Sep. 18, 1890 (A) 28 Y, (B) 1862, (BP) Ireland
Swan G. Swanson: (DI) Nov. 18, 1890 (A) 31 Y, (B) 1859, (BP) Sweden
Thomas Riley: (DI) Oct. 24, 1890 (A) 28 Y, (B) 1862, (BP) England
William Bolte: (DI) Dec. 1, 1890 (A) 39 Y, (B) 1851, (BP) Germany
William Horstmannsdorf: (DI) Nov. 28, 1890 (A) 30 Y, (B) 1860, (BP)
    Germany
William Horstmannspoff*: (DI) Nov. 28, 1890 (A) 30 Y, (B) 1860, (BP)
    Germany
Antonio Porta: (DI) Jul. 11, 1891 (A) 37 Y, (B) 1854, (BP) Italy
Batistta Porta: (DI) Dec. 26, 1891 (A) 30 Y, (B) 1861, (BP) Italy
Bernard Derby: (DI) Mar. 12, 1891 (A) 60 Y, (B) 1831, (BP) Ireland
Carl F. Heiliger: (DI) Mar. 28, 1891 (A) 29 Y, (B) 1862, (BP) Germany
Charles Schauer: (DI) Jul. 17, 1891 (A) 33 Y, (B) 1858, (BP) Austria
Charles Frederick Schlenker: (DI) Jan. 5, 1891 (A) 29 Y, (B) 1862, (BP)
    Germany
Ernst Waele: (DI) Jan. 5, 1891 (A) 28 Y, (B) 1863, (BP) Germany
Eveole Bafummo: (DI) Jan. 23, 1891 (A) 33 Y, (B) 1858, (BP) Italy
Gaetano Natoli: (DI) Feb. 11, 1891 (A) 29 Y, (B) 1862, (BP) Italy
Giovonni Ramoni: (DI) Jul. 11, 1891 (A) 33 Y, (B) 1858, (BP) Italy
James McAuliffe: (DI) Jul. 8, 1891 (A) 27 Y, (B) 1864, (BP) Ireland
John McGrath: (DI) June. 3, 1891 (A) 35 Y, (B) 1856, (BP) Ireland
John Tobermann: (DI) Aug. 3, 1891 (A) 34 Y, (B) 1857, (BP) Bohemia
Karl Fredrick Schlenker: (DI) Jan. 5, 1891 (A) 29 Y, (B) 1862, (BP)
    Germany
Louis Grotz: (DI) June. 13, 1891 (A) 27 Y, (B) 1864, (BP) Germany
Rebecca M. Reavis: (DI) Jan. 3, 1891 (A) 33 Y, (B) 1858, (BP) Ireland
Robert Morrow: (DI) Apr. 24, 1891 (A) 24 Y, (B) 1867, (BP) Ireland
Robert Joseph Alsop: (DI) Jul. 8, 1891 (A) 25 Y, (B) 1866, (BP)
    New Foundland
William Haemmerle: (DI) Jun. 25, 1891 (A) 29 Y, (B) 1862, (BP) Austria
August Feldhaus: (DI) Jan. 4, 1892 (A) 30 Y, (B) 1862, (BP) Germany
August Sontag: (DI) Oct. 17, 1892 (A) 36 Y, (B) 1856, (BP) Germany

Barbato Urbano: (DI) Oct. 31, 1892 (A) 33 Y, (B) 1859, (BP) Italy
Federico Bottinelli: (DI) Feb. 23, 1892 (A) 23 Y, (B) 1869, (BP) Italy
Frederick G.W. Mueller: (DI) Jan. 4, 1892 (A) 51 Y, (B) 1841, (BP) Germany
Herman A. Beuten: (DI) Jan. 4, 1892 (A) 53 Y, (B) 1839, (BP) Germany
Hermann Keppler: (DI) Oct. 17, 1892 (A) 32 Y, (B) 1860, (BP) Germany
Johan Adolf Aaronson: (DI) Jul. 16, 1892 (A) 21 Y, (B) 1871, (BP) Sweden
John Bottinelli: (DI) Feb. 10, 1892 (A) 30 Y, (B) 1862, (BP) Italy
John Feldhaus: (DI) Jan. 4, 1892 (A) 33 Y, (B) 1859, (BP) Germany
John Ramoni: (DI) Feb. 11, 1892 (A) 30 Y, (B) 1862, (BP) Italy
John Sontag: (DI) Oct. 17, 1892 (A) 45 Y, (B) 1847, (BP) Germany
John G. M. Luttenberger: (DI) Apr. 27, 1892 (A) 28 Y, (B) 1864, (BP) Germany
Joseph Nies: (DI) Jan. 4, 1892 (A) 36 Y, (B) 1856, (BP) Germany
Joseph C. Feldmeier: (DI) May. 31, 1892 (A) 23 Y, (B) 1869, (BP) Germany
Louis Appel: (DI) Oct. 6, 1892 (A) 30 Y, (B) 1862, (BP) Germany
Martin Nehemias: (DI) Aug. 25, 1892 (A) 39 Y, (B) 1853, (BP) Germany
Patrick McDermott: (DI) Jun. 20, 1892 (A) 30 Y, (B) 1862, (BP) Ireland
William Giblin: (DI) Oct. 18, 1892 (A) 48 Y, (B) 1844, (BP) Ireland
William Schaefer: (DI) Jan. 11, 1892 (A) 36 Y, (B) 1856, (BP) Germany
William Schweickhardt: (DI) Apr. 18, 1892 (A) 46 Y, (B) 1846, (BP) Germany
Emil F. Stark: (DI) Jul. 14, 1893 (A) 29 Y, (B) 1864, (BP) Germany
George Brug: (DI) Jan. 30, 1893 (A) 26 Y, (B) 1867, (BP) Germany
James Gildea: (DI) Feb. 23, 1893 (A) 33 Y, (B) 1860, (BP) Ireland
John Hornberger: (DI) Jul. 14, 1893 (A) 32 Y, (B) 1861, (BP) Germany
John Smith: (DI) Jun. 12, 1893 (A) 34 Y, (B) 1859, (BP) Ireland
John Frank Gronkonski: (DI) Mar. 31, 1893 (A) 36 Y, (B) 1857, (BP) Germany
Michael Hackett: (DI) Feb. 23, 1893 (A) 24 Y, (B) 1869, (BP) Ireland
Patrick Fahey: (DI) Mar. 22, 1893 (A) 22 Y, (B) 1871, (BP) Ireland
Paul Holtz: (DI) Jul. 15, 1893 (A) 42 Y, (B) 1851, (BP) Germany
William Hunt: (DI) Nov. 8, 1893 (A) 26 Y, (B) 1867, (BP) Canada
Andre Johansen: (DI) Oct. 15, 1894 (A) 45 Y, (B) 1849, (BP) Sweden
Anton Moser: (DI) Oct. 1, 1894 (A) 29 Y, (B) 1865, (BP) Switzerland
August F. Diestelhorst: (DI) Feb. 12, 1894 (A) 25 Y, (B) 1869, (BP) Germany
Caspar Lewing: (DI) Sep. 17, 1894 (A) 40 Y, (B) 1854, (BP) Germany
Charles Freiershaus: (DI) Feb. 3, 1894 (A) 28 Y, (B) 1866, (BP) Germany
David Madson: (DI) Oct. 15, 1894 (A) 40 Y, (B) 1854, (BP) Norway
David Matsen: (DI) Oct. 15, 1894 (A) 40 Y, (B) 1854, (BP) Norway
Erick Johanson Tofte: (DI) Oct. 11, 1894 (A) 37 Y, (B) 1857, (BP) Sweden
Eugene Washington Stern: (DI) Jan. 19, 1894 (A) 28 Y, (B) 1866, (BP)

Canada
Frederick Baer: (DI) Jun. 8, 1894 (A) 37 Y, (B) 1857, (BP) Germany
Jacob Zopfi: (DI) Mar. 7, 1894 (A) 35 Y, (B) 1859, (BP) Switzerland
John Kieser: (DI) Aug. 2, 1894 (A) 31 Y, (B) 1863, (BP) Germany
John Riebel: (DI) Jul. 31, 1894 (A) 25 Y, (B) 1869, (BP) Germany
Lachlan Ferguson: (DI) Aug. 31, 1894 (A) 34 Y, (B) 1860, (BP) Scotland
Mary Brewin: (DI) Jun. 7, 1894 (A) 24 Y, (B) 1870, (BP) England
Robert Bagnell: (DI) Nov. 9, 1894 (A) 53 Y, (B) 1841, (BP) Canada
Robert W. L. Dusing: (DI) Jan. 18, 1894 (A) 26 Y, (B) 1868, (BP) Germany
Battista Bonzani: (DI) Oct. 11, 1895 (A) 33 Y, (B) 1862, (BP) Italy
Fritz Sandmann: (DI) Jul. 9, 1895 (A) 36 Y, (B) 1859, (BP) Germany
Herman Renner: (DI) Jan. 22, 1895 (A) 39 Y, (B) 1856, (BP) Germany
James Harvey McLeod: (DI) Sep. 21, 1895 (A) 26 Y, (B) 1869, (BP) Canada
John F. Harley: (DI) Jul. 19, 1895 (A) 21 Y, (B) 1874, (BP) England
Neil Taylor: (DI) Feb. 13, 1895 (A) 26 Y, (B) 1869, (BP) Scotland
William Hartigan: (DI) Mar. 23, 1895 (A) 29 Y, (B) 1866, (BP) Ireland
Adalbert Bida: (DI) Apr. 6, 1896 (A) 26 Y, (B) 1870, (BP) Bohemia
Adolf Zielinski: (DI) Apr. 4, 1896 (A) 21 Y, (B) 1875, (BP) Russia
Adolph Burg: (DI) Jan. 8, 1896 (A) 24 Y, (B) 1872, (BP) Germany
Adolph Mrockowski: (DI) Apr. 4, 1896 (A) 32 Y, (B) 1864, (BP) Poland
Agation Codoro: (DI) Apr. 6, 1896 (A) 30 Y, (B) 1866, (BP) Italy
Albert Sturma: (DI) Apr. 4, 1896 (A) 42 Y, (B) 1854, (BP) Bohemia
Albert Zuzak: (DI) Apr. 3, 1896 (A) 51 Y, (B) 1845, (BP) Bohemia
Albert E. Graham: (DI) Apr. 4, 1896 (A) 34 Y, (B) 1862, (BP) Ireland
Alfonso Riale: (DI) Apr. 6, 1896 (A) 24 Y, (B) 1872, (BP) Italy
Andreas Pikesh: (DI) Apr. 4, 1896 (A) 34 Y, (B) 1862, (BP) Bohemia
Andrew Mastie: (DI) Apr. 6, 1896 (A) 28 Y, (B) 1868, (BP) Bohemia
Anton Becvar: (DI) Apr. 4, 1896 (A) 46 Y, (B) 1850, (BP) Bohemia
Anton Petrovics: (DI) Apr. 6, 1896 (A) 27 Y, (B) 1869, (BP) Austria
Anton J. Jaworowski: (DI) Apr. 6, 1896 (A) 38 Y, (B) 1858, (BP) Poland
Antonio Detdin: (DI) Apr. 6, 1896 (A) 27 Y, (B) 1869, (BP) Italy
Antonio Russo: (DI) Apr. 6, 1896 (A) 42 Y, (B) 1854, (BP) Italy
Antonio Vollar: (DI) Apr. 4, 1896 (A) 45 Y, (B) 1851, (BP) Italy
Arthur Fairchild: (DI) Apr. 6, 1896 (A) 24 Y, (B) 1872, (BP) England
August Fiedler: (DI) Apr. 2, 1896 (A) 41 Y, (B) 1855, (BP) Germany
August Kaminski: (DI) Apr. 6, 1896 (A) 36 Y, (B) 1860, (BP) Poland
Benjamin Hufker: (DI) Apr. 6, 1896 (A) 27 Y, (B) 1869, (BP) Germany
Bernard Bozechowski: (DI) Apr. 6, 1896 (A) 57 Y, (B) 1839, (BP) Poland
Bernard Wavra: (DI) Apr. 3, 1896 (A) 47 Y, (B) 1849, (BP) Bohemia
Berng Hartmann: (DI) Apr. 6, 1896 (A) 25 Y, (B) 1871, (BP) Germany
Blasius Rekouski: (DI) Apr. 4, 1896 (A) 43 Y, (B) 1853, (BP) Germany
Bryan Neary: (DI) Apr. 1, 1896 (A) 30 Y, (B) 1866, (BP) Ireland
Carmine Caldamone: (DI) Apr. 4, 1896 (A) 34 Y, (B) 1862, (BP) Italy
Charles Duncan: (DI) Apr. 4, 1896 (A) 29 Y, (B) 1867, (BP) Scotland

Charles Halvonson: (DI) Apr. 3, 1896 (A) 28 Y, (B) 1868, (BP) Norway
Charles Sip: (DI) Apr. 3, 1896 (A) 53 Y, (B) 1843, (BP) Bohemia
Clemens Hufker: (DI) Apr. 6, 1896 (A) 56 Y, (B) 1840, (BP) Germany
Conrad Pope: (DI) Apr. 2, 1896 (A) 56 Y, (B) 1840, (BP) Germany
Daniel Kane: (DI) Apr. 1, 1896 (A) 31 Y, (B) 1865, (BP) Ireland
Daniel Keating: (DI) Apr. 1, 1896 (A) 38 Y, (B) 1858, (BP) Ireland
David Barrett: (DI) Apr. 1, 1896 (A) 44 Y, (B) 1852, (BP) Ireland
Dennis Hart: (DI) Apr. 3, 1896 (A) 35 Y, (B) 1861, (BP) Ireland
Dennis McCarthy: (DI) Apr. 3, 1896 (A) 36 Y, (B) 1860, (BP) Ireland
Dennis Murphy: (DI) Apr. 4, 1896 (A) 23 Y, (B) 1873, (BP) Ireland
Domenich Supich: (DI) Apr. 4, 1896 (A) 46 Y, (B) 1850, (BP) Austria
Domenico Liconnili: (DI) Apr. 6, 1896 (A) 35 Y, (B) 1861, (BP) Italy
Edward Cohen: (DI) Apr. 4, 1896 (A) 35 Y, (B) 1861, (BP) Ireland
Edward Hyland: (DI) Apr. 6, 1896 (A) 39 Y, (B) 1857, (BP) Ireland
Edward Johnson: (DI) Apr. 1, 1896 (A) 49 Y, (B) 1847, (BP) Ireland
Edward Johnson: (DI) Apr. 2, 1896 (A) 49 Y, (B) 1847, (BP) England
Edward Kearney: (DI) Apr. 1, 1896 (A) 25 Y, (B) 1871, (BP) Ireland
Edward Linahan: (DI) Apr. 1, 1896 (A) 28 Y, (B) 1868, (BP) Ireland
Eugene Ferriter: (DI) Apr. 3, 1896 (A) 36 Y, (B) 1860, (BP) Ireland
Eugene Terreter: (DI) Apr. 2, 1896 (A) 27 Y, (B) 1869, (BP) Ireland
Filible Landa: (DI) Apr. 4, 1896 (A) 38 Y, (B) 1858, (BP) Bohemia
Florence McAuliffe: (DI) Apr. 6, 1896 (A) 50 Y, (B) 1846, (BP) Ireland
Florence D. McAuliffe: (DI) Apr. 4, 1896 (A) 32 Y, (B) 1864, (BP) Ireland
Frank Cerny: (DI) Apr. 4, 1896 (A) 29 Y, (B) 1867, (BP) Bohemia
Frank Danci: (DI) Apr. 6, 1896 (A) 28 Y, (B) 1868, (BP) Italy
Frank Dillmann: (DI) Apr. 4, 1896 (A) 35 Y, (B) 1861, (BP) Germany
Frank Duhacker: (DI) Apr. 2, 1896 (A) 25 Y, (B) 1871, (BP) Austria
Frank Fiala: (DI) Apr. 6, 1896 (A) 45 Y, (B) 1851, (BP) Bohemia
Frank Kozozimski: (DI) Apr. 6, 1896 (A) 30 Y, (B) 1866, (BP) Poland
Frank Pavlik: (DI) Apr. 3, 1896 (A) 33 Y, (B) 1863, (BP) Bohemia
Frank Radomski: (DI) Apr. 6, 1896 (A) 28 Y, (B) 1868, (BP) Poland
Frank Rekowski: (DI) Apr. 6, 1896 (A) 45 Y, (B) 1851, (BP) Poland
Frank Rupinski: (DI) Apr. 4, 1896 (A) 38 Y, (B) 1858, (BP) Poland
Frank Sasse: (DI) Apr. 4, 1896 (A) 40 Y, (B) 1856, (BP) Germany
Frank Vit: (DI) Apr. 6, 1896 (A) 28 Y, (B) 1868, (BP) Bohemia
Frank Wesolonski: (DI) Apr. 4, 1896 (A) 28 Y, (B) 1868, (BP) Germany
Frank Zib: (DI) Apr. 6, 1896 (A) 30 Y, (B) 1866, (BP) Bohemia
Frederick O. Heller: (DI) Apr. 6, 1896 (A) 33 Y, (B) 1863, (BP) Germany
George Ahrens: (DI) Apr. 4, 1896 (A) 55 Y, (B) 1841, (BP) Germany
George Vogelsang: (DI) Apr. 6, 1896 (A) 32 Y, (B) 1864, (BP) Germany
George M. Kirn: (DI) Apr. 3, 1896 (A) 42 Y, (B) 1854, (BP) Canada
Giovanni Bernardo: (DI) Apr. 6, 1896 (A) 28 Y, (B) 1868, (BP) Italy
Giovanni Pastor: (DI) Apr. 6, 1896 (A) 28 Y, (B) 1868, (BP) Italy
Gottardo Vollar: (DI) Apr. 4, 1896 (A) 28 Y, (B) 1868, (BP) Italy
Guiseppe Riale: (DI) Apr. 6, 1896 (A) 31 Y, (B) 1865, (BP) Italy

Henry Meilert: (DI) Apr. 6, 1896 (A) 43 Y, (B) 1853, (BP) Germany
Henry Sovar: (DI) Apr. 4, 1896 (A) 31 Y, (B) 1865, (BP) Hungary
Henry Weis: (DI) Apr. 6, 1896 (A) 23 Y, (B) 1873, (BP) France
Ignacy Kaszewski: (DI) Apr. 6, 1896 (A) 49 Y, (B) 1847, (BP) Poland
Jacob Butza: (DI) Apr. 4, 1896 (A) 35 Y, (B) 1861, (BP) Germany
James Brosnahan: (DI) Apr. 6, 1896 (A) 21 Y, (B) 1875, (BP) Ireland
James Dyer: (DI) Apr. 3, 1896 (A) 60 Y, (B) 1836, (BP) Ireland
James Halligan: (DI) Apr. 1, 1896 (A) 32 Y, (B) 1864, (BP) Ireland
James McNamara: (DI) Apr. 4, 1896 (A) 28 Y, (B) 1868, (BP) Ireland
James Mernagh: (DI) Apr. 6, 1896 (A) 29 Y, (B) 1867, (BP) Ireland
James Skehan: (DI) Apr. 4, 1896 (A) 35 Y, (B) 1861, (BP) Ireland
James F. Holland: (DI) Apr. 6, 1896 (A) 36 Y, (B) 1860, (BP) England
James J. McAuliff: (DI) Apr. 3, 1896 (A) 26 Y, (B) 1870, (BP) Ireland
Jan Bielicki: (DI) Apr. 6, 1896 (A) 40 Y, (B) 1856, (BP) Poland
Jeremiah Stokes: (DI) Apr. 1, 1896 (A) 32 Y, (B) 1864, (BP) Ireland
Johann Gorski: (DI) Apr. 6, 1896 (A) 25 Y, (B) 1871, (BP) Poland
Johann Kause: (DI) Apr. 6, 1896 (A) 28 Y, (B) 1868, (BP) Poland
Johann Klosienski: (DI) Apr. 6, 1896 (A) 59 Y, (B) 1837, (BP) Poland
John Annis: (DI) Apr. 6, 1896 (A) 43 Y, (B) 1853, (BP) Poland
John Anzalone: (DI) Apr. 6, 1896 (A) 26 Y, (B) 1870, (BP) Italy
John Bariletti: (DI) Oct. 13, 1896 (A) 25 Y, (B) 1871, (BP) Italy
John Barry: (DI) Apr. 4, 1896 (A) 37 Y, (B) 1859, (BP) Ireland
John Burke: (DI) Apr. 6, 1896 (A) 34 Y, (B) 1862, (BP) Ireland
John Daly: (DI) Apr. 1, 1896 (A) 46 Y, (B) 1850, (BP) Ireland
John Direka: (DI) Apr. 6, 1896 (A) 42 Y, (B) 1854, (BP) Poland
John Fahey: (DI) Apr. 6, 1896 (A) 21 Y, (B) 1875, (BP) Ireland
John Fleming: (DI) Apr. 1, 1896 (A) 45 Y, (B) 1851, (BP) Ireland
John Gill: (DI) Apr. 1, 1896 (A) 36 Y, (B) 1860, (BP) Ireland
John Gorkey: (DI) Apr. 3, 1896 (A) 25 Y, (B) 1871, (BP) Germany
John Gray: (DI) Apr. 1, 1896 (A) 28 Y, (B) 1868, (BP) Ireland
John Hackett: (DI) Apr. 1, 1896 (A) 49 Y, (B) 1847, (BP) Ireland
John Harris: (DI) Apr. 6, 1896 (A) 29 Y, (B) 1867, (BP) Ireland
John Hughes: (DI) Apr. 6, 1896 (A) 36 Y, (B) 1860, (BP) Ireland
John Iastizinski: (DI) Apr. 6, 1896 (A) 34 Y, (B) 1862, (BP) Poland
John Lee: (DI) Apr. 6, 1896 (A) 22 Y, (B) 1874, (BP) Ireland
John McAuliffe: (DI) Apr. 1, 1896 (A) 30 Y, (B) 1866, (BP) Ireland
John McNicholas: (DI) Apr. 3, 1896 (A) 32 Y, (B) 1864, (BP) Ireland
John Meehan: (DI) Apr. 1, 1896 (A) 38 Y, (B) 1858, (BP) Ireland
John Morley: (DI) Apr. 1, 1896 (A) 32 Y, (B) 1864, (BP) Ireland
John Nealis: (DI) Apr. 1, 1896 (A) 29 Y, (B) 1867, (BP) Ireland
John Nooter: (DI) Sep. 21, 1896 (A) 29 Y, (B) 1867, (BP) Holland
John O'Connell: (DI) Apr. 6, 1896 (A) 29 Y, (B) 1867, (BP) Ireland
John O'Connor: (DI) Apr. 6, 1896 (A) 33 Y, (B) 1863, (BP) Ireland
John O'Donnell: (DI) Apr. 1, 1896 (A) 54 Y, (B) 1842, (BP) Ireland
John O'Leary: (DI) Apr. 3, 1896 (A) 60 Y, (B) 1836, (BP) Ireland
John Puttmann: (DI) Apr. 6, 1896 (A) 32 Y, (B) 1864, (BP) Bohemia

John Skala: (DI) Apr. 6, 1896 (A) 53 Y, (B) 1843, (BP) Bohemia
John Slattery: (DI) Apr. 1, 1896 (A) 52 Y, (B) 1844, (BP) Ireland
John Soldynski: (DI) Apr. 6, 1896 (A) 47 Y, (B) 1849, (BP) Poland
John Strick: (DI) Apr. 6, 1896 (A) 37 Y, (B) 1859, (BP) Bohemia
John Tracy: (DI) Apr. 6, 1896 (A) 32 Y, (B) 1864, (BP) Ireland
John E. Kaiser: (DI) Oct. 13, 1896 (A) 28 Y, (B) 1868, (BP) Germany
John G. Cairus: (DI) Apr. 4, 1896 (A) 50 Y, (B) 1846, (BP) Ireland
John H. Barrett: (DI) Apr. 1, 1896 (A) 29 Y, (B) 1867, (BP) Ireland
John H. Lambertz: (DI) Apr. 6, 1896 (A) 29 Y, (B) 1867, (BP) Germany
John J. Murphy: (DI) Apr. 1, 1896 (A) 32 Y, (B) 1864, (BP) Ireland
John L. Cummings: (DI) Apr. 2, 1896 (A) 28 Y, (B) 1868, (BP) Ireland
John M. Murphy: (DI) Apr. 3, 1896 (A) 56 Y, (B) 1840, (BP) Ireland
John N. Braun: (DI) Apr. 2, 1896 (A) 34 Y, (B) 1862, (BP) Germany
Josef Bastian: (DI) Apr. 2, 1896 (A) 60 Y, (B) 1836, (BP) Germany
Josef Vejsicky: (DI) Apr. 3, 1896 (A) 38 Y, (B) 1858, (BP) Bohemia
Joseph Acquaviva: (DI) Apr. 6, 1896 (A) 40 Y, (B) 1856, (BP) Italy
Joseph Bleile: (DI) Apr. 4, 1896 (A) 26 Y, (B) 1870, (BP) Switzerland
Joseph Gentile: (DI) Apr. 6, 1896 (A) 33 Y, (B) 1863, (BP) Italy
Joseph Graziano: (DI) Apr. 6, 1896 (A) 25 Y, (B) 1871, (BP) Italy
Joseph Iastizinski: (DI) Apr. 6, 1896 (A) 45 Y, (B) 1851, (BP) Poland
Joseph Laskiewitz: (DI) Apr. 6, 1896 (A) 47 Y, (B) 1849, (BP) Poland
Joseph Lubinski: (DI) Apr. 6, 1896 (A) 28 Y, (B) 1868, (BP) Poland
Joseph Mendeka: (DI) Apr. 6, 1896 (A) 55 Y, (B) 1841, (BP) Germany
Joseph Paluczak: (DI) Apr. 6, 1896 (A) 30 Y, (B) 1866, (BP) Poland
Joseph Smith: (DI) Apr. 4, 1896 (A) 27 Y, (B) 1869, (BP) Hungary
Joseph Smugai: (DI) Apr. 6, 1896 (A) 37 Y, (B) 1859, (BP) Poland
Joseph Tarreyrena: (DI) Apr. 6, 1896 (A) 27 Y, (B) 1869, (BP) Italy
Julian Grenda: (DI) Apr. 4, 1896 (A) 30 Y, (B) 1866, (BP) Poland
Julius Callewaert: (DI) Apr. 1, 1896 (A) 25 Y, (B) 1871, (BP) Belgium
Karle Fassel: (DI) Apr. 6, 1896 (A) 35 Y, (B) 1861, (BP) Austria
Laurence Gaitland: (DI) Apr. 6, 1896 (A) 32 Y, (B) 1864, (BP) Ireland
Louis Issel: (DI) Apr. 6, 1896 (A) 24 Y, (B) 1872, (BP) Germany
Luke Loury: (DI) Apr. 1, 1896 (A) 50 Y, (B) 1846, (BP) Ireland
Marian Wollenberg: (DI) Apr. 6, 1896 (A) 24 Y, (B) 1872, (BP) Poland
Martin Lydon: (DI) Apr. 6, 1896 (A) 26 Y, (B) 1870, (BP) Ireland
Martin Nogalski: (DI) Apr. 6, 1896 (A) 49 Y, (B) 1847, (BP) Poland
Martin Ryan: (DI) Apr. 3, 1896 (A) 54 Y, (B) 1842, (BP) Ireland
Martin Shannon: (DI) Apr. 1, 1896 (A) 38 Y, (B) 1858, (BP) Ireland
Michael Bernal: (DI) Apr. 6, 1896 (A) 63 Y, (B) 1833, (BP) Poland
Michael Coyne: (DI) Apr. 3, 1896 (A) 28 Y, (B) 1868, (BP) Ireland
Michael McAuliffe: (DI) Apr. 6, 1896 (A) 27 Y, (B) 1869, (BP) Ireland
Michael O'Connell: (DI) Apr. 4, 1896 (A) 27 Y, (B) 1869, (BP) Ireland
Michael Quinn: (DI) Apr. 4, 1896 (A) 25 Y, (B) 1871, (BP) Ireland
Michael Scharapinski: (DI) Apr. 4, 1896 (A) 37 Y, (B) 1859, (BP)
    Germany
Michael Sinko: (DI) Apr. 3, 1896 (A) 53 Y, (B) 1843, (BP) Bohemia

Michael Skeffington: (DI) Apr. 1, 1896 (A) 25 Y, (B) 1871, (BP) Ireland
Michael J. O'Keefe: (DI) Apr. 1, 1896 (A) 30 Y, (B) 1866, (BP) Ireland
Michael J. Hartmann: (DI) Apr. 6, 1896 (A) 30 Y, (B) 1866, (BP) Ireland
Michael J. Moriarity: (DI) Apr. 6, 1896 (A) 26 Y, (B) 1870, (BP) Ireland
Michael J. Sullivan: (DI) Apr. 6, 1896 (A) 26 Y, (B) 1870, (BP) Ireland
Mongiat Gottardo: (DI) Apr. 4, 1896 (A) 37 Y, (B) 1859, (BP) Italy
Neal Ruddy: (DI) Apr. 3, 1896 (A) 30 Y, (B) 1866, (BP) Ireland
Nicholas Mazurkiewer: (DI) Apr. 4, 1896 (A) 30 Y, (B) 1866, (BP) Poland
Owen Duggan: (DI) Apr. 3, 1896 (A) 50 Y, (B) 1846, (BP) Ireland
Patrick Barry: (DI) Apr. 6, 1896 (A) 65 Y, (B) 1831, (BP) Ireland
Patrick Bourke: (DI) Apr. 3, 1896 (A) 28 Y, (B) 1868, (BP) Ireland
Patrick Breherry: (DI) Apr. 6, 1896 (A) 30 Y, (B) 1866, (BP) Ireland
Patrick Connors: (DI) Apr. 3, 1896 (A) 36 Y, (B) 1860, (BP) Ireland
Patrick Convey: (DI) Apr. 1, 1896 (A) 31 Y, (B) 1865, (BP) Ireland
Patrick Corrigan: (DI) Apr. 6, 1896 (A) 45 Y, (B) 1851, (BP) Ireland
Patrick Cosgrove: (DI) Apr. 1, 1896 (A) 45 Y, (B) 1851, (BP) Ireland
Patrick Gavin: (DI) Apr. 6, 1896 (A) 47 Y, (B) 1849, (BP) Ireland
Patrick Ghorke: (DI) Apr. 3, 1896 (A) 26 Y, (B) 1870, (BP) Ireland
Patrick Higgins: (DI) Apr. 6, 1896 (A) 34 Y, (B) 1862, (BP) Ireland
Patrick Kane: (DI) Apr. 6, 1896 (A) 26 Y, (B) 1870, (BP) Ireland
Patrick Loughran: (DI) Apr. 6, 1896 (A) 42 Y, (B) 1854, (BP) Ireland
Patrick Martin: (DI) Apr. 4, 1896 (A) 38 Y, (B) 1858, (BP) Ireland
Patrick McDonald: (DI) Apr. 6, 1896 (A) 29 Y, (B) 1867, (BP) Ireland
Patrick McGurn: (DI) Apr. 6, 1896 (A) 28 Y, (B) 1868, (BP) Ireland
Patrick McNamara: (DI) Apr. 3, 1896 (A) 21 Y, (B) 1875, (BP) Ireland
Patrick Meegan: (DI) Apr. 6, 1896 (A) 36 Y, (B) 1860, (BP) Ireland
Patrick Morley: (DI) Apr. 1, 1896 (A) 35 Y, (B) 1861, (BP) Ireland
Patrick O'Connell: (DI) Apr. 3, 1896 (A) 40 Y, (B) 1856, (BP) Ireland
Patrick O'Malley: (DI) Apr. 6, 1896 (A) 27 Y, (B) 1869, (BP) Ireland
Patrick O'Reilly: (DI) Apr. 6, 1896 (A) 34 Y, (B) 1862, (BP) Ireland
Patrick Quinn: (DI) Apr. 6, 1896 (A) 36 Y, (B) 1860, (BP) Ireland
Patrick Slattery: (DI) Apr. 6, 1896 (A) 30 Y, (B) 1866, (BP) Ireland
Patrick Whelan: (DI) Apr. 6, 1896 (A) 22 Y, (B) 1874, (BP) Ireland
Patrick H. Brosnahan: (DI) Apr. 6, 1896 (A) 28 Y, (B) 1868, (BP) Ireland
Patrick M. Burns: (DI) Apr. 1, 1896 (A) 22 Y, (B) 1874, (BP) Ireland
Paul Stizesewski: (DI) Apr. 6, 1896 (A) 53 Y, (B) 1843, (BP) Poland
Peter Connolly: (DI) Apr. 6, 1896 (A) 40 Y, (B) 1856, (BP) Ireland
Peter Garavelli: (DI) Apr. 4, 1896 (A) 24 Y, (B) 1872, (BP) Italy
Peter Lippens: (DI) Apr. 6, 1896 (A) 40 Y, (B) 1856, (BP) Belgium
Peter Rafferty: (DI) May. 1, 1896 (A) 39 Y, (B) 1857, (BP) Ireland
Peter Woblewski: (DI) Apr. 6, 1896 (A) 27 Y, (B) 1869, (BP) Poland
Philip Rush: (DI) Apr. 1, 1896 (A) 35 Y, (B) 1861, (BP) Ireland
Philip TocCo: (DI) Apr. 6, 1896 (A) 21 Y, (B) 1875, (BP) Italy
Philip J. McAuliffe: (DI) Apr. 4, 1896 (A) 24 Y, (B) 1872, (BP) Ireland
Philip M. Cullen: (DI) Apr. 3, 1896 (A) 52 Y, (B) 1844, (BP) Ireland

Pietro Areno: (DI) Apr. 6, 1896 (A) 30 Y, (B) 1866, (BP) Italy
Reinhardt Zollikofer: (DI) Mar. 30, 1896 (A) 30 Y, (B) 1866, (BP)
　　Germany
Robert Frame: (DI) Apr. 3, 1896 (A) 54 Y, (B) 1842, (BP) Ireland
Salvatore Acquaviova: (DI) Apr. 6, 1896 (A) 24 Y, (B) 1872, (BP) Italy
Salvatore Catanzino: (DI) Apr. 6, 1896 (A) 43 Y, (B) 1853, (BP) Italy
Salvatore Lonigro: (DI) Apr. 6, 1896 (A) 46 Y, (B) 1850, (BP) Italy
Salvatore Pairise: (DI) Apr. 6, 1896 (A) 23 Y, (B) 1873, (BP) Italy
Salvatore Prittiri: (DI) Apr. 6, 1896 (A) 30 Y, (B) 1866, (BP) Italy
Samuel Breeze: (DI) Apr. 6, 1896 (A) 23 Y, (B) 1873, (BP) England
Simon Murray: (DI) Apr. 1, 1896 (A) 44 Y, (B) 1852, (BP) Ireland
Stanislau Bielowski: (DI) Apr. 4, 1896 (A) 28 Y, (B) 1868, (BP) Poland
Stanislau Moscicky: (DI) Apr. 4, 1896 (A) 30 Y, (B) 1866, (BP) Poland
Stanislaus Filipiak: (DI) Apr. 4, 1896 (A) 25 Y, (B) 1871, (BP)
　　German Poland
Stephen Maehoiefski: (DI) Apr. 4, 1896 (A) 36 Y, (B) 1860, (BP)
　　Russia Poland
Stifano Colletti: (DI) Apr. 6, 1896 (A) 24 Y, (B) 1872, (BP) Italy
Thomas Blenski: (DI) Apr. 6, 1896 (A) 40 Y, (B) 1856, (BP) Poland
Thomas Bond: (DI) Apr. 1, 1896 (A) 62 Y, (B) 1834, (BP) England
Thomas Brett: (DI) Apr. 3, 1896 (A) 31 Y, (B) 1865, (BP) Ireland
Thomas Broderick: (DI) Apr. 6, 1896 (A) 40 Y, (B) 1856, (BP) Ireland
Thomas Carey: (DI) Apr. 1, 1896 (A) 26 Y, (B) 1870, (BP) Ireland
Thomas Grady: (DI) Apr. 4, 1896 (A) 29 Y, (B) 1867, (BP) Ireland
Thomas Laine: (DI) Apr. 3, 1896 (A) 47 Y, (B) 1849, (BP) Ireland
Thomas Lyons: (DI) Apr. 3, 1896 (A) 34 Y, (B) 1862, (BP) Ireland
Thomas Macken: (DI) Apr. 4, 1896 (A) 24 Y, (B) 1872, (BP) Ireland
Thomas McLarkey: (DI) Apr. 6, 1896 (A) 29 Y, (B) 1867, (BP) England
Thomas McMahon: (DI) Apr. 6, 1896 (A) 35 Y, (B) 1861, (BP) Ireland
Thomas Skredinski: (DI) Apr. 6, 1896 (A) 38 Y, (B) 1858, (BP) Poland
Thomas Slevin: (DI) Apr. 6, 1896 (A) 29 Y, (B) 1867, (BP) Ireland
Thomas Vollar: (DI) Apr. 4, 1896 (A) 25 Y, (B) 1871, (BP) Italy
Timothy Clohosey: (DI) Apr. 3, 1896 (A) 27 Y, (B) 1869, (BP) Ireland
Timothy McCarthy: (DI) Apr. 6, 1896 (A) 21 Y, (B) 1875, (BP) Ireland
Timothy J. Sullivan: (DI) Apr. 6, 1896 (A) 22 Y, (B) 1874, (BP) Ireland
Tony Arena: (DI) Apr. 6, 1896 (A) 21 Y, (B) 1875, (BP) Italy
Vaclao Trantina: (DI) Apr. 3, 1896 (A) 46 Y, (B) 1850, (BP) Bohemia
Venclelaus Vit: (DI) Apr. 6, 1896 (A) 22 Y, (B) 1874, (BP) Bohemia
Vincent Paradowski: (DI) Apr. 6, 1896 (A) 39 Y, (B) 1857, (BP) Poland
Walenty Margulewski: (DI) Apr. 6, 1896 (A) 35 Y, (B) 1861, (BP) Poland
William Dwyer: (DI) Apr. 5, 1896 (A) 21 Y, (B) 1875, (BP) Ireland
William Dwyer: (DI) Apr. 4, 1896 (A) 21 Y, (B) 1875, (BP) Ireland
William Hughes: (DI) Apr. 6, 1896 (A) 30 Y, (B) 1866, (BP) Ireland
William Purcell: (DI) Apr. 6, 1896 (A) 31 Y, (B) 1865, (BP) Ireland
William Vennemann: (DI) Apr. 1, 1896 (A) 29 Y, (B) 1867, (BP)
　　Germany

Woiceh Borowski: (DI) Apr. 6, 1896 (A) 50 Y, (B) 1846, (BP) Poland
Wojciceh Starachawicz: (DI) Apr. 3, 1896 (A) 50 Y, (B) 1846, (BP)
    Austria
B. H. Faillik: (DI) Mar. 16, 1897 (A) 36 Y, (B) 1861, (BP) Bohemia
Ignatz Blaha: (DI) Mar. 15, 1897 (A) 32 Y, (B) 1865, (BP) Austria
John Nekula: (DI) Feb. 16, 1897 (A) 26 Y, (B) 1871, (BP) Moravia
Joseph Hessous: (DI) Mar. 6, 1897 (A) 66 Y, (B) 1831, (BP) Bohemia
Joseph Pecka: (DI) Apr. 29, 1897 (A) 40 Y, (B) 1857, (BP) Bohemia
Joseph Sagstetter: (DI) Feb. 17, 1897 (A) 27 Y, (B) 1870, (BP) Germany
Paul Bernhard Gerhard: (DI) Aug. 10, 1897 (A) 73 Y, (B) 1824, (BP)
    Germany
William H. H Lange: (DI) Feb. 17, 1897 (A) 35 Y, (B) 1862, (BP)
    Germany
Karl Rest: (DI) May. 9, 1898 (A) 23 Y, (B) 1875, (BP) Germany
William Kopatschek: (DI) Aug. 6, 1898 (A) 24 Y, (B) 1874, (BP) Austria
J. O. More: (DI) Dec. 28, 1899 (A) 31 Y, (B) 1868, (BP) Canada
Rudolf Putska: (DI) Jan. 3, 1899 (A) 25 Y, (B) 1874, (BP) Austria

Miscellaneous Railroad Information.
Jay Gould: Stock Certificate Missouri, Kansas, Texas Railroad, 100
    shares, issued Aug. 5, 1881
James Frought: Stock Certificate Mississippi and Missouri Railroad,
    20 shares, issued Apr. 2, 1857
Pamela Beecher: Stock Certificate Mississippi and Missouri Railroad,
    100 shares, issued May 8, 1863
Diana L. Basehart: Stock Certificate Missouri Pacific Railroad, 109
    Shares, issued Nov. 1, 1966
J. S. Grove: Stock Certificate Missouri, Kansas, Texas Railroad, 100
    Shares, cancelled Apr. 3, 1880
H. Fraley: Missouri Pacific Railroad Pass, No. A6714, Inspector
    Forest Procducts, Pennsylvania System.

Clarke County, Missouri Acasto, Business Owners, R. G. Dunn Directory, 1893.

Name	Occupation
John Callee	Wagon Maker
John Deadrick	Blacksmith
William Miller	General Store
F. Hadley	Blacksmith

Clay County, Missouri Acme, Business Owners, R. G. Dunn Directory, 1893.

Name	Occupation
J. E. Bender	General Store

Pike County, Missouri Aberdeen, Business Owners, R. G. Dunn Directory, 1893.

Name	Occupation
Alfred Beall	Grocer

Barry County, Missouri, Antioch Church Cemetery, (Note: Not a complete listing)

Name	Birth	Death
A. E. Anderson	1884	1965
Fern Newman	1914	1966
Bill Newman	1908	1977
Della Bayless	1874	1920
Ava Brunett	Dec. 3, 1911	Feb. 12, 1997
John W. Box	1846	1932
Charles Ray Lasiter	Dec. 3, 1975	Feb. 9, 1976
Bert Catron	Aug. 29, 1885	May 20, 1975
Ann Catron	---	Aug. 25, 1915
Blanch Catron	Dec. 8, 1888	Sep. 17, 1982
Clifford Anderson	1890	1944
Eugene Burnett	Mar. 9, 1908	Mar. 9, 1991
Christopher Columbus Laster	Sep. 27, 1877	Jul. 2, 1937
Rhoda Virginia Laster	Mar. 8, 1904	Mar. 29, 1933
George M. Bayless	Aug. 17, 1850	Feb. 15, 1929
Martha E. Bayless	Feb. 9, 1852	May 14, 1927
Edward Cassidy	May 12, 1928	Aug. 27, 1930
Ethel Anderson	1890	1940
Flora Mattingly	1876	1956
James W. Mattingly	1874	1944
Mary Box	1846	1933
John Talbot Burnett	Apr. 24, 1845	Mar. 26, 1917
Susan Ellen Burnett	Sep. 8, 1850	Feb. 18, 1892
Fred Anderson	1882	1929
Polk Bayless	1874	1927
Viola A. Burnette	1883	1964
Thomas D. Burnette	1878	1915
Thomas G. Burnette	Apr. 19, 1914	Apr. 19, 1963
Loren Catron	Mar. 9, 1907	Nov. 6, 1992
Catron Peter	----	Oct. 31, 1910
William Langston	1847	1936
Loretta Langston	1856	1930

St. Louis County, Missouri, Afton, Business Owners, R. G. Dunn Directory, 1893.

Name	Occupation
Charles Heidel	Blacksmith

Adolph Mead	Blacksmith
Charles Tautphaeus	General Store & Saddler
Henrietta Werner	General Store & Saloon

Buchanan County, Missouri, Agency, Business Owners, R. G. Dunn Directory, 1893.

Name	Occupation
Kirk Blakely	Shoemaker & Gunsmith
Amon Bledsoe	Wagon Maker
Isaac M. Farris	Drugs
G. W. Henley	Blacksmith
H. King	Blacksmith
Peter Klein	Confectioneer
O. D. Kuntz	Confectioneer
Dan C. Miller	General Store
R. M. Moore	General Store
W. H. Ratcliff	Mfr. Stirrups
Charles E. Thompson	Grocery & Mill

St. Louis County, Missouri, Probate Listings, 1881

Ada Vance, Addison T. Weidle, Adolph Wibbing, Adolph C. Huth, Alfred Black, Andreas Edelmann, Angelo Cafferata, Ann Furey, Ann Humphreys, Ann Maria Fletcher, Anna Brand, Annuziata Sabini, Anton Ulinski, Antonia Kuszman, Appolonia Saal, August Ackenhausesn, August F. Beermann, Augusta Schwartz, Augustine Querolo, Balthasar Lorch, Barton Boston, Benjamin Philibert, Benjamin F. Hedges, Benjamin F. Stocker, Bernard Monti, Bertha T. Olshausen, Bridget Fallon, Bridget Howard, C. R. Neale, Caspar Kittenreiner, Casper Greber, Catharine Tenbuelt, Catharine M. Ast, Catherine Fitzsimons, Catherine Schroeder, Catherine Thomas, Charles Frank, Charles Haas, Charles Heynen, Charles Merrick, Charles Michel, Charles Rohrer, Charles Schules, Charles A. Hahn, Charles A. Kuehn, Charles H. Burk, Charles J. Clark, Charles L. Downie, Charles T. Schabe, Charles W. Nehl, Christian Klein, Christiana Schoedel, Christina Zeller, Christopher H. Schnelle, Churchhill J. Selden, Cicero Mendell, Clara V. Whiteman, Claus Dorn, Daniel Keleher, Daniel Mueller, Daniel Schaeffer, Daniel Wilson, Darius Hunkins, Dietrich Schumacher, Duncan S. Carter, E. Gottlob Raaf, E. G. Knowles, Edward Nolan, Edward Traber, Edward B. Sayers, Edward P. McCarty, Elenora Roemmich, Elicalon M. Turner, Elisha Allen, Eliza Bailey, Eliza Redmond, Elizabeth Baumann, Elizabeth Meissner, Elizabeth Schmidt, Elizabeth Winnter, Elizabeth C. Lebourgeois, Ellen Horan, Ellen Meagher, Ernest Gourrier, Ernst Schluter, Ernst H. Docter, Eva Hoffmeister, Federick Haas, Ferdinand Singer, Frances B. Hyde, Frances E. Wall, Francis J. Fidlar Smith, Frank Pluempe, Frank Rocklage, Frank M. Wright, Frederick Bunte, Frederick Muller, Frederick Nedderhut, Frederick Wilms, Frederick W. Picker, Frederick W. Wellemeyer,

Frederick W. Knickmeyer, Fredrick W. Paust, Friedrich A. Driemeyer, G. W. Hoover, George Gebhart, George Gerber, George Kissel, George Link, George Ott, George Shryock, George Traxl, George Wood Platt, Gerard Miller, Gottlieb Altenberend, Gottlieb Dreckshage, Gottlob Feiler, Guiseppi Cloch, Gustav Hogrefe, Gustav G. Sieg, Harriet F. Mcquaid, Heinrich Owermann, Heinrich Scherder, Helen B. Deschapelles, Helena Deck, Henrietta Schillig, Henriette Langsdorf, Henry Brockmann, Henry Furst, Henry Gersie, Henry Goadby, Henry Hilgemann, Henry Hodlenberg, Henry Huchttons, Henry Krull, Henry Morley, Henry Senter, Henry Venderau, Henry Werz, Henry A. Todd, Henry C. Marthens, Henry J. Lueders, Henry R. Niebrugge, Henry S. Boekhoff, Henry S. Turner, Henry W. Muellmann, Herman Bocka, Herman Hake, Herman Pohlmann, Herman Vespermann, Herman H. Laumeier, Herman H. Boewer, Herman H. Fruechte, Hibbert Garrett, Hughey Smith, Hugo Krebs, Ida R. Vollberg, Irwin Z. Smith, Isabella Semple, Jacob Emanuel, Jacob Wastier, James Fea, James Jordan, James O'donnell, James Patrick, James Shaw, James J. Smith, James W. Handfield, Jeffery H. Pybus, Jennie McDonald, Johanna Dieckhoff, Johanna Pabst, Johanna Talleur, John Ackermann, John Betz, John Bruner, John Carroll, John Cauanagh, John Curley, John Kehoe, John Keil, John Martin, John Menown, John Mueller, John O'malley, John Primus, John Pugh, John Schmitt, John Tiche, John Wunderlich, John Wiebusch, John C. Diesel, John F. O'Brien, John Fritz Wirth, John G. Cameron, John Henry Albers, John M. Bass, John M. Cordes, John P. Peters, John Philipp Zurheide, John W. Davidson, Jonathan Richt, Joseph Gentil, Joseph Huhn, Joseph Mathien, Joseph Maurens, Joseph Sentoux, Julius Friedeborn, Julius Mueller, Julius A. Peters, Julius H. Hentter, Julius P. Sunderland, Kate Hession / Gibson, Letitia Parker, Lina Kitzinger, Lizzie M. Edgington, Lola Mason, Louis Bauman, Louis Bruno, Louis Cohen, Louis Ganter, Louis Hudson, Louis C. Koos, Louis O. Beckers, Louis P. Plant, Louis Ulrich Soller, Louisa Urban, Louisa D. Phipps, Luke Lamb, Magdalene Spaenle, Margaret Clancy, Margaret Kronester, Margaret Moran, Margaret Seckel, Margaret Sullivan, Margaret Textor, Margaretha Stueckler, Maria Moeller, Maria Warren, Maria Anna Schilling, Maria Elizabeth Schelter, Maria Elizabeth Zeis, Marie Madeline Masure, Mark Muleeney, Martha A. Briggs, Mary Barry, Mary Block, Mary McCarty, Mary Miller, Mary Oxley, Mary Stalker, Mary Thies, Mary A. Smith, Mary Ann Collins, Mary Ann Duggan, Mary Ann Ely, Mary Ann Maddy, Mary J. Nichols, Mary Magdalene Presley, Mathes Legler, Mathew Walsh, Mathias Weiss, Matthias Ullrich, Mayer Goldsoll, Meinecke Brothers, Michael Buckley, Michael Maguire, Michael Mielke, Michael J. O'Connell, Michael Joseph Faulhaber, Mina Kipp, Moses Stout, Nancy Miriam North, Nicholas Gondolf, Octavia E. Groves, Oliver D. Filley, P.W. Hitchcock, Patrick Barnable, Patrick Fitzgerald, Patrick McGeinn, Patrick Mullaley, Patrick Mulrooney, Patrick Welch, Patrick E. Greene, Patrick R. Brady, Peter Barchi, Peter McEvoy, Peter Steiger, Peter Wiesen, Philip Neufang, Philip

A. Mueller, Philip Lepper, Sr., Phineas J. Thompson, Porter B. Warner, Reuben E. Gezt, Richard Conners, Robert Widensohler, Rosa Renz, Rudolph Schneider, Sallie E. Merritt, Samuel P. Gillespie, Sarah McMurtry, Sarah Wade, Sarah J. Corbett, Sarah J. Russell, Seth A. Ranlett, Stephan H. Wulfemeyer, Stephen Partridge, Theodore Kleibold, Theodore Salorgne, Theodore A. Fischer, Theresa Sawyer, Theresa Sevier, Theresia Ringhoffer, Thomas Coffey, Thomas Hobson, Thomas Kehoe, Thomas Noska, Thomas B. Kelley, Thomas M. Yeats, Thomas T. Richards, Valentine Herrmann, W. F. Peiffer, Walter W. B. Middleton, Wharton T. Labeaume, Wilhelmine Wildeison, William Castello, William Fink, William Miles, William Milford, William Ray, William Staengel, William Thorton, William Wehmueller, William Westholt, William A. Thornburgh, William August Henry Saeger, William C. Blake, William C. Defriez, William H. Fisch, William H. Wehrenberg, William P. Cowperthwait

Linn County, Missouri, Land Patents, Fayette Land Ofice, 1845
William G Alexander : (ID) Jun. 1 , 1845 , (AN) MO2950.212
Thomas Brown : (ID) Jun. 1 , 1845 , (AN) MO2950.004
William Chapman : (ID) Jun. 1 , 1845 , (AN) MO2950.005
William Chapman : (ID) Jun. 1 , 1845 , (AN) MO2950.413
Enoch Fly : (ID) Jun. 1 , 1845 , (AN) MO2950.250
Nicholas Fox : (ID) Jun. 1 , 1845 , (AN) MO2950.443
Abraham Hines : (ID) Jun. 1 , 1845 , (AN) MO2950.136
Elisha Huss : (ID) Jun. 1 , 1845 , (AN) MO2950.288
John D. Locke : (ID) Jun. 1 , 1845 , (AN) MO2950.214
Joseph Mccormick : (ID) Jun. 1 , 1845 , (AN) MO2950.057
Joseph Mccormick : (ID) Jun. 1 , 1845 , (AN) MO2950.306
Lockerd S. Nevins : (ID) Jun. 1 , 1845 , (AN)   MO2950.351
Jackson Newton : (ID) Jun. 1 , 1845 , (AN) MO2950.056
Joseph Newton : (ID) Jun. 1 , 1845 , (AN) MO2950.426
James F. Pendleton : (ID) Jun. 1 , 1845 , (AN) MO2950.428
John Reynolds : (ID) Jun. 1 , 1845 , (AN) MO2950.381
Mason Singleton : (ID) Jun. 1 , 1845 , (AN) MO2950.485
Talton Turner : (ID) Jun. 1 , 1845 , (AN) MO2950.289
Israel Young : (ID) Jun. 1 , 1845 , (AN) MO2950.468
Absalom Glenn : (ID) Oct. 1 , 1845 , (AN) MO2960.072
Henry Latham : (ID) Oct. 1 , 1845 , (AN) MO2960.080
Alexander Ogan : (ID) Oct. 1 , 1845 , (AN) MO2960.041
Richard Pierce : (ID) Oct. 1 , 1845 , (AN) MO2960.037

Missourians in the 1867-1869 Montague County, Texas Voters List
S. Shannon: (CMTS) In state 29 years, in county 5 years, native of Missouri
W. A. Hearn: (CMTS) In state 25year, in county 8 years, native of Missouri

M. Gilbert: (CMTS) Registered to vote, Jul. 27, 1867, in state 30 years, in county 8 years, native of Missouri.
J. J. Willingham: (CMTS) In state 10 years, in county 10 years, native of Missouri
William Holleway: (CMTS) In state 2 years, in county 2 years, native of of Missouri
A. H. Kelly: (CMTS) In state 4 years, in county 1 month, native of Missouri
A. B. Hawkins: (CMTS) In state 13 years, in county 7 years, native of Missouri
W. R. Willigham: (CMTS) In state 9 years, in county 9 years, native of Missouri
James Dennis: (CMTS) In state 7 years, in county 7 years, native of Missouri
William M. Carrell: (CMTS) In state 8 years, in county 1 year, native of issouri
James McFarland: (CMTS) In state 15 years, in county 8 years, native of Missouri
James B. White: (CMTS) In state 5 years, in county 3 years, native of Missouri
John W. McFarland: (CMTS) Registed to vote Jan. 28, 1868, In state 16 Years, in county 12 years, native of Missouri
Thompson Kelly: (CMTS) In state 12 years, in county 11 years, native of Missouri
G. W. Fletcher: (CMTS) In state 25 years, in county 2 years, native of Missouri

Missourians in the 1867-1869 Hood County, Texas Voters List

William Adams: (CMTS) Registered Aug. 27, 1867, in state 7 years, in county 4 years, in precinct 3 years, native of Missouri
A. J. Adams: (CMTS) Registered Aug. 31, 1867, in state 7 years, in county 6 months, in precinct 6 months, native of Missouri
T. B. Atwood: (CMTS) Registered Nov. 22, 1869, in state 15 years, in county 12 months, native of Missouri
James Aust: (CMTS) Registered Nov. 24, 1869, in state 11 years, in county 2 years, native of Missouri
R. Blevins: (CMTS) Registerd Aug. 20, 1867, in state 20 years, in county 8 years, native of Missouri
W. Y. Boyd: (CMTS) Registered Aug. 31, 1868, in state 14 years, in county 2 years, native of Missouri
N. Cornelius: (CMTS) Registered Aug. 22, 1867, in state 9 years, in county 9 years, native of Missouri
A. Crites: (CMTS) Registered Aug. 27, 1867, in state 11 years, in county 9 years, native of Missouri
B. A. Crites: (CMTS) Registered Aug. 30, 1867, in state 7 years, in county 7 years, native of Missouri

E Dalton: (CMTS) Registered Sep. 23, 1867, in state 7 years, in county 1 year, native of Missouri

H. Dennie: (CMTS) Registered Nov. 20, 1869, in state 11 years, in county, 6 months, native of Missouri

J. Dennis: (CMTS) Registered Aug. 31, 1867, in state 11 years, in county 11 years

W. M. Dennis: (CMTS) Registered Aug. 31, 1867, in state 7 years, in county 7 years, native of Missouri

R. T. Foster: (CMTS) Registered Nov. 24, 1869, 3 years in state, 2 years in county, native of Missouri

George Greer: (CMTS) Registered Aug. 27, 1867, in state 7 years, in county 6 years, native of Missouri

W. J. Gregory: (CMTS) Registered Aug. 16, 1867, in state 15 years, in county 13 years, native of Missouri

William P. Gregory: (CMTS) Registered Nov. 26, 1869, in state 15 years, in county 12 years, native of Missouri.

J. M. Gunnel: (CMTS) Registered Nov. 24, 1869, in state 12 years, in county 2 years, native of Missouri.

A. Huffstettler: (CMTS) Registered Nov. 20, 1869, in state 12 years, in county 6 months, native of Missouri

J. Huffsettler: (CMTS) Registered Aug. 20, 1867, in state 2 years, in county 12 months, native of Missouri

Milton Jones: (CMTS) Registered Nov. 23, 1869, in state 12 years, in county 12 years, native of Missouri

David Knutson: (CMTS) Registered Aug. 27, 1867, in state 16 years, in county 3 years, native of Missouri

A. W. Landers: (CMTS) Registered Aug. 16, 1867, in state 9 years, in county 3 years, native of Missouri

J. L. Landers: (CMTS) Registered Sep. 23, 1867, in state 8 years, in county 5 years, native of Missouri

J. A. McCreary: (CMTS) Registered Aug. 31, 1867, in state 14 years, in county 13 years, native of Missouri

J. A. McCreary, Jr.: (CMTS) Registered Jan. 30, 1868, in state 15 years, in county 15 years, native of Missouri

W. R. McCreary: (CMTS) Registered Aug. 31, 1867, in state 16 years, in county 12 years, native of Missouri

W. W. McKenzie: (CMTS) Registered Sep. 23, 1867, in state 7 years, in county 7 years, native of Missouri

J. Mooney: (CMTS) Registered Sep. 23, 1867, in state 21 years, in county 30 days, native of Missouri

J. T. Morton: (CMTS) Registered Nov. 26, 1869, in state 12 years, in county 12 years, native of Missouri

A. P. Nickell: (CMTS) Registered Nov. 26, 1869, in state 12 years, in county 2 years, native of Missouri

T. J. Nolen: (CMTS) Registered Aug. 23, 1867, in state 17 years, in county 1 year, native of Missouri

D. L. Nutt: (CMTS) Registered Nov. 18, 1869, in state 3 years, in county 1 year, native of Missouri

A. H. Oustoll: (CMTS) Rgistered Nov. 26, 1869, in state 22 years, in county 1 year, native of Missouri

G. W. Patton: (CMTS) Registered Aug. 21, 1867, in state 23 years, in county 10 years, native of Missouri

F. M. Pointer: (CMTS) Registered Aug. 31, 1867, in state 15 years, in county 15 years, native of Missouri

Daniel Rhodes: (CMTS) Registered Nov. 24, 1869, in state 10 years, in county 6 month, native of Missouri

Daniel Shipman: (CMTS) Registered Aug. 30, 1867, in state 2 years, in county 1 year, native of Missouri

R. Sneed: (CMTS) Registered Nov. 22, 1869, in state 3 years, in county 12 months, native of Missouri

William B. Tinnin: (CMTS) Registered Aug. 27, 1867, in state 10 years, in county 8 years, native of Missouri

J. T. Walton: (CMTS) Registered Nov. 26, 1869, in state 1 year, in county 1 year, native of Missouri

J. W. Washburne: (CMTS) Registered Nov. 24, 1869, in state 30 years, in county 2 years, native of Missouri

W. R. Weldon: (CMTS) Registered Aug. 31, 1867, in state 18 years, in county 7 months, native of Missouri

S. White: (CMTS) Registered Sep. 23, 1867, in state 26 years, in county 12 years, native of Missouri

G. M. Wright: (CMTS) Nov. 18, 1869, in state 4 years, in county 12 months, native of Missouri

Marriage Notice, *"Fort Worth, TX Democrat,"*
B. Daggett, Forth, to Miss Addie Zimmerman, Lewiston, MO, on Jun. 14, 1874 at the residence of the mother of the bride. Services were performed by Rev, Penn., (I) Jun. 20, 1874

Joseph H. Brown, Forth Worth, to Miss Mary Oliver, St. Louis, MO in St, Louis on Aug. 27, 1874. (I) Sep. 5, 1874

Missouri Songwriters and Lyricists

12th Street Rag: (CP) Euday Louis Bowman, (LY) James S. Sumner, (AR) S. E. Wheeler, (CMTS) Published by J. W. Jenkins & Sons Music Co., Kansas City, MO 1919

Across Loves Great Divide: (CP) Willi E. Skidmore, (LY) J. Everett Moles, (Perf) Southern Harmony Four, B. G. Palmer, E. E. Bell, C E. Few, P. C. Lowery, (CMTS) Published by Skidmore Music Co., Kansas City, MO, 1917

Ada's Favorite Rondo: (CP) Carl Sidus, (CMTS) Published by Kunkel Bros., St. Louis, MO 1885

Adhesive Waltz: (CP) R. F. Cardella, (CMTS) Published by Balmer &

Weber, St. Louis, MO, 1870
Adoration Waltz: (CP) Frank Magine, (LY) A. F. Otis and C. Romano, (Perf) Leo F. Forbstein, (CMTS) Published by J. W. Jenkins Music Co., Kansas City, MO 1924
Areoplane Waltz: (CP) Mamie R. Appler, (CMTS) Published by Alice Martin, St. Louis, MO, 1911
Affinity Rag: (CP) Irene Conzad, (CMTS) Published by J. W. Jenkins & Sons, Kansas City, MO, 1910
Africian Pas': (CP) Maurice Kirwin, (CMTS) John Stark & Son, Missouri, 1902
After the Play: (CP) Thomas M. Bowers, (Perf) William Walling, (CMTS) Published by Thos. M. Bowers & Co., Missouri, 1893
Alice May: (CP) G. Baumfelder, (CMTS) Blamer & Weber, St. Luis, MO, 1870
Alice of the Pines: (CP) G. E. von Hofe, A. J. Hansell, (CMTS) Published by Weil Publishing Co., Missouri, 1916
All For You Dear: (CP) Lucien Denni, (LY) Gwynne Deni, (CMTS) Published by J. W. Jenkson Sons, Kansas City, MO, 1911
All Things Are Beautiful: (CP) Stephen Glover, (LY) Andrew Park, (CMTS) Published 1877 by Wakelam & Luch, St. Louis, MO
All The Candy: (CP) E. Harry Kelly, (CMTS) Published by J. W. Jenkins & Sons, Kansas City, MO, 1907
All The Money: (CP) Raymond Birch, (CMTS) Published by Chas. L. Johnson, Kansas City, 1908
Allan Percy: (AR) W. C. Peters, (Perf) Anna Ablamowiscz, (CMTS) Published by Balmer & Weber, Missouri, 1849
Allegiance to the Red, White & Blue: (CP) Ethel Lee Buxton, (CMTS) Published by Jenkins Music Co., 1942
The Allen Glide: (CP) Louise Allen, (CMTS) Published by Syndicate Music Co., St. Louis, MO, 1915
Ally Ray: (CP) William S. Pitts, (CMTS) Published by J. J. Dobmyer, Missouri, 1864
Alone: (CP) F. Waldo Hargrave, (CMTS) Published by Midland Music Co., St. Louis, MO, 1926
The Amaranth: (CP) A. E. Wimmerstedt, (CMTS) Published by St. Louis Music Co., 1874
America First: (CP) Howard Kocian, (CMTS) Published by Buck & Lowney, St. Louis, MO, 1916
America Is Proud Of You: (CP) Arthur Hiller, (CMTS) Published by Art Hiller, Kansas City, MO, 1921
Amora: (CP) Lucien Denni, (LY) Thomas B. Roberts, (Perf) Myrtle Souders, (CMTS) Published by J. W. Jenkins & Sons, Kansas City, MO, 1913
An Arizona Home: (CP) Mary Goodwin, (LY) William Goodwin, (CMTS) Published by Balmer & Weberm St. Louis, 1904
Angel of Charity: (CP) Frank Fisk, (CMTS) Published by J. R. Bell,

Kansas City, MO, 1885
Angel of My Dreams: (CP) W. Hayes, (CMTS) Published by J. R. Bell, Kansas City, 1885
Angel Visits: (CP) Charles Kinkel, (CMTS) Published by T. A. Boyle, St. Louis, MO
Angelus: (CP) Emile Karst, (CMTS) Published by Balmer & Weber, St. Louis, MO, 1870
Annette and I: (CP) L. F. Johns, (CMTS) Published by Conover Bros., Kansas City, MO, 1882
Answer: (CP) Alfred George Robyn, (CMTS) Published by Balmer & Weber, St. Louis MO, 1885
Answer to Nobody's Darlin' But Mine: (CP) Jimmi Davis, (CMTS) Published by Jenkins Music Co., 1936
Apple Sass Rag: (CP) Harry Belding, (CMTS) Published by Buck & Lowney, St. Louis, MO, 1914
Arbor of Dreams: (CP) C. E. Wheeler, (Ill) H. G. Chilberg, (CMTS) Published by J. W. Jenkins & Sons, Kansas City, MO, 1912
Are You Looking for Someone?: (CP) Donald Yates, (LY) E. L. Knight, (CMTS) Published by E. L. Knight, Kansas City, MO 1956
Are You Waiting for Me, Ila Dear?: (CP) Arthur Dudley, (CMTS) Published by A. Dudley Music Co., 1908
At Parting: (CP) Frank H. Tobey, (CMTS) Dedicated to Mabel Knowles, Published by J. W. Jenkins & Sons, 1898
As Clings the Ivy: (CP) Carson W. White, (CMTS) Dedicated to Bonnie Barstow, (CMTS) Published by Carson W. White, Kansas City, MO, 1920
As Long As I Have You: (CP) Earl Haubrich, Al Lewis and Howard Simon, (CMTS) Published by J. W. Jenkins Sons Music Co., Kansas City, MO 1926
At Our House: (CP) Katherine Marianna Tenner, (CMTS) Published by Dison-Lane, St. Louis, MO, 1928
Attention!: (CP) Lyle Wear Sparks, (CMTS) Published by Ted Sparks Music Co., Kansas City, MO, 1905
Auf Wiedersehn: (CP) Eben H. Bailey, (CMTS) Published by Legg Bros., Agents, Kansas City, MO, 1882
The Aunt Jemina Slide: (CP) Karl Johnson, (LY) Hugh McNutt, (CMTS) Published by Hugh McNutt, St. Joseph, MO, 1917
The Auto Glide: (CP) E. Hardy, (CMTS) Published A. W. Perry & Sons, Sedalia, MO, 1915
The Auto Race Two Step: (CP) Emma B. Sax, (CMTS) Published by A. W. Perry & Sons, 1908
Autumn Leaves: (CP) Henry Bollman, (CMTS) Published by Henry Bollman, St. Louis, 1874
Ave Verum: (CP) Emile Karst, (CMTS) Published by Balmer & Weber, St. Louis, MO, 1870

Avisator's Two Step: (CP) Beulah Brubaker, (CMTS) Published by A. W. Perry's Sons, Sedalia, MO, 1927

Aw, Go By Yourself A. Funeral: (CP) O. E. Sharrat, (CMTS) Published by O. E. Sharrat, Kansas City, MO, 1932

Awake From Thy Slumber: (CP) K.. G. Estabrook, (CMTS) Published by Balmer & Weber, St. Louis, MO, 1870

Baby O. Mine: (CP) Hans Feil. (LY) Rev. Henry B. Tiernan, (CMTS) First Prize in 1928 Kansas City Teachers Associatin Contest, Published by J. W. Jenkins' Sons, Kansas City, MO, 1929

Barny A'Leen: (CP) George W. Persley, (LY) Arthur W. French, (CMTS) Published by T. A. Boyles, St. Louis, 1871

Bachelor's Button: (CP) W. C. Powell, (IL) C. Chilberg, (CMTS) Published by J. W. Jenkins Sons Music Co., Kansas City, MO, 1909

Back to Old Erin: (CP) Joe Hill, (CMTS) Joe Hill Publishing Co., Kansas City, MO 1914

The Bandolero: (CP) Clarice Talot, (CMTS) Published by J. W. Jenkins Sons Music Co., Kansas City, MO, 1909

Beautiful Snow: (CP) Silvio Pratel, (CMTS) Published by Bollman & Schatzman, St. Louis, 1870

Bell Brandon: (CP) Francis Woolcott, (LY) T. E. Garrett, (PF) T. B. Pendergast, Campbell Minstrels, (CMTS) Published by Balmer & Weber, St. Louis, MO, 1854, Name on the plate was E. T. Kirkpatrick

Bell & Everett Polka: (CP) Frederick William Smith, (CMTS) Published By Balmer & Weber, St. Louis, MO, 1860

Ben Bolt: (CP) Nelson Kneass, (CMTS) Published by J. L. Peters, 1848

Berlin Galop: (CP) Phil B. Beyy, (CMTS) Published by A. W. Perry, Sedalia, MO, 1884

Beside the Sea: (CP) William Cummings Peters, (LY) W. Winters, (IL) Donaldson & Elmes, (CMTS) Published J. L. Peters & Co., St. Louis, MO 1864

The Better Land: (CP) Frederic Hymen Cowen, (LY) Felicia Dorothea Browne Hemans, (CMTS) Published by Palmer & Webber, 1878

Black Hawk Waltz & Schottish: (CP) Mary E. Walsh, (IL) ??? Porter, (CMTS) Dedicated to P. H. Brown, Published by J. L. Peters & Co., St. Louis, MO 1869

Bloomer: (CP) Anton Wallerstein, (CMTS) Published by Balmer & Webber, St. Louis, 1851

The Blue Star in the Window: (CP) Albert Simpson Reitz, (CMTS) Published Jenkins Music Co., Kansas City, MO, 1944

The Bohemian Girl: Opera: (CP) Michael William Balfe, (AR) Charles Brunner, (CMTS) Published by H. Bollman & Sons, St. Louis, MO, 1868

Bon Ton Valse Brilliante: (CP) Charles Gimbel, Jr., (CMTS) Dedicated to Miss Emmie Powell, Lee's Summit, MO, Published by A. W.

Perry, Seadalia, MO, 1880
The Bonnie Flag with the Stripes and Stars: (CP) Col. J. L. Geddes, (LY) Henry Werner, (CMTS) Published by Balmer & Weberm St. Louis, MO, 1863, Song was composed while Col. Geddes was a POW in Selma, AL. He was A. member of the 8th Iowa Inf.
Bonnie Scotland I. Adore Thee: (CP) T. Gordon, (CMTS) Published by J. J. Dobmeyer, St. Louis, 1867
Boonville Waltz: (CP) Charles Farringer, (CMTS) Published by Balmer & Weber, St. Louis, MO, 1863
Brighter Than The Star Soft Gleaming: (CP) Giuseppe Verdi, (CMTS) Published by H. Pilcher, St. Louis, 1856
Brush The Frowns Away: (CP) Horace Huron, (CMTS) Published by C. L. Partee, Kansas City, MO, 1897
By-Gone Days: A. Fireside Reverie: (CP) Geo. H. Briggs, (CMTS) Published by, Huyett Bros., St. Joseph, MO, 1885
Call Me Back, Pal, O'Mine: (CP) Harold Dixon, (LY) Morgan Brown, (CMTS) Dixon-Lane Music Publishing Co., St. Louis, MO, 1921
Call Me Darling Once Again: (CP) Charles E. Pratt, (LY) George Cooper, (CMTS) Published by T. A. Boyle, St. Louis, 1871
Call Me No More Mother: (CP) William Shakespeare Hays, (CMTS) Published by Balmer & Weber, St. Louis, 1864
Camille Polka: (CP) Henry Werner, (CMTS) Published by Balmer & Weber, St. Louis, MO, 1856
Cavatine, Op. 43: (CP) Vincenzo Bellini, Published by Wakelam & Lucho, St. Louis, 1855
Daisy Waltz: (CP) Bertha Mathews, (CMTS) Published by J. W. Truxel, Sedalia, MO, 1884
Dat Mornin' in De Sky: (CP) Blind Boone, (CMTS) Published by Carl Hoffman, 1899
Down in Manila Bay: (CP) A. C, Remio, (CMTS) Publiahed by Balmer & Weber, St. Louis, MO, 1898.
Dutch Courtship: (CP) M. Raney, (CMTS) Published by A. W. Perry & Son, Sedalia, MO, 1885
The Egyptian Gil's Song: (CP) E. C. Davis, (LY) Mrs. S. L. Howe, (CMTS) Dedicated to Miss S. Pomeroy, Published by N. Philips, St. Louis, MO, 1850
Elsa Grande Marche Militaire: (CP) H. Victor, (CMTS) Published by A. W. Perry, Sedalia, MO, 1884
Evening Breezes Morceau de Salon: (CP) Henry Bollman, (CMTS) Dedicated to Miss Annie E. Pentecost, Rochester, NY, Published By Bollman & Schatzman, St. Louis, MO, 1871
Face to Face: (CP) Herbert Johnson, (CMTS) Published by Carl Hoffman Music Co., Kansas City, MO, 1897
Fairy Waltz: (CP) Jas. Richards, (CMTS) Published by A. W. Perry & Son, Sedalia, MO, 1885
The Gallant Maine: (CP) Charles Lange, (CMTS) Published by Balmer

& Weber, St. Louis, MO, 1898

General Sigel's Grand March: (CP) Henry Warner alias of Charles Balmer, (CMTS) Published by Charles Balmer & Henry Weber, St. Louis, MO, 1861

Gertie's Waltz: (CP) May Cobine, (CMTS) Published J. W. Tuxel, Sedalia, MO, 1884

Gipsey Countess: (CP) Stephen Glover, (LY) Mrs. Crawford, (CMTS) Dedicated to Miss Fannie Mitchell, St. Louis, MO, Published D. P Fields, Louisville, KY, 1860

The Glide Polka: (CP) Frank Noyes, (CMTS) Published by A. W. Perry & Son, Sedalia, MO, 1885

The Good Bye at the Door: (CP) Stephen Glover, (CMTS) Published by Balmer & Weber, St. Louis, MO, 1850

Hannibal City Waltz: (CP) Frank B. Ray, (CMTS) Published by Balmer Weber, St. Louis, MO, 1862

Happy Hopper: (CP) Mamie Williams, (CMTS) Published by Carl Hoffman Music Co., 1906

Haste Love: (CP) Alfred G. Robyn, (LY) Minnie Gilmore, (CMTS) Published by Balmer & Weber, 1892

Heart's Delight March: (CP) ??? Aurora, (CMTS) Published by A. W. Perry, Sedalia, MO, 1884

Hike to the Pike: (CP) Edward B. Claypoole, (CMTS) Published by Thiebes-Stierlin Music Co., St. Louis, MO, 1904

Holiday March: (CP) Charles Kinkel, (IL) ??? Warren, (CMTS) Dedicated to Miss Katie Bruce, Published by Balmer & Weber, St. Louis, MO, 1869

Homestead Schottische: (CP) D. W. Crist, (CMTS) Published by A. W. Perry & Son, Sedalia, MO, 1885

Hot House Rag: (CP) Paul Pratt, (CMTS) Published by Stark Music Co., St. Louis, MO, 1914

How Can I. Bare to Part From Thee: (CP) Julius C. Meininger, (LY) Thomas B. Long, (CMTS) Dedicated to Mrs. Agnes Toof, Memphis, TN, Published by J. L. Peters & Bro., St. Louis, MO, 1865

If Only I. Had A. Sweetheart: (CP) Chas. L. Johnson, (LY) Robert Spencer, (CMTS) Published by Chas. L. Johnson & Co., Kansas City, MO, 1909

I'm So Fond of Dancing: (CP) R. Frank Cardella, (LY) Hans Patrick le Conner, (IL) A. McLean and J. A. Scholten, (PF) Johnny Allen, (CMTS) Dedicated to Eph. Horn, Published by Compton & Doan, St. Louis, MO 1868

In Vain I. Hope: (CP) Giacamo Meyerberr, (CMTS) Published by Balmer & Weber, St. Louis, MO, 1856

India May: (CP) H. S. Thompson, (CMTS) Published by Balmer & Webber, St. Louis, 1866

Ione Waltz: (CP) Phil B. Perry, (CMTS) Published by A. W. Perry,

Sedalia, MO, 1884

Ireland, I'm For You: (CP) Hale Byers, Hi Wilson, Irving Newhoff, (CMTS) Published Newhoff, Byers & Wilson, Kansas City, MO, 1916

It Takes A. Long Tall Brown Skin Gal to Make A. Preacher Lay His Bible Down: (CP) Will E. Skidmore, (LY) Marshal Walker, (CMTS) Published by Skidmore Music Co., Kansas City, MO, 1917

Jolly Companions: (CP) Robert Vollstedt, (CMTS) Deicated to Miss Alma Goebel, St. Charles, MO, Published by Balmer & Weber, St. Louis, MO, 1892

Kiss Me Goodnight: (CP) Benn Bernie, Vernon Stevens, Gladys Gillette, Elmer Olson, (CMTS) Published by J. W. Jenkins & Sons, Music Co., Kansas City, MO, 1924

La Mode: (CP) E. J. Stark and B. T. Whitlow, (PF) Mrs. Joesph H. Nathan and Rodney Peters at the Dreamland Palace, (CMTS) Published by Stark Music, St. Louis, MO, 1913

Latonia Rag: (CP) Leon Donaldson, (AR) Thomas Sims, (CMTS) Published by American Music Sydicate, St. Louis, MO, 1903

Lauterbacher Waltz: (CP) William Cumming, (CMTS) Dedicated to Miss Ellen Wingate, Published by J. L. Peters & Bro., St. Louis, MO 1865

Legal Tender Polka: (CP) F. Chase, (CMTS) Published by Balmer & Weber, St. Louis, MO, 1865

Lend A. Hand to One Another: (CP) Fred Wilson, (CMTS) Publised by Balmer & Weber, St. Louis, MO, 1866

Let's Make Believe: (CP) Larry Shay, (LY) Harry Harris, (CMTS) Published by Larry Conley Inc., St. Louis, MO, 1927

Lilies of the Valley: (CP) Charles Kinkel, (CMTS) Published by J. L. Peters & Co., St. Louis, MO, 1868

Little Willie: (CP) Lysandra Clemmons, (CMTS) Published by J. W. Truxel Music Co., Sedalia, MO, 1885

Loin du Bal: (CP) Ernest Vital Louis Gillet, (CMTS) Published by Balmer & Weber, St. Louis, MO, 1890

Love, Powder & Pateches: (CP) Rosalie Balmer Smith Cole, (CMTS) Published by Balmer & Weber, St. Louis, MO, 1898

Mabel Boone: (CP) Francis Woolcott, (CMTS) Published by Balmer & Weber, St. Louis, MO, 1860

Maggie's Waltz: (CP) M. Bruner, (CMTS) Published by A. W. Perry, Sedalia, MO, 1884

Magnetic Waltz: (CP) D. C. Weaver, (CMTS) Published by A. W. Perry & Son, Sedalia, MO, 1885

Mammy's Little Blue-Grass Honey: (CP) H. O. Wheeler, (LY) Deamor R. Drake, (PF) Isadore Rush, (CMTS) Published by Brokaw Music, St. Joseph, MO, 1898

Manzanillo: (CP) J. Helmesberger, (CMTS) Published by Balmer & Weber Music House Co., St. Louis, MO, 1891

March of Adelphiennes: (CP) J. T. Conley, (CMTS) Published by Kunkel Bros., St. Louis, MO 1883

Married and Not to Me: (CP) Matthias Keller, (LY) George W. Birdseye, (IL) ??? Warren, (CMTS) Published by John L. Peters, St. Louis, MO, 1869

Mary's Waiting at the Window: (CP) William S. Hays, (CMTS) Published by J. L. Peters & Bros., St. Louis, 1866

Maurice Constello, I. Love a-dat Man: (CP) Charly Brow, (LY) Billy Green and Carter Sidney, (PF) Maurice Consetto and Manny Worth, (CMTS) Published by Buck and Lowney, St. Louis, MO, 1915

Mayflowers: (CP) Joseph Floss, (CMTS) Published by Kinkel Bros., St. Louis, MO, 1870

Mermaids Song from Oberon: (CP) Carl Maria von Weber, (AR) Charles Kinkel, (IL) Gregson, Donaldson & Elmers, (CMTS) Dedicated to Mrs. Agness Toof, Published by J. L. Peters & Bro., St. Louis, MO, 1866

The Mill in the Forest: (CP) by ??? Eilenberg, (CMTS) Published by J. W. Jenkins Sons, Kansas City, MO, 1892

My Copper Colored Squaw: (CP) Peter S. Clark, (IL) ???, Morrison, (CMTS) Published by Thiebes-Stierlin, St. Louis, MO, 1909

My Dear Old Southern Home: (CP) Charles E. Shafer, (LY) E. Edwards, (CMTS) Published by John Stark & Son, St. Louis, MO, 1902

My Sweet Rosita: (CP) Chas. H. Jenne, (LY) Edwin J. Bowrin, (CMTS) Published by Melody Hall, Kansas City, MO, 1943

Nobody's Darlin' But Mine: (CP) Jimmie Davis, (CMTS) Published by Jenkins Music Co., Kansas City MO, 1935

Not Married Yet: (CP) Horatio Dawes Hewitt, (CMTS) Published by Balmer & Weber, St. Louis, MO, 1863

Oh! Say Art Thou Happy: (CP) Mrs. Joseph Bogy, (CMTS) Published by H. Bollman & Sons, St. Louis, MO, 1885

The Old Plantation Songs We used to Sing: (CP) Della Hicks, (LY) Ch. Martin, (CMTS) Published by the Ameican Music Syndicate, St. Louis, MO, 1904

Our Band March: (CP) Leon Everett Simmons, (CMTS) Published by A. W. Perry's Sons, Sedalia, MO, 1932

Pearls of Dew: (CP) Charles Kinkel, (CMTS) Dedicated to Miss Florence Norvell, Published by J. L. Peters & Bros., St. Louis, MO 1864

Penelope Waltz: (CP) leon Everett Simmons, (CMTS) Dedicate to Mr. & Mrs. Luther Palmer, Published by A. W. Perry's Sons, Sedalia, MO, 1926

Perle de L'Amerique: (CP) Charles Kinkel, (CMTS) Dedicated to Miss Kate Redding, Published by J. L. Peters Bros Co., St. Louis, MO, 1866

The Psalms: (CP) J. Faure, (CMTS) Published by Balmer & Weber, St. Louis, 1888

Reasure: A. Collection of Hyms & Chants: (CP) Compiled by Mrs. N. J. Brainard, (CMTS) Published by balmer & Weber, St. Louis, MO, 1871

Red Moon: (CP) Charles Humfeld, (IL) W. M. Young, (PF) Musical Brown Bros., (CMTS) Published by Howard & Browne, St. Louis, MO, 1908

Reve Angelique: (CP) Henri Allard, (CMTS) Dedicated to George Stevens, Published by J. L. Peters & Bro., St. Louis, MO, 1864

Rose Schottish: (CP) E. Rose Besly, (CMTS) Published by J. W. Truxel, Sedalia, MO, 1885

Rosalba Waltz: (CP) Henry Kleber, (IL) ??? Warren, (CMTS) Dedicated to Miss M. A. I. Labouisse, Published by J. L. Peters & Bro., St. Louis, MO, 1866

She's As Lively as A. Rose: (CP) Eddie Fox, (LY) Bobby Newcomb, (AR) Frank Cardella, (IL) A. McLean, (PF) Billy Allen, (CMTS) Published by J. Compton, St. Louis, 1867

Singin' is Prayin': (CP) Helen Pfister Converse, (CMTS) Published by A. W. Perry's SPns, Sedalia, MO, 1937

Sioux March: (CP) Louis Wallis, (CMTS) Published by Balmer & Weber, St. Louis, 1856

Somewhere There's Someone: (CP) Art Gillham, Lillian Madson, (CMTS) Published by J. W. Jenkins& Sons Music Co., Kansas City, MO, 1929

The Song of the Blue & the Gray: (CP) Charles E. Hofmann, (CMTS) Published by Balmer & Weber Music Co., St. Louis, MO, 1898

Songs of the Circle: (CMTS) Collection of children's songs compiled by Clara Beeson Hubbard, Preface by Susan E. Blow, Published by Balmer & Weber, St. Louis, MO, 1881

Sontag Polka: (CP) Charles Louis Napoleon Albert, (IL) E. and C. Robyn, (PF) Henrietta Sontag, (CMTS) Published Balmer & Weber, St. Louis, MO, 1854

Spirit Rapping: (CP) W. W. Rossington, (LY) J. Elwood Garret, (IL) ??? Greene, (CMTS) Punlished by John Gass, St. Louis, MO, 1853

St. Louis Grey's Quick Step March: (CP) J. W. Postwaite, (CMTS) Dedicated to Capt. George Knapp and the St. Louis Greys, Published by Balmer & Weber, St. Louis, MO, 1852

The Sultan's Polka: (CP) Charles Louis Napoleon Albert, (CMTS) Published by Balmer & Weber, St. Louis, MO, 1850

Sunlight Polka: (CP) E. Rose Besley, (CMTS) Published by J. W. Truxel, Sedalia, MO, 1885

Sweet As A. Peach, Sweet Kentucy Girls: (CP) Charles L. Ward, ??? Price, J. W. Parson, (IL) Hart & Mapother, (CMTS) Dedicated to Miss Lena Pratt, St. Louis, MO, Published by Louis Tripp, Louisville, KY, 1869

Sweet Jessie: (CP) Frederick Buckley, (CMTS) Published by Balmer & Weber, St. Louis, MO, 1857

Sweet Thoughts of Home: (CP) A. C. Farnham, (CMTS) Dedicated to Miss Sallie A. Wells, Arcadia, MO, Published by Balme & Weber, St. Louis, MO, 1853

Ta De Da Da De Dum Dangerous Blues: (CP) Billie Brown, (LY) Anna Welker Brown, (CMTS) J. W. Jenkins & Sons Music Co., Kansas City, MO, 1921

There's A. Beautiful Bloom on Thy Cheek my Love: (CP) Thomas Brigham Bishop, (CMTS) Published by Balmer & Weber, St. Louis, MO, 1858

Those Charming Feet: (CP) Henry Hart, (IL) C. Hamilton, (PF) Billy Emerson, (Photo) Jno. A. Scholten, (CMTS) Published by Kunkel Bros., St. Louis, MO, 1870

Twilight Thoughts Waltz: (CP) Fannie Louise King, (CMTS) Published by A. W. Perry, Sedalia, MO, 1884

Two Street Scenes: (CP) Catherine Marianna Tenner, (CMTS) Published By Shattinger Piano & Music, St. Louis, MO, 1927

Vacation Galop: (CP) Phil B. Perry, (CMTS) A. W. Perry, Sedalia, MO, 1884

Way Down East: (CP) Bess Rudisill, (CMTS) Dedicated to Miss Pattie Buchanan, Billings, MT, Published by S. Simon, St. Louis, MO, 1902

We Sing to Abe Our Song: (CP) E. C. Davis, (CMTS) Published by Balmer & Weber, St. Louis, MO, 1887

When I. Take My Vacation in Heaven: (CP) Herbert Buffum, (CMTS) Published by Jenkins Music Co., Kansas City, MO, 1933

When My Great Grand Daddy and My Great Grand Mammy Used to Cuddle and Coo in the Coconut Tree: (CP) Will E. Skidmore, (LY) Marshall Walker, (CMTS) Skidmore Music Co., Kansas City, MO 1917

When the Sallows Homeward Fly: (CP) Franz Abt, (CMTS) Published by Kunkel Bros., St. Louis, 1873

Where are the Friends of my Youth: (OC) George Barker, (LY) Lt. Col. Addison, (AR) Samuel Owen, (IL) ??? Quidor, (CMTS) Published By Balmer & Weber, St. Louis, MO, 1850

While the Leaves Come Drifting Down: (CP) Hattie Nevada, (CMTS) Kansas City Talking Machine Co., Kansas City, MO, 1898

Winnebago Waltz: (CP) Will W. Hinton, (CMTS) Published by A. W. Perry, Sedalia, MO, 1884

Wondering: (CP) Raymond DeWitt, Leroy DeWitt, (CMTS) Published by Weile Publishing CO., St. Louis, MO, 1925

Would You If You Could?: (CP) Herbert Spencer, (LY) Eddie Dustin, (IL) W. M. Young, (PF) Bell's Six Empire Girls, (CMTS) Thiebes-Stierman Music Co., St. Louis, MO, 1906

You: (CP) Alfred George Robyn, (LY) Hannah Daviess Pittman, (CMTS) Published by Thiebes-Stierlin, St. Louis, MO, 1884

Howard County, Missouri, 1840 Heads of Household

Andrew Adams, Minter Adams, Patsy Adams, Sarah Adams, Wilson Adams, Granvill W. Adkins, J. Ainsly, L. Ainsworth, Rewbin Alexander, Wm. Alexander, James Allcorn, D. Allen, G. S. Allen, J. M. Allen, Joseph Allen, Thomas Allen, Elliot Alsop, R. Alverson, S. Alverson, Sidney Alverson, David Amick, William Amick, A. R. Anderson, Benj. Anderson, C. G. Anderson, Green B. Anderson, John Anderson, Moses Andrew, Aaron Andrews, Green Andrews, James Andrews, James Andrews, John Andrews, John Andrews, Joseph Andrews, Martin Andrews, Nancy Andrews, William Andrews, James Ansell, George Anthewise, Jesse Arnett, S. Arnett, Caesor Arnold, Elizabeth Arnold, John Arnold, A. Ashcraft, A. Sr. Ashcraft, Elin Ashcraft, Greenberry Atteberry, Jesse Atteberry, C. Atterberry, Eli Atterberry, Tho. Atterberry, Z. Atterberry, A. Atterbury, Ann Austin, James Averette, Jesse Bailey, L. J. Bailey, Minter H. Bailey, Jesse Ball, B. Ballew, Hiram Ballew, William Ballew, Barnes, Alfred Barnett, Elizabeth Barnett, Solomon Barnett, Zachariah Barnett, Zachias Barnett, Jr., A. Barren, M. M. Barren, J. D. Barton, K. L. Barton, Polly Barton, Henry Basey, Robert Basket, William Basket, G. P. Bass, Nancy Baxter, Bland Becket, J. Belden, Roddy Bell, C. Belmer, Amos Benson, James R. Benson, Rewbin B. Bently, Samuel Bently, Samuel Berby, V. P. Bernard, William Berry, John Best, A. Beverly, J. H. Birch, W. F. Birch, Foster Birmam, F. H. Biswell, Charles Biven, James Biven, Abraham Black, W. E. Black, J. A.. Blackwell, J. A.. Blackwell, J. M. Blakely, John Blakely, John Blakely, Samuel Blane, J. F. Blankenbecket, S. Blankenship, W. L. Blanton, C. Bloom, J. D. Bloys, Rias Blurton, Thomas Bobett, R. W. Boggs, James E. Bolden, John Bondurant, H. L. Boom, W. C. Boon, Henry Boosher, Peter Booth, James Borsley, Willis Boswell, J. Botrite, Jane Botrite, William Botts, E. Bowdrey, Peter Bowmer, T. S. Bowmer, Elijah Bowny, William Boyde, Jonathan Bozarth, Permilla Bozarth, Wm. Bozwell, Alex. Bradley, James Bradley, James Bradley, Nathan Bradley, Rewbin D. Bradley, Squire Bradley, Thomas Bradley, ThomasBradley, Sr., Jesse Bradly, Henry Bragg, Joseph Bragg, Sr., Richard Brannin, J. M. Brashear, Judson Sr. Brashear, W. Brashear, Robert Brashear, A. L. Brasher, Davis J. Brasher, George W. Brasher, John C. Brasher, Neriah Brasher, John Brawdus, Caleb Briggs, K. W. Briggs, R. Briggs, E. F. Broaddus, Jacob Brockman, Hopson Brooks, ?. R. Brown, Hugh Brown, Jacob Brown, James Brown, John C. Brown, Joseph Brown, Nelson Brown, Thomas G. Brown, Thomas Brown, William Brown, James Browning, James Browning, S. P. Browning, John Brundage, John Brunts, William D. Bugby, John Bull, Lewis Bungardar, Joseph Bunnell, Ely. Burckheartt, James Sr. Burge, James Burge, James R. Burkhartt, James Burnett, James M. Burris, Thomas Burris, George Burriss, George Burriss, John Burriss, T. P. Burriss, John Burton, M. Burton, Moses Burton, William Burton, Lemontation Bush, William Buster, James Butler, J. W. Butts, Gray Bynum, Henry Byrnum, C. C. Cady, David J. Caldwell, Chas.

Callaway, S. Callaway, Flanders Calloway, Margaret Calvert, Richard Calvert, T. S. Campbell, Thomas Campbell, Charles Canole, John Canole, J. Canote, Joseph Carey, P. Carnell, G. M. Carney, James Carney, Samuel Carroll, A. Carson, George Carson, George Carson, H. Carson, James Carson, John M. Carson, R. Carson, William Carson, R. W. Carter, Richard M. Carter, Benjamin Cash, George Cason, Sr., John Caspur, Benjamin Caton, Noah G. Caton, D. C. Champion, Isaac Chandler, Isaac Chandler, Benj. Chapman, Benjamin Chapman, George Chapman, William Cherry, D. Cheshire, Thomas Childs, W. G. Childs, W. G. Childs, Mark Chitton, Thomas Chitton, James Chitwood, Henry Chrisman, John B. Clark, Richard Clarkston, Enoch Cleaton, Moses Cleaton, William Cleaton, Jr., William Cleaton, Sr., John T. Cleveland, Nicholas Cline, G. Cloid, Christopher Coats, T. T. Cole, O. S. Coleman, Stephen Collier, William Collier, James Collin, Adelia Collins, Elizabeth Collins, James Collins, John Collins, John D. Colson, Phillip Davis Colson, Madison Colvin, A. W. Compton, Alfred Compton, S. W. Compton, Henry Cook, L. Cook, R. Cooley, John Cooly, Benj. Cooper, Braxton Cooper, Jr., D. F. Cooper, David Cooper, Evert Cooper, Hinly Cooper, John Cooper, John Cooper, Joseph Cooper, William Cooper, William Cooper, Moses Coppage, Thomas N. Corckle, Jesse Cornelius, John Cornelius, Levi Cornelius, E. W. Cose, Stephen Cox, John Coy, Samuel Coy, Archibald Cragg, E. Cravens, Lucintha Cravens, William H. Cravens, R. G. Cregler, George Creson, Andrew Crews, Samuell T. Crews, Temple Crews, Lewis Crigler, James Croff, John Croff, John Crook, L. F. Cropp, William Cropp, Sr., John Cross, Nancy Crows, William Crump, Enoch Cruse, John Cunningham, Th. Cunningham, H. Curtis, James Daily, Lewis Daniel, Charles Danney, James H. Darlington, Mary Daubin, Franklin Daugherty, J. Daugherty, Edward Davis, Edward S. Davis, Joseph Davis, Mary Davis, P. J. Davis, S. H. Davis, T. C. Davis, Thomas Davis, W. C. Davis, W. C. Davis, J. (?) Day, John Dehartt, Benj. Dehaven, James Dempsey, James Denney, George Denoson, Charles Devine, Richard Dickerson, William R. Dickerson, F. W. Diggs, Robt. Diggs, Tho. Dinwiddie, Jacob Ditzler, Enoch Doaty, Isaac Doaty, James Dobson, James H. Dobson, Joseph Dobson, Martin Dobson, Nancy Dobson, W. Dobson, Jr., William Dobson, Stephen Donahoe, Thomas Donoho, John D. Dotson, A. Doty, H. Doty, Edward Douglass, James Douglass, Jeremiah Dowell, William Downey, Chas. Drake, D. R. Drake, David Drake, William Drake, F. Dudgeon, Geo. Duncan, William Duncan, W. F. Dunica, W. F. Dunica, B. F. Dunkin, B. F. Dunkin, John S. Dunn, John Durin, William T. Dyer, Henry Ealy, James Earickson, P. Earickson, Richard Earickson, Laton S. Eddings, Thomas Eddings, John P. Eddins, Francis Edgar, W. H. Edgar, Gustavus Elgin, Sarah Elgin, W. H. Elgin, John G. Elkins, David Elliott, H. S. Elliott, J. W. Elliott, Lewis Elliott, N. G. Elliott, Hary Ellis, Elizabeth Elmore, Lucy Emberson, James Embree, Lewis Engin, A.. Enyart, Jr., David Enyart, Sr., Silas Enyart, Sr., Silas Enyart, Jr., Daniel Estice, B. Estill, John H. Estill, Elijah Estis, Benjamin Evans, John Evans,

John Evans, Pleasant L. Evans, Sarah Evans, Thomas Evans, Thomas Evans, Solomon Everly, Watts D. Ewin, John Ewing, C. B. Fallenstein, Edward Fane, John Fane, Stephen Farland, Will U. Feazle, William Feeland, Thompson Feland, Isham Ferguson, J. Field, Samuel Field, W. C. Field, William B. Field, S. R. Fields, W. Fields, William Finnell, Elijah Fisher, Elijah Fisher, P. P. Fisher, John Fleming, Bion Fly, John Fly, John Ford, Laban Ford, Nathaniel Ford, Polley Ford, William Forrey, M. Forsythe, Norbin Foster, James Fox, Richard L. Fox, Aaron Fray, Thomas Fristoe, C. B. Fullinstine, P. C. Furnish, W. M. Gabbert, W. M. Gabbert, Richmond Gage, Archabold Galbert, C. W. Ganns, G. W. Ganns, Stephen T. Garner, F. A. Garraway, James Garven, Daniel Gates, Augustine Gatewood, William Geery, A. M. George, W. J. George, Andrew Gerrad, William Gess, Isaac Geyhartt, Frederick Gibbs, Stephen Gibbs, Martin Gibson, W. B. Gibson, Joseph Gill, C. M. Gillum, Wm. Gish, Geo. W. Givens, Mary Givens, Heron Golden, Hiram Golden, James Golden, C. Gooch, O. D. Gooch, Daniel B. Goode, Wm. Gradey, N. R. Gragg, David Graves, Richard Graves, Benjamin Green, J. A. Green, John Green, Stephen Green, Wesley S. Green, William Green, William Green, Mr. Gregrey, James Grercy, Henry Griffin, John Griffin, Daniel W. Griffith, T. A. Grigsbey, F. Grishum, Fountain Grissum, William Grubbs, Henry Guin, Jacob Gumm, Jon Gumm, William Gumm, G. L. Hackley, Lott Hackley, W. E. Hackley, James C. Hackly, James Hall, Joshua Hall, Maize Hall, William Hall, S. T. Hamm, Beverly Hamner, John M. Hamner, Nancy Hancock, Robert Hancock, A. Handley, K. P. Hanencamp, R. P. Hanencamp, John Hanes, Thomas Hanley, A. F. Hanna, W. B. Hanna, J. Harden, James Harden, Samuel Hardin, Caleb Hargus, J. D. Hargus, Joshua Hargus, W. C. Hargus, John Harison, Andrew Harris, Moses Harris, S. B. Harris, William Harris, J. Z. Harriss, Jno. Harriss, Charles Harvey, John Harvey, William Harvey, Sr., Thomas Hawkins, William. Hawkins, John T. Haydon, Benjamin Hays, L. E. Hays, Silas Hays, Elizabeth Hayse, Etheldred Hayse, Jesse Haystin, J. H. Hayter, Margaret Head, W. L. Head, Jacob Headrick, W. R. Heath, J. C. Heberling, James Heberling, Allen Hendrix, Robert C. Hendrix, John Henry, R. C. Henry, Allen Hern, Rox Ann Hern, Solomon Hern, A. J. Herndon, J. Herndon, James Herndon, John Herndon, L. A. Herndon, A. Hickerson, Daniel Hickerson, Daniel Hickerson, Harden Hickerson, Thomas Hickman, John Hicks, Otway Hicks, Archibald Hill, J. C. Hill, M. Hill, Abram Hines, W. Hironimus, Joshua Hobbs, Vachel Hobbs, James Hocker, Parkerson Hocker, Wm. Hocker, Joseph Holbert, Benjamin Hollady, Francis Holley, Wm. C. Holley, W. Holms, James Holtsclaw, Westley Homes, Joseph Hopper, M. Hopper, Allen Hord, J. H. Horton, Leonard Horton, Walker Horton, J. S. House, Matthew Howard, Stephen Hubbard, T. E. Hubbard, William F. Hubbard, W. D. Hubbell, Hudson, Isaac Huffman, John Huffman, Allen Hughes, Ann M. Hughes, Charles Hughes, J. F. Hughes, James Hughes, Joseph S. Hughes, Martha Hughes, Roland Hughes, S. M. Hughes, S. T. Hughes, Z. C. Hughes, John Hulett,

Abner Hulitt, Agnis Hulse, William Humphrey, C. W. Hunton, Allen Hurt, Payton L. Hurt, John Hutcherson, A. Hynes, M. Hynes, Samuel Hynes, David Isaacs, Porter Jackman, Thos. Jackman, John Jacks, C. F. Jackson, James Jackson, Sr., James Jackson, Jr., John T. Jackson, John Jackson, Thomas Jackson, Thomas Jackson, Thos. M. Jackson, Wade M. Jackson, Wm. Jackson, E. T. Jacobs, Robt. James, Wm. James, Tilford Jamison, Aerial Jennings, Alex Jennings, J. Jerry, B. F. Jeter, David Johnson, John Johnson, Major H. Johnson, Michael Johnson, Milly Johnson, R. S. Johnson, Rheubin Johnson, Richard Johnson, William Johnson, Sr., Wm. Johnson, Jr., William Johnson, Aquilla Jones, J. H. G. Jones, James Jones, James Jones, Lee Jones, Reese Jones, Thomas Jones, Thomas Jones, William Jones, Wm. Jones, Jas. D. Jourdan, Jas. Jourden, John Jourden, John Kerbey, Jr., Jesse Kerby, John Kerby, Joseph Kerby, Miles Kerby, A. Kertly, Jacob Kerts, J. W. Ketchum, W. J. Key, James King, John King, Wm. King, Horice Kingsberry, Jere Kingsberry, H. Kivett, John Kivett, K. Kivett, Thomas Kivett, W. L. Knight, Catharine Knouse, Henry Knouse, Sr., Henry Knouse, Jr., H. W. Kring, Peter Krogun, David Kunkle, Jacob Kutz, Jr., Stephen Lacy, Daniel Lafley, H. Lamaster, Eli W. Lambert, Felix G. Lame, John R. Lame, John Lamm, William Lamm, R. Lampkins, Henry Lancaster, J. P. Lancaster, Henry Latham, R. H. Law, Jeremiah Lawson, Jeremiah Lawson, W. R. B. Lawson, Alfred Lay, Daniel Lay, John Leach, A. J. Leakey, Jefferson Leaky, Jeremiah Leaky, A. A. Lee, Richard Lee, Sarah Lee, Sarah Lee, Thos. Lee, A. Leonard, David Letts, J. Levelnam, A. Lewis, Adison M. Lewis, Edmund Lewis, T. A. Lewis, Thomas A. Lewis, W. T. Lewis, Enoch Liggett, Johnathan Liggett, Joseph Jr. Liggett, Joseph Liggett, William Liggett, Jr., William Liggett, Sr., Wm. Lile, Sr., Charles Lillert, Hugh L. Linch, James R. Linn, J. Lithartt, D. Litrle, Charles. Litteral, C. Littleton, Charles Littleton, Benj. Lively, Isaac Loathan, J. W. Loid, Danil Long, Reubin Long, John J. Lowry, Neptune Lynch, Robt. Lynch, Samuel Maddox, Jas. M. Major, Overton S. Major, Samuel C. Major, James Malloy, Joseph Mannin, C. C. Markland, Levi Markland, Abel Marley, Wm. T. Marley, T. B. Marsh, Bailey Marshall, J. T. Marshall, D. G. Martin, David Martin, Hudson Martin, John H. Martin, Joseph Martin, John T. Mason, Nicholas Masterats, Nicholas Mastred, Powiton Matson, Benj. Matthews, Dabny Maupin, Daniel C. Maupin, G. W. Maupin, G. D. Maupin, James Maupin, Levi Maupin, M. G. Maupin, Wm M. Maupin, Baswell Maxwell, Daniel Maynard, Daniel Maynard, John McCart, R. McCart, T. S. McCart, Tho. McCart, Joseph McClain, D. H. McClane, A. McCord, Amos McCord, Thomas McCoy, Thos. McCoy, Benjn. McCrary, G. McCrary, Hamilton McCravey, William McCully, H. McDaniel, Jane McDaniel, H. E. W. McDearman, Hugh McDonald, John A. McGerk, Elizabeth McGruder, Thomas McGruder, S. H. McMillan, Calvin McNeese, Wm. McNeese, James P. Meak, John Meals, James Meanes, Letty Meredith, Reub. Messenley, Milton Methers, Haman Millen, James Miller, Lewis Miller, Lewis Miller, Thomas J. Million,

William Million, J. P. Mills, James Mills, George H. Miner, H. Minter, John H. Minter, John Minter, John Minter, Wm. Minter, John Moffitt, John A. Moffitt, James Monroe, Wm. Monroe, David Montgomery, James Montgomery, Jane Montgomery, A. Moon, John A. Moon, Clabourn Moore, George W. Moore, Milton Moore, Mr. Moore, Nathan Moore, T. C. Moore, Wm. J. Moore, Garret Morris, George S. Morris, J. W. Morris, Joel Morris, John P. Morris, N. Morris, Nancy Morris, Saml. Morris, Thomas Morris, Thomas J. Morris, A. W. Morrison, Christopher Morrow, David Morrow, J. W. Morrow, Ambrose Moss, John Moss, Stokley Mott, G. W. Mullins, Lousanna Mullins, Wm. B. Mure, Jeremiah Murhpy, J. W. Murphey, Adam Murry, J. W. Myers, William Myrtle, John Nanson, G. T. Naylor, William Naylor, Presley Neal, Graham Nelson, Frederick Nester, Jacob Nester, Jacob Nester, L. Newcomb, John F. Nichols, John F. Nichols, John Nickson, W. L. Night, W. Night, John T. Norris, E. Norwood, Jonas O'neal, Perry O'neal, Preston O'neal, A. R. Ober, Patrick Orr, Elizabeth Owen, B. Owens, B. Owens, Isaac Owens, James Owens, Sarah Owens, Thomas J. Owens, Hardin Pagdet, John Page, St. Clair Page, Jas. Palmertre, James J. Parks, William Parlin, William Parton, Garrison Patrick, John M. Patrick, L. C. Patrick, Luke Patrick, Samuel Patrick, A. Patterson, B. Patterson, J. A. W. Patterson, John Patterson, Prier Patterson, Rice Patterson, James H. Patton, Nathan Patton, George Payne, George Payne, Mariah? Payne, Unice Payne, A. Peacher, James Peacher, R. Peacher, Wm. Peacher, Charles J. Pearce, John M. Pearce, Rob't Pearcival, Issac Pearson, John Sr. Pearson, Samuel Pearson, David Peeler, John Pemberton, S. Pemberton, T. Pemberton, C. J. Perkins, David Perkins, J. M. Perkins, John Perkins, Michael Perkins, Thos. Perkins, Charles Perryn, Matthew Pettis, Ross Petty, H. Peyton, Henry Peyton, Jackson Peyton, James Pharis, Martin Pharris, Henry Philips, James Phillips, Edward Philpot, W. Pilcher, David Pipes, George Pipes, James Pipes, John Pipes, Simon Pitmore, John Pitney, W. Pitney, M. Pitts, A. Polk, A. Polk, W. H. Porter, Tho. Potter, W. Z. Potter, John Potts, Robert Powell, Willis Powell, Philip Prather, Evan Price, Jno. W. Price, Susan Price, John Prince, Thomas Prince, John Prockter, R. Proctor, Martha Pugh, N. S. Pulliam, S. W. Pulliam, Wm. Pulliam, R. Quinley, J. T. Quisinberry, E. W. Rabertin, William Ranes, John Rawlins, Milly Rawlins, Owen Rawlins, Thos. Rawlins, Samuel Ray, Sr., Samuel Ray, Jr., Thomas Ray, Daniel Rector, J. W. Redman, J. W. Redman, John Redman, J. N. Reed, J. B. Reed, John M. Reed, S. Reed, Sam'l Reed, William L. Reeves, Benj. Reynolds, John C. Reynolds, P. Reynolds, Robert Reynolds, Thomas Reynolds, R. S. Reynon, Briant Rice, Wm. Rice, Elijah Richardson, L. Richardson, John D. Ricketts, Jesse Riddlesbargor, Elijah Ridgway, James Ridgway, Thos. Ridgway, William Ridgway, G. A. Roane, H. Robb, Jonas Robb, Joseph Robb, Michael Robb, Michael Roberts, Michael Roberts, Nicholas Roberts, A. P. Robinson, Gerrard Robinson, W. J. Robinson, John Rooker, Alexander Roseberry, J. C. Ross, John Ross, Jeremiah Rucker, Jr., Jeremiah Rucker,

Sr., John S. Rucker, W. E. Rucker, Matthew Runkel, Matthew Runkle, Pleasant Runnels, Elison Russell, P. Sr. Russell, George Safforans, Henry Saling, Samuel Samington, John Samuels, Joel H. Sanders, R. H. Sanders, R. H. Sanders, Wright Sartin, Wright Sartin, Sally Scott, William Scott, Peter Scotten, Francis D. Searcy, John M. Searcy, Jas. Sears, John Sebree, Uriel Sebree, William Seiburt, Martin Settle, W. H. Settle, J. M. Sexton, J. M. Sexton, E. C. Shackelford, E. E. Shackelford, John Shaffroth, George W. Shaw, Robert Shaw, John Shawman, B. A. Shepherd, J. H. Shepherd, James Shepherd, Licurgus Shepherd, Licurgus Shepherd, Jno. Shields, Thomas Shields, C. Shifflet, Thomas Shifflet, Haslen Shiflett, W. Shiflitt, J. E. Shipley, T. C. Shipley, B. H. Shipp, F. Shipp, F. Shipp, John Shipp, Jas. A. Shirley, Phillip Shirley, William Shores, David Short, G. W. Short, Hezekiah Shugart, Alex. Silvy, James Silvy, Thomas Simmons, M. F. Simons, Isaac Skinner, Lewis Slaughter, Elijah Smallwood, William Smarr, Andrew Smith, Henry Smith, James Smith, James C. Smith, Jesse Smith, Joel Smith, Joseph D. Smith, L. Smith, R. Smith, Samuel Smith, T. S. Smith, W. Smith, William J. Smith, William T. Smith, Isaac Snathen, Jacob Snavely, Joseph Snavely, Wm. Snell, J. W. Snoddy, Syntha Snoddy, James Snyder, J. W. Southworth, James W. Southworth, Wm. Spencer, Weden Sperney, David Spotts, George Sprice, John Spurgeon, Dodson Standerford, John Standiford, Shelton Standiford, M. Standly, Thomas Stanley, Wright Stanley, Elizabeth Stapleton, Harrison Stapleton, Abijah Stapp, Benj. Stapp, James Stapp, James Stapp, John Stapp, John M. Stapp, Joseph M. Stapp, Joseph Stapp, Stephen Stemons, N. H. Stephenson, J. Z. Stern, Lyman Stern, Hugh Stewart, W. W. Stice, S. Stiles, Levi Stipe, Wm. Stipe, Harkiman Stone, Joseph Stone, Stephen Jr. Stone, Stephen Stone, William Stone, Wm. Stone, Corbin J. Street, P. V. Street, William Street, B. F. Stringfellon, Elum Styrn, James T. Sullins, R. Sunderland, James Swane, Obed. Swaringin, J. Swearingin, Lewis Swearingin, Obed. Swearingin, Tho. Swearingin, David Sweazer, John Swetnum, Harison Swinney, Harrison Swinney, Wm. D. Swinney, M. Switzler, M. Switzler, Simeon Switzler, Chas. Swope, M. Taggard, John A. Talbot, A. G. Tatum, Garnett Taylor, Thornton Taylor, W. H. Taylor, William Taylor, William Taylor, James Terrel, F. Terrell, J. Terrell, K. Terrell, Terrell Lyddia A., M. Terrell, Fountain Terrill, John Terrill, John Terrill, Jr., Robert Terrill, Saml. Teter, Jackson Tharp, Thomas Tharp, Richard Thermon, Benj. Thomas, John D. Thomas, Jr., Lawson Thomas, Asa Q. Thompson, Elias Thompson, Elmore Thompson, Ephraim Thompson, Henry Thompson, J. N. Thompson, J. D. Thompson, J. F. Thompson, James Thompson, Nero Thompson, Philip Thompson, Robert Thompson, William Thompson, Randolph Thrasher, Samuel Tilford, Obediah Tindall, Thos. Tindall, James Tindle, A. Titus, E. Titus, G. P. Titus, John Titus, Sr., Joseph Titus, Joseph Titus, B. H. Toalson, James Toalson, Davis Todd, Griffin Todd, Nathan Todd, Neriah Todd, Peter Todd, Rebecca Todd, Thos. Todd, Wm. P. Toles, Danl. Tolson, J. B. Tolson, Polly Tolson, Polly Tolson, Wm. Tolson, C. P. Tooley, C.P. Tooly, Elzy Tracy, James S. Tribble, Casper

Trode, Joseph Tudor, Thomas Tudor, E. W. Turner, Edward Turner, Edward Turner, Edward Turner, Sr., Ephraim Turner, Grezella Turner, Henry Turner, James Turner, Jr., Linch Turner, Matthew Turner, Philip Turner, Talton Turner, J. B. Turrell, Thomas Tyer, J. B. Underwood, Simeon Vanhorn, Frederick Vaughn, R. C. Vaughn, Jesse Vines, Peter Vines, James Viveon, Harvey Vivion, John Wade, A. Wainscott, A. F. Walden, James Waleup, Federal Walker, G. W. Walker, Johnson Walker, Sarah Walker, Thomas J. Walker, James Wallace, Samuel Wallace, St. Clair Wanmouth, Elizabeth Ward, Wm. Ward, Elijah Warden, John Warden, Calebb Ware, E. N. Ware, J. B. Ware, Lucy Ware, William Ware, William Ware, W. B. Warren, William Warren, Henry Watson, Henry Watson, Benj. Watts, George Watts, J. P. Watts, Reubin Watts, Samuel Watts, Joel Wayland, Gideon Weathers, James Weathers, A. White, David White, David White, F. White, Garland C. White, Henry White, Hesekiah White, J. F. White, John R. White, John White, Josiah White, Robert White, Aaron Whitney, W. H. Whitney, F. Whittock, John Wiggington, Louis Wilcoxen, Benj. Wilds, John Wilds, Robt. Wilds, Wm. Wilds, Joshua Wiley, John Wilhoit, Chas. Wilkenson, Charles Wilkerson, Jr., Charles Wilkerson, Henry Wilkerson, John Wilkerson, William Wilkerson, Benj. Williams, Edward Williams, F. E. Williams, Feland Williams, J. Williams, J. C. Williams, James Williams, Joel P. Williams, John Williams, John Williams, Josiah Williams, Powell Williams, Price Williams, Uriah Williams, William Williams, Willoughby Williams, Wm. D. Williams, William Wills, Alfred Wilson, Bennett Wilson, Charles Wilson, Charles Wilson, Christopher Wilson, Clinton Wilson, George Wilson, J. M. Wilson, James C. Wilson, John Wilson, John F. Wilson, John Wilson, John C. Wilson, Mr. Wilson, Plest. Wilson, Rebecca Wilson, William Wilson, Henry Winborn, Elizabeth Winn, William Winn, George Winson, Lewis Wiscom, John A. Wisdom, Jacob Wiseman, Enos Withers, S. Withers, L. B. Witt, William Witt, William Witt, C. Wolfskill, Joseph Wolfskill, M. Wolfskill, J. Woodard, A. Woods, A. C. Woods, J. C. Woods, Wm. Sr. Woods, J. M. Woodson, R. Woodson, David Workman, C. F. Wright, Elizabeth Wright, Joseph Wright, Thomas Wright, Townsend Wright, W. C. Wright, A. Wyandecker, L. Yancey, Henry Yeager, D. Young, Joseph B. Young, William Young, William Young, J. T. Yowell, John Zilhartt, J. Zimmerman, Y. Zimmermann.

<u>Buchanan County, Missouri, Plattsburg Land Office Entries, 1846.</u>
Edward C. Brown: (ID) Feb. 1, 1846, (AN) MO4390.031
Isaac Agee: (ID) Mar. 1, 1846, (AN) MO4390.487
James Anderson: (ID) Mar. 1, 1846, (AN) MO4390.182
Eli Arnold: (ID) Mar. 1, 1846, (AN) MO4390.104
James H. Blackwell: (ID) Mar. 1, 1846, (AN) MO4390.268
Jacob Bohart: (ID) Mar. 1, 1846, (AN) MO4390.354
Peter Boyer: (ID) Mar. 1, 1846, (AN) MO4390.070
Peter Boyer: (ID) Mar. 1, 1846, (AN) MO4390.071

George Brittain: (ID) Mar. 1, 1846, (AN) MO4390.444
Gideon L. Brown: (ID) Mar. 1, 1846, (AN) MO4390.043
Gideon L. Brown: (ID) Mar. 1, 1846, (AN) MO4390.044
Isaac Brown: (ID) Mar. 1, 1846, (AN) MO4390.181
Thomas A. Brown: (ID) Mar. 1, 1846, (AN) MO4390.201
Richard Chany: (ID) Mar. 1, 1846, (AN) MO4390.435
Daniel K. Clark: (ID) Mar. 1, 1846, (AN) MO4390.114
Alford A. Coates: (ID) Mar. 1, 1846, (AN) MO4390.172
Jacob Cogdill: (ID) Mar. 1, 1846, (AN) MO4390.207
Jacob Cogdill: (ID) Mar. 1, 1846, (AN) MO4390.211
John P. Cordonnier: (ID) Mar. 1, 1846, (AN) MO4390.462
Squire S. Cornett: (ID) Mar. 1, 1846, (AN) MO4390.128
John Daniel: (ID) Mar. 1, 1846, (AN) MO4390.400
John Daniel: (ID) Mar. 1, 1846, (AN) MO4390.401
Warner W. Daniel: (ID) Mar. 1, 1846, (AN) MO4390.402
Edward M. Davidson: (ID) Mar. 1, 1846, (AN) MO4390.459
Joseph Davis: (ID) Mar. 1, 1846, (AN) MO4390.164
Peter Deppen: (ID) Mar. 1, 1846, (AN) MO4390.284
Morgan Dryden: (ID) Mar. 1, 1846, (AN) MO4390.130
Morgan Dryden: (ID) Mar. 1, 1846, (AN) MO4390.088
James Ellison: (ID) Mar. 1, 1846, (AN) MO4390.328
Aaron England: (ID) Mar. 1, 1846, (AN) MO4390.388
Weston J. Everett: (ID) Mar. 1, 1846, (AN) MO4390.065
Weston J. Everett: (ID) Mar. 1, 1846, (AN) MO4390.066
David C. Ewing: (ID) Mar. 1, 1846, (AN) MO4390.141
William D. Field: (ID) Mar. 1, 1846, (AN) MO4390.355
Humphrey Finch: (ID) Mar. 1, 1846, (AN) MO4390.083
Zachariah Finney: (ID) Mar. 1, 1846, (AN) MO4390.411
Jesse Fletcher: (ID) Mar. 1, 1846, (AN) MO4390.067
Eli Gabbert: (ID) Mar. 1, 1846, (AN) MO4390.107
George W. Gabbert: (ID) Mar. 1, 1846, (AN) MO4390.106
Michael Gabbert: (ID) Mar. 1, 1846, (AN) MO4390.373
Thomas J. Gabbert: (ID) Mar. 1, 1846, (AN) MO4390.105
Isaac Gann: (ID) Mar. 1, 1846, (AN) MO4390.450
George Gibson: (ID) Mar. 1, 1846, (AN) MO4390.419
George I. Gibson: (ID) Mar. 1, 1846, (AN) MO4390.249
John P. Gibson: (ID) Mar. 1, 1846, (AN) MO4390.385
William D. Gibson: (ID) Mar. 1, 1846, (AN) MO4390.448
William L. Gibson: (ID) Mar. 1, 1846, (AN) MO4390.250
Martin Giddens: (ID) Mar. 1, 1846, (AN) MO4390.204
William Giddens: (ID) Mar. 1, 1846, (AN) MO4390.203
Robert Gilmore: (ID) Mar. 1, 1846, (AN) MO4390.375
Robert Gilmore: (ID) Mar. 1, 1846, (AN) MO4390.376
David Girard: (ID) Mar. 1, 1846, (AN) MO4390.270
James Hall: (ID) Mar. 1, 1846, (AN) MO4390.440
Joseph Hall: (ID) Mar. 1, 1846, (AN) MO4390.441

John S. Hardy: (ID) Mar. 1, 1846, (AN) MO4390.496
William Harrington: (ID) Mar. 1, 1846, (AN) MO4390.208
Stephen Hawley: (ID) Mar. 1, 1846, (AN) MO4390.457
Samuel Hill: (ID) Mar. 1, 1846, (AN) MO4390.347
Robert Irwin: (ID) Mar. 1, 1846, (AN) MO4390.190
Robert Irwin: (ID) Mar. 1, 1846, (AN) MO4390.191
George Jeffers: (ID) Mar. 1, 1846, (AN) MO4390.090
George Jeffers: (ID) Mar. 1, 1846, (AN) MO4390.091
Lewis A. Jeffers: (ID) Mar. 1, 1846, (AN) MO4390.449
Harvey Jones: (ID) Mar. 1, 1846, (AN) MO4390.239
William Kitzmiller: (ID) Mar. 1, 1846, (AN) MO4390.464
William Landis: (ID) Mar. 1, 1846, (AN) MO4390.465
Sampson Langston: (ID) Mar. 1, 1846, (AN) MO4390.127
George W. Layman: (ID) Mar. 1, 1846, (AN) MO4390.116
Joseph Layman: (ID) Mar. 1, 1846, (AN) MO4390.032
Titus Mark: (ID) Mar. 1, 1846, (AN) MO4390.386
Martial N. Martin: (ID) Mar. 1, 1846, (AN) MO4390.187
Daniel McCray: (ID) Mar. 1, 1846, (AN) MO4390.189
William McDowel: (ID) Mar. 1, 1846, (AN) MO4390.241
James McGuire: (ID) Mar. 1, 1846, (AN) MO4390.326
Isaac N. Miller: (ID) Mar. 1, 1846, (AN) MO4390.196
Isaac N. Miller: (ID) Mar. 1, 1846, (AN) MO4390.027
Jesse Miller: (ID) Mar. 1, 1846, (AN) MO4390.118
Thomas D. Montgomery: (ID) Mar. 1, 1846, (AN) MO4390.384
Thomas Moore: (ID) Mar. 1, 1846, (AN) MO4390.329
Silas W. Moreland: (ID) Mar. 1, 1846, (AN) MO4390.307
Gilford Moutray: (ID) Mar. 1, 1846, (AN) MO4390.412
Christopher C. Nichols: (ID) Mar. 1, 1846, (AN) MO4390.258
John Ogle: (ID) Mar. 1, 1846, (AN) MO4390.126
Thomas Ogle: (ID) Mar. 1, 1846, (AN) MO4390.125
Powell S. Owenby: (ID) Mar. 1, 1846, (AN) MO4390.188
John B. Pierson: (ID) Mar. 1, 1846, (AN) MO4390.302
John Ray: (ID) Mar. 1, 1846, (AN) MO4390.425
Mark Ray: (ID) Mar. 1, 1846, (AN) MO4390.086
Alfred M. Rector: (ID) Mar. 1, 1846, (AN) MO4390.324
William Richeson: (ID) Mar. 1, 1846, (AN) MO4390.414
John Ridgeway: (ID) Mar. 1, 1846, (AN) MO4390.269
Cornelius Roberts: (ID) Mar. 1, 1846, (AN) MO4390.352
Farrar A. Robidoux: (ID) Mar. 1, 1846, (AN) MO4390.202
Richard Rogers: (ID) Mar. 1, 1846, (AN) MO4390.397
John Sampson: (ID) Mar. 1, 1846, (AN) MO4390.439
Joseph Sherwood: (ID) Mar. 1, 1846, (AN) MO4390.418
Samuel I. Singleton: (ID) Mar. 1, 1846, (AN) MO4390.398
Scion Singleton: (ID) Mar. 1, 1846, (AN) MO4390.399
Elijah Smith: (ID) Mar. 1, 1846, (AN) MO4390.387
William Southward: (ID) Mar. 1, 1846, (AN) MO4390.459

Robert M. Stockton: (ID) Mar. 1, 1846, (AN) MO4390.453
John Tobin: (ID) Mar. 1, 1846, (AN) MO4390.089
Washington Turner: (ID) Mar. 1, 1846, (AN) MO4390.456
James C. Webb: (ID) Mar. 1, 1846, (AN) MO4390.372
James Wilson: (ID) Mar. 1, 1846, (AN) MO4390.470
James Wilson: (ID) Mar. 1, 1846, (AN) MO4390.471
Nelson Witt: (ID) Mar. 1, 1846, (AN) MO4390.034
Andrew G. Wrinkle: (ID) Mar. 1, 1846, (AN) MO4390.169
Pleasant Yates: (ID) Mar. 1, 1846, (AN) MO4390.117
Daniel Coyle: (ID) Mar. 5, 1846, (AN) MO4390.025
Francis Ducate: (ID) Mar. 5, 1846, (AN) MO4390.024
Levi R. Jackson: (ID) Mar. 5, 1846, (AN) MO4390.024
John Silvers: (ID) Mar. 5, 1846, (AN) MO4390.024
Archibald H. Adams: (ID) Apr. 1, 1846, (AN) MO4410.242
Samuel Agee: (ID) Apr. 1, 1846, (AN) MO4410.117
David Allen: (ID) Apr. 1, 1846, (AN) MO4400.062
John G. Allen: (ID) Apr. 1, 1846, (AN) MO4410.041
Lewis Allen: (ID) Apr. 1, 1846, (AN) MO4420.038
Mary Allen: (ID) Apr. 1, 1846, (AN) MO4400.135
John H. Allison: (ID) Apr. 1, 1846, (AN) MO4410.497
William Allison: (ID) Apr. 1, 1846, (AN) MO4410.093
Joshua Anderson: (ID) Apr. 1, 1846, (AN) MO4410.184
Singleton Asher: (ID) Apr. 1, 1846, (AN) MO4400.453
Thomas J. Auxier: (ID) Apr. 1, 1846, (AN) MO4400.285
Andrew J. Baker: (ID) Apr. 1, 1846, (AN) MO4400.09
John Baker: (ID) Apr. 1, 1846, (AN) MO4400.192
Thomas Baker: (ID) Apr. 1, 1846, (AN) MO4400.191
Aurey Ballard: (ID) Apr. 1, 1846, (AN) MO4410.219
George W. Barnes: (ID) Apr. 1, 1846, (AN) MO4420.131
Doshe Barnett: (ID) Apr. 1, 1846, (AN) MO4420.094
Henry J. Beardsley: (ID) Apr. 1, 1846, (AN) MO4400.039
Lewis W. Bell: (ID) Apr. 1, 1846, (AN) MO4400.081
James Blakeley: (ID) Apr. 1, 1846, (AN) MO4410.026
Elijah H. Bland: (ID) Apr. 1, 1846, (AN) MO4410.276
Austin Bledsoe: (ID) Apr. 1, 1846, (AN) MO4420.350
William Bledsoe: (ID) Apr. 1, 1846, (AN) MO4420.159
Philip Bohart: (ID) Apr. 1, 1846, (AN) MO4400.287
Ratliffe R. Boone: (ID) Apr. 1, 1846, (AN) MO4410.145
Francis D. Bowen: (ID) Apr. 1, 1846, (AN) MO4400.428
Henry Boyer: (ID) Apr. 1, 1846, (AN) MO4410.047
Henry Boyer: (ID) Apr. 1, 1846, (AN) MO4410.048
John W. Bridgeman: (ID) Apr. 1, 1846, (AN) MO4400.210
Thomas Brinton: (ID) Apr. 1, 1846, (AN) MO4400.075
Thomas Brinton: (ID) Apr. 1, 1846, (AN) MO4400.076
John Brittain: (ID) Apr. 1, 1846, (AN) MO4400.234
Squire B. Brooks: (ID) Apr. 1, 1846, (AN) MO4400.074

William R. Brown: (ID) Apr. 1, 1846, (AN) MO4410.348
John S. Burgess: (ID) Apr. 1, 1846, (AN) MO4400.163
Samuel H. Burgess: (ID) Apr. 1, 1846, (AN) MO4410.188
Peter Burk: (ID) Apr. 1, 1846, (AN) MO4410.406
David H. Burnett: (ID) Apr. 1, 1846, (AN) MO4410.274
Robert Burnside: (ID) Apr. 1, 1846, (AN) MO4400.295
Robert R. Bush: (ID) Apr. 1, 1846, (AN) MO4400.139
James Cameron: (ID) Apr. 1, 1846, (AN) MO4420.294
Thomas Campbell: (ID) Apr. 1, 1846, (AN) MO4400.274
William R. Campbell: (ID) Apr. 1, 1846, (AN) MO4420.430
James H. Canter: (ID) Apr. 1, 1846, (AN) MO4410.021
George M. Casey: (ID) Apr. 1, 1846, (AN) MO4420.257
Dyer Cash: (ID) Apr. 1, 1846, (AN) MO4400.426
Ozro Castle: (ID) Apr. 1, 1846, (AN) MO4400.278
Ozro Castle: (ID) Apr. 1, 1846, (AN) MO4400.279
Thomas J. Cate: (ID) Apr. 1, 1846, (AN) MO4400.003
John Chafin: (ID) Apr. 1, 1846, (AN) MO4410.189
Thomas D. Clanton: (ID) Apr. 1, 1846, (AN) MO4400.242
Barnes Clarke: (ID) Apr. 1, 1846, (AN) MO4400.038
William J. Clarke: (ID) Apr. 1, 1846, (AN) MO4410.052
Mary Coatney: (ID) Apr. 1, 1846, (AN) MO4420.267
William Cobb: (ID) Apr. 1, 1846, (AN) MO4410.042
William Cogdill: (ID) Apr. 1, 1846, (AN) MO4400.220
William Combs: (ID) Apr. 1, 1846, (AN) MO4400.493
Hugh Copeland: (ID) Apr. 1, 1846, (AN) MO4420.208
Jonathan Cox: (ID) Apr. 1, 1846, (AN) MO4400.144
Joseph Cox: (ID) Apr. 1, 1846, (AN) MO4420.285
Thomas Cox: (ID) Apr. 1, 1846, (AN) MO4410.315
William T. Crockett: (ID) Apr. 1, 1846, (AN) MO4400.467
Adam Crows: (ID) Apr. 1, 1846, (AN) MO4420.283
Eli Cummins: (ID) Apr. 1, 1846, (AN) MO4420.368
Matthew M. Cummins: (ID) Apr. 1, 1846, (AN) MO4420.370
Christopher Cunningham: (ID) Apr. 1, 1846, (AN) MO4400.281
William Curle: (ID) Apr. 1, 1846, (AN) MO4400.082
William Curle: (ID) Apr. 1, 1846, (AN) MO4400.083
John Daugherty: (ID) Apr. 1, 1846, (AN) MO4410.475
Edward M. Davidson: (ID) Apr. 1, 1846, (AN) MO4410.336
John W. Davidson: (ID) Apr. 1, 1846, (AN) MO4410.328
Henry C. Davis: (ID) Apr. 1, 1846, (AN) MO4420.290
Ishamel Davis: (ID) Apr. 1, 1846, (AN) MO4420.347
Ishmael Davis: (ID) Apr. 1, 1846, (AN) MO4420.348
James Davis: (ID) Apr. 1, 1846, (AN) MO4420.432
Joseph Davis: (ID) Apr. 1, 1846, (AN) MO4410.158
Isaac Deppin: (ID) Apr. 1, 1846, (AN) MO4400.078
John J. Devorss: (ID) Apr. 1, 1846, (AN) MO4420.015
John J. Devorss: (ID) Apr. 1, 1846, (AN) MO4420.449

Joseph Devorss: (ID) Apr. 1, 1846, (AN) MO4410.356
Joseph Devorss: (ID) Apr. 1, 1846, (AN) MO4420.014
Benjamin H. Dixon: (ID) Apr. 1, 1846, (AN) MO4410.195
James Dixon: (ID) Apr. 1, 1846, (AN) MO4410.164
James Dixon: (ID) Apr. 1, 1846, (AN) MO4420.388
Alexander Dobkins: (ID) Apr. 1, 1846, (AN) MO4410.386
Robert Donnell: (ID) Apr. 1, 1846, (AN) MO4410.035
Robert W. Donnell: (ID) Apr. 1, 1846, (AN) MO4420.350
Robert W. Donnell: (ID) Apr. 1, 1846, (AN) MO4420.387
Robert W. Donnell: (ID) Apr. 1, 1846, (AN) MO4420.389
Robert W. Donnell: (ID) Apr. 1, 1846, (AN) MO4420.390
Robert W. Donnell: (ID) Apr. 1, 1846, (AN) MO4420.391
John Dooley: (ID) Apr. 1, 1846, (AN) MO4400.034
Thomas Dronenburg: (ID) Apr. 1, 1846, (AN) MO4400.441
Anna Dryden: (ID) Apr. 1, 1846, (AN) MO4400.073
Samuel Dryden: (ID) Apr. 1, 1846, (AN) MO4400.072
Edward P. Duncan: (ID) Apr. 1, 1846, (AN) MO4400.478
William Dunning: (ID) Apr. 1, 1846, (AN) MO4410.408
William Dunning: (ID) Apr. 1, 1846, (AN) MO4420.431
William J. Earixson: (ID) Apr. 1, 1846, (AN) MO4410.097
Samuel C. Edwards: (ID) Apr. 1, 1846, (AN) MO4410.491
William H. Elliott: (ID) Apr. 1, 1846, (AN) MO4410.241
Willis Elliott: (ID) Apr. 1, 1846, (AN) MO4420.046
Robert C. Ellipit: (ID) Apr. 1, 1846, (AN) MO4420.314
William Estes: (ID) Apr. 1, 1846, (AN) MO4400.204
John T. Evans: (ID) Apr. 1, 1846, (AN) MO4400.233
John A. Ewell: (ID) Apr. 1, 1846, (AN) MO4410.069
David C. Ewing: (ID) Apr. 1, 1846, (AN) MO4420.384
David C. Ewing: (ID) Apr. 1, 1846, (AN) MO4420.386
Sandford Feland: (ID) Apr. 1, 1846, (AN) MO4400.161
Sandford Feland: (ID) Apr. 1, 1846, (AN) MO4400.162
Sarah Feland: (ID) Apr. 1, 1846, (AN) MO4420.149
Matthew C. Ferrell: (ID) Apr. 1, 1846, (AN) MO4400.416
Jefferson Ferrill: (ID) Apr. 1, 1846, (AN) MO4400.148
John Fitzhugh: (ID) Apr. 1, 1846, (AN) MO4420.186
John B. Flanary: (ID) Apr. 1, 1846, (AN) MO4410.322
Dugan Fouts: (ID) Apr. 1, 1846, (AN) MO4420.182
Dugan Fouts: (ID) Apr. 1, 1846, (AN) MO4420.186
Dugan Fouts: (ID) Apr. 1, 1846, (AN) MO4420.457
John Fowler: (ID) Apr. 1, 1846, (AN) MO4420.393
John Fowler: (ID) Apr. 1, 1846, (AN) MO4400.241
Welcome Fowler: (ID) Apr. 1, 1846, (AN) MO4410.319
William Fowler: (ID) Apr. 1, 1846, (AN) MO4410.328
William Fowler: (ID) Apr. 1, 1846, (AN) MO4400.230
Nathan T. Frakes: (ID) Apr. 1, 1846, (AN) MO4410.482
William Frakes: (ID) Apr. 1, 1846, (AN) MO4400.397

David Fulton: (ID) Apr. 1, 1846, (AN) MO4410.409
Duncan Fulton: (ID) Apr. 1, 1846, (AN) MO4410.218
James Fulton: (ID) Apr. 1, 1846, (AN) MO4410.217
Thomas Gabbert: (ID) Apr. 1, 1846, (AN) MO4400.237
Daniel Gallaway: (ID) Apr. 1, 1846, (AN) MO4410.211
William Gallaway: (ID) Apr. 1, 1846, (AN) MO4410.210
James Galloway: (ID) Apr. 1, 1846, (AN) MO4420.489
Nathaniel Garlin: (ID) Apr. 1, 1846, (AN) MO4400.115
James Gibson: (ID) Apr. 1, 1846, (AN) MO4420.177
James Gibson: (ID) Apr. 1, 1846, (AN) MO4420.272
Jesse Gilliam: (ID) Apr. 1, 1846, (AN) MO4420.190
Richard Gillman: (ID) Apr. 1, 1846, (AN) MO4420.152
James J. Gilmore: (ID) Apr. 1, 1846, (AN) MO4400.320
Joseph Gilmore: (ID) Apr. 1, 1846, (AN) MO4400.116
Milford Gilmore: (ID) Apr. 1, 1846, (AN) MO4420.025
Joseph Gladden: (ID) Apr. 1, 1846, (AN) MO4410.171
Silas S. Glenn: (ID) Apr. 1, 1846, (AN) MO4400.105
Tobias Goodwin: (ID) Apr. 1, 1846, (AN) MO4410.216
Hardin G. Gordon: (ID) Apr. 1, 1846, (AN) MO4420.479
Charles H. Grable: (ID) Apr. 1, 1846, (AN) MO4400.226
Martin Green: (ID) Apr. 1, 1846, (AN) MO4400.399
Abel Griffith: (ID) Apr. 1, 1846, (AN) MO4420.030
James Guthrie: (ID) Apr. 1, 1846, (AN) MO4410.005
Daniel Haddix: (ID) Apr. 1, 1846, (AN) MO4410.278
Isaac H. Haines: (ID) Apr. 1, 1846, (AN) MO4420.250
Isaac H. Haines: (ID) Apr. 1, 1846, (AN) MO4420.339
David M. Hall: (ID) Apr. 1, 1846, (AN) MO4420.293
James B. Hall: (ID) Apr. 1, 1846, (AN) MO4410.275
Samuel C. Hall: (ID) Apr. 1, 1846, (AN) MO4420.200
John Hamon: (ID) Apr. 1, 1846, (AN) MO4420.297
Thomas Hardy: (ID) Apr. 1, 1846, (AN) MO4420.033
Jacob Harlan: (ID) Apr. 1, 1846, (AN) MO4410.029
Reuben Harris: (ID) Apr. 1, 1846, (AN) MO4400.014
William T. Harris: (ID) Apr. 1, 1846, (AN) MO4420.279
John Hays: (ID) Apr. 1, 1846, (AN) MO4410.093
Silvester Hays: (ID) Apr. 1, 1846, (AN) MO4420.344
James Highley: (ID) Apr. 1, 1846, (AN) MO4410.246
Richard Hill: (ID) Apr. 1, 1846, (AN) MO4410.055
Harlow Hinkston: (ID) Apr. 1, 1846, (AN) MO4420.075
Parker A. Hooper: (ID) Apr. 1, 1846, (AN) MO4420.477
Charles B. Huddleston: (ID) Apr. 1, 1846, (AN) MO4400.243
James Hudgins: (ID) Apr. 1, 1846, (AN) MO4410.229
George W. Hudspeth: (ID) Apr. 1, 1846, (AN) MO4420.217
George W. Hudspeth: (ID) Apr. 1, 1846, (AN) MO4420.443
James Huffman: (ID) Apr. 1, 1846, (AN) MO4420.236
Silvester Hughlitt: (ID) Apr. 1, 1846, (AN) MO4400.174

Silvester S. Hughlitt: (ID) Apr. 1, 1846, (AN) MO4400.221
Newmeris Humber: (ID) Apr. 1, 1846, (AN) MO4400.386
Andrew J. Hunter: (ID) Apr. 1, 1846, (AN) MO4400.229
Armsterd Hurst: (ID) Apr. 1, 1846, (AN) MO4400.122
Charles Hurst: (ID) Apr. 1, 1846, (AN) MO4410.190
Harman Hurst: (ID) Apr. 1, 1846, (AN) MO4420.164
David James: (ID) Apr. 1, 1846, (AN) MO4410.486
James James: (ID) Apr. 1, 1846, (AN) MO4420.320
John Johnson: (ID) Apr. 1, 1846, (AN) MO4420.193
Lewis Johnson: (ID) Apr. 1, 1846, (AN) MO4410.318
Ambrose Jones: (ID) Apr. 1, 1846, (AN) MO4400.149
Harvey Jones: (ID) Apr. 1, 1846, (AN) MO4410.034
Harvey Jones: (ID) Apr. 1, 1846, (AN) MO4410.140
Harvey Jones: (ID) Apr. 1, 1846, (AN) MO4420.350
Harvey Jones: (ID) Apr. 1, 1846, (AN) MO4420.387
Harvey Jones: (ID) Apr. 1, 1846, (AN) MO4420.389
Harvey Jones: (ID) Apr. 1, 1846, (AN) MO4420.390
Harvey Jones: (ID) Apr. 1, 1846, (AN) MO4420.391
Holland Jones: (ID) Apr. 1, 1846, (AN) MO4400.084
Holland Jones: (ID) Apr. 1, 1846, (AN) MO4400.085
Jonathan Jones: (ID) Apr. 1, 1846, (AN) MO4410.308
William Jones: (ID) Apr. 1, 1846, (AN) MO4410.307
Evans Jordan: (ID) Apr. 1, 1846, (AN) MO4420.268
Frances Jordon: (ID) Apr. 1, 1846, (AN) MO4400.253
George Kames: (ID) Apr. 1, 1846, (AN) MO4400.212
George Karnes: (ID) Apr. 1, 1846, (AN) MO4420.369
James G. Karnes: (ID) Apr. 1, 1846, (AN) MO4420.114
Daniel G. Keedy: (ID) Apr. 1, 1846, (AN) MO4420.041
Daniel G. Keedy: (ID) Apr. 1, 1846, (AN) MO4420.424
Simeon Kemper: (ID) Apr. 1, 1846, (AN) MO4400.214
Stephen W. Kennedy: (ID) Apr. 1, 1846, (AN) MO4410.379
Stephen W. Kennedy: (ID) Apr. 1, 1846, (AN) MO4420.462
Adam Kerns: (ID) Apr. 1, 1846, (AN) MO4420.468
Charles Kinnaird: (ID) Apr. 1, 1846, (AN) MO4410.096
James Kirkwood: (ID) Apr. 1, 1846, (AN) MO4420.385
John Lamb: (ID) Apr. 1, 1846, (AN) MO4420.028
John Lamb: (ID) Apr. 1, 1846, (AN) MO4420.392
Joseph Lanes: (ID) Apr. 1, 1846, (AN) MO4420.282
Samuel A. Lee: (ID) Apr. 1, 1846, (AN) MO4420.482
Samuel A. Lee: (ID) Apr. 1, 1846, (AN) MO4400.239
John Lemon: (ID) Apr. 1, 1846, (AN) MO4420.261
Solomon L. Leonard: (ID) Apr. 1, 1846, (AN) MO4420.423
William Lichliter: (ID) Apr. 1, 1846, (AN) MO4410.172
Ann Lilly: (ID) Apr. 1, 1846, (AN) MO4420.353
Abraham Linville: (ID) Apr. 1, 1846, (AN) MO4400.009
Peter Loar: (ID) Apr. 1, 1846, (AN) MO4400.424

Peter Loar: (ID) Apr. 1, 1846, (AN) MO4420.421
Elizabeth Long: (ID) Apr. 1, 1846, (AN) MO4400.413
Henry Long: (ID) Apr. 1, 1846, (AN) MO4410.154
Lewis Long: (ID) Apr. 1, 1846, (AN) MO4420.079
Solomon Long: (ID) Apr. 1, 1846, (AN) MO4420.071
Hugh D. Louthan: (ID) Apr. 1, 1846, (AN) MO4420.269
Joseph Lucas: (ID) Apr. 1, 1846, (AN) MO4420.206
Joshua H. Lucas: (ID) Apr. 1, 1846, (AN) MO4400.291
James B. Mackey: (ID) Apr. 1, 1846, (AN) MO4420.153
John Marachal: (ID) Apr. 1, 1846, (AN) MO4410.377
Joseph Mark: (ID) Apr. 1, 1846, (AN) MO4400.238
Christopher Martin: (ID) Apr. 1, 1846, (AN) MO4400.485
James C. Martin: (ID) Apr. 1, 1846, (AN) MO4400.486
Jesse Martin: (ID) Apr. 1, 1846, (AN) MO4420.016
John Martin: (ID) Apr. 1, 1846, (AN) MO4400.218
Luda W. Martin: (ID) Apr. 1, 1846, (AN) MO4400.267
David May: (ID) Apr. 1, 1846, (AN) MO4420.098
Isaac May: (ID) Apr. 1, 1846, (AN) MO4420.097
Robert McCain: (ID) Apr. 1, 1846, (AN) MO4400.077
Benjamin F. McClary: (ID) Apr. 1, 1846, (AN) MO4400.064
Henry H. McClary: (ID) Apr. 1, 1846, (AN) MO4400.065
Benjamin McCrary: (ID) Apr. 1, 1846, (AN) MO4420.195
Philip McCray: (ID) Apr. 1, 1846, (AN) MO4420.300
Ambrose D. McDaniel: (ID) Apr. 1, 1846, (AN) MO4400.138
Silas McDonald: (ID) Apr. 1, 1846, (AN) MO4410.033
Cornelius McGuire: (ID) Apr. 1, 1846, (AN) MO4420.050
William McGuire: (ID) Apr. 1, 1846, (AN) MO4410.018
James McKinney: (ID) Apr. 1, 1846, (AN) MO4400.473
James McMahan: (ID) Apr. 1, 1846, (AN) MO4410.252
Esther McNeeley: (ID) Apr. 1, 1846, (AN) MO4410.054
Francis J. Meadows: (ID) Apr. 1, 1846, (AN) MO4420.277
George W. Means: (ID) Apr. 1, 1846, (AN) MO4400.197
Herald W. Miller: (ID) Apr. 1, 1846, (AN) MO4410.147
Isaac Miller: (ID) Apr. 1, 1846, (AN) MO4420.422
Jacob Miller: (ID) Apr. 1, 1846, (AN) MO4420.198
James Miller: (ID) Apr. 1, 1846, (AN) MO4420.095
Matthias Miller: (ID) Apr. 1, 1846, (AN) MO4400.094
Michael Miller: (ID) Apr. 1, 1846, (AN) MO4420.120
Peggy C. Miller: (ID) Apr. 1, 1846, (AN) MO4410.148
Andrew J. Mills: (ID) Apr. 1, 1846, (AN) MO4420.260
Frederick Mitchell: (ID) Apr. 1, 1846, (AN) MO4400.110
Robert Modrel: (ID) Apr. 1, 1846, (AN) MO4400.314
John Modrell: (ID) Apr. 1, 1846, (AN) MO4420.351
David C. Montgomery: (ID) Apr. 1, 1846, (AN) MO4410.342
Benjamin Moore: (ID) Apr. 1, 1846, (AN) MO4410.222
Drury Moore: (ID) Apr. 1, 1846, (AN) MO4410.221

Starling Morgan: (ID) Apr. 1, 1846, (AN) MO4410.127
Henry B. Morris: (ID) Apr. 1, 1846, (AN) MO4400.207
Charles M. Moss: (ID) Apr. 1, 1846, (AN) MO4410.478
James Moutrie: (ID) Apr. 1, 1846, (AN) MO4400.147
Philip P. Mudgett: (ID) Apr. 1, 1846, (AN) MO4420.334
Daniel Mulkey: (ID) Apr. 1, 1846, (AN) MO4410.074
James L. Mulkey: (ID) Apr. 1, 1846, (AN) MO4420.144
James Muncy: (ID) Apr. 1, 1846, (AN) MO4400.457
Absalom Munkers: (ID) Apr. 1, 1846, (AN) MO4400.142
Joseph Nash: (ID) Apr. 1, 1846, (AN) MO4410.206
Claiborne Neil: (ID) Apr. 1, 1846, (AN) MO4410.223
Alexander Newby: (ID) Apr. 1, 1846, (AN) MO4410.203
William Noble: (ID) Apr. 1, 1846, (AN) MO4420.219
Thomas K. Norris: (ID) Apr. 1, 1846, (AN) MO4400.491
William O'Bannon: (ID) Apr. 1, 1846, (AN) MO4420.282
Patrick O'Connor: (ID) Apr. 1, 1846, (AN) MO4410.227
Thomas Oldham: (ID) Apr. 1, 1846, (AN) MO4420.138
James B. Otoole: (ID) Apr. 1, 1846, (AN) MO4400.361
Greenberry Overton: (ID) Apr. 1, 1846, (AN) MO4410.260
William Payne: (ID) Apr. 1, 1846, (AN) MO4410.043
Allen Pearson: (ID) Apr. 1, 1846, (AN) MO4400.284
Stanislas Pelkier: (ID) Apr. 1, 1846, (AN) MO4410.161
Joel J. Penick: (ID) Apr. 1, 1846, (AN) MO4400.136
William D. Penny: (ID) Apr. 1, 1846, (AN) MO4410.174
James Pierson: (ID) Apr. 1, 1846, (AN) MO4410.066
Reuben Pigg: (ID) Apr. 1, 1846, (AN) MO4420.121
Morris Pile: (ID) Apr. 1, 1846, (AN) MO4410.053
Ephraim Porter: (ID) Apr. 1, 1846, (AN) MO4400.450
Ephraim Porter: (ID) Apr. 1, 1846, (AN) MO4400.282
William R. Powe: (ID) Apr. 1, 1846, (AN) MO4400.086
Charles K. Powell: (ID) Apr. 1, 1846, (AN) MO4420.302
Ann Preston: (ID) Apr. 1, 1846, (AN) MO4400.478
Peter Price: (ID) Apr. 1, 1846, (AN) MO4420.233
Peter Price: (ID) Apr. 1, 1846, (AN) MO4420.234
William Purrott: (ID) Apr. 1, 1846, (AN) MO4400.280
Frederick Rantel: (ID) Apr. 1, 1846, (AN) MO4410.350
John Ray: (ID) Apr. 1, 1846, (AN) MO4420.1
James M. Rector: (ID) Apr. 1, 1846, (AN) MO4420.478
William C. Rector: (ID) Apr. 1, 1846, (AN) MO4420.199
Joshua W. Redman: (ID) Apr. 1, 1846, (AN) MO4420.438
Stephen Reeves: (ID) Apr. 1, 1846, (AN) MO4400.088
James Reynolds: (ID) Apr. 1, 1846, (AN) MO4400.117
James J. Reynolds: (ID) Apr. 1, 1846, (AN) MO4400.451
William W. Reynolds: (ID) Apr. 1, 1846, (AN) MO4400.433
John M. Rhodes: (ID) Apr. 1, 1846, (AN) MO4410.007
Branston Ridge: (ID) Apr. 1, 1846, (AN) MO4400.203

Ransom Ridge: (ID) Apr. 1, 1846, (AN) MO4400.223
John D. Ritchie: (ID) Apr. 1, 1846, (AN) MO4400.227
Samuel Robb: (ID) Apr. 1, 1846, (AN) MO4400.091
Emanuel Roberson: (ID) Apr. 1, 1846, (AN) MO4410.020
Hugh Robertson: (ID) Apr. 1, 1846, (AN) MO4410.247
John Robertson: (ID) Apr. 1, 1846, (AN) MO4410.248
Joseph Robidoex: (ID) Apr. 1, 1846, (AN) MO4410.377
John Robinett: (ID) Apr. 1, 1846, (AN) MO4410.343
Asa Rockhold: (ID) Apr. 1, 1846, (AN) MO4400.469
Michael Rogers: (ID) Apr. 1, 1846, (AN) MO4420.049
Jacob Ross: (ID) Apr. 1, 1846, (AN) MO4410.151
John Ross: (ID) Apr. 1, 1846, (AN) MO4410.162
Samuel Rowntree: (ID) Apr. 1, 1846, (AN) MO4420.077
John B. Roy: (ID) Apr. 1, 1846, (AN) MO4400.179
John C. Rusel: (ID) Apr. 1, 1846, (AN) MO4410.417
Elijah Russell: (ID) Apr. 1, 1846, (AN) MO4410.335
Henry Sager: (ID) Apr. 1, 1846, (AN) MO4420.064
Edward M. Samuel: (ID) Apr. 1, 1846, (AN) MO4400.282
James Sanders: (ID) Apr. 1, 1846, (AN) MO4410.287
Charles C. Sanganett: (ID) Apr. 1, 1846, (AN) MO4420.205
John Saunders: (ID) Apr. 1, 1846, (AN) MO4400.292
Jane Scarbrough: (ID) Apr. 1, 1846, (AN) MO4400.119
William A. Scott: (ID) Apr. 1, 1846, (AN) MO4420.186
William Shearer: (ID) Apr. 1, 1846, (AN) MO4420.039
John B. Sherwood: (ID) Apr. 1, 1846, (AN) MO4410.254
Jordan Silvus: (ID) Apr. 1, 1846, (AN) MO4400.418
Phenehas Skinner: (ID) Apr. 1, 1846, (AN) MO4420.277
Phinehas Skinner: (ID) Apr. 1, 1846, (AN) MO4400.450
John Slaybaugh: (ID) Apr. 1, 1846, (AN) MO4410.280
Elijah Smith: (ID) Apr. 1, 1846, (AN) MO4400.486
Frederick W. Smith: (ID) Apr. 1, 1846, (AN) MO4410.165
George Smith: (ID) Apr. 1, 1846, (AN) MO4410.185
Hiram Smith: (ID) Apr. 1, 1846, (AN) MO4420.472
Hiram Smith: (ID) Apr. 1, 1846, (AN) MO4420.487
James C. Smith: (ID) Apr. 1, 1846, (AN) MO4410.324
Simpson Smith: (ID) Apr. 1, 1846, (AN) MO4410.415
Edward Snyder: (ID) Apr. 1, 1846, (AN) MO4410.185
Elisha Sollars: (ID) Apr. 1, 1846, (AN) MO4410.158
Benedict Spear: (ID) Apr. 1, 1846, (AN) MO4420.249
Obadiah M. Spencer: (ID) Apr. 1, 1846, (AN) MO4400.456
William W. Spratt: (ID) Apr. 1, 1846, (AN) MO4400.376
John Steel: (ID) Apr. 1, 1846, (AN) MO4420.466
Allen Stephens: (ID) Apr. 1, 1846, (AN) MO4410.140
William Stephenson: (ID) Apr. 1, 1846, (AN) MO4420.130
Isaac Stobaugh: (ID) Apr. 1, 1846, (AN) MO4410.311
Thomas Strickland: (ID) Apr. 1, 1846, (AN) MO4420.229

William Strickland: (ID) Apr. 1, 1846, (AN) MO4420.110
James Stultz: (ID) Apr. 1, 1846, (AN) MO4410.062
Thornton S. Talbott: (ID) Apr. 1, 1846, (AN) MO4410.458
Elvis Taylor: (ID) Apr. 1, 1846, (AN) MO4420.109
George W. Taylor: (ID) Apr. 1, 1846, (AN) MO4420.060
Joseph H. Thomas: (ID) Apr. 1, 1846, (AN) MO4400.301
Turpin T. Thomas: (ID) Apr. 1, 1846, (AN) MO4400.358
David V. Thompson: (ID) Apr. 1, 1846, (AN) MO4420.196
Isaac Thompson: (ID) Apr. 1, 1846, (AN) MO4400.454
James T. Thompson: (ID) Apr. 1, 1846, (AN) MO4420.292
William N. Thompson: (ID) Apr. 1, 1846, (AN) MO4420.018
Rebecca Thorp: (ID) Apr. 1, 1846, (AN) MO4400.434
Albert Tipton: (ID) Apr. 1, 1846, (AN) MO4410.118
Nathan Turner: (ID) Apr. 1, 1846, (AN) MO4410.255
Peter Venlemans: (ID) Apr. 1, 1846, (AN) MO4420.470
Isaac W. Voorhies: (ID) Apr. 1, 1846, (AN) MO4410.238
Samuel Wade: (ID) Apr. 1, 1846, (AN) MO4400.335
Michael Wallace: (ID) Apr. 1, 1846, (AN) MO4410.220
Michael Wallace: (ID) Apr. 1, 1846, (AN) MO4420.464
Elias F. Wells: (ID) Apr. 1, 1846, (AN) MO4410.163
James W. Whitehead: (ID) Apr. 1, 1846, (AN) MO4410.180
John H. Whitehead: (ID) Apr. 1, 1846, (AN) MO4410.179
George W. Whitsun: (ID) Apr. 1, 1846, (AN) MO4410.484
John C. Whittington: (ID) Apr. 1, 1846, (AN) MO4410.301
Hiram Wilburn: (ID) Apr. 1, 1846, (AN) MO4410.486
John Wilfley: (ID) Apr. 1, 1846, (AN) MO4420.069
John Wilfley: (ID) Apr. 1, 1846, (AN) MO4420.201
Ross Wilkerson: (ID) Apr. 1, 1846, (AN) MO4420.197
Ross Wilkinson: (ID) Apr. 1, 1846, (AN) MO4420.051
Joel Willard: (ID) Apr. 1, 1846, (AN) MO4420.266
Henry Williams: (ID) Apr. 1, 1846, (AN) MO4400.429
Jinkins Williams: (ID) Apr. 1, 1846, (AN) MO4400.107
Joseph Williams: (ID) Apr. 1, 1846, (AN) MO4400.430
William Williams: (ID) Apr. 1, 1846, (AN) MO4400.108
William Williams: (ID) Apr. 1, 1846, (AN) MO4400.109
Martin Wilson: (ID) Apr. 1, 1846, (AN) MO4400.472
Robert Wilson: (ID) Apr. 1, 1846, (AN) MO4400.224
Joseph Wonderly: (ID) Apr. 1, 1846, (AN) MO4410.237
Bird Wood: (ID) Apr. 1, 1846, (AN) MO4410.235
Jeremiah Wood: (ID) Apr. 1, 1846, (AN) MO4420.176
Thomas Wood: (ID) Apr. 1, 1846, (AN) MO4410.239
Abigail Woolen: (ID) Apr. 1, 1846, (AN) MO4410.352
Levin Woolen: (ID) Apr. 1, 1846, (AN) MO4410.076
Russell H. Wrinkle: (ID) Apr. 1, 1846, (AN) MO4420.059
Cyrus Young: (ID) Apr. 1, 1846, (AN) MO4400.455
William J. Young: (ID) Apr. 1, 1846, (AN) MO4400.435

William Abbit: (ID) May 1, 1846, (AN) MO4440.377
John Adams: (ID) May 1, 1846, (AN) MO4440.480
James Agee: (ID) May 1, 1846, (AN) MO4430.047
Ruth Agee: (ID) May 1, 1846, (AN) MO4430.046
Humphrey P. Allison: (ID) May 1, 1846, (AN) MO4430.213
William Allison: (ID) May 1, 1846, (AN) MO4430.214
William Anderson: (ID) May 1, 1846, (AN) MO4440.362
James A. Anthony: (ID) May 1, 1846, (AN) MO4450.367
Landon Bagby: (ID) May 1, 1846, (AN) MO4450.086
Andrew Baker: (ID) May 1, 1846, (AN) MO4450.316
William M. Balew: (ID) May 1, 1846, (AN) MO4440.305
Henry Ballard: (ID) May 1, 1846, (AN) MO4430.386
James Barnes: (ID) May 1, 1846, (AN) MO4440.422
David Barris: (ID) May 1, 1846, (AN) MO4450.279
Francis Bazergue: (ID) May 1, 1846, (AN) MO4460.175
Edward A. Beauchamp: (ID) May 1, 1846, (AN) MO4440.387
Stephen Bedford: (ID) May 1, 1846, (AN) MO4430.130
John Bell: (ID) May 1, 1846, (AN) MO4440.437
Anthony Beller: (ID) May 1, 1846, (AN) MO4430.348
Samuel J. Best: (ID) May 1, 1846, (AN) MO4430.240
Samuel J. Best: (ID) May 1, 1846, (AN) MO4450.022
Thomas Bilderback: (ID) May 1, 1846, (AN) MO4460.048
John W. Blakeley: (ID) May 1, 1846, (AN) MO4440.381
Valentine Bledsoe: (ID) May 1, 1846, (AN) MO4430.449
John Bohannon: (ID) May 1, 1846, (AN) MO4440.180
John Bombarger: (ID) May 1, 1846, (AN) MO4440.227
William G. Boon: (ID) May 1, 1846, (AN) MO4450.318
Thomas Boydstun: (ID) May 1, 1846, (AN) MO4450.405
William Boydstun: (ID) May 1, 1846, (AN) MO4460.023
Daniel Boyer: (ID) May 1, 1846, (AN) MO4440.013
Jacob Boyer: (ID) May 1, 1846, (AN) MO4440.318
Jacob Boyer: (ID) May 1, 1846, (AN) MO4460.027
Peter Boyer: (ID) May 1, 1846, (AN) MO4460.278
David G. Brooks: (ID) May 1, 1846, (AN) MO4440.082
Thomas Brooks: (ID) May 1, 1846, (AN) MO4430.439
Alexander Brown: (ID) May 1, 1846, (AN) MO4430.344
Alexander Brown: (ID) May 1, 1846, (AN) MO4440.399
Alexander Brown: (ID) May 1, 1846, (AN) MO4460.240
John Brown: (ID) May 1, 1846, (AN) MO4450.392
William S. Brown: (ID) May 1, 1846, (AN) MO4430.168
Daniel Brumley: (ID) May 1, 1846, (AN) MO4430.407
James Burnes: (ID) May 1, 1846, (AN) MO4440.206
Brinsley Burns: (ID) May 1, 1846, (AN) MO4450.333
James Burns: (ID) May 1, 1846, (AN) MO4440.459
Ennis Burris: (ID) May 1, 1846, (AN) MO4440.418
John Burris: (ID) May 1, 1846, (AN) MO4450.280

Lindsey Butler: (ID) May 1, 1846, (AN) MO4450.114
William Callahan: (ID) May 1, 1846, (AN) MO4440.032
McKinsey Carlyle: (ID) May 1, 1846, (AN) MO4440.206
McKinsey Carlyle: (ID) May 1, 1846, (AN) MO4440.459
John T. Cate: (ID) May 1, 1846, (AN) MO4460.020
Benjamin Catlet: (ID) May 1, 1846, (AN) MO4450.474
Richard Chaney: (ID) May 1, 1846, (AN) MO4450.254
William Chaney: (ID) May 1, 1846, (AN) MO4430.165
Daniel Chitwood: (ID) May 1, 1846, (AN) MO4430.415
Campbell E. Chrisman: (ID) May 1, 1846, (AN) MO4430.443
John D. Clagsby: (ID) May 1, 1846, (AN) MO4430.437
Hiram Clark: (ID) May 1, 1846, (AN) MO4450.257
Jesse A. Clark: (ID) May 1, 1846, (AN) MO4460.065
John R. Clark: (ID) May 1, 1846, (AN) MO4430.411
William J. Clark: (ID) May 1, 1846, (AN) MO4440.355
Witten J. Clark: (ID) May 1, 1846, (AN) MO4450.258
Edward C. Clarke: (ID) May 1, 1846, (AN) MO4440.005
William H. Clasby: (ID) May 1, 1846, (AN) MO4440.298
Daniel Cogdill: (ID) May 1, 1846, (AN) MO4430.021
John H. Colyer: (ID) May 1, 1846, (AN) MO4460.196
Jacob Combs: (ID) May 1, 1846, (AN) MO4440.124
Husselton Compton: (ID) May 1, 1846, (AN) MO4440.021
John Conner: (ID) May 1, 1846, (AN) MO4450.420
Eli Copeland: (ID) May 1, 1846, (AN) MO4460.195
Hugh Copeland: (ID) May 1, 1846, (AN) MO4430.172
James Copeland: (ID) May 1, 1846, (AN) MO4450.207
John Copeland: (ID) May 1, 1846, (AN) MO4440.187
John Copeland: (ID) May 1, 1846, (AN) MO4440.406
John Corby: (ID) May 1, 1846, (AN) MO4460.394
John Corby: (ID) May 1, 1846, (AN) MO4460.395
John Corby: (ID) May 1, 1846, (AN) MO4460.396
Green R. Cordry: (ID) May 1, 1846, (AN) MO4460.125
John Cordry: (ID) May 1, 1846, (AN) MO4450.292
Benjamin Cornelius: (ID) May 1, 1846, (AN) MO4430.153
Benjamin Cornelius: (ID) May 1, 1846, (AN) MO4440.062
James B. Cornelius: (ID) May 1, 1846, (AN) MO4430.284
John H. Cox: (ID) May 1, 1846, (AN) MO4440.351
Joseph Cox: (ID) May 1, 1846, (AN) MO4460.115
Matthew Coy: (ID) May 1, 1846, (AN) MO4450.417
William Crocker: (ID) May 1, 1846, (AN) MO4450.035
John Croy: (ID) May 1, 1846, (AN) MO4440.423
Ely Crumply: (ID) May 1, 1846, (AN) MO4440.343
Matthew M. Cummins: (ID) May 1, 1846, (AN) MO4450.006
Robert Cunningham: (ID) May 1, 1846, (AN) MO4450.186
Elisha K. Davis: (ID) May 1, 1846, (AN) MO4460.326
John Davis: (ID) May 1, 1846, (AN) MO4430.212

Sarah Davis: (ID) May 1, 1846, (AN) MO4440.142
Sarah Davis: (ID) May 1, 1846, (AN) MO4440.417
Absalom Deakins: (ID) May 1, 1846, (AN) MO4430.185
George Deppen: (ID) May 1, 1846, (AN) MO4430.367
James Dix: (ID) May 1, 1846, (AN) MO4450.281
John Donell: (ID) May 1, 1846, (AN) MO4440.206
Alfred G. Donovan: (ID) May 1, 1846, (AN) MO4440.247
James Donovan: (ID) May 1, 1846, (AN) MO4440.479
Morgan Dryden: (ID) May 1, 1846, (AN) MO4460.024
Robert Duncan: (ID) May 1, 1846, (AN) MO4430.390
James C. Dunlap: (ID) May 1, 1846, (AN) MO4440.302
William Dunlap: (ID) May 1, 1846, (AN) MO4450.268
John Earixson: (ID) May 1, 1846, (AN) MO4450.335
John Ellison: (ID) May 1, 1846, (AN) MO4440.319
David M. Evans: (ID) May 1, 1846, (AN) MO4430.108
David Ewing: (ID) May 1, 1846, (AN) MO4450.091
David C. Ewing: (ID) May 1, 1846, (AN) MO4440.266
Stephen Fields: (ID) May 1, 1846, (AN) MO4440.214
William Flanery: (ID) May 1, 1846, (AN) MO4430.443
Charles Fletcher: (ID) May 1, 1846, (AN) MO4430.188
William P. Flint: (ID) May 1, 1846, (AN) MO4460.097
Erastus D. Ford: (ID) May 1, 1846, (AN) MO4430.170
Dugan Fouts: (ID) May 1, 1846, (AN) MO4440.123
William Fowler: (ID) May 1, 1846, (AN) MO4430.110
Joseph T. Frakes: (ID) May 1, 1846, (AN) MO4440.229
Willis C. Frakes: (ID) May 1, 1846, (AN) MO4440.230
Tazewell Frans: (ID) May 1, 1846, (AN) MO4450.018
John Freeland: (ID) May 1, 1846, (AN) MO4460.389
Arthur R. Frogge: (ID) May 1, 1846, (AN) MO4450.023
William R. Frogge: (ID) May 1, 1846, (AN) MO4450.024
Alexander Fudge: (ID) May 1, 1846, (AN) MO4440.073
Richard Fulton: (ID) May 1, 1846, (AN) MO4430.408
Thomas J. Gabbert: (ID) May 1, 1846, (AN) MO4430.219
John Gann: (ID) May 1, 1846, (AN) MO4440.007
Isom Gardner: (ID) May 1, 1846, (AN) MO4440.293
David Garred: (ID) May 1, 1846, (AN) MO4430.324
Nathaniel Gartin: (ID) May 1, 1846, (AN) MO4450.372
Uriah Gartin: (ID) May 1, 1846, (AN) MO4440.174
Zachariah Garton: (ID) May 1, 1846, (AN) MO4440.426
Henry Gelling: (ID) May 1, 1846, (AN) MO4440.375
Arthur Gibson: (ID) May 1, 1846, (AN) MO4430.186
Arthur Gibson: (ID) May 1, 1846, (AN) MO4450.233
Henry T. Gill: (ID) May 1, 1846, (AN) MO4440.416
Robert P. Gilliam: (ID) May 1, 1846, (AN) MO4430.446
James M. Givens: (ID) May 1, 1846, (AN) MO4460.044
Hugh Glenn: (ID) May 1, 1846, (AN) MO4440.134

Samuel N. Gordan: (ID) May 1, 1846, (AN) MO4460.383
Samuel N. Gordon: (ID) May 1, 1846, (AN) MO4460.182
Andrew W. Graham: (ID) May 1, 1846, (AN) MO4430.413
Andrew W. Graham: (ID) May 1, 1846, (AN) MO4450.293
Boston Graves: (ID) May 1, 1846, (AN) MO4430.002
Robert U Gray: (ID) May 1, 1846, (AN) MO4430.366
Solomon Groom: (ID) May 1, 1846, (AN) MO4440.411
Rufus Guinn: (ID) May 1, 1846, (AN) MO4450.342
James Hall: (ID) May 1, 1846, (AN) MO4440.228
James F. Hamilton: (ID) May 1, 1846, (AN) MO4440.386
John S. Hardy: (ID) May 1, 1846, (AN) MO4450.091
John S. Hardy: (ID) May 1, 1846, (AN) MO4460.173
John Hargrove: (ID) May 1, 1846, (AN) MO4430.231
Lewis Harness: (ID) May 1, 1846, (AN) MO4460.387
William Harrington: (ID) May 1, 1846, (AN) MO4430.181
Isaac Harris: (ID) May 1, 1846, (AN) MO4440.350
Joshua C. Hays: (ID) May 1, 1846, (AN) MO4440.038
Jesse C. Henderson: (ID) May 1, 1846, (AN) MO4440.400
John H. Henry: (ID) May 1, 1846, (AN) MO4430.262
John F. Henshaw: (ID) May 1, 1846, (AN) MO4450.015
Creed Herring: (ID) May 1, 1846, (AN) MO4430.109
George W. Herring: (ID) May 1, 1846, (AN) MO4430.108
John Herring: (ID) May 1, 1846, (AN) MO4430.108
Caleb Hesemyer: (ID) May 1, 1846, (AN) MO4440.376
Thomas Hickman: (ID) May 1, 1846, (AN) MO4440.428
William Hickman: (ID) May 1, 1846, (AN) MO4450.344
John Hill: (ID) May 1, 1846, (AN) MO4440.176
Joseph Hill: (ID) May 1, 1846, (AN) MO4440.479
James R. Holeman: (ID) May 1, 1846, (AN) MO4440.104
William S. Holeman: (ID) May 1, 1846, (AN) MO4440.061
John Holland: (ID) May 1, 1846, (AN) MO4440.263
Amos Horn: (ID) May 1, 1846, (AN) MO4440.301
John Howard: (ID) May 1, 1846, (AN) MO4450.277
James M. Howe: (ID) May 1, 1846, (AN) MO4430.436
Thomas Howsk: (ID) May 1, 1846, (AN) MO4460.018
Joseph Hughart: (ID) May 1, 1846, (AN) MO4440.353
John Huntsucker: (ID) May 1, 1846, (AN) MO4440.219
John Huntsucker: (ID) May 1, 1846, (AN) MO4460.277
Anliff C. Hyde: (ID) May 1, 1846, (AN) MO4450.116
James L. Hyde: (ID) May 1, 1846, (AN) MO4450.115
Calvin James: (ID) May 1, 1846, (AN) MO4460.107
Nelson James: (ID) May 1, 1846, (AN) MO4430.275
George Jessee: (ID) May 1, 1846, (AN) MO4430.003
John Johnson: (ID) May 1, 1846, (AN) MO4430.377
John Johnson: (ID) May 1, 1846, (AN) MO4440.356
Harvey Jones: (ID) May 1, 1846, (AN) MO4440.407

James H. Jones: (ID) May 1, 1846, (AN) MO4430.072
John M. Jones: (ID) May 1, 1846, (AN) MO4460.241
Josiah Jones: (ID) May 1, 1846, (AN) MO4440.115
Leander W. Jones: (ID) May 1, 1846, (AN) MO4450.071
Ely Judah: (ID) May 1, 1846, (AN) MO4430.406
Abraham Karnes: (ID) May 1, 1846, (AN) MO4440.135
Abel Keener: (ID) May 1, 1846, (AN) MO4440.060
Jacob Kennedy: (ID) May 1, 1846, (AN) MO4440.481
Absalom Kent: (ID) May 1, 1846, (AN) MO4430.375
Robert G. Kercheval: (ID) May 1, 1846, (AN) MO4430.069
Silas H. Kernes: (ID) May 1, 1846, (AN) MO4440.409
Spencer A. Lacefield: (ID) May 1, 1846, (AN) MO4460.193
Joseph P. Lapsley: (ID) May 1, 1846, (AN) MO4450.143
Robert L. Lassater: (ID) May 1, 1846, (AN) MO4440.407
George W. Layman: (ID) May 1, 1846, (AN) MO4430.346
Elgan J. Layne: (ID) May 1, 1846, (AN) MO4460.190
Elgan J. Layne: (ID) May 1, 1846, (AN) MO4460.323
Thomas M. Lear: (ID) May 1, 1846, (AN) MO4440.037
John Legerwood: (ID) May 1, 1846, (AN) MO4440.446
Aaron Lewis: (ID) May 1, 1846, (AN) MO4430.462
George H. Linville: (ID) May 1, 1846, (AN) MO4440.432
Robert Loveland: (ID) May 1, 1846, (AN) MO4440.361
Humberson Lyon: (ID) May 1, 1846, (AN) MO4450.388
James B. Mackey: (ID) May 1, 1846, (AN) MO4450.052
Frederick Marker: (ID) May 1, 1846, (AN) MO4430.202
Phillip Marker: (ID) May 1, 1846, (AN) MO4430.203
James J. Marshall: (ID) May 1, 1846, (AN) MO4440.255
Abraham Martin: (ID) May 1, 1846, (AN) MO4440.153
John T. Martin: (ID) May 1, 1846, (AN) MO4430.227
Samuel Martin: (ID) May 1, 1846, (AN) MO4430.231
Michie Maupin: (ID) May 1, 1846, (AN) MO4460.021
Edward Maxwell: (ID) May 1, 1846, (AN) MO4450.329
Hugh Maxwell: (ID) May 1, 1846, (AN) MO4430.376
Logan Maxwell: (ID) May 1, 1846, (AN) MO4440.393
Logan Maxwell: (ID) May 1, 1846, (AN) MO4440.395
Isaac May: (ID) May 1, 1846, (AN) MO4460.162
Lankford McCain: (ID) May 1, 1846, (AN) MO4450.341
Robert McCain: (ID) May 1, 1846, (AN) MO4440.282
William McCarty: (ID) May 1, 1846, (AN) MO4430.332
Alexander McCorkle: (ID) May 1, 1846, (AN) MO4430.325
Alexander McCorkle: (ID) May 1, 1846, (AN) MO4430.326
Benjamin McCray: (ID) May 1, 1846, (AN) MO4440.466
Benjamin McCray: (ID) May 1, 1846, (AN) MO4460.022
Daniel McCray: (ID) May 1, 1846, (AN) MO4450.144
Elizabeth McCubbin: (ID) May 1, 1846, (AN) MO4440.138
William McDowell: (ID) May 1, 1846, (AN) MO4460.252

William McKeever: (ID) May 1, 1846, (AN) MO4430.356
James McKown: (ID) May 1, 1846, (AN) MO4430.412
James McKown: (ID) May 1, 1846, (AN) MO4460.332
Thomas McKown: (ID) May 1, 1846, (AN) MO4450.390
William McNeal: (ID) May 1, 1846, (AN) MO4430.189
John Meers: (ID) May 1, 1846, (AN) MO4440.424
Joshua Michael: (ID) May 1, 1846, (AN) MO4440.429
Archibald Millen: (ID) May 1, 1846, (AN) MO4450.291
Isaac Miller: (ID) May 1, 1846, (AN) MO4440.076
Isaac Miller: (ID) May 1, 1846, (AN) MO4440.106
Jennetta Miller: (ID) May 1, 1846, (AN) MO4460.192
Silas Mitchell: (ID) May 1, 1846, (AN) MO4430.314
William Moore: (ID) May 1, 1846, (AN) MO4430.168
John Morris: (ID) May 1, 1846, (AN) MO4430.103
John Morris: (ID) May 1, 1846, (AN) MO4440.384
Willaba P. Morris: (ID) May 1, 1846, (AN) MO4430.248
Robert C. Moseley: (ID) May 1, 1846, (AN) MO4460.122
Thomas P. Moss: (ID) May 1, 1846, (AN) MO4440.028
George Mufly: (ID) May 1, 1846, (AN) MO4440.123
Isham Nance: (ID) May 1, 1846, (AN) MO4440.170
Hardin J. Noland: (ID) May 1, 1846, (AN) MO4450.361
Oliver Norman: (ID) May 1, 1846, (AN) MO4440.325
Oliver Norman: (ID) May 1, 1846, (AN) MO4460.239
John Norris: (ID) May 1, 1846, (AN) MO4430.274
Joseph Ogle: (ID) May 1, 1846, (AN) MO4430.184
Greenberry Overton: (ID) May 1, 1846, (AN) MO4460.302
Martha Owen: (ID) May 1, 1846, (AN) MO4440.272
John C. Parker: (ID) May 1, 1846, (AN) MO4440.012
Andrew Parnell: (ID) May 1, 1846, (AN) MO4440.172
Isaac Parnell: (ID) May 1, 1846, (AN) MO4440.173
Green Patterson: (ID) May 1, 1846, (AN) MO4450.106
Anderson E. Patton: (ID) May 1, 1846, (AN) MO4440.031
Elizabeth Pearson: (ID) May 1, 1846, (AN) MO4430.094
William Pearson: (ID) May 1, 1846, (AN) MO4430.095
Calvin Pell: (ID) May 1, 1846, (AN) MO4450.187
Richard Pell: (ID) May 1, 1846, (AN) MO4460.311
Conrad L. Peters: (ID) May 1, 1846, (AN) MO4440.452
Jeremiah Petit: (ID) May 1, 1846, (AN) MO4430.048
John S. Pickett: (ID) May 1, 1846, (AN) MO4430.210
Jacob D. Pierce: (ID) May 1, 1846, (AN) MO4430.068
John B. Pierson: (ID) May 1, 1846, (AN) MO4440.467
William Pile: (ID) May 1, 1846, (AN) MO4430.294
Thomas Poteet: (ID) May 1, 1846, (AN) MO4440.356
William Potter: (ID) May 1, 1846, (AN) MO4450.240
William R. Powe: (ID) May 1, 1846, (AN) MO4430.017
John Price: (ID) May 1, 1846, (AN) MO4460.291

William Pritchett: (ID) May 1, 1846, (AN) MO4430.328
John Purdue: (ID) May 1, 1846, (AN) MO4440.257
William Purrott: (ID) May 1, 1846, (AN) MO4440.168
William Purrott: (ID) May 1, 1846, (AN) MO4440.169
George Rainey: (ID) May 1, 1846, (AN) MO4460.138
Charles Ramsey: (ID) May 1, 1846, (AN) MO4460.106
Joseph Rawls: (ID) May 1, 1846, (AN) MO4440.427
James M. Rector: (ID) May 1, 1846, (AN) MO4440.434
Jacob Reece: (ID) May 1, 1846, (AN) MO4440.294
Hugh B. Reynolds: (ID) May 1, 1846, (AN) MO4440.454
Levi W. Reynolds: (ID) May 1, 1846, (AN) MO4450.244
Yerby W. Reynolds: (ID) May 1, 1846, (AN) MO4450.243
Joseph Rice: (ID) May 1, 1846, (AN) MO4460.325
John Ritchie: (ID) May 1, 1846, (AN) MO4450.350
John Robb: (ID) May 1, 1846, (AN) MO4450.357
James Roberts: (ID) May 1, 1846, (AN) MO4440.178
James Roberts: (ID) May 1, 1846, (AN) MO4450.336
Richard Roberts: (ID) May 1, 1846, (AN) MO4430.420
Joseph Robidoux: (ID) May 1, 1846, (AN) MO4460.411
Julius C. Robidoux: (ID) May 1, 1846, (AN) MO4460.412
Stephen Robnett: (ID) May 1, 1846, (AN) MO4430.191
Andrew Russell: (ID) May 1, 1846, (AN) MO4440.299
Robert R. Russell: (ID) May 1, 1846, (AN) MO4450.358
Benjamin Sampson: (ID) May 1, 1846, (AN) MO4430.369
Benjamin Sampson: (ID) May 1, 1846, (AN) MO4430.370
Glenn P. Sampson: (ID) May 1, 1846, (AN) MO4440.292
John Sampson: (ID) May 1, 1846, (AN) MO4430.371
Taylor Sargent: (ID) May 1, 1846, (AN) MO4440.352
William Saunders: (ID) May 1, 1846, (AN) MO4450.169
Labault Sela: (ID) May 1, 1846, (AN) MO4450.490
Waider A. Shannon: (ID) May 1, 1846, (AN) MO4450.416
Martin Shultz: (ID) May 1, 1846, (AN) MO4440.236
James Sidler: (ID) May 1, 1846, (AN) MO4430.466
Goalden Silvers: (ID) May 1, 1846, (AN) MO4440.478
Johnson Simmons: (ID) May 1, 1846, (AN) MO4450.295
Allen Skouten: (ID) May 1, 1846, (AN) MO4440.137
Elijah W. Smith: (ID) May 1, 1846, (AN) MO4440.175
Hiram Smith: (ID) May 1, 1846, (AN) MO4440.022
Hugh Smith: (ID) May 1, 1846, (AN) MO4450.366
John M. Smith: (ID) May 1, 1846, (AN) MO4430.052
Richard A. Smith: (ID) May 1, 1846, (AN) MO4440.486
Washington Smith: (ID) May 1, 1846, (AN) MO4440.474
James Spencer: (ID) May 1, 1846, (AN) MO4440.396
Ralph M. Stafford: (ID) May 1, 1846, (AN) MO4450.220
William Staley: (ID) May 1, 1846, (AN) MO4430.354
Isaac H. Stanley: (ID) May 1, 1846, (AN) MO4450.355

John A. Steel: (ID) May 1, 1846, (AN) MO4450.002
Joseph Y Steel: (ID) May 1, 1846, (AN) MO4430.440
Zaddock Stevenson: (ID) May 1, 1846, (AN) MO4430.131
James Stultz: (ID) May 1, 1846, (AN) MO4450.110
James Stultz: (ID) May 1, 1846, (AN) MO4450.134
John D. Sullivan: (ID) May 1, 1846, (AN) MO4450.102
Thornton S. Talbot: (ID) May 1, 1846, (AN) MO4430.097
James S. Talbott: (ID) May 1, 1846, (AN) MO4430.112
Jacob Tarwater: (ID) May 1, 1846, (AN) MO4450.008
Alfred C. Taylor: (ID) May 1, 1846, (AN) MO4430.235
James Taylor: (ID) May 1, 1846, (AN) MO4450.229
William Thomas: (ID) May 1, 1846, (AN) MO4430.166
Frank Thompson: (ID) May 1, 1846, (AN) MO4430.036
Lemuel Thornburgh: (ID) May 1, 1846, (AN) MO4440.467
Isaac Thornton: (ID) May 1, 1846, (AN) MO4430.149
William Thornton: (ID) May 1, 1846, (AN) MO4460.342
David J. Thorp: (ID) May 1, 1846, (AN) MO4440.306
John Thurman: (ID) May 1, 1846, (AN) MO4440.437
John Tobin: (ID) May 1, 1846, (AN) MO4460.019
John Tobin: (ID) May 1, 1846, (AN) MO4460.151
James Toney: (ID) May 1, 1846, (AN) MO4440.103
Samuel Trower: (ID) May 1, 1846, (AN) MO4460.017
Winslow Turner: (ID) May 1, 1846, (AN) MO4430.093
Abel Tyler: (ID) May 1, 1846, (AN) MO4460.183
John Underwood: (ID) May 1, 1846, (AN) MO4440.147
William Underwood: (ID) May 1, 1846, (AN) MO4440.385
Isaac Vanhoozer: (ID) May 1, 1846, (AN) MO4440.431
Daniel Vestal: (ID) May 1, 1846, (AN) MO4460.400
David Vestal: (ID) May 1, 1846, (AN) MO4450.394
Isaac W. Voorhies: (ID) May 1, 1846, (AN) MO4460.279
William Wade: (ID) May 1, 1846, (AN) MO4440.359
William M. Wadsworth: (ID) May 1, 1846, (AN) MO4450.239
Michael Wallace: (ID) May 1, 1846, (AN) MO4430.385
Jonathan Waller: (ID) May 1, 1846, (AN) MO4430.435
Daniel P. Wallingford: (ID) May 1, 1846, (AN) MO4460.170
William P. Wallingford: (ID) May 1, 1846, (AN) MO4430.182
Isaac Waymire: (ID) May 1, 1846, (AN) MO4440.412
Joseph Waymire: (ID) May 1, 1846, (AN) MO4450.491
Joseph Waymire: (ID) May 1, 1846, (AN) MO4460.091
Joel Weddle: (ID) May 1, 1846, (AN) MO4450.057
William D. Weir: (ID) May 1, 1846, (AN) MO4430.175
Charles Wetzel: (ID) May 1, 1846, (AN) MO4450.049
James White: (ID) May 1, 1846, (AN) MO4440.377
William S. White: (ID) May 1, 1846, (AN) MO4450.084
Henry Widner: (ID) May 1, 1846, (AN) MO4460.171
Samuel Widner: (ID) May 1, 1846, (AN) MO4460.172

Samuel C. Wiley: (ID) May 1, 1846, (AN) MO4450.170
Margaret Wilhelm: (ID) May 1, 1846, (AN) MO4450.414
Alexander Williams: (ID) May 1, 1846, (AN) MO4440.358
Newell Willis: (ID) May 1, 1846, (AN) MO4430.368
Gilbert Wilson: (ID) May 1, 1846, (AN) MO4460.313
Hermon Wiskerger: (ID) May 1, 1846, (AN) MO4460.238
John Wiskirchen: (ID) May 1, 1846, (AN) MO4430.347
Abram Womack: (ID) May 1, 1846, (AN) MO4440.215
William Womack: (ID) May 1, 1846, (AN) MO4440.373
Joseph Wonderly: (ID) May 1, 1846, (AN) MO4430.144
John Wood: (ID) May 1, 1846, (AN) MO4460.306
Mary Wood: (ID) May 1, 1846, (AN) MO4430.051
James Workman: (ID) May 1, 1846, (AN) MO4450.391
Benjamin Yocum: (ID) May 1, 1846, (AN) MO4430.008

St. Louis County, MO, Death Records, January, 1901

Frances Bell	Jan. 1, 1901
Mary Brewer	Jan. 1, 1901
Thomas Brown	Jan. 1, 1901
Joseph W. C0ssmann	Jan. 1, 1901
John J. Coffey	Jan. 1, 1901
Meurel Davis	Jan. 1, 1901
James Duraud	Jan. 1, 1901
Mathias Emmerich	Jan. 1, 1901
Alexander Fletcher	Jan. 1, 1901
Martin Furgeson	Jan. 1, 1901
Rebecca Gast	Jan. 1, 1901
Celia Hade	Jan. 1, 1901
Frank Johns	Jan. 1, 1901
Augustine Jones	Jan. 1, 1901
Jessie J. Jones	Jan. 1, 1901
Henry Lechtreck	Jan. 1, 1901
Letha Lederer	Jan. 1, 1901
Mary Mahon	Jan. 1, 1901
Mandy Manteaitta	Jan. 1, 1901
Patrick Nickols	Jan. 1, 1901
Edward Niehans	Jan. 1, 1901
Anton Obermeier	Jan. 1, 1901
Elizabeth Olenstead	Jan. 1, 1901
Lena Plate	Jan. 1, 1901
Joseph Schnorr	Jan. 1, 1901
Maria A. Schraeder	Jan. 1, 1901
Clara Schwarneck	Jan. 1, 1901
Frank Shapleigh	Jan. 1, 1901
George Stoll	Jan. 1, 1901
Tillie Werner	Jan. 1, 1901

Matilda C Westmann	Jan. 1, 1901
Helen Young	Jan. 1, 1901
William Brown	Jan. 2, 1901
Mattew J. Cole	Jan. 2, 1901
Alonzo Raphael Flanagan	Jan. 2, 1901
Joseph H. Glass	Jan. 2, 1901
Julia Grasch	Jan. 2, 1901
Charles G. Haltman	Jan. 2, 1901
Mary Hasamer	Jan. 2, 1901
Otto Haslerlik	Jan. 2, 1901
Herman Hesling	Jan. 2, 1901
George Jend	Jan. 2, 1901
Ray R. Keisker	Jan. 2, 1901
Hettie Ryan Lanigan	Jan. 2, 1901
John Lewis	Jan. 2, 1901
Mamie Mc Carthy	Jan. 2, 1901
Catherine Mc Gregor	Jan. 2, 1901
Harriet B. Mc Iutine	Jan. 2, 1901
John Ames Moellmann	Jan. 2, 1901
George J. Niedt	Jan. 2, 1901
Kate O'dell	Jan. 2, 1901
James O'toole	Jan. 2, 1901
Fred Pfeiffer	Jan. 2, 1901
Frances Placht	Jan. 2, 1901
Irvin Albert Reinhold	Jan. 2, 1901
George Schneider	Jan. 2, 1901
George C Sennewald	Jan. 2, 1901
Lucy Sharp	Jan. 2, 1901
Henry Simcox	Jan. 2, 1901
Franklin J. Smith	Jan. 2, 1901
Mary Smith	Jan. 2, 1901
Robert Smith	Jan. 2, 1901
Osmond Taylor	Jan. 2, 1901
Ida May Thomas	Jan. 2, 1901
Catherine Winkler	Jan. 2, 1901
David Alexander Wood	Jan. 2, 1901
Clara Wunderlich	Jan. 2, 1901
John Baily	Jan. 3, 1901
E, O. Bartholomew	Jan. 3, 1901
Vincent William Dainey	Jan. 3, 1901
James C Fisher	Jan. 3, 1901
Henry Frederick	Jan. 3, 1901
Beatrice Anna Hebener	Jan. 3, 1901
Catherine E. Horrigen	Jan. 3, 1901
William T. Koken	Jan. 3, 1901
John P. Mc Grath	Jan. 3, 1901

James W. Morris	Jan. 3, 1901
Willetta Ollham	Jan. 3, 1901
William Pallmeier	Jan. 3, 1901
Harry Ringling	Jan. 3, 1901
Christ Schlueter	Jan. 3, 1901
Gladys Seelig	Jan. 3, 1901
Maria E. Stueve	Jan. 3, 1901
Hazel Widener	Jan. 3, 1901
John Wienecke	Jan. 3 1890
Victory Frances Wifers	Jan. 3, 1901
Henry Casper	Jan. 4, 1901
Jacob Christman	Jan. 4, 1901
Lawrence Cody	Jan. 4, 1901
James L. Donnelly	Jan. 4, 1901
Virginia Eaton	Jan. 4, 1901
John B. Fitzgerald	Jan. 4, 1901
Josie Gray	Jan. 4, 1901
A. H. Green	Jan. 4, 1901
David W. Guernsey	Jan. 4, 1901
Fanny Hawkins	Jan. 4, 1901
Frank J. Hoops	Jan. 4, 1901
Anna J. Horstkoette	Jan. 4, 1901
Pat Hughes	Jan. 4, 1901
W. B. Jones	Jan. 4, 1901
Bridget Lanagan	Jan. 4, 1901
Raymond Manz	Jan. 4, 1901
John B. Marschal	Jan. 4, 1901
John Mc Namara	Jan. 4, 1901
Nellie Murphy	Jan. 4, 1901
Marie O'Connel	Jan. 4, 1901
Henry N. Pies	Jan. 4, 1901
Johanna Rolf	Jan. 4, 1901
Ella Elson Ropes	Jan. 4, 1901
Henry Royal	Jan. 4, 1901
John Ruthsatz	Jan. 4, 1901
Bernard Schindler	Jan. 4, 1901
Johanna Schmidt	Jan. 4, 1901
Sophia Schwenker	Jan. 4, 1901
Anne Mary Seimers	Jan. 4, 1901
John Smith	Jan. 4, 1901
Myra J. Smith	Jan. 4, 1901
Samuel Smith	Jan. 4, 1901
Louise F. Stiffel	Jan. 4, 1901
George Thein	Jan. 4, 1901
Frederick Thompson	Jan. 4, 1901
Regulv Treichler	Jan. 4, 1901

Malcolm Venderhagen	Jan. 4, 1901
Anna Voelker	Jan. 4, 1901
Maria Waldon	Jan. 4, 1901
George Weimann	Jan. 4, 1901
William Wendel	Jan. 4, 1901
Caroline Ahrens	Jan. 5, 1901
Katy Allen	Jan. 5, 1901
William E. Atenone	Jan. 5, 1901
Emma Barney	Jan. 5, 1901
Charles Lee Baumhoff	Jan. 5, 1901
Lucy Bohn	Jan. 5, 1901
Timothy Canty	Jan. 5, 1901
Charles P. Chouteau	Jan. 5, 1901
Margaret Coump	Jan. 5, 1901
Grace Cunninghan	Jan. 5, 1901
William Dinan	Jan. 5, 1901
August Eggers	Jan. 5, 1901
Katherine Feraro	Jan. 5, 1901
Ellen M. Glant	Jan. 5, 1901
William Green	Jan. 5, 1901
Minna Haffner	Jan. 5, 1901
Wilhelimnia Harding	Jan. 5, 1901
Henrietta Hermann	Jan. 5, 1901
Elizabeth Hill	Jan. 5, 1901
Lanro C Hoberg	Jan. 5, 1901
Ida Johnson	Jan. 5, 1901
David Kelly	Jan. 5, 1901
Barbara Knopfle	Jan. 5, 1901
Henry Larson	Jan. 5, 1901
Annie M. Lieuemann	Jan. 5, 1901
Daniel A. McCarthy	Jan. 5, 1901
Anthony Miller	Jan. 5, 1901
Charles Johann Pabst	Jan. 5, 1901
Isaac Preston	Jan. 5, 1901
Julius Rothschild	Jan. 5, 1901
Maria Ann Sack	Jan. 5, 1901
John Shaver	Jan. 5, 1901
Catherine Slezak	Jan. 5, 1901
Frank C. Stewart	Jan. 5, 1901
Josephine Stradel	Jan. 5, 1901
Lorenzo Gasten Wells	Jan. 5, 1901
Annie Whitinore	Jan. 5, 1901
Grace Cervantes	Jan. 6, 1901
John Clark	Jan. 6, 1901
Frederick Clements	Jan. 6, 1901
Jacob Dernand	Jan. 6, 1901

Edna Dickson	Jan. 6, 1901
Sarah Doriocourt	Jan. 6, 1901
Annie Feher	Jan. 6, 1901
Lillie Graham	Jan. 6, 1901
Edward W. Griener	Jan. 6, 1901
Maria Hall	Jan. 6, 1901
Benjamine F. Hudson	Jan. 6, 1901
Richard C Jr Lewis	Jan. 6, 1901
John M. Martin	Jan. 6, 1901
Charles Mc Donald	Jan. 6, 1901
John W. Mc Donald	Jan. 6, 1901
John Doyle Mc Dowell	Jan. 6, 1901
Harry A. Meinhardh	Jan. 6, 1901
Thomas M. Moriarty	Jan. 6, 1901
Anton L. Otten	Jan. 6, 1901
William Parke	Jan. 6, 1901
John Perkins	Jan. 6, 1901
Margaret Redmond	Jan. 6, 1901
George Schneider	Jan. 6, 1901
Henry Schnelkes	Jan. 6, 1901
Bernard G. Seever	Jan. 6, 1901
G. B. Shaw	Jan. 6, 1901
Patrick Shea	Jan. 6, 1901
Mary Shields	Jan. 6, 1901
Sister Anastasia	Jan. 7, 1901
Grace Bauer	Jan. 7, 1901
Minnie Berk	Jan. 7, 1901
Timothy Bryan	Jan. 7, 1901
John Butz	Jan. 7, 1901
G. A. Colesworthy	Jan. 7, 1901
Jennie Conroy	Jan. 7, 1901
Flossie Cooper	Jan. 7, 1901
Louise Doding	Jan. 7, 1901
Barbara Enles	Jan. 7, 1901
Leroy Clarence Ford	Jan. 7, 1901
Joseph Fox	Jan. 7, 1901
Leonard Frame	Jan. 7, 1901
Ferdinand F. Gehring	Jan. 7, 1901
August Hallming	Jan. 7, 1901
Louisa Hauptmann	Jan. 7, 1901
Carl Hogemann	Jan. 7, 1901
Pearl Johnson	Jan. 7, 1901
Henry Keefe	Jan. 7, 1901
J. M. Kelly	Jan. 7, 1901
Edward William Kershaw	Jan. 7, 1901
Henry Koetter	Jan. 7, 1901

Garrat N. Kregar	Jan. 7, 1901
Sarah Lafsan	Jan. 7, 1901
James Lathan	Jan. 7, 1901
Mary Lemkowitz	Jan. 7, 1901
William G. Mahaney	Jan. 7, 1901
Frank Malisszewski	Jan. 7, 1901
Catherine Mc Coy	Jan. 7, 1901
Alexander Mc Mullen	Jan. 7, 1901
Loretta Murphy	Jan. 7, 1901
Peter Oppermann	Jan. 7, 1901
Bessie Parker	Jan. 7, 1901
Anna Ridings	Jan. 7, 1901
John Ritchie	Jan. 7, 1901
Edwin W. Rossiter	Jan. 7, 1901
Mary Francis Sisco	Jan. 7, 1901
Eva Stancell	Jan. 7, 1901
Christian Stern	Jan. 7, 1901
May Stewart	Jan. 7, 1901
Rose Strining	Jan. 7, 1901
Henry Theirauf	Jan. 7, 1901
Edgar White	Jan. 7, 1901
Jennie Williams	Jan. 7, 1901
Ellen Willis	Jan. 7, 1901
Jacob Zimmerman	Jan. 7, 1901
Johanna Backendorf	Jan. 8, 1901
Victor J. Bush	Jan. 8, 1901
Ed Carmody	Jan. 8, 1901
Anna M. Dix	Jan. 8, 1901
Sandy Doaks	Jan. 8, 1901
Elizabeth Glaser	Jan. 8, 1901
William F. Grant	Jan. 8, 1901
Jessie Patterson Hoover	Jan. 8, 1901
Martha King	Jan. 8, 1901
John Larky	Jan. 8, 1901
Henry Lippert	Jan. 8, 1901
William H. Markham	Jan. 8, 1901
Fred Mc Donald	Jan. 8, 1901
Annie Mc Lean	Jan. 8, 1901
Alice Mesly	Jan. 8, 1901
Charles Metz	Jan. 8, 1901
Charles Mullane	Jan. 8, 1901
Joseph Ossendorf	Jan. 8, 1901
Mary Pajaces	Jan. 8, 1901
Herman Pechel	Jan. 8, 1901
Margareth Marie Price	Jan. 8, 1901
Richard Roach	Jan. 8, 1901

Stephen Elmer Ruth	Jan. 8, 1901
Mary Scanlan	Jan. 8, 1901
Frank Schuengel	Jan. 8, 1901
George Stechford	Jan. 8, 1901
Leo Steins	Jan. 8, 1901
Alfred Thompson	Jan. 8, 1901
James Timmis	Jan. 8, 1901
William Veal	Jan. 8, 1901
Nettie Adams	Jan. 9, 1901
Nora Barrett	Jan. 9, 1901
Lena Bernius	Jan. 9, 1901
Sophie Bine	Jan. 9, 1901
Julia Cashman	Jan. 9, 1901
Annie Blanche Conway	Jan. 9, 1901
Charles Doat	Jan. 9, 1901
Herman Fichtenmeyer	Jan. 9, 1901
John Henry Fleer	Jan. 9, 1901
Edward Otis Goodman	Jan. 9, 1901
Allen Harris	Jan. 9, 1901
George Heine	Jan. 9, 1901
Fredfrick Hettiker	Jan. 9, 1901
Herman Leo Hivbe	Jan. 9, 1901
Celesta Augusta Houser	Jan. 9, 1901
James P. Kelly	Jan. 9, 1901
Laura Koehler	Jan. 9, 1901
Catherina Kramer	Jan. 9, 1901
Joseph Mc Grath	Jan. 9, 1901
Hattie W. Middleton	Jan. 9, 1901
Patrick O'Flaherty	Jan. 9, 1901
John William Pamflne	Jan. 9, 1901
Peter Rembor	Jan. 9, 1901
Adolph Rohnbach	Jan. 9, 1901
Mary Shines	Jan. 9, 1901
Margaret Tivy	Jan. 9, 1901
William Weaver	Jan. 9, 1901
Charles L. Wefferling	Jan. 9, 1901
Susanna Welsh	Jan. 9, 1901
Peter Andres	Jan. 10, 1901
Marie Annie Baumle	Jan. 10, 1901
Albert Baxter	Jan. 10, 1901
William Brandhorst	Jan. 10, 1901
J. L. Dickinson	Jan. 10, 1901
Elick Frodenburgh	Jan. 10, 1901
John Henry Harfor	Jan. 10, 1901
Charlotte Herbers	Jan. 10, 1901
Williams Higgs	Jan. 10, 1901

William Johnson	Jan. 10, 1901
Mary Montroy	Jan. 10, 1901
Flora Neiman	Jan. 10, 1901
Henry Nelle	Jan. 10, 1901
Christ Peterson	Jan. 10, 1901
Augustus M. Pococke	Jan. 10, 1901
Ida Rinimeline	Jan. 10, 1901
William Ruler	Jan. 10, 1901
Sarah Ellen Sanguinet	Jan. 10, 1901
Robert Schnedding	Jan. 10, 1901
H E. Sharp	Jan. 10, 1901
Frank Steeg	Jan. 10, 1901
James Stills	Jan. 10, 1901
Elizabeth Alice Twist	Jan. 10, 1901
John C Wagner	Jan. 10, 1901
Sylvester White	Jan. 10, 1901
Roberta Bwesing	Jan. 11, 1901
Barbara Deugler	Jan. 11, 1901
Mary Ebert	Jan. 11, 1901
August H. Elz	Jan. 11, 1901
Marguard Forster	Jan. 11, 1901
Nettie Galloway	Jan. 11, 1901
Louis M. Hellmann	Jan. 11, 1901
Clara Koers	Jan. 11, 1901
Louis Meyer	Jan. 11, 1901
Frank Joseph Navo	Jan. 11, 1901
Herman Praedicon	Jan. 11 1891
Mary Jane Sanders	Jan. 11, 1901
Mary Schemerhores	Jan. 11, 1901
Louis A. Shepard	Jan. 11, 1901
Martha Hester Von Clossman	Jan. 11, 1901
Louise C. Wagelein	Jan. 11, 1901
William Henry Watson	Jan. 11, 1901
Barbara Weber	Jan. 11, 1901
Mary Whelan	Jan. 11, 1901
John Wiedner	Jan. 11, 1901
Pauline Berger	Jan. 12, 1901
Louis Breggeman	Jan. 12, 1901
Margaret Clancy	Jan. 12, 1901
Angelina Desoto	Jan. 12, 1901
William Deyhle	Jan. 12, 1901
Joseph Doyle	Jan. 12, 1901
Catherine Engelhardt	Jan. 12, 1901
John G. Fennessy	Jan. 12, 1901
John Garvey	Jan. 12, 1901
Lewis Gnash	Jan. 12, 1901

Max Ernest Grams	Jan. 12, 1901
Emma Green	Jan. 12, 1901
John Grnen	Jan. 12, 1901
Ella Hamilton	Jan. 12, 1901
Peter Heag	Jan. 12, 1901
Robert Hutawa	Jan. 12, 1901
Jacob Isancs	Jan. 12, 1901
Charles Johnson	Jan. 12, 1901
Timothy Keating	Jan. 12, 1901
Philip Kuntz	Jan. 12, 1901
Mabel Leay	Jan. 12, 1901
Alaina Lerche	Jan. 12, 1901
Elizabeth Lingelbach	Jan. 12, 1901
Sadie A. Morris	Jan. 12, 1901
Walter Mumm	Jan. 12, 1901
Louise Murphy	Jan. 12, 1901
George Noonan	Jan. 12, 1901
Wilhelmina Ottensmeyer	Jan. 12, 1901
William Reichmann	Jan. 12, 1901
Alice Robinson	Jan. 12, 1901
James H. Ross	Jan. 12, 1901
Charles F. Stefel	Jan. 12, 1901
Dovil Sutton	Jan. 12, 1901
Peter C Thomas	Jan. 12, 1901
Josephine Turner	Jan. 12, 1901
John Van Cluf	Jan. 12, 1901
Charles Vermeersch	Jan. 12, 1901
Adelaide Vetter	Jan. 12, 1901
Gerhard Wallenick	Jan. 12, 1901
Fannie Wedler	Jan. 12, 1901
Adelia Mary White	Jan. 12, 1901
Lawson White	Jan. 12, 1901
Cora H. Williams	Jan. 12, 1901
Sarah E. Wilson	Jan. 12, 1901
Margaret Albrecht	Jan. 13, 1901
Marvin Allan	Jan. 13, 1901
Hermina Bechtlen	Jan. 13, 1901
Anastasia Bold	Jan. 13, 1901
Frederick William Brann	Jan. 13, 1901
Emma Coddey	Jan. 13, 1901
Howard M. Dinsmore	Jan. 13, 1901
Theresa Goddell	Jan. 13, 1901
Lyndon H. Keogh	Jan. 13, 1901
Infant King	Jan. 13, 1901
Eleanor Kolafa	Jan. 13, 1901
Stephen Lee	Jan. 13, 1901

Jacob Leiendecker	Jan. 13, 1901
Robert Miller	Jan. 13, 1901
Estella Naun	Jan. 13, 1901
Bridget Neville	Jan. 13, 1901
Mamie O'brien	Jan. 13, 1901
Ellen Reiley	Jan. 13, 1901
Rena Rush	Jan. 13, 1901
Lena Sartori	Jan. 13, 1901
Christopher Schmetzer	Jan. 13, 1901
Bell M. Stephens	Jan. 13, 1901
Nannie Theresa Taake	Jan. 13, 1901
Garret M. Vallandingham	Jan. 13, 1901
Florence Wedle	Jan. 13, 1901
Isabel H. Wilson	Jan. 13, 1901
Robert L. Baldanf	Jan. 14, 1901
James Balsamo	Jan. 14, 1901
Minnie Bledsoe	Jan. 14, 1901
Gustav Bohres	Jan. 14, 1901
Louisa Bremenkamp	Jan. 14, 1901
John Capestro	Jan. 14, 1901
Christ Cardnall	Jan. 14, 1901
Lizzie Carney	Jan. 14, 1901
Cecil C Cole	Jan. 14, 1901
Elizabeth Davis	Jan. 14, 1901
Charles E. Degge	Jan. 14, 1901
Ellen Dumer	Jan. 14, 1901
Henry Elm	Jan. 14, 1901
Michael Fitzgerald	Jan. 14, 1901
Thomas French	Jan. 14, 1901
James Goodwin	Jan. 14, 1901
Anna Mary Gores	Jan. 14, 1901
Frederick Gorsmann	Jan. 14, 1901
Louisa Grossheider	Jan. 14, 1901
Elizabeth Haenni	Jan. 14, 1901
Mary Hanson	Jan. 14, 1901
Catherine Hennessy	Jan. 14, 1901
Henry Highway	Jan. 14, 1901
Clemens Hofmann	Jan. 14, 1901
Permelia Hogue	Jan. 14, 1901
Dennis Hurley	Jan. 14, 1901
Edward Johannson	Jan. 14, 1901
Henry Kemper	Jan. 14, 1901
Maria Gertrude Lahm	Jan. 14, 1901
John George Lay	Jan. 14, 1901
Mary Loftus	Jan. 14, 1901
John Quirk	Jan. 14, 1901

John F. Ransser	Jan. 14, 1901
Henry Rathers	Jan. 14, 1901
Mary E. Ritter	Jan. 14, 1901
Mary Jane Rundell	Jan. 14, 1901
Bridget Russell	Jan. 14, 1901
Frank J. Russell	Jan. 14, 1901
Joseph Salemrnig	Jan. 14, 1901
Agatha Schafferle	Jan. 14, 1901
Clarence A. Sinclair, Jr.	Jan. 14, 1901
John Skelly	Jan. 14, 1901
George Spinner	Jan. 14, 1901
Christiana Steiniuges	Jan. 14, 1901
Katie Wilkins	Jan. 14, 1901
Johanna Zimmermann	Jan. 14, 1901
Frederick Aschmore	Jan. 15, 1901
Florence Aubuchon	Jan. 15, 1901
Alfred G. Bauer	Jan. 15, 1901
William Bell	Jan. 15, 1901
Wilhelminia F. Bernard	Jan. 15, 1901
Mary Brannigan	Jan. 15, 1901
William Bruder	Jan. 15, 1901
John Dekock	Jan. 15, 1901
Augusta Diebal	Jan. 15, 1901
Paul Farrington	Jan. 15, 1901
Kirk D. Gordner	Jan. 15, 1901
Jacob Hager	Jan. 15, 1901
Louis Harney	Jan. 15, 1901
Elizabeth Hofstetter	Jan. 15, 1901
Julia C Howse	Jan. 15, 1901
W. J. Hutchison	Jan. 15, 1901
Ernst Johnson	Jan. 15, 1901
John Kelly	Jan. 15, 1901
Edward H. Kempfer	Jan. 15, 1901
Bridget Kennedy	Jan. 15, 1901
Paul Herman Keppel	Jan. 15, 1901
Catherine Lohbeck	Jan. 15, 1901
Margaret Mc Mahan	Jan. 15, 1901
Louis Grant Meyers	Jan. 15, 1901
Thomas Moore	Jan. 15, 1901
Mary Sachse	Jan. 15, 1901
Leopold Samuels	Jan. 15, 1901
Mary Schneined	Jan. 15, 1901
Annie Schultz	Jan. 15, 1901
Mary Sherlock	Jan. 15, 1901
D. V. Stebins	Jan. 15, 1901
James Michael Vaughn	Jan. 15, 1901

Ann Walsh	Jan. 15, 1901
Joseph Whitaker	Jan. 15, 1901
Dok Kee Wong	Jan. 15, 1901
Arthur Baldwin	Jan. 16, 1901
Mary Bentrof	Jan. 16, 1901
Edmund Casey	Jan. 16, 1901
Joseph Dugruen	Jan. 16, 1901
Oliver J. Flachs	Jan. 16, 1901
Henry Flier	Jan. 16, 1901
Joseph Haefner	Jan. 16, 1901
Annie Jones	Jan. 16, 1901
Margaretha Kimm	Jan. 16, 1901
John Klemberg	Jan. 16, 1901
Joseph Knopp	Jan. 16, 1901
August Kretschmann	Jan. 16, 1901
John W. Loosmore	Jan. 16, 1901
Susie Miller	Jan. 16, 1901
William Muegge	Jan. 16, 1901
Bridget Mullaney	Jan. 16, 1901
Paul Morris O'bryan	Jan. 16, 1901
Anna Marie Obermeyer	Jan. 16, 1901
John R. Pitts	Jan. 16, 1901
Moss Schnermann	Jan. 16, 1901
Robert Sheldon	Jan. 16, 1901
Agnas Sikorski	Jan. 16, 1901
George Thomas	Jan. 16, 1901
Raymond Van Cleef	Jan. 16, 1901
Isaac Walker	Jan. 16, 1901
Leslie William Weston	Jan. 16, 1901
William Anheuser	Jan. 17, 1901
Dora Bradhack	Jan. 17, 1901
Patrick Derley	Jan. 17, 1901
Francisca Dumbach	Jan. 17, 1901
Virginia Hatfield	Jan. 17, 1901
John Hertrich	Jan. 17, 1901
Bernard Hitcamp	Jan. 17, 1901
Henry Hubeli	Jan. 17, 1901
Christina Ingrund	Jan. 17, 1901
Veronicka Kamadulski	Jan. 17, 1901
Frederick Klinger	Jan. 17, 1901
Minnie Kzaemer	Jan. 17, 1901
Mary Miller	Jan. 17, 1901
Emma Mohrman	Jan. 17, 1901
Elizabeth Norton	Jan. 17, 1901
Sidney Nye	Jan. 17, 1901
Clara Peterson	Jan. 17, 1901

Eva A. Ritzdorf	Jan. 17, 1901
George A. Ruggles	Jan. 17, 1901
Oliver Slayton	Jan. 17, 1901
William Tolley	Jan. 17, 1901
Anna C Vable	Jan. 17, 1901
Albertina Vetter	Jan. 17, 1901
John White	Jan. 17, 1901
Mary J. Wyatt	Jan. 17, 1901
Andrew Bell	Jan. 18, 1901
John H. Borgess	Jan. 18, 1901
Anna Brachtendorf	Jan. 18, 1901
Conrad Brady	Jan. 18, 1901
Jodocus Brockleman	Jan. 18, 1901
Elizabeth Clever	Jan. 18, 1901
Ervin A. Drier	Jan. 18, 1901
Edward Dunkmann	Jan. 18, 1901
Peter Gallagher	Jan. 18, 1901
John T. Havener	Jan. 18, 1901
Louis Hoeber	Jan. 18, 1901
Mary Jane Lake	Jan. 18, 1901
Mary B. Machles	Jan. 18, 1901
Bridget Maloney	Jan. 18, 1901
John Mc Carthy	Jan. 18, 1901
Charles B. Murphy	Jan. 18, 1901
Genevieave Murray	Jan. 18, 1901
Anthony Niehaus	Jan. 18, 1901
Johnnie Ratay	Jan. 18, 1901
Margaret Ryan	Jan. 18, 1901
August Seibel	Jan. 18, 1901
Elizabeth Simon	Jan. 18, 1901
Kirk Smith	Jan. 18, 1901
Maria D. Snell	Jan. 18, 1901
Martin Stamps	Jan. 18, 1901
Harry R. Trefny	Jan. 18, 1901
Adolph Wunsch	Jan. 18, 1901
Valentine Abel	Jan. 19, 1901
Mabel Bessa	Jan. 19, 1901
Bert Boyer	Jan. 19, 1901
Mabel Brewer	Jan. 19, 1901
William H. Davies	Jan. 19, 1901
Thomas H. Fulkerson	Jan. 19, 1901
Julia Glanzman	Jan. 19, 1901
Margaret Green	Jan. 19, 1901
Theresa Hertel	Jan. 19, 1901
Annie Imhof	Jan. 19, 1901
Theophil Jeutter	Jan. 19, 1901

Lee Johnson	Jan. 19, 1901
Edward Lee	Jan. 19, 1901
Theophile Maliszewski	Jan. 19, 1901
Mary McGlynn	Jan. 19, 1901
Mary McLaughlin	Jan. 19, 1901
Ernest Meyer	Jan. 19, 1901
Frank Mouinges	Jan. 19, 1901
Calvin O. Nessler	Jan. 19, 1901
Sarah Norton	Jan. 19, 1901
Angela Pellegrinl	Jan. 19, 1901
Joseph Perrine	Jan. 19, 1901
Frank Schroeder	Jan. 19, 1901
Robert Strange	Jan. 19, 1901
John Jacob Strubel	Jan. 19, 1901
John Sullivan	Jan. 19, 1901
John Teichmann	Jan. 19, 1901
Slethere J. Turner	Jan. 19, 1901
Katherine Wiethuchter	Jan. 19, 1901
Benjamin Wilson	Jan. 19, 1901
Catherine Beitze	Jan. 20, 1901
Peter Benda	Jan. 20, 1901
Hector Camerin	Jan. 20, 1901
Laura M. Cooke	Jan. 20, 1901
Sarah Creviston	Jan. 20 1892
Infs/o Arthur Davis	Jan. 20, 1901
Travis Davis	Jan. 20, 1901
Anna L. Eberhard	Jan. 20, 1901
Pat Ferrigan	Jan. 20, 1901
William Gallagher	Jan. 20, 1901
Gladys Hamilton	Jan. 20, 1901
Mary Harkelrude	Jan. 20, 1901
William Herkenhoff	Jan. 20, 1901
Patrick Kelly	Jan. 20, 1901
Maud Marie Klee	Jan. 20, 1901
Maggie Koch	Jan. 20, 1901
John Martini	Jan. 20, 1901
Mary May	Jan. 20, 1901
John Mc Hugh	Jan. 20, 1901
Catherine Mc Nealey	Jan. 20, 1901
Arthur Muller	Jan. 20, 1901
Alexander Niehoff	Jan. 20, 1901
John Quail	Jan. 20, 1901
Pasquales Rebori	Jan. 20, 1901
Hosateo B. Rogerson	Jan. 20, 1901
Celia Elizabeth Schrouder	Jan. 20, 1901
Anna Viola Sorg	Jan. 20, 1901

Matilda Taylor	Jan. 20, 1901
Arthur Urban	Jan. 20, 1901
Louisa Wheeler	Jan. 20, 1901
George Wiley	Jan. 20, 1901
Maxiumilian Birkenmieier	Jan. 21, 1901
George Henry Bruemner	Jan. 21, 1901
Henry Collins	Jan. 21, 1901
Agnes Daly	Jan. 21, 1901
Wesley Gilespie	Jan. 21, 1901
Clara Gorden	Jan. 21, 1901
Henry Hayes	Jan. 21, 1901
Cora Huff	Jan. 21, 1901
Henry John Kamp	Jan. 21, 1901
Isabel Kane	Jan. 21, 1901
Herman Kelhing	Jan. 21, 1901
John Kelly	Jan. 21, 1901
Fritz Koch	Jan. 21, 1901
Harriett Lecompe	Jan. 21, 1901
Robert Monroe	Jan. 21, 1901
William E. Philips	Jan. 21, 1901
Henry William Richwein	Jan. 21, 1901
Albert Schoenfeld	Jan. 21, 1901
Anna M. Spengemann	Jan. 21, 1901
John Washington	Jan. 21, 1901
Annie White	Jan. 21, 1901
Berhardina Baumgartner	Jan. 22, 1901
George Burke	Jan. 22, 1901
Henry Doering	Jan. 22, 1901
Dolly Evans	Jan. 22, 1901
Jobst H. Fuenborn	Jan. 22, 1901
Wilhelmina Ganges	Jan. 22, 1901
Agnes Halbruegger	Jan. 22, 1901
George Hamenstead	Jan. 22, 1901
Magdelena Jaroshik	Jan. 22, 1901
Margaret Kelly	Jan. 22, 1901
Kate Matteson	Jan. 22, 1901
Howard P. Mc Cosland	Jan. 22, 1901
Catherine Nolting	Jan. 22, 1901
Henner Oelrich	Jan. 22, 1901
Bridget Oschae	Jan. 22, 1901
Edward Parrat	Jan. 22, 1901
Jane Mobley Ridgeway	Jan. 22, 1901
Mathilda Schaefer	Jan. 22, 1901
Cresentia Sister Cresentia	Jan. 22, 1901
Ida Suess	Jan. 22, 1901
Lena Weikart	Jan. 22, 1901

Sisa Young	Jan. 22, 1901
Frank Batzinski	Jan. 23, 1901
Ann Bell	Jan. 23, 1901
Andrew Chilton	Jan. 23, 1901
Ellen Dillon	Jan. 23, 1901
Jennie Dixon	Jan. 23, 1901
Walthen Ehrhardt	Jan. 23, 1901
Frank Fuchs	Jan. 23, 1901
Aaron Green	Jan. 23, 1901
Fredk W. Gussoskey	Jan. 23, 1901
Molly Hall	Jan. 23, 1901
Babette Hellman	Jan. 23, 1901
Victon'a Amelia Hellrwig	Jan. 23, 1901
Clara Hilgemann	Jan. 23, 1901
Elizabeth Hites	Jan. 23, 1901
George Hoell	Jan. 23, 1901
William Johnson	Jan. 23, 1901
George L. Knipfenberger	Jan. 23, 1901
William Milward	Jan. 23, 1901
Catherine Okineke	Jan. 23, 1901
C. J. Payne	Jan. 23, 1901
Rudolph Pfeifer	Jan. 23, 1901
Earl P. Sanders	Jan. 23, 1901
Mary Scharisdick	Jan. 23, 1901
Barbara Schiman	Jan. 23, 1901
Veronica Shymkewich	Jan. 23, 1901
William Taylor	Jan. 23, 1901
Frank Timeluan	Jan. 23, 1901
Emily Weird	Jan. 23, 1901
Clarence Young	Jan. 23, 1901
John Young	Jan. 23, 1901
James F. Aglar	Jan. 24, 1901
John W. Andrews	Jan. 24, 1901
Helen Anson	Jan. 24, 1901
Michael Berger	Jan. 24 1888
Herman Boel	Jan. 24, 1901
Frank Broermann	Jan. 24, 1901
John J. Ciunmiskey	Jan. 24, 1901
August Doering	Jan. 24, 1901
John Finn	Jan. 24, 1901
William Gilmortin	Jan. 24, 1901
Leonardo Giovannini	Jan. 24, 1901
Luella Green	Jan. 24, 1901
Charles Heckler	Jan. 24, 1901
Cornelius Hester	Jan. 24, 1901
Lee Hunt	Jan. 24, 1901

Joseph Kaspar	Jan. 24, 1901
Louise Lemens	Jan. 24, 1901
Josephine Lieberman	Jan. 24, 1901
Mary Mason	Jan. 24, 1901
Nannie Cora Myerson	Jan. 24, 1901
Margaret Scott	Jan. 24, 1901
Catherine Stansbury	Jan. 24, 1901
William Storbeck	Jan. 24, 1901
Elizabeth Thomas	Jan. 24, 1901
J. F. Williams	Jan. 24, 1901
Martin Boettscher	Jan. 25, 1901
D. G. Borrick	Jan. 25, 1901
Joseph Cadenazzi	Jan. 25, 1901
John P. Cooper	Jan. 25, 1901
Victor E. Dewey	Jan. 25, 1901
Fred Droege	Jan. 25, 1901
Frank Fechtel	Jan. 25, 1901
James Gallagher	Jan. 25, 1901
Elias Gzami	Jan. 25, 1901
Mary Heil	Jan. 25, 1901
Lucy Horton	Jan. 25, 1901
Malinda Howard	Jan. 25, 1901
Inf/o Joseph Kattler	Jan. 25, 1901
James Maher	Jan. 25, 1901
Frank Niederschmidt	Jan. 25, 1901
Frank Ortemann	Jan. 25, 1901
Margaret Phelan	Jan. 25, 1901
Arthur Popp	Jan. 25, 1901
Chester Raymond	Jan. 25, 1901
Meilech Saffier	Jan. 25, 1901
Arthur Schalarmann	Jan. 25, 1901
Julius Mersman Schwarz	Jan. 25, 1901
Martha L. Smith	Jan. 25, 1901
Joseph Taylor	Jan. 25, 1901
Isabelle Valstin	Jan. 25, 1901
Mary Volling	Jan. 25, 1901
Fannie Walker	Jan. 25, 1901
Louis Weise	Jan. 25, 1901
Amelia Prudence Wilkinson	Jan. 25, 1901
T. H. Ball	Jan. 26, 1901
Archie Brockhan	Jan. 26, 1901
Martha Chappell	Jan. 26, 1901
Mary Condow	Jan. 26, 1901
Jacob Endres	Jan. 26, 1901
Edward Martin Flachmeier	Jan. 26, 1901
James Heffernan	Jan. 26, 1901

Kate Heinsius	Jan. 26, 1901
Charles Henry	Jan. 26, 1901
Marie Cynthia Hillman	Jan. 26, 1901
Laura Keller	Jan. 26, 1901
Martin Kennelly	Jan. 26, 1901
Lucy Lipcomb	Jan. 26, 1901
Helen Mole	Jan. 26, 1901
Mary Newby	Jan. 26, 1901
Elmer J. O'Brien	Jan. 26, 1901
Amanda Rhoads	Jan. 26, 1901
Barbara Rittenbach	Jan. 26, 1901
Herman W. Schwaebe	Jan. 26 1893
Elizabeth Westlake	Jan. 26, 1901
Bettie Williams	Jan. 26, 1901
Anton Zatorski	Jan. 26, 1901
George Blake	Jan. 27, 1901
Thomas Carter	Jan. 27, 1901
Mary Eagan	Jan. 27, 1901
Louis Sr Faszholz	Jan. 27, 1901
Charles Garret	Jan. 27, 1901
Cecelia Gleitz	Jan. 27, 1901
Maria Hatcher	Jan. 27, 1901
William Hurley	Jan. 27, 1901
Thomas Knidischek	Jan. 27, 1901
August J. Lager	Jan. 27, 1901
James Lankford	Jan. 27, 1901
Patrick Lowey	Jan. 27, 1901
Peter Lyons	Jan. 27, 1901
Michael McElroy	Jan. 27, 1901
Mary M. Ohler	Jan. 27, 1901
Mabel C Palmer	Jan. 27, 1901
Edward Regan	Jan. 27, 1901
Earl Seidel	Jan. 27, 1901
Abel Williams	Jan. 27, 1901
Harriet Woodey	Jan. 27, 1901
Catherine Agnew	Jan. 28, 1901
Elizabeth R. Andrae	Jan. 28, 1901
Alfred H. Bruer	Jan. 28 1892
Maurice Callahan	Jan. 28, 1901
Mary A. Carten	Jan. 28, 1901
Louis Chechenovsky	Jan. 28, 1901
Victoria Collins	Jan. 28, 1901
John Costly	Jan. 28, 1901
Samuel L. Cramer	Jan. 28, 1901
Tomesina Dblase	Jan. 28, 1901
Ruby Emory	Jan. 28, 1901

George Esili	Jan. 28, 1901
Martz Fostler	Jan. 28, 1901
Annie Irene Gallagher	Jan. 28, 1901
Mary Gardner	Jan. 28, 1901
Orlando F. Guthrie	Jan. 28, 1901
Lucy Haynes	Jan. 28, 1901
Blanche Heinecke	Jan. 28, 1901
John J. Hennesey	Jan. 28, 1901
William Hoppel	Jan. 28, 1901
Kate Ischer	Jan. 28, 1901
Julia Grace Kissler	Jan. 28, 1901
Viola Anna Knott	Jan. 28, 1901
Julius Edward Koch	Jan. 28, 1901
Adam G. Kohl	Jan. 28, 1901
Mattie Lewis	Jan. 28, 1901
Philip Martin	Jan. 28, 1901
Joseph H. Otten	Jan. 28, 1901
Julius A. Schneider	Jan. 28, 1901
Elizabeth M. Schutten	Jan. 28, 1901
Vincent Schwartz	Jan. 28, 1901
E. M. Smurr	Jan. 28, 1901
Henry Steinmeyer	Jan. 28, 1901
Dotti Swain	Jan. 28, 1901
Eva Swift	Jan. 28, 1901
Henry Swope	Jan. 28, 1901
John Tullard	Jan. 28, 1901
John Ulrich	Jan. 28, 1901
Stephen Volz	Jan. 28, 1901
Alexander Williamson	Jan. 28, 1901
John Ambruster	Jan. 29, 1901
William H. Anemow	Jan. 29, 1901
John Born	Jan. 29, 1901
Marion Brown	Jan. 29, 1901
Russell Powell Brown	Jan. 29, 1901
W C Butterfield	Jan. 29, 1901
Henry Markhan Cooke	Jan. 29, 1901
Charles Dahlberg	Jan. 29, 1901
Mary Donnelly	Jan. 29, 1901
Katie Flaherty	Jan. 29, 1901
Catherine Green	Jan. 29, 1901
John Heilman	Jan. 29, 1901
Harry Hogan	Jan. 29, 1901
Samuel Hults	Jan. 29, 1901
Oliver Karl	Jan. 29, 1901
Thelma Keister	Jan. 29, 1901
Minnie Lucks	Jan. 29, 1901

Conrad Molkenbur	Jan. 29, 1901
Kate Noble	Jan. 29, 1901
Michael O'malley	Jan. 29, 1901
Mary Otto	Jan. 29, 1901
David Parkes	Jan. 29, 1901
Frank Patts	Jan. 29, 1901
Minnie Porch	Jan. 29, 1901
John Purnhagen	Jan. 29, 1901
Elsa Rambach	Jan. 29, 1901
John Reoescomb, Jr.	Jan. 29, 1901
Bella Ryan	Jan. 29, 1901
John Schaefer	Jan. 29, 1901
William M. Senter	Jan. 29, 1901
Lydia Truetzel	Jan. 29, 1901
Wilhelminia Mary Umgelter	Jan. 29, 1901
Benjamin Wilkes	Jan. 29, 1901
Mary Armbruster	Jan. 30, 1901
Cora D. Bratton	Jan. 30, 1901
Kate Connors	Jan. 30, 1901
Esther Cowlishaw	Jan. 30, 1901
Nicholas Ford	Jan. 30, 1901
Arthur Goodlaw	Jan. 30, 1901
Margaret Gorg	Jan. 30, 1901
David Jaffe	Jan. 30, 1901
Lena Jands	Jan. 30, 1901
Frederick Koberg	Jan. 30, 1901
Mary E. Punshon	Jan. 30, 1901
Ernst A. Rueger	Jan. 30, 1901
Frank Schejbal	Jan. 30, 1901
Franziska Schmitz	Jan. 30, 1901
Charles B. Schonebeck	Jan. 30, 1901
William Smith	Jan. 30, 1901
Ignatz Stack	Jan. 30, 1901
Annie Staneck	Jan. 30, 1901
Samuel Steck	Jan. 30, 1901
Clara Stublmeyer	Jan. 30, 1901
Carolina Weinreich	Jan. 30, 1901
John Weiter	Jan. 30, 1901
Gertrude White	Jan. 30, 1901
Frank Worth	Jan. 30, 1901
Jacob Yaeger	Jan. 30, 1901
August Adams	Jan. 31, 1901
Virginia Brittain	Jan. 31, 1901
Frank Brynda	Jan. 31, 1901
Harriet A. Campbell	Jan. 31, 1901
Harold Crump	Jan. 31, 1901

Timothy Driscoll	Jan. 31, 1901
Adam Eckert	Jan. 31, 1901
Lilly Hattie Eckert	Jan. 31, 1901
John Fleming	Jan. 31, 1901
Lucina Garrison	Jan. 31, 1901
Lizetta Graff	Jan. 31, 1901
Harry Hamilton	Jan. 31, 1901
Jessie E. Hooffer	Jan. 31, 1901
Raymond Johnson	Jan. 31, 1901
Fulton H. Johnston	Jan. 31, 1901
John Kelly	Jan. 31, 1901
Emannel Kettener	Jan. 31, 1901
Anton Lipps	Jan. 31, 1901
Lawrence Mc Coy	Jan. 31, 1901
Michael Mc Murray	Jan. 31, 1901
Bernhard Menke	Jan. 31, 1901
Ed Mesler	Jan. 31, 1901
Bertha Minder	Jan. 31, 1901
Charles Hy Schiorner	Jan. 31, 1901
Sibylls Schoppe	Jan. 31, 1901
Thomas Smith	Jan. 31, 1901
Frederick William Zachritz	Jan. 31, 1901

Linn County, Missouri, Individuals on the Veterans Census 1890.

John W. Abel, Richard S. Abell, Druffield Adam, Riley Adams, William Adams, James R. Albert, Nathaniel Allen, Albert A. Altman, Daniel Ambs, Henry W. Angus, James A. Arbathnaty, Horacio N. Armstrong, Theoffilson Atterbury, John F. Aullman, Jeremiah Austin, Jeremiah Austin, John N. Austin, Russell Austin, Abraham Bachelor, Silas H. Bagley, William Bagley, Andrew J. Bailey, Harrison Bailey, Jacob Bailey, Lewis H. Bailey, David Baker, George Baker, James Baker, John Baker, Joseph Baker, Robert J. Baker, Edward S. Baldwin, George W. Ball, William Ballow, Joseph G. Baning, John Barber, Daniel W. Barclay, Henry C. Bargar, Jacob G. Bargar, George P. Bassett, William S. Baughman, Ceyphus J. Bean, Anna C. Beaver, F. M. Beers, James H. Beller, Daniel R. Bemer, Charles D. Bennett, Tho. Bennett, John W. Blunt, C. B. Boaz, Henry Bollman, Benjamin F. Bond, Jessie D. Bond, Van Buren Bowers, John C. Boyle, Davis M. Boyles, David C. Brakey, David C. Brakey, John B. Brand, Martin M. Bratner, Lafayette W. Breanel, Carlos M. Brott, Chas. E. Brott, Edwin Brott, Eliha C. Brott, William J. Brower, Duncan Brown, George Brown, Washington Brown, Washington Brown, Zachariah Brown, James Brownlee, Quincy R. Bruce, Vincent C. Bruce, Ephram Bryan, Cornelius Buckley, Jesse Buckman, D. Burch, Hugo Burk, Thomas B. Burk, John Burns, Thomas Burt, Charles O. Bushnell, John P. Butterfield, John P. Butterfield, Deloss H. Cadey, Daniel M. Carey, Jacob C. Carriker, James M. Carroll, Caleb C. Carter,

Luke L. Carter, William H. Carter, Joshua M. Cash, Andrew Cassity, John W. Cassity, Henry B. Chandler, Rice W. Chapman, Stephen W. Chapman, Ambrose S. Christy, Harlow C. Clark, Hiram H. Clark, William D. Clark, Elias Cleveland, William H. Clifton, Joseph Cline, William Comer, William H. Cook, Daniel W. Cooley, Jerrie Cooper, James Cortkins, John A. Couch, Joseph M. Couch, George L. Coulson, William W. Coulson, Thomas Crampton, Thomas Sr. Crampton, Samuel B. Crandall, Watson E. Crandall, Watson E. Crandall, William E. Crane, William E. Crane, Charles P. Craven, David R. Crecelius, Richard W. Crump, William G. Cuberly, Alonzo J. Cumming, Benjamin Cunningham, Isaac Cunningham, John S. Curtlieb, Clinton T. Cutler, William E. Cutler, Gerard A. Dangherty, James Darling, Simeon Darling, J. C. Davis, J. S. Davis, Jacob Davis, Jacob Davis, Joseph H. Davis, William R. Davis, Wm. Davis, James H. Day, Ezra Dean, Daniel D. Decker, Tobias Dennett, John Dennis, Wm. A. Determan, Charles L. Devine, Nelson Dickinson, Libbus Dillman, John F. Doan, Thomas E. Doan, Vincent Green Dodge, Edward F. Dougen, Warner O. Dougherty, I. W. Dow, Robert W. Dow, Jay Drake, Jay Drake, Hiram Drury, Joseph Eads, Joseph Eads, John Easley, John Easley, Thornton Easley, Burl Edington, Burl Edington, Charles Ellis, James Fagan, Richard J. Fanin, Joseph M. Farmer, Harrison Fasher, John Fasher, Hugh W. Faulkner, Clinton W. Fenton, William H. Fenton, Thomas M. Fergeson, Thomas M. Fergeson, Cummins G. Fields, Peter Foster, Samuel H. Foster, Frank Franklin, William J. Furbey, Henry Gaines, B. F. Gallitan, Johnson C. Gardner, Obadiah B. Gardner, John Garswich, Thomas J. Gillham, Thomas Gillispie, James M. Gilson, D. C. Godfry, James W. Gooch, David Gordon, John H. Gordon, James B. Gray, James B. Gray, Charles Green, William Green, Albert Grider, S. Grier, Jacob Gross, John P. Grossharth, George Gucker, George Gucker, Richard M. Hair, Riley S. Hall, Charles Hallett, George W. Hammond, William Hanson, Thomas B.L. Hardin, Jasper N. Hardy, John Hardy, John P. Harker, Alfred Hatfield, William H. Hatfield, Edward A. Hawkins, James M. Hawkins, Henry W. Haws, John T. Hayes, Fredrick M. Haymaker, George H. Hazelrigg, William R. Hedges, John Henning, John Henning, Robert T. Henry, William Henry, William Hilbrand, William Hinkle, William H. Hinton, Cornelius Honeycut, Enoch Hooker, Jermiah Hooker, Wm. H. Hortin, Perry Hoskins, George R. Hover, Nathaniel Howard, John M. Howe, Lorenzo Howe, Dwight P. Hubbard, Dwight P. Hubbard, Hart Hubbard, Rebeca J. Hulten, Charles H. Humphrey, John W. Hunt, Alfred M. Hunter, Levi Huston, Charles Jacobs, Austin R. Jenkins, Henry Jenkins, J. B. Johnson, John Johnson, S. McNeal Johnson, William Johnson, Wm. N. Johnson, Elijah A. Jones, Hanly Jones, John T. Jones, L. C. Jones, William Alisa Jones, William H. Jones, William S. Kemp, Samuel Kemptes, Joel B. Ketchem, Beverly Keyes, Hiram Kimbell, Charlie L. King, William Kingsland, Franklin Kinman, George L. Kost, George L. Kost, Charles LaBarr, Abner Lambert, Harry Landen, Cyrus Landhart, Alexander Landon, Elijah Lawson, Martin V. Lawson, Christian

Leffler, Morgan Leonard, Christian Lewis, Fielding Lewis, Fielding Lewis, Fielding Lewis, George F. Lewis, Thomas Lewis, William H. Lewis, John W. Lindsey, Emery Lockwood, Andrew Long, Charles Long, William H. Long, John F. Looh, T. A. Loomis, W. L. Loomis, Nephi Lord, Burr C. Lottridge, Henry Love, James A. Love, Levi W. Lyons, John N. Manning, George Manory, Charles Manuel?, Elisha S. Marain, Frank Marlett, John Marshall, George W. Martin, Josiah V. Martin, Mathew Martin, William C. Mathus, Lawson S. Maulsby, John D. Maupin, William Maynard, James M. McClintock, Daniel McCollum, James R. McCollum, John McCollum, Reuben McCollum, William McConnell, Mathes McCormick, J. W. McFall, William McIntyre, William McKin, Peter McShane, S. G. Merchant, Jacob J. Meyers, Levi Miles, Jeptha S. Miller, Jeptha S. Miller, Lester Miller, James Mills, John F. Mills, P. B. Molloy, Joseph Monroe, Henry O. Moon, Henry H. Moore, Henry H. Moore, Elisha Morely, Abraham Morgan, Rice Morris, Augustus Mowrey, Asher Moxley, Alexander W. Mullins, Andrew Murrance, Benjamin F. Murrance, Isaac H. Murrell, M. Murry, Abram W. Myers, John Myers, George Nagle, James Newman, Benjamin Northcutt, Nicholas Northrup, Charles Nottrott, William O. Sr. Null, John Nutter, Eli R. Overman, Andrew J. Painter, John C. Palmer, William H. Panter, William C. Patrick, Rufus Peck, L. C. Pendleton, Columbus Penn, H. Phillipps, Loyd Phillips, John R. Pickens, Joseph Pixler, N. C. Pomeroy, Frederick W. Powers, Frederick W. Powers, Frederick W. Powers, Silas Powers, William W. Prather, Thomas Pulliam, William Pulliam, Allen W. Purdin, James r. Ramsey, William S. Ramsey, Felix Randall, Josiah M. RRandolph, Wilhaus H. Ready, Wilhaus H. Ready, William S. Reece, Hugh Reed, James Reid, Samuel O. Renshaw, Daniel E. Reynolds, John B. Reynolds, Frank Ricket, Abell Rickett, Charles Rieck, John W. Robbinson, Frederick G. Robinson, Samuel M. Robinson, Lewis H. Rodgers, A. James Rose, George Rose, James K. Rose, James Runyan, Richard Russell, George Rutherford, John Ryan, Willis Salta, John W. Sapington, Nathan D. Sattler, William H. Schener, John G. Schick, J. M. Scott, John B. Scrivener, John G. Seeley, Gideon W. Shane, Merritt Sheldon, Henry Shook, Henry Shook, Henry Shook, Henry Shook, Isaac Shook, James B. Shook, Isaac N. Shore, Hiram M. Shreckhise, Joshua M. Shuts, James Sibert, Charles B. Simpson, Elisha Sims, Michael F. Sims, Lacy Sipple, Joseph E. Slader, Cornelius Slaughter, Joshua Sliver, Dennis Smith, Franklin P. Smith, J. A. Smith, Joseph R. Smith, Martin Smith, William Smith, Silas Snow, Christopher Spiese, Christopher Spiese, John R. Sportsman, Thomas A. Standley, William N. Stanley, William Stein, Hamilton G. Stephens, Wilson T. Stephens, Thomas J. Stephenson, Sam Sterling, Benjamin F. Stone, David C. Stone, G. H. Stone, Hezekiah G. Stone, Robert Stone, Oscar F. Story, Thaddeus J. Struber, Louis Stuckel, Leyman Studevant, Leyman Studevant, John T. Sturges, John Suder, John H. Sugar, Thomas J. Sugar, William B. Summers, Frank A. Tabler, George W. Taylor, George W. Taylor, Ephram P. Teter, David W. Tharp,

Thomas J. Tharp, John F. Thompson, Permenious M. Thompson, James Tomilson, Adam G. Torrance, William T. Towas, Charles W. Tragdon, David Triplett, William Trippeer, Shelton Trumbo, Lee C. Turner, Wilson Turner, Benjamin F. Turpin, Henry Ulrich, Joseph Vance, Christopher D. Veal, Jefferson C. Vincent, William W. Wade, George M. Walsh, George M. Walsh, George M. Walsh, George M. Walsh, Thomas A. Walters, Albert E. Ward, Marcellus E. Ware, Erastus G. Warner, Richard C. Waters, Frank Watkins, Hugh Watson, F. M. Watts, Carlos Weikel, S. Wellman, David Wheeler, James Whismand, Thomas Whitaker, Thomas Whitaker, Hugh White, James E. White, Wm. L. White, S. S. Whitesel, John Wilhaus, Edward W. William, George Williams, Andrew F. Wilson, Frederick Wilson, Hiram Wilson, John Wilson, Johnson A. Wilson, Sheldon Wilson, Sylvania Wilson, John F. Winship, John F. Winship, Thomas Wolf, Warren Wolf, Warren Wolf, Peter M. Woolf, William R. Worth, Ezdail F. Wright, Ezdail F. Wright, Henry B. Wright, James H. Wyatt, James A. Wylie, Francis M. Young, Levis Young, William J. Young, Charles Youngman, Benjamin W. Yount, Silas M. Yount, Stephen G. Yount

Buchanan County, Missouri, 1883 Pensioners List
James M. Stewart: (PO) Agency, (CMTS) inj. r. leg, (FD) Aug. 1881
Mary A. McCray: (PO) Agency, (CMTS) widow 1812, (FD) Jul. 1879
Angeline McGaughey: (PO) Agency, (CMTS) widow, (FD) May 1867
Zclora Crumpacker: (PO) DeKalb, (CMTS) gsw rt. breast & shoulder
Parmelia E. Parnell: (PO) DeKalb, (CMTS) widow
William R. Oliver: (PO) DeKalb, (CMTS) gsw of left hand, (FD) Aug. 1872
Mary Bittick: (PO) Easton, (CMTS) widow
Nelson Tuck: (PO) Easton, (CMTS) disease of eyes
William T. Tuck: (PO) Easton, (CMTS) curv. of spine, par. loss of hearing, & debility
William M. Daniels: (PO) Easton, (CMTS) inj. to right knee
George M. Loomis: (PO) Easton, (CMTS) injury to abdomen
William B. Pelham: (PO) Easton, (CMTS) gsw of rt. thigh & hip
Benjamin F. Boyer: (PO) Easton, (CMTS) wd of left groin, (FD) Feb. 1869
Mary A. Rapp: (PO) Easton, (CMTS) widow & minor child, (FD) Jul. 1877
Elizabeth Hudson: (PO) Frazer, (CMTS) do
Andrew Blair: (PO) Frazer, (CMTS) wd. of left shoulder & head
Charity Lane: (PO) Frazer, (CMTS) dep. mother, (FD) Jul. 1865
Mary A. Workman: (PO) Frazer, (CMTS) widow, (FD) Mar. 1870
Elizabeth Whitson: (PO) Garrettsburg, (CMTS) widow 1812, (FD) Jun. 1880
Isaac Foote: (PO) Halleck, (CMTS) rheu. & dis. of heart, (FD) May 1882
Priscilla Cogdell: (PO) Halleck, (CMTS) widow 1812, (FD) Sep. 1879

Rebecca McDowell: (PO) Platte River, (CMTS) widow 1812, (FD) Feb.1879
Elizabeth Brown: (PO) Rushville, (CMTS) widow
John Pollock: (PO) Rushville, (CMTS) wd. rt. leg
Esther McKinney: (PO) Rushville, (CMTS) dep. mother, (FD) Jul. 1865
Jacob B. Thomas: (PO) Rushville, (CMTS) gsw of l. shoulder & l. leg, (FD) Oct. 1881
Charles C. Crawford: (PO) Saint Joseph, (CMTS) wd. of right hip
Philip Mack: (PO) Saint Joseph, (CMTS) chr. rheu. of back & limbs
Lyman C. Bradley: (PO) Saint Joseph, (CMTS) gsw of right thigh
George K. Donnelly: (PO) Saint Joseph, (CMTS) wd. chest, rt. shldr.,& left side
Richard B. Hemstreet: (PO) Saint Joseph
Waldo A. Stearnes: (PO) Saint Joseph, (CMTS) inj. rt. molar bone
Charles H. House: (PO) Saint Joseph, (CMTS) gsw right leg
Charles R. B. Thomas: (PO) Saint Joseph, (CMTS) wd. of left wrist
Geo. H. Moore: (PO) Saint Joseph, (CMTS) neuralgia
August Aubuchon: (PO) Saint Joseph, (CMTS) gsw of right hand
Thomas Allen: (PO) Saint Joseph, (CMTS) wd. of left side
William Atkinson: (PO) Saint Joseph, (CMTS) gsw rt. hand & left arm
Franklin Butler: (PO) Saint Joseph, (CMTS) gsw rt. shoulder
John Bonham: (PO) Saint Joseph, (CMTS) gsw of left hand
Linzy Butler: (PO) Saint Joseph, (CMTS) chron. diarr
Lucius C. Booth: (PO) Saint Joseph, (CMTS) loss 1st finger rt. hand
William Saare: (PO) Saint Joseph, (CMTS) gsw of forearm
William H. Stratton: (PO) Saint Joseph, (CMTS) loss of rt. arm ab. elbow
Elias Timerson: (PO) Saint Joseph, (CMTS) injury to abdomen
John N. Thomas: (PO) Saint Joseph, (CMTS) amp. rt. arm ab. elbow
Anton Wanger: (PO) Saint Joseph, (CMTS) fracture of 3 ribs
Enoch G. Warhurst: (PO) Saint Joseph, (CMTS) gsw of head
Charles F. Schoeneck: (PO) Saint Joseph, (CMTS) chron. diarr. & debility
Christopher Schreiber: (PO) Saint Joseph, (CMTS) injury to abdomen
Frank Steever: (PO) Saint Joseph, (CMTS) inj. to left ribs
Annie B. Blanton: (PO) Saint Joseph, (CMTS) widow
Ruth Branson: (PO) Saint Joseph, (CMTS) widow
George W. Wilson: (PO) Saint Joseph, (CMTS) chr.rheum
George W. McDaniel: (PO) Saint Joseph, (CMTS) wd. left breast & chest
William Washington: (PO) Saint Joseph, (CMTS) gsw of right knee
Pembroke V. Wise: (PO) Saint Joseph, (CMTS) gsw of right leg
Reuben Williams: (PO) Saint Joseph, (CMTS) disease of eyes
George F. Rose: (PO) Saint Joseph, (CMTS) wd. of left breast
Anna Hamilton: (PO) Saint Joseph, (CMTS) widow
Evaleen Holcomb: (PO) Saint Joseph, (CMTS) widow
Sarah Garner: (PO) Saint Joseph, (CMTS) widow
George T. Newcomb: (PO) Saint Joseph, (CMTS) ulcers of rt. leg
Frederick K. Noyes: (PO) Saint Joseph, (CMTS) injury to abdomen

Charles Roth: (PO) Saint Joseph, (CMTS) frac. of ribs
John D. Ogelsby: (PO) Saint Joseph, (CMTS) gsw of left hand
Elizabeth A. Castle: (PO) Saint Joseph, (CMTS) widow
Sarah Smith: (PO) Saint Joseph, (CMTS) widow
Rosina Sutler: (PO) Saint Joseph, (CMTS) widow
Anna H. Stinsman: (PO) Saint Joseph, (CMTS) widow
Mary Warburton: (PO) Saint Joseph, (CMTS) widow
Genoveza Weipert: (PO) Saint Joseph, (CMTS) widow
Sindrilla Vaughn: (PO) Saint Joseph, (CMTS) widow
Caroline Uhl: (PO) Saint Joseph, (CMTS) widow
Ann Casey: (PO) Saint Joseph, (CMTS) widow
William R. Deakins: (PO) Saint Joseph, (CMTS) gsw l. hand & loss of thumb
Burnham M. Decker: (PO) Saint Joseph, (CMTS) loss of rt. forearm
Frederick G. Doebelin: (PO) Saint Joseph, (CMTS) disease of heart
Peter Dutton: (PO) Saint Joseph, (CMTS) injury to abdomen
Conrad Folche: (PO) Saint Joseph, (CMTS) gsw of rt. shoulder, both thighs & legs
David Frendenthal: (PO) Saint Joseph, (CMTS) injury right leg
Wilhelmina Maria Rodde: (PO) Saint Joseph, (CMTS) widow
Joseph W. Nay: (PO) Saint Joseph, (CMTS) gsw l. thigh & r. leg
Thomas Lee: (PO) Saint Joseph, (CMTS) injury to abdomen
Amos A. McIninch: (PO) Saint Joseph, (CMTS) gsw r. side of face & shldr.
Austin McClurg: (PO) Saint Joseph, (CMTS) gsw r. side
John A. Wheeler: (PO) Saint Joseph, (CMTS) gsw of rt. sh'ld'r & chest
John Young: (PO) Saint Joseph, (CMTS) shell wd. left arm
Joseph Wiehl: (PO) Saint Joseph, (CMTS) loss 2d finger rt. hand
Maria Ann Mollett: (PO) Saint Joseph, (CMTS) widow
Charlotte Inman: (PO) Saint Joseph, (CMTS) widow
Patrick Mears: (PO) Saint Joseph, (CMTS) wd. of rt. thigh
Seno Heaston: (PO) Saint Joseph, (CMTS) gsw of left side
William B. Kemper: (PO) Saint Joseph, (CMTS) wd. of right thigh, & c
Robert Killen: (PO) Saint Joseph, (CMTS) gsw of right thigh
George Hull: (PO) Saint Joseph, (CMTS) gsw of rt. leg
John Cross: (PO) Saint Joseph, (CMTS) gsw of rt. thigh
John Gellottly: (PO) Saint Joseph, (CMTS) w.r. thigh, left arm, & chest
Anderson Hill: (PO) Saint Joseph, (CMTS) injury to abdomen
Joseph R. Harris: (PO) Saint Joseph, (CMTS) amp. r. thigh
Thomas F. Skeed: (PO) Saint Joseph, (CMTS) loss finger l. hand
Dallas S. Lewis: (PO) Saint Joseph, (CMTS) gsw r. arm
Samuel O. Beatty: (PO) Saint Joseph, (CMTS) gsw left groin, (FD) Apr. 1873
Joseph Kerner: (PO) Saint Joseph, (CMTS) injury to abdomen, (FD) Apr. 1875
Elizabeth Sommer: (PO) Saint Joseph, (CMTS) widow, (FD) Apr. 1876

Peter Van Volkenburgh: (PO) Saint Joseph, (CMTS) gsw of back & l'ft thigh, (FD) Apr. 1878
John S. Hanlin: (PO) Saint Joseph, (CMTS) gsw l. hip, (FD) Apr. 1880
James P. Moore: (PO) Saint Joseph, (CMTS) hypertrophy of heart, (FD) Aug. 1864
Seril P. Hyde: (PO) Saint Joseph, (CMTS) bronchitis, (FD) Aug. 1866
Mary J. Smith: (PO) Saint Joseph, (CMTS) dep. mother, (FD) Aug. 1870
Benjamin C. Eddy: (PO) Saint Joseph, (CMTS) gsw of right arm, (FD) Aug. 1872
Frederick Ludwig: (PO) Saint Joseph, (CMTS) disease of eyes, (FD) Aug.1876
Daniel Honisher: (PO) Saint Joseph, (CMTS) injury to abdomen, (FD) Aug. 1880
Amanda Phelps: (PO) Saint Joseph, (CMTS) widow, (FD) Dec. 1868
Nancy Crocker: (PO) Saint Joseph, (CMTS) dep mother, (FD) Dec. 1869
Thomas F. Roberts: (PO) Saint Joseph, (CMTS) gsw of left wrist joint, (FD) Dec. 1873
Margaret F. Friend: (PO) Saint Joseph, (CMTS) widow, (FD) Feb. 1868
Vina Shadrick: (PO) Saint Joseph, (CMTS) widow, (FD) Feb. 1869
John C. Register: (PO) Saint Joseph, (CMTS) surv. 1812, (FD) Feb. 1872
Annie Hollman: (PO) Saint Joseph, (CMTS) widow, (FD) Feb. 1881
Mary B. Cushing: (PO) Saint Joseph, (CMTS) dep. mother, (FD) Jan. 1864
William Striblen: (PO) Saint Joseph, (CMTS) gsw right foot, (FD) Jan. 1871
Rudolf Haas: (PO) Saint Joseph, (CMTS) gsw of rt. knee, (FD) Jan. 1873
William H. Carpenter: (PO) Saint Joseph, (CMTS) gsw of right thigh, (FD) Jan. 1874
Zarilda Bass: (PO) Saint Joseph, (CMTS) widow, (FD) Jan. 1877
Lucinda Sage: (PO) Saint Joseph, (CMTS) widow 1812, (FD) Jan. 1880
David B. Peabody: (PO) Saint Joseph, (CMTS) gsw of left thigh, (FD) Jan. 1881
Penina Hunt: (PO) Saint Joseph, (CMTS) widow, (FD) Jan. 1881
John Frank: (PO) Saint Joseph, (CMTS) gsw of right leg, (FD) Jan. 1881
Robert C. Bradshaw: (PO) Saint Joseph, (CMTS) wd. sh'ld'r,thigh, & c, (FD) Jul. 1866
Anna M. Lushbaugh: (PO) Saint Joseph, (CMTS) mother, (FD) Jul. 1875
Wilson P. Lucas: (PO) Saint Joseph, (CMTS) gsw left side of abdomen, (FD) Jul. 1876
Hannah Davis: (PO) Saint Joseph, (CMTS) widow 1812, (FD) Jul. 1879
Annie Dunning: (PO) Saint Joseph, (CMTS) widow 1812, (FD) Jul. 1880
James G. Young: (PO) Saint Joseph, (CMTS) partial deafness both eyes, (FD) Jul. 1881
Sarah A. Lancaster: (PO) Saint Joseph, (CMTS) dep. mother, (FD) Jul. 1881
Lydia Bumeson: (PO) Saint Joseph, (CMTS) dep. mother, (FD) Jun. 1865

Albert Palmer: (PO) Saint Joseph, (CMTS) sunstroke & result. paralysis, (FD) Jun. 1865

James H. Blagg: (PO) Saint Joseph, (CMTS) gsw of left hand, (FD) Jun. 1874

Herman Mantler: (PO) Saint Joseph, (CMTS) gsw of left foot, (FD) Jun. 1874

Margaret Gibson: (PO) Saint Joseph, (CMTS) widow 1812, (FD) Jun. 1880

Richard Horrigan: (PO) Saint Joseph, (CMTS) gsw rt. groin, (FD) Jun. 1882

James L. Cline: (PO) Saint Joseph, (CMTS) gsw of left thigh, (FD) Jun. 1882

James M. Gibson: (PO) Saint Joseph, (CMTS) wd. of right hand, (FD) Mar. 1866

Honora Dinnehy: (PO) Saint Joseph, (CMTS) widow, (FD) Mar. 1868

Mary A. Cogdell: (PO) Saint Joseph, (CMTS) dep. mother, (FD) Mar. 1868

Lucinda McClurg: (PO) Saint Joseph, (CMTS) widow, (FD) Mar. 1869

Martha J. Witten: (PO) Saint Joseph, (CMTS) widow, (FD) Mar. 1872

John Ruberson: (PO) Saint Joseph, (CMTS) gsw of abdomen, (FD) Mar. 1877

Miriam Wilson: (PO) Saint Joseph, (CMTS) dep. mother, (FD) Mar. 1880

William Day: (PO) Saint Joseph, (CMTS) inj. to right hip & both hds, (FD) Mar. 1880

William W. Berris: (PO) Saint Joseph, (CMTS) dis. of abdominal viscera, (FD) Mar. 1881

Joseph Hansen: (PO) Saint Joseph, (CMTS) bayonet wd. rt. hand, (FD) May 1866

Amanda Jones: (PO) Saint Joseph, (CMTS) widow, (FD) May 1869

Frank Randall: (PO) Saint Joseph, (CMTS) gsw rt. arm, (FD) May 1874

Margaret Kessler: (PO) Saint Joseph, (CMTS) widow and minor, (FD) May 1878

William V. Scull: (PO) Saint Joseph, (CMTS) injury to abdomen, (FD) May 1881

John W. Scott: (PO) Saint Joseph, (CMTS) disease of lungs, (FD) May 1882

Egbert O. Hill: (PO) Saint Joseph, (CMTS) gsw of r. thigh & chr. diar., (FD) May 1882

Peter Wolfer: (PO) Saint Joseph, (CMTS) gsw of face, (FD) Nov. 1865

Martin L. Vigus: (PO) Saint Joseph, (CMTS) minor, (FD) Nov. 1878

John T. Warburton: (PO) Saint Joseph, (CMTS) goitre, (FD) Nov. 1881

Mary L. Sterling: (PO) Saint Joseph, (CMTS) widow & minors, (FD) Nov. 1882

Alfred Elliott: (PO) Saint Joseph, (CMTS) gsw of right shoulder, (FD) Nov. 1882

Frank M. Tracy: (PO) Saint Joseph, (CMTS) gsw & disease, (FD)

Oct. 1863
Laura Francis: (PO) Saint Joseph, (CMTS) dep. mother, (FD) Oct. .1866
Mary Bell: (PO) Saint Joseph, (CMTS) widow, (FD) Oct. 1869
Nathan Reynolds: (PO) Saint Joseph, (CMTS) minor, (FD) Oct. 1877
Robert Stewart: (PO) Saint Joseph, (CMTS) gsw of throat & breast, (FD) Oct. 1877
Francis M. Hinds: (PO) Saint Joseph, (CMTS) injury to abdomen, (FD) Oct. 1880
Catharine Garsting: (PO) Saint Joseph, (CMTS) dep. mother, (FD) Oct. 1882
Sarah J. Cameron: (PO) Saint Joseph, (CMTS) widow, (FD) Oct. 1882
Adolph Phildius: (PO) Saint Joseph, (CMTS) gsw of left leg, (FD) Sep. 1863
Thomas McKinnie: (PO) Saint Joseph, (CMTS) gsw rt. arm, (FD) Sep. 1865
Calvin P. Kingsbury: (PO) Saint Joseph, (CMTS) gsw of left leg, (FD) Sep. 1865
Robert Harvey: (PO) Saint Joseph, (CMTS) injury to abdomen, (FD) Sep, 1873
Gustav Zunkel: (PO) Saint Joseph, (CMTS) gsw of right arm, (FD) Sep. 1877
Nancy A. Wolverton: (PO) Saint Joseph, (CMTS) widow & minors, (FD) Sep. 1880
Lucy Bush Todd: (PO) Saint Joseph, (CMTS) widow 1812, (FD) Sep. 1880
Robert Taylor: (PO) Saint Joseph, (CMTS) heart disease, (FD) Sep. 1881
Bruno Bemm: (PO) Saint Joseph, (CMTS) disease of eyes
Anna J. Kiger: (PO) Saxton, (CMTS) widow 1812, (FD) Mar. 1880
Martha Chaney: (PO) Stanley, (CMTS) widow 1812, (FD) Apr. 1880
Charles C. Dail: (PO) Wallace, (CMTS) disease of the lungs, (FD) Jan. 1881
Frances Frailey: (PO) Winthrop, (CMTS) widow

Lafayette County, Missouri, *Lexington News, January 12, 1893,*
At St. Louis, MO, January 5, 1893, after A. long illness, Mrs. Mary Virginia, widow of the late William Smith, in the 41st year of her age. Her remains were brought to this city Sunday morning and interred beside her husband in Machpelah. Her two sons, Messers William E. and Ralph Smith Accompanied her remains here. Brief services were held at the grave by Rev W. A. Carpenter, of the Methodist church of which church the deceased was A. member. Mrs. Smith was A. sister-in-law of Mrs. W. F. Kerdolff, and was A. resident of this city for A. few months.

Jackson County, Missouri, Obituary of Francis P. Reddington, *Holy Cross Magazine, 2001.*

Francis P. Reddington on April 29, 2001 at St. Luke's Hospital, Kansas City, Mo., at 82. Prior to his retirement in 1984, Mr. Reddington had been the superintendent of the Willbraham, MAHampden Regional School District for 18 years; In the past he was superintendent of the Williamsburg School District. During his career, Mr. Reddington also taught at Drury High School, North Adams, MA., and served as principal of West Stockbridge, MA Junior High School. An Army veteran of World War II, he had been a. member of the Army Reserves as well. He retired in 1977 with the rank of lieutenant colonel. Mr. Reddington is survived by his wife, Pauline; two sons; three daughters; two brothers, including John B., a sister; nine grandchildren; and A. great-grandchild.

Nodaway County, Missouri, 1883 Pensioners List
John McKee: (PO) Maryville, (CMTS) gsw rt. thigh & groin
Charles M. Messenger: (PO) Maryville, (CMTS) injury to abdomen
John Moore: (PO) Maryville, (CMTS) gsw lft. arm
William H. Walker: (PO) Maryville, (CMTS) gsw lft. thigh
Elias Pittman: (PO) Maryville, (CMTS) amp. lft. arm above elbow
Henry M. Carver: (PO) Maryville, (CMTS) ch. laryng
Francis A. Coleman: (PO) Maryville, (CMTS) gsw lft. hand
William A. Bailey: (PO) Maryville, (CMTS) wd. knee
John G. Honnold: (PO) Maryville, (CMTS) gsw lft. knee
Scribner R. Beech: (PO) Maryville, (CMTS) gsw lft. arm
John Gwin: (PO) Maryville, (CMTS) gsw lft. thigh
Byron A. Dunn: (PO) Maryville, (CMTS) gsw rt. shoulder
Sarah A. Trusty: (PO) Maryville, (CMTS) widow
Philip E. Sellers: (PO) Maryville, (CMTS) gsw lft. thigh
Isaac A. Bennett: (PO) Maryville, (CMTS) gsw lft. arm & rt. thigh
William D. Ashford: (PO) Maryville, (CMTS) gsw rt. side abdomen
Wulebald Tehle: (PO) Maryville, (CMTS) injury to abdomen
William H. Stewart: (PO) Maryville, (CMTS) wd rt. hip
Christopher Weaver: (PO) Maryville, (CMTS) dis. eyes
Silas R. Rowley: (PO) Maryville, (CMTS) injury to abdomen & gsw rt. shoulder
Samuel B. Cook: (PO) Maryville, (CMTS) gsw lft. ankle
Gain M. Bartlett: (PO) Maryville, (CMTS) gsw both thighs
Andrew Byers: (PO) Maryville, (CMTS) gsw rt. leg, var. veins, & ulcer
Joseph Jackson: (PO) Maryville, (CMTS) loss rt. leg
David Knee: (PO) Maryville, (CMTS) gsw l. breast r. shr. & foot
John B. Kildow: (PO) Maryville, (CMTS) gsw lft. foot
Stephen G. Ackerman: (PO) Maryville, (CMTS) wd. head
Thomas P. Graves: (PO) Maryville, (CMTS) ch. diar.
Thomas Smith: (PO) Maryville, (CMTS) gsw lft. hand
Edmond W. Anderson: (PO) Maryville, (CMTS) gsw lft. breast & arm

William M. Renshaw: (PO) Maryville, (CMTS) heart dis.
Abraham Walk: (PO) Maryville, (CMTS) wd. l. forearm & inj. to abd.
William C. Patterson: (PO) Maryville, (CMTS) wd. lft. arm
Richard H. Speake: (PO) Maryville, (CMTS) wd. rt. leg & inj. to abdomen
John Bruce: (PO) Maryville, (CMTS) gsw lft. hip
James R. Shultz: (PO) Maryville, (CMTS) ch. diar
Jacob Brown: (PO) Maryville, (CMTS) wd. rt. leg
Benjamin F. Shawn: (PO) Maryville, (CMTS) gsw lft. thigh
Charles S. Cooper: (PO) Maryville, (CMTS) gsw r. arm
John Slusser: (PO) Maryville, (CMTS) gsw r. leg & l. hd.
John Herron: (PO) Maryville, (CMTS) w. r. arm
James McKnight: (PO) Barnard, (CMTS) gsw rt. leg
Henry Hubbard: (PO) Barnard, (CMTS) gsw lft. thigh
John Duncan: (PO) Barnard, (CMTS) inj. lft. elbow
Albert Ulman: (PO) Barnard, (CMTS) gsw lft. shoulder & leg
Ira B. Jobe: (PO) Barnard, (CMTS) gsw lft. arm, affecting han. l.&gsw of groin
James Birtwistle: (PO) Barnard, (CMTS) gsw lft. Leg
Andrew S. Moore: (PO) Barnard, (CMTS) gsw l. shoul.
Londus O. Gallup: (PO) Barnard, (CMTS) chr. diar.
James F. Gregory: (PO) Barnard, (CMTS) chr. diar.
Perry J. Perkins: (PO) Barnard, (CMTS) dis. eyes
Samuel W. Ripley: (PO) Clearmont, (CMTS) gsw lft. arm & rt. ankle
John M. Evans: (PO) Clearmont, (CMTS) loss rt. arm
James M. Summers: (PO) Clyde, (CMTS) wd. lft. shoulder
Oliver P. Bogart: (PO) Clyde, (CMTS) gsw rt. thigh & inj. to abd
Charles W. Miles: (PO) Dawson, (CMTS) rheum
Robert D. Brown: (PO) Ebony, (CMTS) heart dis.
Wm. H. Melton: (PO) Gaynor City, (CMTS) gsw shoul.
Charles E. Bowen: (PO) Graham, (CMTS) gsw rt. thigh
Orson M. Markcum: (PO) Graham, (CMTS) injury to abdomen
Andrew A. Milligan: (PO) Graham, (CMTS) inj. palate bone
Sarah Moody: (PO) Hopkins, (CMTS) widow
Luther Whitney: (PO) Hopkins, (CMTS) wd. abdomen
Zachariah Coffin: (PO) Hopkins, (CMTS) gsw rt. forearm
Washington Durant: (PO) Hopkins, (CMTS) gsw rt. thigh
Nathaniel Atkins: (PO) Hopkins, (CMTS) dis. hip & back
John W. Jones: (PO) Hopkins, (CMTS) dis. heart, lungs, & spine
Howard H. Hensley: (PO) Hopkins, (CMTS) gsw chest
Luther Stewart: (PO) Hopkins, (CMTS) inj. l. hand
John W. Auders: (PO) Hughes, (CMTS) wd. rt. leg
Ezekiel Awalt: (PO) Pickering, (CMTS) amp. 3 fingers lft. hand, with dis. stumps
John L. Alexander: (PO) Pickering, (CMTS) gsw rt. arm
William J. Hewitt: (PO) Pickering, (CMTS) frac. rt. leg
Milton B.W. Harman: (PO) Pickering, (CMTS) gsw lft. arm & rt. s. face

Edward M. Manning: (PO) Quitman, (CMTS) gsw lft. foot
Allen Butner: (PO) Quitman, (CMTS) gsw lft. foot
George J. Smith: (PO) Quitman, (CMTS) rheum
Peter Roney: (PO) Quitman, (CMTS) wd. rt. hand
Jonathan Graves: (PO) Quitman, (CMTS) result prison life
Francis M. White: (PO) Quitman, (CMTS) wd. lft. arm
Milly Colwell: (PO) Quitman, (CMTS) widow
Richard Dove: (PO) Quitman, (CMTS) wd. rt. leg
Joseph V. Parrish: (PO) Skidmore, (CMTS) ch. diar.
Bartley Dunn: (PO) Skidmore, (CMTS) wd. lft. thigh
Thos. L. Howden: (PO) Skidmore, (CMTS) wd. rt. leg
James A. Gustine: (PO) Skidmore, (CMTS) dis. eyes
Delaplain Millard: (PO) Skidmore, (CMTS) gsw rt. shoulder
Henry Ross: (PO) Sweet Home, (CMTS) ch. rheum
Thomas McWhorter: (PO) Sweet Home, (CMTS) gsw both feet
Phineas Bird: (PO) Sweet Home, (CMTS) gsw head
Eliza Ann James: (PO) Sweet Home, (CMTS) widow
Reason A. Burge: (PO) Wilcox, (CMTS) chr. spinitis
Sarah J. Higerson: (PO) Barnard, (CMTS) widow, (FD) Apr. 1865
Scott K. Snively: (PO) Arkoe, (CMTS) wd. body, lft. leg, (FD) Apr. 1866
Marion Sturgeon: (PO) Hopkins, (CMTS) gsw rt. shoulder, (FD) Apr. 1873
Robert S. Stockton: (PO) Maryville, (CMTS) gsw rt. wrist, (FD) Apr. 1874
John F. Bainum: (PO) Barnard, (CMTS) gsw lft. forearm, (FD) Apr. 1877
Jeremiah Mills: (PO) Barnard, (CMTS) w.l.hd, (FD) Apr. 1878
Phebe Black: (PO) Skidmore, (CMTS) widow 1812, (FD) Apr. 1879
Silas R. Gates: (PO) Maryville, (CMTS) dis. lungs & ch. diar., (FD) Apr. 1880
Sarah McFarland: (PO) Hopkins, (CMTS) mother, (FD) Apr. 1880
Nancy E. Nichols: (PO) Pickering, (CMTS) widow 1812, (FD) Apr. 1881
George W. Gill: (PO) Quitman, (CMTS) mutilation lft. hand, gsw, (FD) Apr. 1881
John S. Miller: (PO) Maryville, (CMTS) gsw r. side abdomen, (FD) Apr. 1882
Daniel Cook: (PO) Maryville, (CMTS) inj. lft. shoulder & clavicle, (FD) Apr. 1882
James H. Dyer: (PO) Maryville, (CMTS) dis. lungs, (FD) Apr. 1882
William Ingram: (PO) Barnard, (CMTS) bronchitis, (FD) Apr. 1882
Josiah Brolyer: (PO) Skidmore, (CMTS) gsw rt. hip, (FD) Apr. 1882
George W. Nicholas: (PO) Barnard, (CMTS) gen'l debil, (FD) Aug. 1868
George W. Murray: (PO) Skidmore, (CMTS) gsw lft. side, (FD) Aug. 1872
Eli D. Adams: (PO) Barnard, (CMTS) gsw rt, side abdomen, (FD) Aug. 1874
Alonzo O. Spargur: (PO) Maryville, (CMTS) gsw lft. leg, (FD) Aug. 1876

Henry A. Herring: (PO) Sweet Home, (CMTS) ch. diar., (FD) Aug. 1876
Maria Rapalje: (PO) Maryville, (CMTS) widow 1812, (FD) Aug. 1878
James H. Smith: (PO) Pickering, (CMTS) gsw lft. leg, (FD) Aug. 1878
Rebecca Myers: (PO) Barnard, (CMTS) widow 1812, (FD) Aug. 1879
William A. Baker: (PO) Maryville, (CMTS) injury to abdomen, (FD) Aug. 1881
William S. Kennedy: (PO) Skidmore, (CMTS) ch. diar., (FD) Aug. 1881
Oliver Ridgeway: (PO) Maryville, (CMTS) gsw lft. thigh, (FD) Aug. 1882
Peter Noblet: (PO) Graham, (CMTS) gsw face, (FD) Dec. 1866
James McVey: (PO) Maryville, (CMTS) surv. 1812, (FD) Dec. 1871
W. H. Copper: (PO) Maryville, (CMTS) gsw abdomen, (FD) Dec. 1877
John O. McGee: (PO) Hopkins, (CMTS) gsw r. elbow, (FD) Dec. 1877
Daniel K. Joyclin: (PO) Graham, (CMTS) dis of abd. vis. & part'l loss rt. gt. toe, (FD) Dec. 1879
Norris H. Herbert: (PO) Hopkins, (CMTS) gsw lft. thigh, (FD) Dec. 1879
Absalom Miller: (PO) Maryville, (CMTS) ch. diar., (FD) Dec. 1881
John W. S. Bland: (PO) Hopkins, (CMTS) gsw forehead, (FD) Dec. 1881
Charles F. Porter: (PO) Hopkins, (CMTS) gsw rt. hip, (FD) Dec. 1882
Jacob V. Gallion: (PO) Maryville, (CMTS) ch. myelitis, (FD) Feb. 1867
Amanda Helmer: (PO) Hopkins, (CMTS) mother, (FD) Feb. 1882
Mary Ann McMillan: (PO) Maryville, (CMTS) widow, (FD) Jan. 1865
Mary L. Middleton: (PO) Maryville, (CMTS) widow, (FD) Jan. 1868
James J. Miller: (PO) Barnard, (CMTS) gsw lft. arm, (FD) Jan. 1876
William Baringer: (PO) Barnard, (CMTS) gsw rt. thigh, (FD) Jan. 1882
James Bracken: (PO) Barnard, (CMTS) dis. eyes, (FD) Jan. 1882
Joseph Acres: (PO) Guilford, (CMTS) gsw rt. foot & side, (FD) Jan. 1882
Stacy J. Thompson: (PO) Arkoe, (CMTS) widow, (FD) Jul. 1867
Robert M. Benbow: (PO) Maryville, (CMTS) sh. wd., causing irritation spine & kid., (FD) Jul. 1870
Elizabeth C. Saunders: (PO) Graham, (CMTS) widow 1812, (FD) Jul. 1879
Hannah Bond: (PO) Graham, (CMTS) widow 1812, (FD) Jul. 1880
Mariah Young: (PO) Quitman, (CMTS) widow 1812, (FD) Jul. 1880
Rebecca Crosson: (PO) Maryville, (CMTS) mother, (FD) Jul. 1881
Joseph F. Randolph: (PO) Hopkins, (CMTS) gsw rt. hip, (FD) Jul. 1881
Jennie E. Heald: (PO) Hopkins, (CMTS) widow, (FD) Jun. 1863
John T. Scantling: (PO) Quitman, (CMTS) gsw lft. eye & rt. shoulder, (FD) Jun. 1872
Alfred H. Karns: (PO) Maryville, (CMTS) wd. rt. arm, (FD) Jun. 1877
Hamilton Roth: (PO) Clearmont, (CMTS) sh. wd. lft. hip, (FD) Jun. 1877
John L. Stafford: (PO) Maryville, (CMTS) gsw rt. hip, (FD) Jun. 1878
Thomas Corken: (PO) Quitman, (CMTS) surv. 1812, (FD) Jun. 1878
Lyman Parcher: (PO) Maryville, (CMTS) gs wds. rt. leg & thigh, (FD) Jun. 1880
David Laughlin: (PO) Maryville, (CMTS) gsw lft. hand, (FD) Jun. 1881
Frederick Morse: (PO) Pickering, (CMTS) injury to abdomen, (FD) Jun.

1881
Mary Weaver: (PO) Maryville, (CMTS) mother, (FD) Jun. 1882
John H. Jones: (PO) Maryville, (CMTS) injury to abdomen, (FD) Jun. 1882
Francis Conlin: (PO) Barnard, (CMTS) dis. lungs, (FD) Jun. 1882
William L. Smith: (PO) Barnard, (CMTS) diar. & dis. of abd. vis.,result measles, (FD) Jun. 1882
James A. Friend: (PO) Barnard, (CMTS) dis. lungs, (FD) Jun. 1882
George W. May: (PO) Barnard, (CMTS) inj. lft. arm, (FD) Jun. 1882
George W. Greenlee: (PO) Hopkins, (CMTS) ch. diar. & rheum., & sh. wd. rt. foot, (FD) Jun. 1882
Lorenzo Deets: (PO) Hopkins, (CMTS) gsw lft. hip, (FD) Jun. 1882
Sylvester V. Dooley: (PO) Maryville, (CMTS) dis. of abdominal viscera, (FD) Mar. 1868
Ellen Cunningham: (PO) Maryville, (CMTS) widow, (FD) Mar. 1869
Jean Maria Mott: (PO) Pickering, (CMTS) wd. rt. shoulder, (FD) Mar. 1869
Elizabeth Ruhl: (PO) Maryville, (CMTS) widow 1812, (FD) Mar. 1879
Wm. E. Wehmer: (PO) Hopkins, (CMTS) gsw r. thigh, (FD) Mar. 1879
Elizabeth Burkhart: (PO) Pickering, (CMTS) widow 1812, (FD) Mar. 1880
Daniel Kingsley: (PO) Wilcox, (CMTS) rheum, (FD) Mar. 1880
Joseph M. Green: (PO) Maryville, (CMTS) dis. stomach & bowels, (FD) Mar. 1881
Mary W. Jones: (PO) Maryville, (CMTS) widow 1812, (FD) Mar. 1881
John Montgomery: (PO) Maryville, (CMTS) dis. lungs, (FD) Mar. 1882
David M. Crawford: (PO) Maryville, (CMTS) gsw rt. leg, (FD) Mar. 1882
Lewis Patterson: (PO) Maryville, (CMTS) injury to abdomen, (FD) Mar. 1882
James Tippie: (PO) Hopkins, (CMTS) gsw lft. shoulder, (FD) Mar. 1882
Joseph A. Mall: (PO) Maryville, (CMTS) gsw back, (FD) May 1865
Nathaniel Latimer: (PO) Pickering, (CMTS) surv 1812, (FD) May 1872
Caroline J. Murray: (PO) Maryville, (CMTS) widow, (FD) May 1873
George W. Moore: (PO) Maryville, (CMTS) ch. diar., (FD) May 1880
Christopher C. Baker: (PO) Barnard, (CMTS) var. veins both legs, (FD) May 1880
Valentine Korell: (PO) Barnard, (CMTS) part'l deafness both ears & dis. heart & lungs, (FD) May 1881
Isaac B. Woodard: (PO) Barnard, (CMTS) chr. diar., (FD) May 1881
Donald C. Glasgow: (PO) Barnard, (CMTS) chr. diar. & sunstroke, (FD) May 1881
William Hughes: (PO) Hopkins, (CMTS) gsw rt. foot, (FD) May 1881
Henry C. Pearson: (PO) Maryville, (CMTS) bronchitis, (FD) May 1882
Joshua Seyster: (PO) Maryville, (CMTS) gsw head, (FD) May 1882
Wm. Colter: (PO) Ebony, (CMTS) w. body, (FD) Nov. 1866
Frances Miller: (PO) Maryville, (CMTS) widow, (FD) Nov. 1867

George Cobb: (PO) Hopkins, (CMTS) gsw rt. shoulder, (FD) Nov. 1870
Mary Blagg: (PO) Barnard, (CMTS) widow 1812, (FD) Nov. 1879
Susan Hudelson: (PO) Maryville, (CMTS) widow 1812, (FD) Nov. 1880
Annis M.A. Kinsela: (PO) Maryville, (CMTS) widow, minor children, (FD) Nov. 1880
Morris Supple: (PO) Conception, (CMTS) inj. of spine, (FD) Nov. 1880
George B. Steffler: (PO) Maryville, (CMTS) var. vein lft. leg, (FD) Nov. 1881
William H. Ward: (PO) Barnard, (CMTS) gsw lft. arm, (FD) Oct. 1876
William McVicker: (PO) Maryville, (CMTS) injury to abdomen, (FD) Oct. 1878
John A. Leffler: (PO) Clyde, (CMTS) gsw r. thigh, (FD) Oct. 1878
Samuel Zaucker: (PO) Graham, (CMTS) gsw rt. arm, (FD) Oct. 1880
Harrison Smith: (PO) Quitman, (CMTS) gsw lft. thigh, (FD) Oct. 1880
James F. Wallace: (PO) Dawson, (CMTS) dis. lungs & heart, (FD) Oct. 1881
Cornelius Hull: (PO) Hopkins, (CMTS) injury to abdomen, (FD) Oct. 1882
Thomas Gray: (PO) Barnard, (CMTS) surv 1812, (FD) Sep. 1871
Isom Cordill: (PO) Barnard, (CMTS) surv. 1812, (FD) Sep. 1871
Benjamin F. Livengood: (PO) Skidmore, (CMTS) loss rt. eye from smallpox, (FD) Sep. 1873
Philip H. Walker: (PO) Clearmont, (CMTS) gsw face, (FD) Sep. 1878
Thomas H. Collins: (PO) Arkoe, (CMTS) var. veins both legs, (FD) Sep. 1881
John W. Herren: (PO) Maryville, (CMTS) chr. diar. & dis. of abd. vis, (FD) Sep. 1882
John Swinford: (PO) Maryville, (CMTS) ch. diarr. & dis. of abd. vis, (FD) Sep. 1882

Andrew County, Missouri, Democratic County Committee, 1936-1938

Name	Township	Residence
J. F. Wilcox (Chairman)	Jefferson	St. Joseph
Mrs. Gladys Rhoades (Vice Chariman)	Benton	Rosendale
Geo. Lambert (Secretary)	Nodaway	Savannah
Minnie D. Limerick (Treasurer)	Nodaway	Savanah
Gene Middleton	Benton	Bolckow
W. S. Miller	Platte	Bolckow
Riva Potts	Platt	Bolckow
C. M. Smith	Empire	Union Star
Lillian Wyss	Empire	Savannah
J. A. Slade	Rochester	Helena
Mrs. Wm. Sims	Rochester	Helena
Orley Tate	Monroe	Helena
Mrs. Chas. Patton	Monroe	Cosby
Lucille Lambright	Savannah	Savannah

Chas. Lambright	Clay	Bolckow
Mona Wood	Clay	Bolckow
Glenn Tipton	Jackson	Rosendale
Estella Todd	Jackson	Rosendale
Ghas. Gibson	Lincoln	Amazonia
Mrs. A. J. Zimmerman	Lincoln	Amazonia
Mrs. J. F. Wilcox	Jefferson	St. Joseph

Atchison County, Missouri, Democratic Committee, 1936-1938

Name	Township	Residence
Henry B. Hunt (Chairman)	Clay	Rock Port
Mrs. James Thomson (Vice Chairman)	Dale	Fairfax
Mrs. Minnie Templeton (Secretary)	Clay	Rock Port
John T. Wells (Treasurer)	---	Rock Port
John Rosenbohm	Benton	Langdon
Mrs. Anna Cooper	Benton	Langdon
Harmon Harmes, Jr.	Buchanan	Hamburg, IA
Mrs. Cabell Brown	Buchanan	Hamburg, IA
B. F. Portis	Clark	Fairfax
Edith Ottman	Clark	Fairfax
Harry Clement	Colfax	Tarkio
Mrs. Lillie Clement	Colfax	Tarkio
James Thomson	Dale	Fairfax
Hugh Doyle, Jr.	Lincoln	Westboro
Chas. Ramsay	Nishnabotna	Watson
Mrs. June Hays	Nishnabotna	Watson
Ray Matkin	Polk	Rock Port
Mrs. Frances Wolf	Polk	Rock Port
Theo. J. Wulber	Tarkio	Tarkio
Mrs. Andrew Campbell	Tarkio	Tarkio
J. L. Mulvania	Templeton	Phelps City
Mrs. Thelma Hames	Templeton	Pheps City

Atchison County, Missouri, *"Atchison County Mail,"* August 31, 1917
John Gaunce died on Aug 24th, 1917, after years in poor health and as A. cripple. We have just been thinking that those pioneers, F.W. Walter and H.A. Dankers, had the record for long residence in this section, but here was A. man who had lived hereabouts longer than they. In his seventy-ninth year, he had lived here since he was 2 years old, his father having located in the timber, about 4 miles northwest of Rock Port, along the bluff and near the Mishnabotna River, seventy-seven years ago. There his brother Hiram Gaunce, former merchant at Linden, was born and that locality and in and near Rock Port, John Gaunce passed the whole of his life, and saw about all there was to be seen in the development of this country. He is survived by his wife and one son--James Hiram Gaunce. Two daughters are dead. His brother, Hiram Gaunce, is post master and

merchant at Wise, Mo. Funeral services were conducted at the home at 10:30 o'clock a.m. on Sunday, by Rev. Orlo Jeffrey of the Baptist Church, and the remains were interred in Linden Cemetery.

Barry County, Missouri, Democratic Committee, 1936-1938

Name	Township	Residence
Hugh Brixey (Chairman)	Flat Creek 2	Cassville
Mrs. Marie Martin (Vice Chairman)		Monett
Jess Preddy (Secretary)	Flat Creek 3	Cassville
Mrs. Eva Chandler (Treasurer)		Cassville
Pete Webb	Ash No. 1	Garfield, AR
Sophia Webb	Ash No. 1	Garfield, AR
E. T. Weathers	Ash No. 2	Washburn
Mamie Weathers	Ash No. 2	Washburn
C. K. Lowe	Butterfield	Butterfield
Grace Lowe	Butterfield	Butterfield
Alex Kenski	Capps Creek	Pierce City
Mary West	Capps Creek	Pierce City
Bill Linebarger	Corsicana	Purdy
Mrs. Earl Black	Corsicana	Purdy
J. C. Blythe	Crane Creek 1	Crane
Celia Blythe	Crane Creek 1	Crane
P. O. Bassett	Crane Creek 2	Crane
P. O. Antle	Exeter	Exeter
Mrs. W. P. Searcy	Exeter	Exeter
Frank Hefley	Flat Creek 1	Cassville
Mabel Ward	Flat Creek 1	Cassville
Hugh Brixey	Flat Creek 2	Cassville
Gladys Baker	Flat Creek 2	Cassville
Omi Manley	Flat Creek 3	Cassville
W. B. Garris	Jenkins	Jenkins
Ella Garris	Jenkins	Jenkins
Clint Marbut	Kings Praire 1	Monett
Bessie Marbut	Kings Praire 1	Monett
Frank Birkenbach	Kings Praire 2	Monett
Mrs. Lawrence Roetto	Kings Praire 2	Monett
Orbie Brown	Liberty 1	Exeter
Alma Stamps	Liberty 1	Exeter
T. H. B. Smith	Liberty 2	Exeter
Mrs. Eva Smith	Liberty 2	Exeter
Claud Wooten	Liberty 3	Exeter
Alvia Packwood	Liberty 3	Exeter
Chester Stever	McDonald 1	Purdy
Fannie Webb	McDonald 1	Purdy
Henry Roller	McDonald 2	Purdy
Tennie Roller	McDonald 2	Purdy

E. E. Marbut	McDowell	Monett
Mollie Marbut	McDowell	Monett
Ralph Loftin	Mineral 1	Mineral Spgs.
Grace Sanders	Mineral 1	Cassville
John Hudson	Mineral 2	Cassville
Mrs. Ben Reno	Mineral 2	Cato
Arch Long	Monett 1	Monett
Mrs. J. P. Martin	Monett 1	Monett
Carl D. Sullinger	Monett 2	Monett
Mrs. Vie Willaims	Monett 2	Monett
Mont Bentley	Monett 3	Monett
Mrs. Anna Ryan	Monett 3	Monett
W. E. Schafnitt	Monett 4	Monett
Fannie Larkin	Monett 4	Monett
G. A, Cope	Mountain	Crane
Dessie Cope	Mountain	Jenkins
Joe Cline	Ozark	Aurora
Thelma McCallah	Ozark	Aurora
W. J. MacDougal	Pioneer	Purdy
Mrs. Joe Wrobleski	Pioneer	Purdy
George Eckman	Pleasant Rdg.	Verona
Mrs. Faye Kent	Pleasant Rdg.	Verona
Roy Daniels	Purdy	Purdy
Mrs. Agnes Baker	Purdy	Purdy
Frank Fogg	Roaring River	Eagle Rock
Alma Ayres	Roaring River	Eagle Rock
Frank Easley	Roaring River	Eagle Rock
Lucille Easley	Roaring River	Eagle Rock
John T. Easley	Roaring River	Eureka Springs, AR
Gale Cope	Shell Knob	Shell Knob
Mrs. G. C. Ledgerwood	Sugar Creek	Seligman
Virgil McGlothin	Sugar Creek	Seligman
Frank Webb	Washburn	Washburn
Cleo Edens	Washburn	Washburn
Bryan Wolfenbarger	Wheaton	Wheaton
Mrs. Tom Gahn	Wheaton	Wheaton
H. H. Hardwock	White River 1	Golden
Mrs. Slade Johnson	White River 1	Golden
J. T. Hardman	White River 2	Shell Knob
Lola Curry	White River 2	Viola

<u>Winfield, KS, " *Courier,* "Aug. 20, 2001, Jackson County, MO, Connection, Obituary of Alpha May Seimears Thurman</u>

Alpha May Seimears-Thurman, 92, formerly of Severy, died Aug. 19, 2001, at Susan B. Allen Memorial Hospital in El Dorado. Services will be at 2 p.m. Wednesday at Severy Baptist Church. The Rev. Tony Pameticky, Allen Seimears and George Seimears will officiate. Burial will be in Grace Lawn Cemetery in Howard. Mrs.Seimears-Thurman was born Dec. 13, 1908, in Rudy, Ark., to Gertrude Emily Morrison and James VanZandt. When she was A. child, the family moved to Kansas where she attended school in Beaumont. On Feb. 1, 1932, she married George Walter Wesley Seimears in Eureka. They made their home in the Fiat community southeast of Severy. Her husband died Sept. 26, 1964. On Oct. 15, 1972, she married Asa Bryant Thurman. They made their home in Elk Falls before moving to Aline, Okla., where they remained for 20 years. Thurman died March 28, 1983. Mrs. Seimears-Thurman was A. former member of the Order of Eastern Star and A. member of the Christian Church of Aline, Okla. Survivors include her sons, George Seimears, Lone Jack, Mo., Allen Seimears, LaCygne, Leon Seimears, Howard, Charles Seimears, Derby, and Steven Seimears, Sedan; her daughters, Maisie Rodenbaugh, Blue Springs, Mo., Ella Huffman, Denver, Mo., Frances Barrier and Gertrude Jessogne, both of El Dorado, June Lakin, Kaw City, Okla., and Cora Sue Thornton, Kincaid; her stepsons, Bob Thurman, Garfield, Ark., and John Thurman, Rock Hills, S.C.; her stepdaughters, Karen Gray, Garfield, Ark., and Kay Howell, Howard; A. sister, Marie Colyer, Amarillo, Texas; 30 grandchildren, 54 great-grandchildren, 37 great-great-grandchildren and one great-great-great-grandchild.

Amarillo, TX, "*Daily News,*"Mar. 3, 2001, Barry County, Missouri Connection

Frances Jewell Patton, 81, died Wednesday, Feb. 28, 2001, in Elkhart. Services will be at 2 p.m. today in the First Christian Church with the Rev. Larry Bradford officiating. Burial will be in Hugoton Cemetery by Paul's Funeral Home. Mrs. Patton was born at Golden, Mo. She had lived in Hugoton since 1947, moving from Vilas, Colo. She was A. cook for the Senior Citizens at Hugoton. She attended First Christian Church, was A. member of the Glow Worm Band and A. past member of the Rebekah Lodge of Hugoton. She married Aubry R. Patton in 1941 at Exeter, Mo. He died in 1981. Survivors include three sons, Ronnie Lee Phillips of Springdale, Ark., Robert Patton of Amarillo and Charles Patton of Cooper, Texas; A. daughter, Judy Sap of Hugoton; A. brother, James Sisco of Raytown, Mo.; two sisters, Helen Spain of Monett, Mo., and Louise Crim of Gladstone, Mo.; 15 grandchildren; and 15 great-grandchildren.

Attendees of the Schoenhal Family Reunion, Shattuck, OK, "*Northwest Oklahoman,*"Aug. 21, 2003, Connection with New Franklin, Howard County, Missouri.

August 3, 2003, the Schoenhals family had their 33rd annual reunion at Shattuck Senior Citizens Center. Mark Schoenhals called for the election of officers for the following year. Norman Bay was elected president, Sue Ann Schoenhals was re-elected treasurer and Anneva Sander was re-elected secretary.

Attendees: Henry Schoenhals family: Robert D. Bishop, Tena C. Kirk, Deborah and John Whitaker, Wichita, Kansas; Gail Petree, Chad Petree, Shattuck; Leona Schoenhals, Mark and Margy Schoenhals, Spearman, TX.; Alviana Kliewer, LaVeta Bucher, Martha Herberl, Follett, TX; Carl, Linda and Michael White, Broken Arrow; OK, Allen and Esther Schoenhals, Doug A. Schoenhals, Jim Schoenhals, Fred Schoenhals, Shattuck; Don Schoenhals, David Schoenhals, Oklahoma City; OK, Dennis, Pam, Ty and Trev Schoenhals, Enid; OK Rick and Sondra Schoenhals, Weatherford; Sharron and Floria Schoenhals, Wichita, KS; Carrol and Sarah Schoenhals, New Franklin, MO; Ruby Myers, Fred and Carolyn Goddard, New Martinsville, WV; Michael and Joanna Myers, Jared Myers, Palmlyra, PA; Katheeen Myers, Hummelstown, PA.

George Schoenhals and Marie Elizabeth Kelln family:Gloria Griggs, Perryton, TX.; Elmer Helfenbein, Amarillo, TX; Ruth Yauck, Follett, TX; and Harry Schoenhals, Darrouzett, TX; and Beverly Long, Shattuck.

The Fred Schoenhals and Katherine Meier family: Valentine Schoenhals, Donald Schoenhals, Higgins, TX; and Ophelia Schoenhals, Shattuck.

John and Schoenhals and Eva Hefley: Norman and Anita Schoenhals, Stacey and Jeannette Schoenhals, Martha Schoenhals, Earl and Marilyn Schoenhals, Doug and Sue Ann Schoenhals, Larry and Jusy Schoenhals, Reuben and Elma Schoenhals, Hulda Kelln, Clayton and Marilyn DePriest, Patty, Grey and Dane DePriest, all of Shattuck; Joyce Dowling, Oakwood; Kevin Schoenhals, Oklahoma City; OK, Adolph and Clara Repp, Weatherford, OK, and John and Anneva Sander, Seiling, OK

Katherine Schoenals and Frack Yauck family: Ira Lee Meller, Leona Bush, Kerie, Cierra and Larissa Bland,

Maria Schoenhals and Alex Bay family: Norman and Helen Bay, Shattuck; Harold and Dorothy Schoenhals, Elmer and Elizabeth Schoenhals, Perryton, TX, and Ed and Wilma Schoenhals

Maria Katherine Schoenhals and Carl Miller family: Gate Haskell Sturtz

Other Guests : Monica Kirby, Oklahoma City, OK; Joan Beck, Darrouzett, TX.; T. J. Littlejohn, Wichita, KS; Clara Kraft, Follett, TX; Roy Kretz, Norman, OK, and Joan Kelln, Shattuck; OK, Allene Albers and Junior, Zollinger, Woodward, OK

<u>Clark County, Missouri, Democratic Committee, 1936-1938</u>

Name	Township	Residence
Wilford Orr (Chairman)	Des Moines	Alexandria
Mrs. Edna L. Weaver (Vice Chariman)	Lincoln	Kahoka
Mrs. Edgar F. Smith (Secretary)	Madison	Kahoka

R. C. Murphy (Treasurer)	---	Kahoka
A. C. Baugher	Sweet Home	Revere
Mrs. Bertha Christy	Sweet Home	Revere
J. B. Wood	Jefferson	Revere
Mrs. Harry Gutting	Jefferson	Kahoka
Frank Philip	Folker	Luray
Mrs. Mary Mills	Folker	Luray
Lynn Gregory	Madison	Kahoka
E. D. Baugher	Grant	Farmington, IA
Mrs. E. D. Baugher	Grant	Farmington, IA
Pearl J. Smith	Wyaconda	Wyaconda
Mrs. Edgar Mosier	Wyaconda	Luray
R. L. Boulware	Clay	Canton
Mrs. N. N. Frazee	Clay	Alexandria
S. P. Fetters	Jackson	Kahoka
Mrs. Ruth Logsdon	Jackson	Canton
Mrs. Roy Campbell	Des Moines	Alexandria
Mrs. Edna Weaver	Lincoln	Kahoka
Lee Norris	Union	Kahoka
Mrs. Carrie McLaughlin	Union	Kahoka
C. L. Carrol	Washington	Wyaconda
Mrs. Chas. Hudson	Washington	Wyaconda
G. W. Hill	Vernon	Alexandria
Mrs. Florence Bryant	Vernon	AlexandrI

<u>Clarke County, Missouri Luray, Business Owners, R. G. Dunn Directory, 1893.</u>

Name	Occupation
W. S. Belows	Grocery & Hardware
John W. Bibb	Drugs
William B. Bradly	Jeweler
Noe Combs	Grocery
J. V. Falkenburg	Miller & Coal
J. W. Fonda	Genl. Store
William Hamilton	Waggon Maker
William Harkness	Hotel
William Hill	Builder
McWilliams & McWilliams	Livery & Hotel
William Randal	Wagon Maker
Mrs. J. M. Shore	Millinery
L. J. Shore	Genl. Store
Stafford & Co.	Dry Goods
Stevens Bros.	Blacksmiths
J. W. Tinsman	Stationer

Clark County, Missouri, Land Patents, 1841-1849

Abraham C. Baldwin: (ID) May 20, 1841, (AN) MO2340.469
Emily F. Baldwin: (ID) May 20, 1841, (AN) MO2340.469
Abraham C. Baldwin: (ID) May 20, 1841, (AN) MO2340.470
Emily F. Baldwin: (ID) May 20, 1841, (AN) MO2340.470
Timothy W. Baldwin: (ID) May 20, 1841, (AN) MO2340.471
Isaiah T. Hayman: (ID) May 20, 1841, (AN) MO2340.497
Samuel Zeller: (ID) May 20, 1841, (AN) MO2340.498
Samuel Zeller: (ID) May 20, 1841, (AN) MO2340.499
Samuel Zeller: (ID) Jul. 1, 1841, (AN) MO2350.001
Joseph R. Schnelly: (ID) Jul. 1, 1841, (AN) MO2350.002
Joseph R. Schnebly: (ID) Jul. 1, 1841, (AN) MO2350.003
Joseph R. Schnebly: (ID) Jul. 1, 1841, (AN) MO2350.004
Joseph R. Schnebly: (ID) Jul. 1, 1841, (AN) MO2350.005
David S. Haslett: (ID) Jul. 1, 1841, (AN) MO2350.010
Thomas Wells: (ID) Jul. 1, 1841, (AN) MO2350.022
Thomas Wells: (ID) Jul. 1, 1841, (AN) MO2350.023
Thomas Wells: (ID) Jul. 1, 1841, (AN) MO2350.024
Abraham C. Baldwin: (ID) Jul. 1, 1841, (AN) MO2350.025
Emily F. Baldwin: (ID) Jul. 1, 1841, (AN) MO2350.025
Abraham C. Baldwin: (ID) Jul. 1, 1841, (AN) MO2350.026
Emily F. Baldwin: (ID) Jul. 1, 1841, (AN) MO2350.026
Abraham C. Baldwin: (ID) Jul. 1, 1841, (AN) MO2350.027
Emily F. Baldwin: (ID) Jul. 1, 1841, (AN) MO2350.027
William G. Kerfott: (ID) Jul. 1, 1841, (AN) MO2350.028
James M. Burton: (ID) Jul. 1, 1841, (AN) MO2350.052
William Walker: (ID) Jul. 1, 1841, (AN) MO2350.063
Lydia A. Martin: (ID) Jul. 1, 1841, (AN) MO2350.072
Mary R. Martin: (ID) Jul. 1, 1841, (AN) MO2350.073
Samuel Zeller: (ID) Jul. 1, 1841, (AN) MO2350.074
Joseph R. Schnebly: (ID) Jul. 1, 1841, (AN) MO2350.075
Joseph R. Schnebly: (ID) Jul. 1, 1841, (AN) MO2350.076
Joseph R. Schnelly: (ID) Jul. 1, 1841, (AN) MO2350.077
Peter Conkle: (ID) Jul. 1, 1841, (AN) MO2350.097
Peter Conkle: (ID) Jul. 1, 1841, (AN) MO2350.098
Peter Conkle: (ID) Jul. 1, 1841, (AN) MO2350.099
Verdner Suter: (ID) Jul. 1, 1841, (AN) MO2350.110
Preston H. Burch: (ID) Jul. 1, 1841, (AN) MO2350.111
Preston H. Burch: (ID) Jul. 1, 1841, (AN) MO2350.112
Walton P. Smith: (ID) Jul. 1, 1841, (AN) MO2350.117
Alva H. Wells: (ID) Jul. 1, 1841, (AN) MO2350.189
Alva H. Wells: (ID) Jul. 1, 1841, (AN) MO2350.190
John Sisson: (ID) Jul. 1, 1841, (AN) MO2350.205
James Doyle: (ID) Jul. 1, 1841, (AN) MO2350.429
William L. Slaughter: (ID) Jul. 1, 1841, (AN) MO2360.031
David Kennedy: (ID) Jul. 1, 1841, (AN) MO2360.133

James M. Inskeep: (ID) Jul. 1, 1841, (AN) MO2360.171
Samuel Musgrove: (ID) Jul. 1, 1841, (AN) MO2360.217
Elizabeth Dawson: (ID) Jul. 1, 1841, (AN) MO2360.332
John Lapsley: (ID) Jul. 1, 1841, (AN) MO2360.338
John A. Lapsley: (ID) Jul. 1, 1841, (AN) MO2360.363
John A. Lapsley: (ID) Jul. 1, 1841, (AN) MO2360.364
Owen R. Dean: (ID) Jul. 1, 1841, (AN) MO2360.385
Isaiah T. Hayman: (ID) Jul. 1, 1841, (AN) MO2360.447
Robert Q. Stark: (ID) Jul. 1, 1841, (AN) MO2360.479
Jesse Blanton: (ID) Jul. 1, 1841, (AN) MO2360.480
William Bay: (ID) Jul. 1, 1841, (AN) MO2360.493
Samuel C. Sloan: (ID) Nov. 10, 1841, (AN) MO2370.011
Temple H. Davis: (ID) Nov. 10, 1841, (AN) MO2370.061
Mahatible HamMOnd: (ID) Nov. 10, 1841, (AN) MO2370.143
Mahatible HamMOnd: (ID) Nov. 10, 1841, (AN) MO2370.144
Justin E. Falley: (ID) Nov. 10, 1841, (AN) MO2370.145
Ephraim Grimes: (ID) Nov. 10, 1841, (AN) MO2370.153
Mahatible HamMOnd: (ID) Nov. 10, 1841, (AN) MO2370.200
Samuel G. Medley: (ID) Nov. 10, 1841, (AN) MO2370.295
Samuel G. Medley: (ID) Nov. 10, 1841, (AN) MO2370.296
Samuel G. Medley: (ID) Nov. 10, 1841, (AN) MO2370.297
Veranus P. Stevens: (ID) Nov. 10, 1841, (AN) MO2370.328
Veranus P. Stevens: (ID) Nov. 10, 1841, (AN) MO2370.329
John E. Howell: (ID) Nov. 10, 1841, (AN) MO2370.330
John E. Howell: (ID) Nov. 10, 1841, (AN) MO2370.331
John E. Howell: (ID) Nov. 10, 1841, (AN) MO2370.332
Isaiah T. Hayman: (ID) Nov. 10, 1841, (AN) MO2370.370
Isaiah T. Hayman: (ID) Nov. 10, 1841, (AN) MO2370.371
Joseph Carman: (ID) Nov. 10, 1841, (AN) MO2370.374
John A. Rench: (ID) Jun. 17, 1841, (AN) MO2370.408
Elias Houser: (ID) Nov. 10, 1841, (AN) MO2370.409
Elias Houser: (ID) Nov. 10, 1841, (AN) MO2370.410
William S. Gregory: (ID) Nov. 10, 1841, (AN) MO2370.430
John A. Rench: (ID) Nov. 10, 1841, (AN) MO2370.440
John A. Rench: (ID) Nov. 10, 1841, (AN) MO2370.441
John A. Rench: (ID) Nov. 10, 1841, (AN) MO2370.442
John A. Rench: (ID) Jun. 17, 1841, (AN) MO2370.443
Robert E. Lee: (ID) Nov. 10, 1841, (AN) MO2370.445
Benjamin M. Mills: (ID) Nov. 10, 1841, (AN) MO2370.477
Benjamin M. Mills: (ID) Nov. 10, 1841, (AN) MO2370.478
Nicholas Conkle: (ID) Nov. 10, 1841, (AN) MO2370.481
Nicholas Conkle: (ID) Nov. 10, 1841, (AN) MO2370.482
John Barnes: (ID) Nov. 10, 1841, (AN) MO2370.483
John Wade: (ID) Nov. 10, 1841, (AN) MO2370.492
Daniel Doyle: (ID) Nov. 10, 1841, (AN) MO2370.493
Thomas Wells: (ID) Nov. 10, 1841, (AN) MO2380.017

John W. Ward: (ID) Nov. 10, 1841, (AN) MO2380.030
William M. Newman: (ID) Nov. 10, 1841, (AN) MO2380.036
William M. Newman: (ID) Nov. 10, 1841, (AN) MO2380.037
William M. Newman: (ID) Nov. 10, 1841, (AN) MO2380.038
Isaiah T. Hayman: (ID) Nov. 10, 1841, (AN) MO2380.039
Samuel Johnston: (ID) Nov. 10, 1841, (AN) MO2380.065
Samuel Johnston: (ID) Nov. 10, 1841, (AN) MO2380.066
Thomas J. Calvert: (ID) Nov. 10, 1841, (AN) MO2380.093
Greenbury Story: (ID) Nov. 10, 1841, (AN) MO2380.098
Mercer Moodey: (ID) Nov. 10, 1841, (AN) MO2380.112
Mercer Moodey: (ID) Nov. 10, 1841, (AN) MO2380.113
Barry Caldwell: (ID) Nov. 10, 1841, (AN) MO2380.121
Barry Caldwell: (ID) Nov. 10, 1841, (AN) MO2380.122
Patrick McDerMOtt: (ID) Nov. 10, 1841, (AN) MO2380.136
John Roberts: (ID) Nov. 10, 1841, (AN) MO2380.137
John Roberts: (ID) Nov. 10, 1841, (AN) MO2380.138
Margaret R. Houston: (ID) Nov. 10, 1841, (AN) MO2380.159
Margaret R. Houston: (ID) Nov. 10, 1841, (AN) MO2380.160
Mahala J. Worthington: (ID) Nov. 10, 1841, (AN) MO2380.164
Clement White: (ID) Nov. 10, 1841, (AN) MO2380.179
William B. Feagan: (ID) Nov. 10, 1841, (AN) MO2380.200
Clement White: (ID) Nov. 10, 1841, (AN) MO2380.224
David Kennedy: (ID) Nov. 10, 1841, (AN) MO2380.225
Jerome B. Bibb: (ID) Nov. 10, 1841, (AN) MO2380.226
Davis Piersol: (ID) Nov. 10, 1841, (AN) MO2380.246
Samuel Hammond: (ID) Nov. 10, 1841, (AN) MO2380.293
Veranus P. Stevens: (ID) Nov. 10, 1841, (AN) MO2380.294
Joseph Carman: (ID) Nov. 10, 1841, (AN) MO2380.343
Joseph Carman: (ID) Nov. 10, 1841, (AN) MO2380.344
Nancy Carman: (ID) Nov. 10, 1841, (AN) MO2380.345
John Wade: (ID) Nov. 10, 1841, (AN) MO2380.346
Thomas F. Nelson: (ID) Nov. 10, 1841, (AN) MO2380.421
Thomas F. Nelson: (ID) Nov. 10, 1841, (AN) MO2380.422
Thomas F. Nelson: (ID) Nov. 10, 1841, (AN) MO2380.423
Thomas F. Nelson: (ID) Nov. 10, 1841, (AN) MO2380.424
Thomas F. Nelson: (ID) Nov. 10, 1841, (AN) MO2380.425
Thomas F. Nelson: (ID) Nov. 10, 1841, (AN) MO2380.426
Jesse Sisson: (ID) Nov. 10, 1841, (AN) MO2380.436
Richard Callaway: (ID) May 19, 1841, (AN) MO2390.073
Joseph Scott: (ID) Mar. 10, 1843, (AN) MO2390.084
Joseph Scott: (ID) Mar. 10, 1843, (AN) MO2390.085
William O. Peake: (ID) Mar. 10, 1843, (AN) MO2390.089
Reuel Murphy: (ID) Mar. 10, 1843, (AN) MO2390.100
James McClure: (ID) Mar. 10, 1843, (AN) MO2390.101
Joseph Burtle: (ID) Mar. 10, 1843, (AN) MO2390.109
Ezra S. Ely: (ID) Aug. 20, 1842, (AN) MO2390.132

Jeptha S. Smith: (ID) Mar. 10, 1843, (AN) MO2390.168
Collin C. Holmes: (ID) Mar. 10, 1843, (AN) MO2390.182
William B. Feagan: (ID) Mar. 10, 1843, (AN) MO2390.209
William B. Feagan: (ID) Mar. 10, 1843, (AN) MO2390.210
John Legg: (ID) Mar. 10, 1843, (AN) MO2390.229
Clement White: (ID) Mar. 10, 1843, (AN) MO2390.231
Joab Hill: (ID) Mar. 10, 1843, (AN) MO2390.276
Joab Hill: (ID) Mar. 10, 1843, (AN) MO2390.277
John McCoy: (ID) Mar. 10, 1843, (AN) MO2390.320
John McCoy: (ID) Mar. 10, 1843, (AN) MO2390.321
William Hill: (ID) Mar. 10, 1843, (AN) MO2390.333
Colin C. Holmes: (ID) Mar. 10, 1843, (AN) MO2390.388
Joseph Davis: (ID) Mar. 10, 1843, (AN) MO2390.410
James S. Markell: (ID) Jul. 10, 1844, (AN) MO2400.291
W L. Webb: (ID) Jul. 10, 1844, (AN) MO2400.291
William Bedell: (ID) Jul. 10, 1844, (AN) MO2400.301
George D. Barnes: (ID) Jul. 10, 1844, (AN) MO2400.306
Christopher Schvaar: (ID) Jul. 10, 1844, (AN) MO2400.307
Christopher Schvaar: (ID) Jul. 10, 1844, (AN) MO2400.308
William Wooden: (ID) Jul. 10, 1844, (AN) MO2400.309
Joseph J. Benning: (ID) Jul. 10, 1844, (AN) MO2400.325
William H. Thompson: (ID) Jul. 10, 1844, (AN) MO2400.332
William J. Floyd: (ID) Mar. 25, 1845, (AN) MO2400.354
Robert Wooden: (ID) Sep. 10, 1844, (AN) MO2400.357
James Johnson: (ID) Sep. 10, 1844, (AN) MO2400.393
James Johnson: (ID) Sep. 10, 1844, (AN) MO2400.394
James Johnson: (ID) Sep. 10, 1844, (AN) MO2400.395
Oscar F. Hampton: (ID) Sep. 10, 1844, (AN) MO2400.412
Oscar F. Hampton: (ID) Sep. 10, 1844, (AN) MO2400.413
John E. Howell: (ID) Sep. 10, 1844, (AN) MO2400.422
Robert E. Lee: (ID) Sep. 10, 1844, (AN) MO2400.473
Robert E. Lee: (ID) Sep. 10, 1844, (AN) MO2400.474
Robert E. Lee: (ID) Sep. 10, 1844, (AN) MO2400.475
Clifton G. Thompson: (ID) Sep. 10, 1844, (AN) MO2400.502
Adison Barn: (ID) Sep. 10, 1844, (AN) MO2410.006
Jeremiah Lewis: (ID) Sep. 10, 1844, (AN) MO2410.141
William Phelps: (ID) Sep. 10, 1844, (AN) MO2410.172
John B. Hogan: (ID) Sep. 10, 1844, (AN) MO2410.216
John B. Hogan: (ID) Sep. 10, 1844, (AN) MO2410.217
Andrew J. Daggs: (ID) Sep. 10, 1844, (AN) MO2410.232
Andrew J. Daggs: (ID) Sep. 10, 1844, (AN) MO2410.233
Kinsey Holcomb: (ID) Sep. 10, 1844, (AN) MO2410.248
Murdock Cooper: (ID) Sep. 10, 1844, (AN) MO2410.249
Abijah Coldiron: (ID) Sep. 10, 1844, (AN) MO2410.267
Horatio P. Arnold: (ID) Sep. 10, 1844, (AN) MO2410.320
Horatio P. Arnold: (ID) Sep. 10, 1844, (AN) MO2410.321

George Watkins: (ID) Sep. 10, 1844, (AN) MO2410.361
Jochim Lafrenz: (ID) Sep. 10, 1844, (AN) MO2410.378
Parthenia Wells: (ID) Sep. 10, 1844, (AN) MO2410.406
Parthenia Wells: (ID) Sep. 10, 1844, (AN) MO2410.407
Susan Mcbee: (ID) Sep. 10, 1844, (AN) MO2410.419
James A. Mclaughlin: (ID) Sep. 10, 1844, (AN) MO2410.420
James Shoeman: (ID) Sep. 10, 1844, (AN) MO2410.423
Alexander Keith: (ID) Sep. 10, 1844, (AN) MO2410.446
Alexander Keith: (ID) Sep. 10, 1844, (AN) MO2410.447
Jacob Senseney: (ID) Mar. 9, 1846, (AN) MO2420.016
Robert Jenkins: (ID) Aug. 21, 1846, (AN) MO2420.019
Joseph R. Schnebly: (ID) Aug. 21, 1846, (AN) MO2420.020
Rice Smith: (ID) Apr. 1, 1848, (AN) MO2420.054
Joseph G. Wilson: (ID) Apr. 1, 1848, (AN) MO2420.058
Francis Smith: (ID) Apr. 1, 1848, (AN) MO2420.068
Francis Smith: (ID) Apr. 1, 1848, (AN) MO2420.069
Samuel Cox: (ID) Apr. 1, 1848, (AN) MO2420.076
Thomas Harrison: (ID) Apr. 1, 1848, (AN) MO2420.077
William Seaton: (ID) Apr. 1, 1848, (AN) MO2420.089
John MOseley: (ID) Apr. 1, 1848, (AN) MO2420.094
Frederick Hauptman: (ID) Apr. 1, 1848, (AN) MO2420.096
Reuel Murphy: (ID) Apr. 1, 1848, (AN) MO2420.100
William Lambirth: (ID) Apr. 1, 1848, (AN) MO2420.113
Squire G. Shropshire: (ID) Apr. 1, 1848, (AN) MO2420.115
Thomas H. Davidge: (ID) Apr. 1, 1848, (AN) MO2420.119
George Quigley: (ID) Apr. 1, 1848, (AN) MO2420.120
Samuel Cox: (ID) Apr. 1, 1848, (AN) MO2420.127
Wyatt Mayfield: (ID) Apr. 1, 1848, (AN) MO2420.139
Wyatt Mayfield: (ID) Apr. 1, 1848, (AN) MO2420.140
Hugh M. Lyle: (ID) Apr. 1, 1848, (AN) MO2420.142
William F. Northcraft: (ID) Apr. 1, 1848, (AN) MO2420.164
Lewis Drew: (ID) Apr. 1, 1848, (AN) MO2420.165
Jefferson Jordan: (ID) Apr. 1, 1848, (AN) MO2420.174
Wyatt Mayfield: (ID) Apr. 1, 1848, (AN) MO2420.177
Robert Jenkins: (ID) Apr. 1, 1848, (AN) MO2420.178
William F. Dixon: (ID) Apr. 1, 1848, (AN) MO2420.209
William F. Dixon: (ID) Apr. 1, 1848, (AN) MO2420.210
Reuel Murphy: (ID) Apr. 1, 1848, (AN) MO2420.219
Robert E. Lee: (ID) Jun. 23, 1847, (AN) MO2420.221
Bernard Brogan: (ID) Jul. 1, 1848, (AN) MO2420.291
Bernard Brogan: (ID) Jul. 1, 1848, (AN) MO2420.292
John Weaver: (ID) Mar. 1, 1848, (AN) MO2420.360
Rice Price: (ID) Mar. 1, 1848, (AN) MO2420.375
Rice Price: (ID) Mar. 1, 1848, (AN) MO2420.376
Rice Price: (ID) Mar. 1, 1848, (AN) MO2420.377
John Burke: (ID) Mar. 1, 1848, (AN) MO2420.386

John Burke: (ID) Mar. 1, 1848, (AN) MO2420.387
Adman Howard: (ID) Mar. 1, 1848, (AN) MO2420.398
Jane Ford: (ID) Mar. 1, 1848, (AN) MO2420.425
Jacob Schnebly: (ID) Mar. 1, 1848, (AN) MO2420.438
Julia A. Sullivan: (ID) Mar. 1, 1848, (AN) MO2420.476
Abigail Doud: (ID) Mar. 1, 1848, (AN) MO2420.485
Isaac N. Lewis: (ID) Mar. 1, 1848, (AN) MO2420.500
William C. Sullivan: (ID) Jun. 1, 1848, (AN) MO2430.012
Henry Heald: (ID) Jun. 1, 1848, (AN) MO2430.022
Samuel G. Scovern: (ID) Jun. 1, 1848, (AN) MO2430.036
Hiram D. Sanders: (ID) Jun. 1, 1848, (AN) MO2430.058
Hiram D. Sanders: (ID) Jun. 1, 1848, (AN) MO2430.059
Julia A. Sullivan: (ID) Jun. 1, 1848, (AN) MO2430.080
Jacob Bias: (ID) Jun. 1, 1848, (AN) MO2430.116
Abdell Miller: (ID) Jun. 1, 1848, (AN) MO2430.119
John Shafer: (ID) Jun. 1, 1848, (AN) MO2430.132
Philander Reed: (ID) Jun. 1, 1848, (AN) MO2430.185
Philander Reed: (ID) Jun. 1, 1848, (AN) MO2430.186
James Turtle: (ID) Jun. 1, 1848, (AN) MO2430.201
James Turtle: (ID) Jun. 1, 1848, (AN) MO2430.202
Finton Brock: (ID) Jun. 1, 1848, (AN) MO2430.221
Reuben Crow: (ID) Jun. 1, 1848, (AN) MO2430.251
William H. Todd: (ID) Jun. 1, 1848, (AN) MO2430.252
William Macdonald: (ID) Jun. 1, 1848, (AN) MO2430.439
Rice Price: (ID) Jun. 1, 1848, (AN) MO2430.444
John M. Liles: (ID) Jun. 1, 1848, (AN) MO2430.449
James Gary: (ID) Jun. 1, 1848, (AN) MO2430.461
James F. Forman: (ID) Jun. 1, 1848, (AN) MO2430.465
George W. Combs: (ID) Mar. 1, 1848, (AN) MO2440.001
William Jeffries: (ID) Mar. 1, 1848, (AN) MO2440.011
Andrew Hunt: (ID) Mar. 1, 1848, (AN) MO2440.016
James Gary: (ID) Mar. 1, 1848, (AN) MO2440.020
George Clark: (ID) Mar. 1, 1848, (AN) MO2440.026
Bazilliam Etzler: (ID) Mar. 1, 1848, (AN) MO2440.045
John K. Ball: (ID) Mar. 1, 1848, (AN) MO2440.059
Benjamin W. Hunt: (ID) Mar. 1, 1848, (AN) MO2440.078
William C. Sullivan: (ID) Mar. 1, 1848, (AN) MO2440.080
Samuel Zeller: (ID) Mar. 1, 1848, (AN) MO2440.097
Jacob Bias: (ID) Mar. 1, 1848, (AN) MO2440.098
Charles Etzler: (ID) Mar. 1, 1848, (AN) MO2440.125
Thomas J. Calvert: (ID) Mar. 1, 1848, (AN) MO2440.140
Thomas J. Calvert: (ID) Mar. 1, 1848, (AN) MO2440.141
Edward Baly: (ID) Mar. 1, 1848, (AN) MO2440.147
Ensign B. Wells: (ID) Mar. 1, 1848, (AN) MO2440.153
Hezekiah Foree: (ID) Mar. 1, 1848, (AN) MO2440.168
Bartholomew Herrington: (ID) Mar. 1, 1848, (AN) MO2440.175

Daniel Fee: (ID) Mar. 1, 1848, (AN) MO2440.187
Rice Price: (ID) Mar. 1, 1848, (AN) MO2440.191
Daniel Sickels: (ID) Mar. 1, 1848, (AN) MO2440.206
Adam S. Kennedy: (ID) Mar. 1, 1848, (AN) MO2440.209
Benjamin W. Hunt: (ID) Mar. 1, 1848, (AN) MO2440.210
Thomas J. Calvert: (ID) Mar. 1, 1848, (AN) MO2440.211
John Wilson: (ID) Mar. 1, 1848, (AN) MO2440.212
Diderick Mangels: (ID) Mar. 1, 1848, (AN) MO2440.222
Nicholas Mangels: (ID) Mar. 1, 1848, (AN) MO2440.223
Uriah L. Shaffer: (ID) Mar. 1, 1848, (AN) MO2440.229
George Perkins: (ID) Mar. 1, 1848, (AN) MO2440.234
George M. Carlock: (ID) Mar. 1, 1848, (AN) MO2440.241
George Watkins: (ID) Mar. 1, 1848, (AN) MO2440.243
James Raybourn: (ID) Mar. 1, 1848, (AN) MO2440.244
Micajah Weber: (ID) Mar. 1, 1848, (AN) MO2440.251
Charles Devance: (ID) Mar. 1, 1848, (AN) MO2440.256
William Clark: (ID) Mar. 1, 1848, (AN) MO2440.265
Isaac N. Lewis: (ID) Mar. 1, 1848, (AN) MO2440.267
Samuel W. Athy: (ID) Mar. 1, 1848, (AN) MO2440.277
Oscar F. Hampton: (ID) Mar. 1, 1848, (AN) MO2440.298
John Weaver: (ID) Mar. 1, 1848, (AN) MO2440.299
Elliot Brandon: (ID) Mar. 1, 1848, (AN) MO2440.301
George W. Stoveall: (ID) Mar. 1, 1848, (AN) MO2440.302
Daniel Fee: (ID) Aug. 10, 1849, (AN) MO2440.466
Isaac Renfro: (ID) Aug. 10, 1849, (AN) MO2450.037
Thomas J. Calvert: (ID) Aug. 10, 1849, (AN) MO2450.051
Reuben Nichols: (ID) Aug. 10, 1849, (AN) MO2450.055
Jacob Bias: (ID) Aug. 10, 1849, (AN) MO2450.082
Lewis D. Kent: (ID) Aug. 10, 1849, (AN) MO2450.093
Branson B. Pearson: (ID) Aug. 10, 1849, (AN) MO2450.114
James Pitney: (ID) Aug. 10, 1849, (AN) MO2450.144
John H. Folker: (ID) Aug. 10, 1849, (AN) MO2450.184
John M. Childress: (ID) Aug. 10, 1849, (AN) MO2450.214
Moses D. Carter: (ID) Aug. 10, 1849, (AN) MO2450.216
Michael Grenell: (ID) Nov. 14, 1849, (AN) MO2450.245

Holt County, Missouri, Democratic County Committee, 1936-1938

Name	Township	Residence
R. G. Ruley (Chairman)	Lewis	Oregon
Mrs. Will Henning (Vice Chairman)		Mound City
Mrs. Cleo Smith (Secretary)	Hickory	Oregon
Joe Catron (Tresurer)	Minton	Fortescue
Otho Hinkle	Bigelow	Craig
Mrs. Everett Catron	Bigelow	Bigelow
H. R. Feil	Benton	Mound City
Mrs. W. E. Henning	Benton	Mound City

George Link	Clay	Maitland
Rosa Patterson	Clay	Maitland
Carl Harrison	Forbes	Forbes
Maggie Worley	Forbes	Forbes
R. W. Fawks	Forest	ForestCity
Mrs. C. C. France	Forest	Forest City
Fred D. Patterson	Hickory	Maitland
Mrs. Cleo Smith	Hickory	Oregon
Juanita Patterson	Lewis	Oregon
Elmer Nauman	Liberty	Mound City
Clyde Nauman	Liberty	Mound City
J. O. Swan	Lincoln	Corning
Susie Swan	Lincoln	Corning
Mrs. May Dodson	Minton	Fortescue
Hugh Brohan	Nodaway	Oregon
Myrtle Derr	Nodaway	Oregon
C. R Steffey	Union	Craig
Vinta Anderson	Union	Craig

<u>Howard County, Missouri, Democratic County Committee, 1936-1938</u>

Name	Township	Residence
R. P. Spencer (Chairman)		Fayette
Mrs. J. W. Stevenson (Vice Chairman)	Chariton	Glasgow
Ada Potts (Secretary)	Richmond	Fayette
Mrs. Rogers Strickland (Secretary)	Boons Lick	Boonsboro
Shelby Ware	Burton	Fayette
Mrs. Eugene Williams	Burton	Fayette
Thos. W. Snoddy	Prairie	Armstrong
Mrs. W. W. Harvey	Prairie	Armstrong
W. B. Nivert	Chariton	Glasgow
Mrs. J. W. Stevenson	Chariton	Glasgow
Frank Dockins	Boons Lick	Boonsboro
J. Boulton Settle	Franklin	New Franklin
Mrs. Herndon Bowman	Franklin	New Franklin
Denny T. Johnson	Moniteau	Fayette
Gladys Minor	Moniteau	New Franklin
Guy Dougherty	Bonne Femme	Highbee
Mrs. Paul Naylor	Bonne Femme	Fayette
Richard Perry Spencer	Richmond	Fayette

<u>St. Louis County, Missouri, Clerks in the Branch Office of the Driver's License Department, 1837-1838, St. Louis</u>

Agnes Cheeley: (POL) Democrat, (POC) School Teacher, (OC) Clerk, (RES) St. Louis

Marie Clark: (POL) Democrat, (POC) Stenographer, (OC) Clerk, (RES) St. Louis

Dorothy Grieble: (POL) Democrat, (POC) Stenographer, (OC) Clerk, (RES) St. Louis

V. Mulvihill: (POL) Democrat, (POC) Clerk, (OC) Clerk, (RES) St. Louis

Margaret Murphy: (POL) Democrat, (POC) Telephone Operator, (OC) Clerk, (RES) St. Louis

Virginia McKim: (POL) Democrate, (POC) Stenographer, (OC) Clerk, (RES) St. Louis

C. O'Connor: (POL) Democrat, (POC) Clerk, (OC) Clerk, (RES) St. Louis

Catherine Roden: (POL) Democrat, (POC) Clerk, (OC) Clerk, (RES) St. Louis

Mae Sheehan: (POL) Deomcrat, (POC) Stenographer, (OC) Clerk, (RES) St. Louis

Helen Sugrue: (POL) Democrat, (POC) Stenographer, (OC) Clerk, (RES) St. Louis

Mary Walsh: (POL) Democrat, (POC) Clerk, (OC) Clerk, (RES) St. Louis

Mary Whalen: (POL) Democrat, (POC) Clerk, (OC) Clerk, (RES) St. Louis

Shelby County, Missouri, Democratic County Committee, 1936-1938

Name	Township	Residence
Earl Garrison (Chairman)	Bethel	Bethel
Dixie Dean (Vice Chairman)	Salt River	Shelbina
Mrs. Mary Jane Drennan (Secretary)	Bethel	Shelbyville
Mrs. Mabel Wood (Treasurer)	--	Emden
Omer R. Dye	Tiger Fork	Shelbyville
Mrs. Edgar Rife	Tiger Fork	Bethel
Chas. Killen	Taylor	Leonard
Mrs. Otis McCully	Taylor	Leonard
John A. O'Daniel	Jackson	Hunnewell
Ruth Jordan	Jackson	Shelbina
E. W. Ragland	Clay	Clarence
Mrs. Etta Dorrell	Clay	Clarence
Tom Weatherford	Jefferson	Clarence
Mrs. Anna Ash	Jefferson	Clarence
W. T. Dimmitt	Black Creek	Shelbyville
Mrs. Arthur Burk	Black Creek	Shelbyville
Lewis Carroll	Lentner	Lentner
Clunette Wood	Lentner	Lentner
H. J. Turner	North River	Emden
Mrs. R. A. Wood	North River	Emden
E. W. Jewett	Salt River	Shelbina

St. Louis County, Missouri, June, 1916, Graduates Soldan High School
Mildred Candy, Anita Hall, Marquise Klepper, William Coburn, Frances Stevens, Evadne Alden, Sylvia Walden, Richard McCullen, Frannces Murch, Martha Casey, Van Deniso, Edythe Brown, Ellizabeth Moore, Lucien M. Brigham, Paul Wilkerson, Mildred Murch, Henry Schwenk, Ruby Mason, Martha Potts, Welles Pullen, Eugenenia Cayce, Katherine Jordan, Harvey Luley, Doris Deucke, Edmund Marx, Sarah Subovitz, Jeannette Lebermuth, Lottiemae Logan, Harold Brinkman, Katherine Bain, Marshall Cree, Irene Wooster, Kenneth Chroa, Howard Preston, Alma Wightman, Edward Coleman Barnidge, Harold Landau, Mildred James, Martin Connelly, Kenneth Flint, Concordia Bode, Arthur Nash, Louis Loeb, Johanna Harris, Leo Mayer, Ernestine Biby, Harold V. Leslie, Edwina Luckey, Robert Arthur, Beth Barnett, Anson Keller, InezHellman, Jamerson McCormack, Allie Vere Davis, Roberta Woodson, Marion Strauss, Marguerite Brod, Edith Smith, Barclay Meador, Helen Moll, Rothwell Watts, Alice Chamberlain, Rex Dewhirst, Florence Jacobson, Rosalind Eberson, Renate Schweig, Lucile Glazebrook, Staley Rathbun, Louise Trask, George Kroenlein, Marjorie Brockmiller, William Stroeter, Urilla Eckert, Herbert Mundt, Hannah Adamsky, Julia Jonah, Mortimer Mears, Charlotte Sands, Paul S. Loomis, Josephine Parker, Edgar Harras (sic), Helen Lugenbeel, Ladis Offofy

Johnson County, Missouri, Officers of the Bar Association, 1919-1920

Name	Office	Residence
Nick M. Bradly	President	Warrensburg
John Beyers	Vice President	Warrensburg
W. L. Chaney	Secretary	Warrensburg
A. Musser	Treasurer	Holden

Andrew County, Missouri, Officers of the Bar Association, 1919-1920

Name	Office	Residence
Peter C. Brett	President	Savannah
K. D. Cross	Vice President	Savannah
Grover C. Sparks	Secretary-Treasurer	Savannah

Clark County, Missouri, Officers of the Bar Association, 1919-1920

Name	Office	Residence
T. L. Montgomery	President	Kahoka
John M. Dawson	Vice President	Kahoka
C. T. Llewellyn	Secretary-Treasurer	Kahoka

Clay County, Missouri, Officers of the Bar Association, 1919-1920

Name	Office	Residence
W A. Craven	President	Excelsior Springs
M. E. Lawson	Vice President	Liberty
James S. Simball	Secretary-Treasurer	Liberty

Holt County, Missouri, Officers of the Bar Association, 1919-1920

Name	Office	Residence
John A. Gilbreath	President	Clinton
Walter G. Davis	Vice President	Windsor
Henry F. Poague	Clinton	Secretary
N. B. Conrad	Montrose	Treasurer

INDEX

AARONSON, 115
ABBIT, 80 157
ABEL, 25 177 185
ABELL, 185
ABERNATHY, 9
ABERSON, 27
ABLAMAWISCZ, 130
ABT, 138
ACKENHAUSESN, 124
ACKERMAN, 194
ACKERMANN, 125
ACKERSON, 104
ACKLUM, 97
ACQUAVIOVA, 121
ACQUAVIVA, 119
ACRES, 197
ACTON, 37
ADAM, 35 185
ADAMS, 5 25-29 31-37 63 68 74 80 83 92 104 127 139 148 157 171 184-185 196
ADAMSKY, 215
ADCOCK, 104
ADDISON, 138
ADDUDLE, 2
ADELUNG, 37
ADKINS, 139
ADKISSON, 37
AGEE, 145 148 157
AGEN, 30-31
AGNEW, 182
AHRENS, 117 168
AILER, 27
AINGE, 74
AINSLY, 139
AINSWORTH, 139
AIRD, 16
ALBALT, 114
ALBERS, 37 125 204
ALBERT, 137 185
ALBRECHT, 173
ALBURT, 25
ALDEN, 215
ALDERS, 93
ALDERSON, 26
ALDREDGE, 32
ALEXANDER, 30-32 85 90 104 126 139 195
ALLAN, 173
ALLARD, 137
ALLCORN, 139
ALLEN, 3 5 13 21 26 33 37 65 92 94 103-104 124 130 134 137 139 148 168 185 189
ALLEY, 99

ALLISON, 2 5 30 68 72 148 157
ALLMAN, 104
ALMOND, 93
ALSOP, 114 139
ALTENBEREND, 125
ALTMAN, 185
ALVERSON, 139
ALYEA, 81
AMBROSE, 67
AMBRUSTER, 183
AMBS, 185
AMICK, 139
AMMERMAN, 8
AMMERSON, 31
AMMON, 37
AMOS, 37
AMSBARY, 31
ANASTASIA, 169
ANDERS, 9
ANDERSEN, 37
ANDERSON, 2 7 11 25-26 29-30 32-35 37 69 98 104 123 139 145 148 157 194 213
ANDRAE, 182
ANDRES, 171
ANDREW, 2 139
ANDREWS, 5 27 37 83 139
ANEMOW, 183
ANFINSON, 37
ANGELL, 28
ANGUS, 185
ANHEUSER, 176
ANNIS, 118
ANSELL, 139
ANSELMENT, 37
ANTHEWISE, 139
ANTHONY, 157
ANTINE, 27
ANTLE, 201
ANVILLE, 38
ANZALONE, 118
APPEL, 115
APPLEBEE, 38
APPLEGATE, 14
APPLER, 130
ARBATHNATY, 185
ARCHER, 18
ARENA, 121
ARENO, 121
ARGABRIGHT, 11
ARKFELD, 38
ARMBRUSTER, 184
ARMSTRONG, 15 185
ARNETT, 2 139

ARNEY, 38
ARNHART, 104
ARNOLD, 24-25 82 84 92 139 145 209
ARSTIP, 69
ARTERBERRY, 31
ARTHUR, 215
ARTHURS, 38
ASCHE, 38
ASCHMORE, 175
ASH, 214
ASHCRAFT, 139
ASHER, 148
ASHFORD, 194
ASHLEY, 4 35
ASKINS, 38
AST, 124
ATENONE, 168
ATHERTON, 2
ATHY, 212
ATKERSON, 104
ATKINS, 195
ATKINSON, 17 189
ATON, 5
ATTEBERRY, 139
ATTERBERRY, 139
ATTERBURY, 185
ATWOOD, 127
AUBUCHON, 175 189
AUDERS, 195
AULLMAN, 185
AULT, 38
AURORA, 134
AUST, 127
AUSTEN, 35
AUSTIN, 5 139 185
AUSTON, 33
AUTH, 84
AUTHOR, 2
AUXIER, 148
AVERETTE, 139
AWALT, 195
AYERS, 202
AYLE, 38
AYRES, 103
BABB, 2
BACHELOR, 185
BACKENDORF, 170
BADDOCK, 96
BAER, 116
BAFUMMO, 114
BAFUNNO, 113
BAGBY, 157
BAGLEY, 185
BAGNELL, 116

BAILEY, 2 36 38 80 124 131 139 185 194
BAILY, 26 166
BAIN, 22 215
BAINES, 26
BAINTER, 20
BAINUM, 196
BAIRD, 19 28
BAJECK, 38
BAKER, 2 5-6 17 25 27 32 36 38 81 98 148 157 185 197-198 201-202
BALAD, 25
BALDANF, 174
BALDWIN, 2 176 185 206
BALES, 33
BALEW, 157
BALFE, 132
BALL, 139 181 185 211
BALLARD, 38 148 157
BALLE, 2
BALLENGER, 102
BALLEW, 139
BALLOW, 185
BALM, 91
BALME, 138
BALMER, 129-138
BALSAMO, 174
BALTER, 101
BALTHROPE, 2
BALY, 211
BANING, 185
BANKS, 9 38
BANN, 146
BANTZ, 38
BARADA, 95
BARBER, 25 102 185
BARCHI, 125
BARCLAY, 185
BARFOOT, 38
BARGAR, 185
BARGSTADT, 38
BARHENDT, 76
BARILETTI, 118
BARKER, 2 38 138
BARKSDOL, 32
BARN, 209
BARNABLE, 125
BARNES, 2 101 139 148 157 207 209
BARNET, 33
BARNETT, 3 30 37-38 73 85 98 139 148 215
BARNEY, 168
BARNIDGE, 215
BARR, 2
BARREN, 139
BARRETT, 38 117 119 171
BARRIER, 203
BARRINGER, 197
BARRIS, 157

BARRY, 38 69 103 118 120 125
BARSTOW, 131
BARTHOLOMEW, 166
BARTLETT, 38 194
BARTON, 27-28 139
BARTSCH, 38
BARTUP, 2
BASEHART, 122
BASEY, 139
BASKER, 26
BASKET, 139
BASS, 38 125 139 191
BASSER, 99
BASSETT, 23 185 201
BASTIAN, 119
BATEMAN, 38
BATES, 38
BATTIN, 38
BATTON, 25
BAUER, 63 169 175
BAUGH, 26
BAUGHER, 205
BAUGHMAN, 185
BAUM, 4
BAUMAN, 125
BAUMANN, 124
BAUMBACK, 1
BAUMFELDER, 130
BAUMGARTNER, 179
BAUMHOFF, 168
BAUMLE, 171
BAXTER, 34 104 139 171
BAY, 204 207
BAYLESS, 123
BAYS, 25
BAZERGUE, 157
BEACH, 38
BEADLE, 38
BEALL, 123
BEAN, 185
BEARD, 33 35
BEARDON, 26
BEARDSLEY, 148
BEASHERS, 26
BEASLEY, 67
BEATTY, 190
BEAUCHAMP, 157
BEAVER, 185
BECCARD, 38
BECHTLEN, 173
BECK, 10 30 84 204
BECKER, 38
BECKERS, 125
BECKET, 25 139
BECKETT, 104
BECVAR, 116
BEDELL, 209
BEDFORD, 157
BEECH, 194
BEECHER, 122

BEERBOHN, 38
BEERMANN, 124
BEERS, 185
BEERY, 38
BEESON, 38
BEETHE, 38
BEGLY, 77
BEHLERS, 38
BEHLING, 38
BEHRENDS, 38
BEHRGINAN, 84
BEITZE, 178
BELCH, 2
BELDEN, 2 139
BELDING, 131
BELL, 2 4 39 129-131 138-139 148 157 165 175 177 193
BELLER, 157 185
BELLINI, 133
BELMER, 139
BELOWS, 205
BEMER, 185
BEMM, 193
BENBOW, 197
BENCHEL, 72
BENDA, 39 178
BENDER, 122
BENNET, 25
BENNETT, 39 104 185 194
BENNING, 209
BENSON, 19 39 88 139
BENTLEY, 85 202
BENTLY, 139
BENTROF, 176
BERBY, 139
BERGER, 65 172
BERGMAN, 68 82
BERGOM, 65
BERK, 169
BERKETT, 4
BERKEY, 39
BERNAL, 119
BERNARD, 39 139 175
BERNARDO, 117
BERNET, 27
BERNIE, 135
BERNIUS, 171
BERRIS, 192
BERRY, 1-2 26 32 104 139
BERWICK, 20
BESLEY, 137
BESLY, 137
BESSA, 177
BEST, 39 139 157
BETE, 15
BETHARDS, 2
BETTEYS, 20
BETTS, 21
BETZ, 125
BEUTEN, 115
BEVERLY, 139

BEVINS, 39 69 72
BEVRIDGE, 23
BEWHURST, 1
BEYERS, 215
BEYY, 132
BIAS, 211-212
BIBB, 25 205 208
BIBLE, 39
BIBY, 215
BIDA, 116
BIELICKI, 118
BIELOWSKI, 121
BIERCE, 39
BIERE, 39
BILDERBACK, 157
BILLINGS, 2 68
BILLIPS, 72
BINE, 171
BINGHAM, 39
BIRCH, 130 139
BIRD, 26 39 196
BIRDSEYE, 136
BIRKENBACH, 201
BIRKENMIEIER, 179
BIRMAM, 139
BIRMINGHAM, 15 104
BIRTWISTLE, 195
BISBEE, 75
BISHOP, 2 12 84 138 204
BISWELL, 139
BIT, 117
BITELLO, 33
BITTICK, 188
BIVEN, 139
BLACK, 25 27 124 139 196 201
BLACKBURN, 2
BLACKWELL, 139 145
BLAGG, 192 199
BLAHA, 122
BLAIR, 37 188
BLAISDELL, 39
BLAISE, 39
BLAKE, 63 70 126 182
BLAKELEY, 148 157
BLAKELY, 5 72 124 139
BLAKESLEE, 39
BLAKEY, 2
BLAMER, 130
BLAND, 148 197 204
BLANE, 139
BLANKENBECKET, 139
BLANKENSHIP, 139
BLANTON, 139 189 207
BLATTEN, 2
BLEDSOE, 4 124 148 157 174
BLEILE, 119
BLENSKI, 121
BLEVINS, 5 28 30 36 127
BLINE, 16
BLIZZARD, 2

BLOCK, 39 125
BLOMENKAMP, 39
BLOOM, 139
BLOOMER, 100
BLOUNT, 90
BLOW, 137
BLOXHAM, 39
BLOYS, 139
BLUBACH, 103
BLUMER, 39
BLUNT, 185
BLURTON, 139
BLYE, 25
BLYTHE, 201
BOAZ, 185
BOBETT, 139
BOCKA, 125
BODE, 215
BOEHE, 14
BOEKHOFF, 125
BOENCEKE, 113
BOETTSCHER, 181
BOEWER, 125
BOGART, 104 195
BOGGS, 139
BOGY, 136
BOHANNON, 157
BOHART, 145 148
BOHLING, 39
BOHN, 168
BOHRES, 174
BOILSTON, 4
BOISSEAU, 28
BOLD, 173
BOLDEN, 139
BOLEN, 66
BOLLAR, 121
BOLLMAN, 131-133 136 185
BOLTE, 114
BOLTS, 39
BOMBARGER, 157
BOMBECK, 88
BOND, 66 121 185 197
BONDENBOUCHY, 78
BONDURANT, 17 139
BONES, 31
BONHAM, 189
BONSACK, 39
BONSEY, 25
BONTA, 39
BONZANI, 116
BOOKEE, 2
BOOKER, 2 28
BOOM, 139
BOON, 139 157
BOONE, 133 148
BOOSHER, 139
BOOTH, 39 97 139 189
BOREL, 103
BOYD, 25 39 127
BOYDE, 139

BOYDSTUN, 157
BOYER, 5 145 148 157 177 188
BOYLE, 131 133 185
BOYLES, 30 132 185
BOZARTH, 139
BOZECHOWSKI, 116
BOZWELL, 139
BRACHTENDORF, 177
BRACKEN, 197
BRADBURY, 4
BRADFORD, 23 203
BRADHACK, 176
BRADLEY, 2 17 29-33 35-36 139 189
BRADLY, 139 205 215
BRADSHAW, 30 191
BRADWAY, 82
BRADY, 2 97 102 125 177
BRAGG, 5 139
BRAHMSTEADT, 39
BRAINARD, 137
BRAKEY, 185
BRALMANN, 103
BRAMBLETTE, 39
BRANCLEAVE, 81
BRAND, 39 102 124 185
BRANDHORST, 171
BRANDON, 30 212
BRANDT, 39
BRANK, 1
BRANN, 75 173
BRANNIGAN, 175
BRANNIN, 139
BRANSON, 189
BRASHEAR, 139
BRASHER, 139
BRASHERS, 105
BRATCHER, 9
BRATNER, 185
BRATTON, 39 184
BRAUN, 18 119
BRAWDUS, 139
BRAZZIL, 35
BREANEL, 185
BREDEMEIER, 39
BREEDEN, 39
BREEZE, 121
BREGGEMAN, 172
BREHERRY, 120
BREMENKAMP, 174
BRENER, 36
BRENNEN, 40
BRESTEL, 40
BRETT, 121 215
BREWER, 35 165 177
BREWIN, 116
BRICK, 36
BRIDGEMAN, 148
BRIDGEMON, 37
BRIDGES, 105

BRIGGS, 125 133 139
BRIGHAM, 2 215
BRIGHT, 25
BRILL, 82
BRINEY, 25
BRING, 24
BRINKERHOFF, 2
BRINKMAN, 103 215
BRINTON, 148
BRISTON, 25
BRITTAIN, 146 148 184
BRIXEY, 201
BROADDUS, 139
BROCK, 211
BROCKHAN, 181
BROCKLEMAN, 177
BROCKMAN, 28-29 32 34 139
BROCKMANN, 125
BROCKMILLER, 215
BROD, 215
BRODERICK, 121
BRODZINSKY, 113
BROGAN, 40 210
BROHAN, 213
BROKAW, 135
BROLLIAR, 40
BROLYER, 196
BROMLEY, 66
BRONSON, 40
BROOKS, 2 32-33 139 148 157
BROSNAHAN, 118 120
BROTHERS, 125
BROTT, 185
BROW, 136
BROWER, 185
BROWLE, 90
BROWN, 2-5 10 17 25-27 29 33-36 40 65 68 76 95 100-102 105 126 129 132-133 137-139 145-146 149 157 165-166 183 185 189 195 200-201 215
BROWNE, 137
BROWNING, 2 26 31 105 139
BROWNLEE, 185
BROZ, 40
BRUBAKER, 132
BRUCE, 74 134 185 195
BRUDER, 175
BRUEMNER, 179
BRUER, 182
BRUESEKE, 113
BRUG, 115
BRUMBACK, 105
BRUMBECK, 87
BRUMLE, 87
BRUMLEY, 157
BRUNDAGE, 139
BRUNER, 125 135
BRUNETT, 123
BRUNING, 103

BRUNNER, 132
BRUNO, 125
BRUNS, 40 103
BRUNTS, 139
BRUNZ, 40
BRYAN, 169 185
BRYANT, 19 26 35 40 93 102 205
BRYNDA, 184
BUCHANAN, 101 138
BUCHER, 204
BUCK, 130-131 136
BUCKLAND, 5
BUCKLEY, 125 137 185
BUCKMAN, 185
BUCKNELL, 40
BUCKNER, 2
BUETER, 113
BUFF, 29-30
BUFFUM, 138
BUFORD, 2
BUGBY, 139
BUHRMAN, 40
BULL, 139
BUMBARGER, 5
BUMESON, 191
BUMGARDNER, 40
BUNCHELBERGER, 18
BUNGARDAR, 139
BUNNELL, 139
BUNTE, 124
BUNTING, 5 100
BURCE, 73
BURCH, 40 185 206
BURCKHEARTT, 139
BURES, 40
BURG, 116
BURGE, 139 196
BURGESS, 149
BURK, 40 80 124 149 185 214
BURKE, 96 118 179 210-211
BURKHARD, 40
BURKHART, 198
BURKHARTT, 139
BURNAN, 5
BURNES, 157
BURNET, 25
BURNETT, 29 31 89 105 123 139 149
BURNETTE, 123
BURNS, 40 65 120 157 185
BURNSIDE, 149
BURRIS, 79 139 157
BURRISS, 139
BURROW, 105
BURT, 185
BURTLE, 208
BURTON, 25 32 139 206
BUSH, 9 20 66 101 149 170 204
BUSHNELL, 185

BUSKIRK, 68
BUSTER, 139
BUTLER, 24 29 67 139 158 189
BUTNER, 196
BUTSHER, 83
BUTTERFIELD, 183 185
BUTTS, 11 34 70 139
BUTZ, 169
BUTZA, 118
BUXTON, 130
BUZZARD, 2 85
BWESING, 172
BYERS, 135 194
BYNUM, 139
BYRNE, 40
BYRNUM, 139
CABINESO, 83
CACEY, 67
CACHELIN, 7
CADDE, 82
CADENAZZI, 181
CADEY, 185
CADY, 139
CAFFERATE, 124
CAGLE, 105
CAHILL, 40
CAIN, 98
CAIRUS, 119
CALDAMONE, 116
CALDWELL, 2 105 139 208
CALFEE, 2
CALHOUN, 2 99-100
CALKINS, 40
CALL, 88 105
CALLAHAN, 158 182
CALLAWAY, 140 208
CALLEE, 122
CALLEWAERT, 119
CALLIHAN, 93
CALVERT, 140 208 211-212
CAMERIN, 178
CAMERON, 125 149 193
CAMPBELL, 2 11 30 35 71 80 96 105 132 140 149 184 200 205
CANALL, 2
CANDY, 215
CANFIELD, 6
CANINE, 105
CANNON, 94
CANOLE, 140
CANOTE, 140
CANTER, 149
CANTY, 168
CAPESTRO, 174
CAPP, 2
CAPPEN, 40
CAPPS, 26
CARDELLA, 129 134 137
CARDNALL, 174

CAREW, 35
CAREY, 121 140 185
CARGILL, 84
CARLIN, 114
CARLOCK, 212
CARLSON, 13 40 86
CARLSTEN, 40
CARLTON, 25
CARLYLE, 158
CARMAN, 17 207-208
CARMICHAEL, 28
CARMODY, 170
CARNELL, 140
CARNETTE, 105
CARNEY, 140 174
CAROTHERS, 2
CARPENTER, 31 40 64 191 193
CARPER, 86
CARR, 2 25 40 105
CARRELL, 127
CARRICO, 2
CARRIKER, 185
CARRINGTON, 97
CARRITY, 95
CARROL, 24 205
CARROLL, 2 25 40 75 125 140 185 214
CARRY, 25
CARSE, 40
CARSNER, 25
CARSON, 24 105 140
CARTEN, 182
CARTER, 25-26 30 40 66 82 105 124 140 182 185-186 212
CARTHA, 101
CARTRIGHT, 2
CARTZENDERFER, 71
CARVER, 2 40 194
CASE, 18
CASEY, 149 176 190 215
CASH, 140 149 186
CASHMAN, 171
CASON, 140
CASPER, 103 167
CASPERS, 40
CASPUR, 140
CASS, 78
CASSELL, 95
CASSERLY, 114
CASSICY, 123
CASSIDY, 186
CASTLEY, 105
CAST, 40
CASTEEL, 26 88 102
CASTELLO, 126
CASTILE, 11
CASTILLER, 105
CASTILLO, 2
CASTONGN, 103

CASTLE, 3 30 149 190
CATANZINO, 121
CATCHING, 3
CATE, 149 158
CATHON, 24
CATLET, 158
CATON, 140
CATREL, 27
CATRON, 123 212
CAUANAGH, 125
CAUEDY, 93
CAULEY, 83
CAULTON, 104
CAVENY, 40
CAVITT, 29
CAYCE, 215
CERNY, 117
CERVANTES, 168
CESTERSON, 34
CHADDOCK, 11
CHADICK, 2
CHADWICH, 40
CHAFIN, 149
CHALUPA, 40
CHAMBERLAIN, 27-28 30 35 215
CHAMBERS, 5 26
CHAMPION, 140
CHANDLER, 78 105 140 186 201
CHANEY, 24 66 158 193 215
CHANY, 146
CHEYNEY, 41
CHICKLAW, 94
CHILBERG, 131-132
CHILDERS, 25
CHILDRESS, 212
DORRELL, 25 214
DORSCH, 42
DORSEY, 87
DOSS, 106
DOTSON, 140
DOTY, 25 140
DOUD, 42 211
DOUGEN, 186
DOUGHERTY, 101 186 213
DOUGLAS, 27 29
DOUGLASS, 2 36 140
DOVE, 196
DOW, 140
DOWELL, 140
DOWLING, 204
DOWNEY, 106 140
DOWNIE, 124
DOWNING, 26 42 82
DOYLE, 16 68 83 96 172 200 206-207
DRAKE, 4 135 140 186
DRECKSHAGE, 125
DREDGE, 42
DRENNAN, 214

DREW, 210
DRIEMEYER, 125
DRIER, 177
DRISCOLL, 185
DROEGE, 181
DROESCHER, 42
DRONENBURG, 150
DRUEN, 106
DRURY, 186
DRYDEN, 2 146 150 159
DUANE, 99
DUBLIN, 69
DUBOIS, 114
DUCATE, 148
DUDGEON, 140
DUDLEY, 34 106 131
DUECKE, 215
DUFF, 26
DUGEON, 2
DUGGAN, 120 125
DUGGER, 106
DUGLASS, 31
DUGRUEN, 176
DUHACKER, 117
DUKE, 5
DULANY, 43
DUMBACH, 176
DUMER, 174
DUNAWAY, 29 31 33 36 43
DUNBAR, 95
DUNCAN, 2 26 28-29 31-33 43 64 79 87-88 116 140 150 159 195
DUNGAN, 37
DUNGEON, 2
DUNHAM, 25
DUNICA, 140
DUNKIN, 140
DUNKMANN, 177
DUNLAP, 77-78 159
DUNN, 2 43 65 140 194 196
DUNNE, 70
DUNNING, 4 77 150 191
DURALL, 32
DURANT, 195
DURAUD, 165
DURBIN, 2
DURIN, 140
DURKIN, 69
DUSING, 116
DUSTIN, 138
DUTCHER, 20
DUTTON, 190
DUVAL, 73
DUVAULT, 106
DWYER, 2 121
DYE, 2 43 214
DYER, 118 140 196
DYKES, 43
DYSART, 63 77
EADS, 186

EAGAN, 182
EAGEN, 36
EAKLE, 2
EALY, 140
EARHART, 75
EARICKSON, 140
EARIXSON, 4 150 159
EARLS, 3
EARLY, 29 89
EARNEST, 2
EARSOM, 22
EASLEY, 2 186 202
EASLY, 25
EASTESS, 106
EATINGER, 43
EATON, 2 167
EBBEKA, 43
EBERHARD, 178
EBERSON, 215
EBERT, 172
ECKART, 103
ECKERT, 185 215
ECKMAN, 202
EDDINGS, 140
EDDINS, 140
EDDY, 191
EDELMANN, 124
EDENS, 202
EDGAR, 2 140
EDGINGTON, 43 125
EDINGTON, 186
EDMONDS, 82
EDWARDS, 3 28-30 33 37 43 70-71 136 150
EELLS, 43
EFNER, 87
EGAN, 29
EGBERT, 35
EGGERS, 168
EGGLESTON, 43
EHMEN, 43
EIBETT, 89
EICHELBERGER, 43
EICKMEIER, 43
EIKER, 43
EILENBERG, 136
EILERS, 7
ELAM, 15
ELDER, 98
ELGIN, 2 140
ELISON, 4
ELKINS, 26 140
ELLIGOOD, 2
ELLINGER, 95
ELLIOTT, 2 5 7 140 150 192
ELLIPIT, 150
ELLIS, 1 26 34 43 106 140 186
ELLISON, 4 43 146 159
ELLISTON, 75
ELM, 174
ELMERS, 136

ELMES, 132
ELMORE, 43 140
ELSHIRE, 43
ELY, 125 208
ELZ, 172
EMAN, 43
EMANUEL, 125
EMBERSON, 140
EMBREE, 140
EMERICK, 5
EMERSON, 43 138
EMICK, 43
EMMERICH, 165
EMMONS, 32 36
EMON, 28
EMORY, 182
ENDRES, 181
ENGELHARDT, 172
ENGELMAN, 78
ENGIN, 140
ENGLAND, 25 34 146
ENGLEMAN, 15 43
ENGLERT, 43
ENLES, 169
ENLOW, 31-32
ENNEN, 2
ENNIS, 2
ENSLEY, 43
ENYART, 5 140
EPBRIGHT, 28
EPMAN, 31
EPPNER, 86
EPRIGHT, 30 34
ERICKSON, 43 106
ERNST, 43
ERVIN, 33
ERWIN, 35
ESCHER, 43
ESEMAN, 36
ESHERTON, 89
ESHOM, 43
ESILI, 183
ESKRIDGE, 2
ESTABROOK, 132
ESTEL, 2
ESTES, 150
ESTICE, 140
ESTILL, 140
ESTIS, 140
ETHERIDGE, 25
ETHRIDGE, 106
ETLING, 2
ETZLER, 211
EUBANK, 25
EVANS, 2 25 35 43 140-141 150 159 179 195
EVELAND, 43
EVERETT, 146
EVERLY, 141
EWELL, 150
EWIN, 141

EWING, 141 146 150 159
FAGAN, 186
FAHEY, 115 118
FAILLIK, 122
FAIRBAIN, 22
FAIRCHILD, 116
FALKE, 43
FALKENBURG, 205
FALLEY, 207
FALLON, 124
FAR, 32
FARLEY, 22 30 35
FARNHAM, 138
FARNSWORTH, 70
FARRELL, 63
FARRIGNTON, 43
FARRINGER, 133
FARRINGTON, 175
FARRIS, 17 124
FASS, 43
FASSEL, 119
FASZHOLZ, 182
FAULHABER, 43 125
FAULKNER, 186
FAURE, 136
FAWKS, 213
FEA, 125
FEAGAN, 208-209
FEATHER, 43
FEE, 212
FEENEY, 44
FEES, 44
FEHER, 169
FEICHT, 44
FEIL, 132 212
FEILER, 125
FEILINGS, 44
FELAND, 94 141 150
FELDHAUS, 114-115
FELDMAN, 44
FELDMEIER, 115
FELLING, 101
FELLWOCK, 106
FENNESSY, 172
FENTON, 186
FERARO, 168
FERGASON, 32
FERGERSON, 28
FERGESON, 186
FERGUSON, 3 24-25 28 30 33 141
FERRELL, 88 150
FERRIGAN, 178
FERRILL, 150
FERRITER, 117
FETLOR, 103
FETTERS, 205
FEW, 129
FIALA, 117
FICHTENMEYER, 171
FICKAS, 30 33 36

FIDDLER, 82 103
FIECKER, 74
FIEDLER, 116
FIELD, 141 146
FIELDS, 141 159 186
FIFFER, 10
FILIPIAK, 121
FILLEY, 125
FILMER, 44
FILTER, 44
FINCH, 4 21 90 146
FINDLEY, 13
FINDLING, 2
FINE, 27 32
FINELY, 63
FINK, 126
FINLEY, 26
FINN, 2
FINNEGAN, 44
FINNELL, 141
FINNEY, 2
FINTEL, 44
FIRMAN, 2
FISCH, 126
FISCHER, 126
FISHBURN, 26
FISHCER, 44
FISHER, 8 26-27 36 44 93-94 97 141 166
FISK, 130
FITCH, 8 44
FITZGERALD, 23 29 37 44 76 100 125 167 174
FITZGERELL, 34
FITZHUGH, 4 150
FITZPATRICK, 31 102
FITZSIMONS, 124
FIX, 44
FLACHMEIER, 181
FLACHS, 176
FLAHERTY, 183
FLANAGAN, 166
FLANARY, 5 150
FLANERY, 159
FLEER, 171
FLEMING, 29 79 118 141 185
FLETCHER, 2 13 124 127 146 159 165
FLIER, 176
FLINT, 13 23 159 215
FLOCK, 44
FLOSS, 136
FLOURNEY, 106
FLOURNOY, 106-107
FLOYD, 79 209
FLY, 25 126 141
FOGG, 202
FOGLESONG, 107
FOLCHE, 190
FOLEY, 2
FOLKER, 212

FONDA, 205
FOOTE, 188
FORBES, 27 44
FORBSTEIN, 130
FORD, 2 44 94 141 159 169 184 211
FOREE, 211
FOREMAN, 2
FORESTER, 2
FORKNER, 102
FORLINES, 107
FORMAN, 2 211
FORREY, 141
FORSTER, 172
FORSYTHE, 2 141
FORTNER, 107
FOSKET, 44
FOSTER, 2-3 28 30-31 34-35 97 128 141 186
FOSTERMAKER, 44
FOSTLER, 183
FOUTS, 150 159
FOWKES, 44
FOWLER, 2 26 86 150 159
FOX, 2 33-34 36 126 137 141 169
FOY, 44
FOYE, 93
FRAILEY, 193
FRAISER, 107
FRAKES, 3 5 21 63 87 95 150 159
FRALEY, 122
FRAME, 121 169
FRANCE, 213
FRANCIS, 29 77 81 193
FRANCISCO, 80
FRANK, 124 191
FRANKLIN, 27 186
FRANS, 159
FRANZEN, 44
FRASS, 103
FRAY, 141
FRAZEE, 205
FRAZELL, 44
FRAZER, 37
FRAZIER, 10
FREAR, 44
FREDERICK, 166
FREE, 26
FREELAND, 26 159
FREEMAN, 26 44
FREEOUF, 44
FREIERSHAUS, 115
FRENCH, 44 99 132 174
FRENDENTHAL, 190
FRIEDEBORN, 125
FRIEDRICKSEN, 44
FRIEMANN, 103
FRIEND, 73 107 191 198
FRIES, 103

FRIESMAN, 44
FRIMPLE, 12
FRINK, 44
FRISKA, 113
FRISTOE, 141
FRITZ, 44
FRODENBURGH, 171
FROGGE, 159
FROMONG, 44
FROSCHHEISER, 44
FROST, 34 36
FROUGHT, 122
FRUECHTE, 125
FRUIT, 44
FUDGE, 159
FUENBORN, 179
FULKERSON, 32 177
FULLBRIGHT, 107
FULLER, 2 26
FULLINSTINE, 141
FULTON, 3 23 33 151 159
FUNK, 26
FUNKHOUSER, 44
FURBEY, 186
FUREY, 124
FURGESON, 28 165
FURGUSON, 30
FURNISH, 141
FURST, 125
GABBERT, 93 141 146 151 159
GABELL, 23
GACSON, 92
GADDIS, 15
GAGE, 44 101 141
GAGNEBIN, 7
GAHAN, 103
GAHN, 202
GAINES, 186
GAITHER, 26
GAITLAND, 119
GALBERT, 141
GALBREATH, 44
GALE, 44
GALLAGHER, 177-178 181 183
GALLAHER, 37
GALLAWAY, 25 151
GALLENSTEIN, 141
GALLION, 197
GALLITAN, 186
GALLOWAY, 77 172
GALLUP, 195
GALVIN, 100 102
GAMBLE, 2
GAMMEL, 44
GANE, 141
GANGES, 179
GANIN, 186
GANN, 3-4 159
GANNS, 141

GANT, 32 94
GANTER, 125
GARAVELLI, 120
GARBER, 9
GARDNER, 37 44 74 90 107 159 183 186
GARLAND, 141
GARLIN, 151
GARLON, 84
GARMAN, 45
GARMER, 186
GARNER, 141 189
GARNETT, 2
GARRAWAY, 141
GARRED, 159
GARRET, 36 137 182
GARRETT, 45 125 132
GARRIS, 201
GARRISON, 22 107 185 214
GARSTING, 193
GARSWICH, 186
GARTES, 5
GARTH, 101
GARTIN, 159
GARTNER, 4
GARTON, 69 159
GARTRELL, 2
GARTSBY, 92
GARVEN, 141
GARVEY, 172
GARY, 211
GASHER, 186
GASKILL, 37
GASS, 137
GAST, 165
GASTON, 45
GATES, 73 87 141 196
GATEWOOD, 141
GAUGHAN, 21
GAULDIN, 5
GAULT, 45
GAUNCE, 200
GAVIS, 120
GAW, 107
GAY, 100
GEAR, 45
GEARHARD, 14
GEAZLE, 141
GEBHARD, 45
GEBHART, 125
GECHTEL, 181
GEDDES, 133
GEELAND, 141
GEERY, 141
GEHRING, 169
GEIGKEY, 2
GELLETT, 69
GELLING, 159
GELLOTTLY, 190
GENNUG, 13
GENTIL, 125

GENTILE, 119
GENTRY, 2
GEORGE, 24 45 100 107 141
GERARD, 45
GERBER, 125
GERDEMANN, 103
GERDES, 45
GERGUSON, 2 116
GERHARD, 122
GERRAD, 141
GERSIE, 125
GESS, 141
GEST, 32
GETTER, 106
GEYHARTT, 141
GEZT, 126
GHOLSTON, 107
GHORKE, 120
GIBBONS, 2
GIBBS, 141
GIBLIN, 115
GIBSON, 4 26 31 65 125 141 146 151 159 192 200
GIDDENS, 146
GIDNEY, 2
GIESY, 2
GILBERT, 107 127
GILBREATH, 216
GILCHRIST, 45
GILDEA, 115
GILESPIE, 179
GILKERSON, 35
GILKESON, 45
GILL, 45 118 141 159 196
GILLASPIE, 14
GILLELAND, 29
GILLESPIE, 2 90 126
GILLET, 135
GILLETTE, 135
GILLHAM, 137 186
GILLIAM, 151 159
GILLIAND, 19
GILLILAND, 8 27
GILLIS, 2
GILLISPIE, 186
GILLMORE, 3
GILLOCK, 26
GILLUM, 30 141
GILMAN, 2 100
GILMORE, 36 45 98 134 146 151
GILS, 31
GILSON, 186
GIMBEL, 132
GINDER, 45
GIPE, 2
GIRARD, 146
GISH, 141
GIVAN, 2
GIVENS, 141 159
GLADDEN, 33 151

GLADWISH, 17
GLAMPE, 45
GLANT, 168
GLANZMAN, 177
GLASER, 170
GLASGOW, 198
GLASS, 166
GLASSCOCK, 2
GLATHER, 45
GLAZEBROOK, 215
GLEAVES, 95
GLEITZ, 182
GLEMING, 92
GLENN, 29 37 71 89 126 151 159
GLESSNER, 2
GLOVER, 25 45 130 134
GLOYD, 29
GNASH, 172
GOADBY, 125
GOADING, 71
GODDARD, 20 204
GODDELL, 173
GOEBEL, 135
GOEKING, 45
GOEMANN, 14
GOEN, 36
GOERGEN, 45
GOESHAN, 30
GOETZEN, 45
GOFF, 45
GOINGS, 29
GOINNS, 81
GOLAY, 2
GOLDEN, 141
GOLDFISH, 45
GOLDSOLL, 125
GONDOLF, 125
GONEWOLD, 46
GOOCH, 141 186
GOOD, 28 45
GOODE, 141
GOODFELLOW, 11
GOODHUE, 2
GOODIN, 35
GOODLAW, 184
GOODMAN, 171
GOODRICH, 107
GOODWIN, 24 31 45 130 151 174
GOOLSBY, 45
GORDAN, 160
GORDEN, 32 179
GORDNER, 175
GORDON, 2 30 64 91-92 133 151 160 186
GORES, 174
GORG, 184
GORING, 67 70
GORKEY, 118
GORSKI, 118

GORSMANN, 174
GOSDA, 45
GOSLIN, 37
GOSS, 82
GOTTARDO, 120
GOULD, 45 122
GOURRIER, 124
GRABER, 113
GRABLE, 151
GRADEN, 32
GRADEY, 141
GRADY, 121
GRAFF, 6 45 185
GRAGG, 32 141
GRAHAM, 2 27 33 35 37 45 107 116 160 169
GRAINGER, 28 30 33 36
GRAMS, 173
GRANER, 45
GRANGER, 28-29
GRANNIS, 45
GRANT, 2 35 45 170
GRASCH, 166
GRAVES, 2 32 45 95 141 160 194 196
GRAY, 2 11 26 77 92 96 118 160 167 186 199 203
GRAZIANO, 119
GREBER, 124
GREEN, 2 26 28 34 36 45 90 96 107 136 141 151 167-168 173 177 183 186 198
GREENE, 2 125 137
GREENLEE, 198
GREER, 107 128
GREGORY, 2 63 72 128 195 205 207
GREGREY, 141
GREGSON, 136
GRENDA, 119
GRENELL, 212
GRERCY, 141
GRESHAM, 29 32
GREVENSTEDE, 103
GREYS, 137
GRICE, 33
GRIDER, 186
GRIEBLE, 214
GRIENER, 169
GRIER, 186
GRIFFIN, 141
GRIFFITH, 2 63 107 141 151
GRIFFITHS, 45
GRIGGS, 204
GRIGSBEY, 141
GRIM, 45
GRIMES, 46 85 207
GRISHAM, 27
GRISHUM, 141
GRISSOM, 107
GRISSON, 33

GRISSUM, 141
GRIST, 68
GROESBECK, 37
GRONKONSKI, 115
GROOM, 4 160
GROOMS, 4
GROSS, 186
GROSSHARTH, 186
GROSSHEIDER, 174
GROSSMAN, 7
GROSSNICKLAUS, 46
GROSSOEHME, 46
GROTTS, 14
GROTZ, 114
GROUT, 2
GROVE, 2 122
GROVER, 33 91
GROVES, 125
GRUBBS, 141
GRUBER, 46
GRUEN, 103
GRUPE, 46
GRURSHAIER, 66
GUCKER, 186
GUERNSEY, 167
GUILLIAMS, 37
GUIN, 141
GUINN, 5 160
GULLIT, 26
GUM, 107
GUMM, 141
GUNBY, 2
GUNDERSON, 46
GUNN, 25
GUNNEL, 128
GUNSOLLY, 46
GUNTER, 107
GUNTHERLESS, 46
GUPTON, 25
GURNSEY, 46
GUSTINE, 196
GUTHERIE, 26
GUTHERY, 5
GUTHRIE, 151 183
GUTTING, 205
GUYTON, 13
GUYUN, 34
GWIN, 194
GYLES, 23
GYLFE, 46
GZAMI, 181
HAAS, 124 191
HACKETT, 78 115 118
HACKLER, 28 31
HACKLEY, 141
HACKLY, 141
HACKNELL, 73
HACKNEY, 32
HADDIX, 151
HADDOCK, 25
HADE, 165

HADLEY, 122
HADRICK, 4
HAEFNER, 176
HAEMMERLE, 114
HAENNI, 174
HAFFNER, 2 46 168
HAGAR, 2 68
HAGARMAN, 2
HAGEMEIR, 46
HAGER, 175
HAGERTY, 26
HAHER, 66
HAHN, 124
HAINES, 2 151
HAIR, 186
HAJEK, 46
HAKE, 125
HALBRUEGGER, 179
HALE, 2 33 91
HALL, 2 4 8 27 33-34 46 72 79 85 99 141 146 151 160 169 186 215
HALLETT, 186
HALLIGAN, 118
HALLMING, 169
HALLS, 2
HALTERMAN, 46
HALTMAN, 166
HALVONSON, 117
HAMENSTEAD, 179
HAMER, 46
HAMERICK, 2
HAMERNIK, 46
HAMERS, 46
HAMES, 200
HAMILTON, 1 4 18 22 24-26 46 84 138 160 173 178 185 189 205
HAMM, 102 141
HAMMER, 46 107
HAMMOND, 186 207-208
HAMNER, 141
HAMON, 151
HAMPTON, 6 13 209 212
HANAWALD, 46
HANCHETTE, 46
HANCOCK, 72 141
HANDFIELD, 125
HANENCAMP, 141
HANES, 141
HANEY, 16
HANGERFORD, 5
HANIKA, 46
HANKINS, 25 46 107
HANLEY, 141
HANLIN, 191
HANNA, 8 29 37 141
HANNAH, 27 35 107
HANNERS, 46
HANSBERRY, 16
HANSELL, 130

HANSEN, 46 192
HANSLERRY, 7
HANSON, 46 90 174 186
HANSSEN, 46
HANY, 4
HARBAUGH, 46
HARDEN, 107 141
HARDIN, 28 100 141 186
HARDING, 168
HARDMAN, 202
HARDON, 85
HARDT, 46
HARDWOCK, 202
HARDY, 2 46 97 131 147 151 160 186
HARFOR, 171
HARGRAVE, 37 130
HARGROVE, 4 100 107 160
HARGUS, 141
HARISON, 141
HARKELRUDE, 178
HARKER, 186
HARKINS, 46
HARKNESS, 205
HARLAN, 151
HARLAND, 46
HARLEY, 116
HARMAN, 195
HARMES, 200
HARMON, 33
HARN, 12
HARNESS, 160
HARNEY, 175
HARNISH, 46
HARPER, 26 46
HARRAS, 215
HARRASS, 34
HARRIE, 80
HARRINGTON, 5 147 160
HARRIS, 3 10 26 31 34-36 46 89 107 118 135 141 151 160 171 190 215
HARRISON, 10 27-28 30-31 33 35-36 46 96 210 213
HART, 14 117 137-138
HARTIGAN, 116
HARTLEY, 46
HARTMAN, 4
HARTMANN, 116 120
HARTSHORN, 69
HARTSOCH, 81
HARTUNG, 46
HARTWELL, 5
HARVEY, 11 46 84 141 193 213
HASAMER, 166
HASELOH, 13
HASH, 26
HASHAW, 26
HASK, 26
HASKINGS, 2

HASKINS, 2 69
HASLERLIK, 166
HASLETT, 206
HASS, 47
HASTINGS, 2
HASWELL, 47
HATCHER, 182
HATFIELD, 72 107 176 186
HAUBRICH, 131
HAUGHT, 47
HAULEY, 66
HAUPTMAN, 210
HAUPTMANN, 169
HAUSSLER, 47
HAVENER, 177
HAVERKAMP, 113
HAWKINS, 2 26 66 127 141 167 186
HAWKS, 69
HAWLEY, 5 147
HAWS, 186
HAYDEN, 17 47
HAYDON, 141
HAYES, 5 35 47 65 70 131 179 186
HAYMAKER, 186
HAYMAN, 206-208
HAYNES, 183
HAYS, 27 29-30 32 87 133 136 141 151 160 200
HAYSE, 141
HAYSTIN, 141
HAYTER, 141
HAYWORTH, 26
HAZELRIGG, 186
HAZLIP, 31
HAZZARD, 79
HEAD, 141
HEADLEY, 47
HEADRICK, 141
HEAG, 173
HEALD, 47 197 211
HEAMELNI, 91
HEAPS, 77
HEARN, 126
HEASTON, 190
HEATH, 47 141
HEATON, 107
HEBENER, 166
HEBERLING, 141
HECKARD, 2
HECKART, 2
HEDENBURG, 69
HEDGES, 124 186
HEEKS, 25
HEESCH, 47
HEFFERNAN, 181
HEFLEY, 201 204
HEFTY, 47
HEGAN, 97
HEIDEL, 123

HEIDEN, 47
HEIER, 47
HEIL, 181
HEILIGER, 114
HEILMAN, 183
HEIMES, 47
HEINE, 171
HEINECKE, 183
HEINEMANN, 47
HEINEN, 47
HEINKEN, 47
HEINSIUS, 182
HEIRONYMUS, 19
HEITERICH, 2
HELFENBEIN, 204
HELLER, 117
HELLMAN, 215
HELLMANN, 172
HELMER, 197
HELMESBERGER, 135
HELMS, 34
HELVAS, 6
HEMANS, 132
HEMPHILL, 79
HEMSTREET, 189
HENDERSON, 4 9 26 29 36 160
HENDOTT, 26
HENDRIX, 141
HENLEY, 124
HENLINE, 47
HENNECKE, 47
HENNESEY, 183
HENNESSY, 174
HENNING, 186 212
HENNOE, 26
HENRY, 2 4 10 47 141 160 182 186
HENSENGER, 76
HENSHAW, 31 160
HENSKE, 86
HENSLEY, 195
HENSON, 26
HENTGES, 47
HENTTER, 125
HERBERL, 204
HERBERS, 171
HERBERT, 197
HERDFORD, 25
HERDON, 2
HERGAN, 26
HERKENHOFF, 178
HERMANN, 168
HERMSMEYER, 47
HERN, 141
HERNDON, 29-30 34 141
HERREL, 25
HERREN, 199
HERRING, 160 197
HERRINGTON, 211
HERRMANN, 126

HERRON, 1 195
HERSHBERGER, 47
HERTEL, 177
HERTRICH, 176
HESEMYER, 160
HESLING, 166
HESSION, 125
HESSOUS, 122
HETHERINGTON, 72
HETTIKER, 171
HETTMENN, 113
HEUN, 103
HEWITT, 2 136 195
HEWLETT, 107-108
HEYNEN, 124
HIATT, 31
HICK, 26
HICKAM, 25
HICKENBOTTOM, 47
HICKERSON, 141
HICKMAN, 2 26 67 81 86 98 141 160
HICKOK, 77
HICKS, 31 66 71 136 141
HIGDON, 26
HIGERSON, 196
HIGGINS, 25 47 120
HIGGS, 171
HIGHLANE, 101
HIGHLEY, 151
HIGHWAY, 174
HIGLEY, 47
HILBRAND, 186
HILCHER, 2
HILGEMANN, 125
HILL, 17 26 31 47 91 132 141 147 151 160 168 190 192 205 209
HILLER, 130
HILLHOUSE, 25 108
HILLMAN, 182
HILPERT, 21
HILTON, 2 25
HIMES, 30
HIMPLE, 28
HINCKLE, 28 36
HINCLE, 29
HINDLE, 2
HINDLEY, 65 86 93
HINDS, 193
HINES, 126 141
HINKLE, 186 212
HINKSTON, 151
HINTON, 70 138 186
HIRONIMUS, 141
HIRST, 2
HITCAMP, 176
HITCHCOCK, 125
HITCHENS, 34
HITE, 80
HIVBE, 171
HIX, 101
HIXON, 17
HOARL, 3
HOBBS, 141
HOBERG, 168
HOBLITZELL, 37
HOBSON, 27 29 32 126
HOCKER, 141
HODGE, 32
HODGES, 33 47
HODKINS, 17
HODLENBERG, 125
HODTONS, 26
HOEBER, 177
HOFFMAN, 133-134
HOFFMEISTER, 124
HOFMANN, 137 174
HOFSTETTER, 175
HOGAN, 25 94 183 209
HOGEMANN, 169
HOGREFE, 37 125
HOGUE, 174
HOHMANN, 47
HOHNBAUM, 47
HOINS, 8
HOLBERT, 141
HOLCOMB, 189 209
HOLEMAN, 160
HOLLADY, 141
HOLLAND, 108 118 160
HOLLEWAY, 127
HOLLEY, 141
HOLLIDAY, 2
HOLLMAN, 191
HOLLY, 96
HOLLYMAN, 2
HOLM, 47
HOLMES, 2 76 108 209
HOLMS, 141
HOLSBACH, 103
HOLSTEN, 19
HOLTSCLAW, 141
HOLTZ, 115
HOLVERSON, 47
HOLZ, 47
HOMER, 36
HOMES, 141
HOMOLKA, 47
HONEYCUT, 186
HONISHER, 191
HONNOLD, 194
HOOD, 108
HOOFER, 2
HOOFFER, 185
HOOKER, 108 186
HOOPER, 151
HOOPS, 167
HOOTEN, 47
HOOVER, 74 108 125 170
HOPE, 2
HOPKINS, 18 81 108
HOPPEL, 183
HOPPER, 30 35 141
HORAN, 124
HORD, 141
HORDS, 26
HORN, 2 19 27 35-36 134 160
HORNBERGER, 115
HORNBUCKLE, 30 32-33
HORNE, 5
HORNSBY, 30-31
HORRIGAN, 192
HORRIGEN, 166
HORSTKOETTE, 167
HORSTMANNSDORF, 114
HORSTMANNSPOFF, 114
HORTIN, 186
HORTON, 141 181
HOSCHOUER, 47
HOSEA, 82
HOSKINS, 186
HOSS, 103
HOTTMAN, 2
HOUCHINS, 29
HOUGHTON, 47
HOUSE, 141 189
HOUSEMAN, 78
HOUSER, 171 207
HOUSTON, 29 34 208
HOUTS, 36
HOUX, 29-30 33
HOVER, 186
HOW, 32
HOWARD, 22 24 30-31 34 92 124 137 141 160 181 186 211
HOWDEN, 196
HOWDERM, 9
HOWE, 2 133 160 186
HOWEL, 30
HOWELL, 203 207 209
HOWERTON, 16 25
HOWSE, 175
HOWSK, 160
HOY, 47
HOYE, 15
HUBBARD, 25 30 34 86 137 141 186 195
HUBBELL, 141
HUBELI, 176
HUCHTTONS, 125
HUDDER, 25
HUDDLESTON, 151
HUDELSON, 199
HUDGINS, 151
HUDSON, 25 27 47 125 141 169 188 202 205
HUDSPETH, 5 151
HUEBNER, 47
HUELLE, 47
HUFF, 27 29 34 48 179
HUFFMAN, 48 141 151 203

HUFFSETTLER, 128
HUFFSTETTLER, 128
HUFKER, 116-117
HUGES, 2
HUGHART, 160
HUGHES, 15 48 83 118 121 141 167 198
HUGHLITT, 151-152
HUHN, 125
HULETT, 141
HULFEMEYER, 113
HULITT, 142
HULL, 89 190 199
HULLEN, 190
HULSE, 142
HULTEN, 186
HULTMAN, 48
HULTS, 183
HUMAN, 48
HUMBER, 152
HUMFELD, 137
HUMM, 85
HUMPAL, 48
HUMPHREY, 142 186
HUMPHREYS, 48 124
HUNDLEY, 83 108
HUNELS, 25
HUNGAFORD, 4
HUNGATE, 16
HUNKINS, 124
HUNKLE, 47
HUNNING, 212
HUNSUCKER, 36
HUNT, 17 30 79 94 101 108 115 186 191 200 211-212
HUNTER, 3 48 84 152 186
HUNTLY, 26
HUNTON, 142
HUNTSMAN, 28
HUNTSUCKER, 4 160
HUPP, 48
HURLEBAUS, 2
HURLEY, 15 174 182
HURLY, 85
HURON, 133
HURST, 83 152
HURT, 142
HUSLY, 26
HUSS, 126
HUSSEY, 103
HUSTON, 108 186
HUTAWA, 173
HUTCHERSON, 142
HUTCHISON, 175
HUTH, 124
HUTTON, 21
HUYETT, 133
HY, 42
HYDE, 2 5 76 124 160 191
HYLAND, 117
HYNES, 142

HYRE, 103
IASTIZINSKI, 118-119
IDEN, 80 87
IGLER, 92
IMEL, 69
IMHOF, 177
INGRAHAM, 48
INGRAM, 196
INGRUND, 176
INLOW, 25
INMAN, 190
INSKEEP, 207
IRBY, 108
IRELAND, 12
IRVING, 2
IRWIN, 2 69 147
ISAACS, 142
ISANCS, 173
ISBELL, 48 108
ISCHER, 183
ISSEL, 119
ITTNER, 6
ITZEN, 48
JACKMAN, 142
JACKS, 142
JACKSON, 2-3 25 30 32 34-35 48 148 194
JACOBS, 6 48 142 186
JACOBSON, 48 215
JAFFE, 184
JAMES, 26 32 87 142 152 160 196 215
JAMISON, 142
JANDS, 184
JANECEK, 48
JANNSEN, 48
JANZEN, 48
JAROSHIK, 179
JAWOROWSKI, 116
JAY, 108
JEFFERS, 5 68 147
JEFFERSON, 2 48
JEFFREY, 201
JEFFRIES, 102 108 211
JEMISON, 108
JEND, 166
JENKINS, 99 104 129-132 135-138 186 210
JENKSON, 130
JENNE, 136
JENNINGS, 2 25-26 35-36 142
JENSEN, 48
JERIS, 96
JERRY, 142
JESSEE, 160
JESSOGNE, 203
JESSUP, 2
JETER, 142
JETT, 2
JETTER, 48
JEWETT, 48 214

JEZ, 48
JOB, 34
JOBE, 195
JOHANNSON, 174
JOHANSEN, 115
JOHNS, 2 5 131 165
JOHNSON, 1-3 9 11-12 18 21 26 29-31 48 66-67 83 90 96 108 114 117 130-131 133-134 142 152 160 168-169 172-173 175 178 185-186 202 209 213
JOHNSTON, 6 49 114 185 208
JOHNSTUN, 37
JONAL, 215
JONES, 2 6 16 18 20-21 32-35 49 62 64 72 74-75 79-80 91 100 102 108 128 142 147 152 160-161 165 167 176 186 192 195 198
JORDAN, 27 88 92 125 152 210 214-215
JORDON, 152
JORGENSEN, 49 93
JOURA, 49
JOURDAN, 142
JOURDEN, 142
JOYCLIN, 197
JUDAH, 87 161
JUDSON, 64
JUEDES, 49
JUETTER, 177
JUNGEK, 49
JUNKEL, 129
JURNESS, 86
JUTON, 78
JUTTON, 81
KADLEC, 49
KAHNY, 49
KAISER, 119
KALINA, 49
KAMADULSKI, 176
KAMES, 152
KAMINSKI, 116
KAMP, 179
KANE, 72 87 117 120 179
KANZELMEYER, 49
KAPPEN, 64
KAREL, 15
KARL, 183
KARNES, 152 161
KARNS, 197
KARPISEK, 49
KARST, 131
KASPAR, 181
KASSEBAUM, 49
KASZEWSKI, 118
KATTLER, 181
KATZ, 49
KAUCHER, 37
KAUFFMAN, 49

KAUFMAN, 49
KAUSE, 118
KAUTZ, 49
KEAL, 2
KEALLPER, 9
KEARN, 24
KEARNEY, 49 117
KEARNS, 49
KEATING, 49 117 173
KEATON, 98
KEECH, 49
KEEDY, 152
KEEFE, 169
KEEGAN, 2
KEENAN, 49
KEENER, 161
KEENY, 27 34
KEET, 24
KEHOE, 125-126
KEIL, 2 125
KEINGREY, 26
KEISKER, 166
KEISTER, 183
KEITH, 210
KELAND, 81
KELEHER, 124
KELHING, 179
KELING, 75
KELL, 82
KELLER, 86-87 136 182 215
KELLEY, 33 126
KELLN, 204
KELLOGG, 49
KELLY, 17 25 67 83 99 127 130 168-169 171 175 178-179 185
KELREY, 17
KELSER, 5
KELTON, 2
KEMP, 186
KEMPER, 152 174 190
KEMPFER, 175
KEMPTES, 186
KENNEDY, 2 49 71 75 88 152 161 175 197 206 208 212
KENNELLY, 182
KENSKI, 201
KENT, 161 202 212
KENYON, 70 101
KEOGH, 173
KEOWN, 13
KEPPEL, 175
KEPPLER, 115
KERBEY, 142
KERBY, 36 142
KERCHEVAL, 161
KERDOLFF, 193
KERFOTT, 206
KERLY, 36
KERN, 49
KERNER, 190

KERNES, 161
KERNS, 72 152
KERR, 25 34
KERRIGAN, 49 65
KERSHAW, 169
KERTLY, 142
KERTS, 142
KESSLER, 91 94 192
KETCHEM, 186
KETCHUM, 142
KETTENER, 185
KETTMENN, 113
KEY, 36 142
KEYES, 186
KEYS, 103
KIEFFE, 49
KIENE, 90
KIESER, 116
KIGER, 193
KILDER, 87
KILDOW, 194
KILLEAN, 11
KILLEN, 190 214
KIMBELL, 186
KIMM, 176
KIMMONS, 108
KIMSEY, 28 30 35
KINCHLOE, 2
KINDER, 36
KINDRICK, 33
KING, 2 6 8 10 16 25 28-29 31 34 49 66 71 91 101 124 138 142 170 173 186
KINGSBERRY, 142
KINGSBURRY, 89
KINGSBURY, 6 193
KINGSLAND, 186
KINGSLEY, 198
KINGSOLVER, 12
KINGSTON, 86
KINKEL, 131 134-136
KINKIDE, 73
KINMAN, 186
KINNAIRD, 152
KINNAN, 49
KINSELA, 199
KIPP, 125
KIRBY, 49 108 204
KIRK, 4 204
KIRKMAN, 77 95
KIRKPATRICK, 25 34 49 132
KIRKWOOD, 152
KIRN, 117
KIRWIN, 130
KISLING, 49
KISSEL, 125
KISSLER, 183
KITCHEL, 20
KITHNE, 4
KITTENREINER, 124
KITZINGER, 125

KITZMILLER, 147
KIVETT, 142
KLEBER, 137
KLEE, 178
KLEIBOLD, 126
KLEIN, 49 124
KLEMBERY, 176
KLEPPER, 215
KLIEWER, 204
KLIMEK, 49
KLINE, 84
KLINGER, 176
KLIPPEL, 37
KLONSKI, 98
KLOSIENSKI, 118
KLUNDER, 49
KNAPP, 4 72 77 91 137
KNEASS, 132
KNECHT, 103
KNEPPEPPER, 2
KNICKMEYER, 125
KNIDISCHEK, 182
KNIGHT, 2 30-31 131 142
KNOCH, 103
KNOPFLE, 168
KNOPP, 99 176
KNOTT, 183
KNOTTS, 78
KNOUSE, 142
KNOWLES, 49 124 131
KNUTSON, 49 128
KOBERG, 184
KOCH, 49 71 178-179 183
KOCIAN, 130
KOEHLER, 171
KOENIG, 113
KOERS, 172
KOETTER, 169
KOHL, 183
KOHLER, 49
KOKEN, 166
KOLAFA, 173
KOLAR, 49
KOOS, 125
KOPATSCHEK, 122
KOPIETZ, 49
KORELL, 50 198
KORN, 103
KORNS, 8
KOST, 186
KOSTAL, 50
KOTTICH, 50
KOZOZIMSKI, 117
KRACH, 93
KRAFT, 204
KRAMER, 171
KRATOCVIL, 50
KRAUSH, 71
KREBS, 125
KREGAR, 170
KREINHEDER, 17

KREINKAMP, 113
KRENING, 103
KREPPER, 68
KRETSCHMANN, 176
KRETZ, 204
KRING, 142
KROCKER, 50
KROEGER, 50
KROENLEIN, 215
KROGUN, 142
KROHN, 50
KRONESTER, 125
KRONOUGH, 2
KRUEGER, 50
KRULL, 125
KRUSE, 8
KRUTSINGER, 50
KUEHN, 124
KUENKER, 113
KUMM, 50
KUNKEL, 37 136 138
KUNKLE, 142
KUNTZ, 124 173
KUSKER, 102
KUSTER, 50
KUSZMAN, 124
KUTSCH, 50
KUTZ, 142
KYLE, 2
KZAEMER, 176
LABARR, 186
LABEAUME, 126
LABOUISSE, 137
LACEFIELD, 161
LACY, 142
LADAGE, 62 64
LADD, 63
LAFLEY, 142
LAFON, 2
LAFRENZ, 210
LAFSAN, 170
LAGER, 182
LAHM, 174
LAINE, 121
LAIR, 2
LAKE, 177
LAKIN, 203
LAMASTER, 142
LAMB, 125 152
LAMBERT, 108 142 186 199
LAMBERTZ, 119
LAMBIE, 50
LAMBIRTH, 210
LAMBRIGHT, 199-200
LAME, 142
LAMING, 104
LAMM, 50 142
LAMMERS, 50
LAMPKINS, 142
LANAGAN, 167
LANCASTER, 142 191

LAND, 50
LANDA, 117
LANDAU, 215
LANDEN, 186
LANDERS, 128
LANDHART, 186
LANDIS, 147
LANDON, 186
LANDWEHR, 50
LANE, 2 4 24 73 131 133 188
LANEIR, 33
LANES, 152
LANG, 25 50
LANGDON, 2 50 91
LANGE, 50 122 133
LANGSDORF, 125
LANGSTON, 123 147
LANIER, 35
LANIGAN, 166
LANKFORD, 182
LANSHAW, 2
LANTIS, 6
LANTZ, 50 85
LAPSLEY, 27-29 35 161 207
LARIMER, 22
LARKIN, 202
LARKY, 170
LARMAN, 2
LARSON, 50 168
LARTOR, 25
LASEE, 88
LASHAWAY, 90
LASITER, 123
LASKIEWITZ, 119
LASSATER, 161
LASTER, 123
LATHAM, 2 126 142
LATHAN, 170
LATHROP, 5
LATIMER, 2 198
LAUGHLIN, 50 197
LAUMEIER, 125
LAUP, 18
LAW, 96 142
LAWE, 8
LAWLESS, 75 80
LAWNEY, 131
LAWPORT, 89
LAWSON, 50 142 186 215
LAY, 142 174
LAYFATTE, 73
LAYMAN, 147 161
LAYNE, 161
LE CONNER, 134
LEA, 33
LEACH, 20 142
LEAKEY, 142
LEAKY, 142
LEAR, 2 161
LEAY, 173
LEBAW, 26

LEBERMUTH, 215
LEBOURGEOIS, 124
LECHLITER, 50
LECHTRECK, 165
LECOMPE, 179
LEDERER, 165
LEDGERWOOD, 202
LEDORAS, 22
LEE, 3 24-26 32 108 118 142
   152 173 178 190 207 209-
   210
LEEP, 50
LEFFLER, 187 199
LEFLET, 2
LEGERWOOD, 161
LEGG, 50 131 209
LEGLER, 125
LEGRAND, 78
LEIENDECKER, 174
LEM, 8
LEMASTER, 108
LEMBURG, 50
LEMENS, 181
LEMKOWITZ, 170
LEMON, 3 86 152
LENEUR, 97
LENGER, 10
LEON, 50
LEONARD, 24 29 142 152 187
LEPPER, 126
LERCHE, 173
LERNER, 78
LESLIE, 21 50 215
LESTER, 50 108
LETTS, 142
LEVELNAM, 142
LEWING, 115
LEWIS, 15 50 65 82 131 142
   161 166 169 183 187 190
   209 211-212
LIBBY, 37 50
LICHLITER, 152
LICHTE, 50
LICHTI, 50
LICONNILI, 117
LIEBERMAN, 181
LIERMANN, 50
LIESNER, 50
LIEUEMANN, 168
LIGGETT, 142
LILE, 142
LILES, 211
LILLERT, 142
LILLIE, 2 50
LILLY, 5 152
LIMBIRD, 37
LIMERICK, 199
LINABERY, 50
LINAHAN, 117
LINCH, 35 142
LINDSEY, 187

LINE, 50
LINEBARGER, 201
LING, 74
LINGELBACH, 173
LINGO, 25
LINISBY, 65
LINK, 2 25 125 213
LINN, 142
LINNVILLE, 89
LINVILLE, 5 152 161
LIPCOMB, 182
LIPKER, 50
LIPPENS, 120
LIPPERT, 170
LIPPOLD, 50
LIPPONCOTT, 50
LIPPS, 185
LISKA, 51
LITHARTT, 142
LITRLE, 142
LITTERAL, 142
LITTLE, 2 7
LITTLETON, 142
LIVELY, 142
LIVENGOOD, 29 199
LLEWELLYN, 215
LOAR, 152-153
LOATHAN, 142
LOCK, 25
LOCKE, 126
LOCKHART, 51
LOCKWOOD, 51 187
LODL, 51
LOEB, 215
LOEDING, 51
LOFTIN, 202
LOFTUS, 174
LOGAN, 24-25 27 215
LOGSDON, 205
LOHBECK, 175
LOHMANN, 51
LOID, 142
LOLLAR, 103
LONCON, 3
LONG, 11-12 37 51 79-80 108 134 142 153 187 202 204
LONGACRE, 28 31-33 36
LONGFELLOW, 51
LONGMYRE, 26
LONIGRO, 121
LONKUM, 25
LOOCK, 51
LOOH, 187
LOOMIS, 187-188 215
LOONEY, 2 25
LOOSMORE, 176
LORANCE, 19
LORCH, 124
LORD, 74 79 187
LORENS, 83
LOTTRIDGE, 22 187

LOUDON, 75
LOUGHBRIDGE, 19
LOUGHRAN, 120
LOURY, 119
LOUSE, 71
LOUSINGMOUNT, 5
LOUTHAN, 2 153
LOVE, 187
LOVELAND, 161
LOVELESS, 51
LOVING, 51
LOW, 15 51
LOWDER, 26
LOWE, 201
LOWERY, 129
LOWEY, 182
LOWNEY, 130 136
LOWQUIST, 1
LOWRY, 27 31 142
LUBINSKI, 119
LUCAS, 4 26 153 191
LUCE, 96
LUCH, 130
LUCHO, 133
LUCKEY, 215
LUCKS, 183
LUDWIG, 51 191
LUEDERS, 51 125
LUETHGE, 114
LUGENBEEL, 51 215
LUKEFAHR, 51
LULEY, 215
LUMKIN, 51
LUND, 51
LUNDAY, 29
LUNDBERG, 51
LUNINGHOHNER, 20
LUSHBAUGH, 191
LUSK, 108
LUTTENBERGER, 115
LUTZ, 21
LYDON, 119
LYKINS, 88
LYLE, 2 210
LYNCH, 25 142
LYNDE, 32
LYON, 51 65 161
LYONS, 85 121 182 187
MACDONALD, 211
MACDOUGAL, 202
MACHLES, 177
MACK, 189
MACKEN, 121
MACKEY, 153 161
MACUMBER, 51
MADDOX, 2 142
MADDY, 125
MADKINS, 2
MADSON, 115 137
MAEHOIEFSKI, 121
MAFFLEY, 3

MAGEE, 51
MAGILL, 51 78
MAGINE, 130
MAGRESS, 92
MAGUIRE, 125
MAHAN, 2 114
MAHANEY, 79 90 170
MAHER, 181
MAHLMAN, 51
MAHON, 165
MAIN, 51
MAJOR, 27 142
MAJORS, 28-29 31 36
MALACK, 51
MALISSZEWSKI, 170
MALISZEWSKI, 178
MALL, 198
MALLOY, 142
MALONE, 2
MALONEY, 18 177
MAMAHAN, 28
MANG, 81
MANGELS, 212
MANLEY, 201
MANN, 65 77 93
MANNAN, 88
MANNIN, 142
MANNING, 187 196
MANORY, 187
MANSFIELD, 2
MANTEAITTA, 165
MANTLER, 192
MANUEL, 2 187
MANZ, 167
MAPTHER, 137
MARACHAL, 153
MARAIN, 187
MARBUT, 201-202
MARCLINE, 103
MARCUM, 27
MARGULEWSKI, 121
MARK, 100 147 153
MARKCUM, 195
MARKELL, 209
MARKER, 161
MARKEY, 51
MARKHAM, 170
MARKLAND, 37 142
MARKS, 2 51
MARKWOOD, 5
MARLETT, 187
MARLEY, 142
MARMADUKE, 2
MARR, 28 30 32 34-36
MARRION, 4
MARS, 36 113
MARSCHAL, 167
MARSEE, 68
MARSH, 142
MARSHAFFER, 71

MARSHALL, 26-29 34-36 76 95 142 161 187
MARSHHALL, 6
MARTAIN, 84
MARTHENS, 125
MARTIN, 2 5 26 29 31 36-37 51 120 125 130 136 142 147 153 161 169 183 187 201-202 206
MARTINI, 178
MARY, 27
MARX, 215
MASHEK, 51
MASON, 2 24 51 125 142 181 215
MASSMAN, 19
MASTER, 4
MASTERATS, 142
MASTERS, 25
MASTERSON, 27 30 33
MASTIE, 116
MASTRED, 142
MASURE, 125
MATHENY, 5
MATHEWS, 133
MATHIEN, 125
MATHUS, 26 187
MATKIN, 200
MATKINS, 2
MATLOCK, 66
MATSEN, 115
MATSON, 142
MATTESON, 179
MATTHEWS, 34 94 142
MATTINGLY, 123
MATTISON, 51
MATTLEY, 13
MATTSON, 51
MATZING, 96
MATZOFF, 90
MAU, 51
MAULSBY, 187
MAUPIN, 67 142 161 187
MAURENS, 125
MAXWELL, 5 28 78 142 161
MAY, 51 153 161 178 198
MAYBURY, 26
MAYER, 215
MAYFIELD, 210
MAYHAN, 26
MAYHEW, 51 109
MAYNARD, 142 187
MAYNE, 18
MAYS, 27-28 30
MAYSE, 34
MAZURKIEWER, 120
MCADAM, 12
MCADAMS, 22
MCAFEE, 3
MCALESTER, 31
MCAULIFF, 118
MCAULIFFE, 114 117 119-120
MCBEE, 210
MCBEY, 197
MCBRIDE, 94
MCCABE, 25 88
MCCAFFREE, 53
MCCAFFREY, 103
MCCAIN, 5 153 161
MCCALL, 20
MCCALLAH, 202
MCCAN, 25
MCCART, 53 142
MCCARTHY, 117 121 166 168 177
MCCARTIN, 64
MCCARTNEY, 53
MCCARTY, 124-125 161
MCCARY, 5 24-25
MCCAULLY, 5
MCCAULY, 88
MCCLAIN, 81 142
MCCLANAHAN, 53
MCCLANE, 142
MCCLARSEY, 32
MCCLARY, 153
MCCLINTOCK, 187
MCCLOUD, 53 109
MCCLUNEY, 33
MCCLURE, 16 25 109 208
MCCLURG, 190 192
MCCOLERY, 19
MCCOLLUM, 187
MCCOMB, 53
MCCONNAUGHEY, 53
MCCONNELL, 187
MCCORD, 22 53 142
MCCORKLE, 53 161
MCCORMACK, 109 215
MCCORMICK, 29 126 187
MCCOSLAND, 179
MCCOY, 33-34 37 142 170 185 209
MCCRACKEN, 53
MCCRARY, 27 30 76 142 153
MCCRAVEY, 142
MCCRAY, 147 153 161 188
MCCREARY, 128
MCCROSKEY, 3
MCCRUMB, 29
MCCUBBIN, 161
MCCULLEN, 215
MCCULLY, 142 214
MCCUNE, 109
MCCURDY, 28
MCDANIEL, 26 68 142 153 189
MCDEARMAN, 142
MCDERMOTT, 115 208
MCDONALD, 3 25 37 68 90 120 125 142 153 169-170
MCDOWEL, 147
MCDOWELL, 92 161 169 189
MCDYE, 92
MCELROY, 3 182
MCENTEE, 53
MCEVOY, 125
MCFADDEN, 53
MCFALL, 109 187
MCFARLAND, 29 32-33 53 127 196
MCGAHER, 26
MCGEE, 3 197
MCGEHER, 26
MCGEINN, 125
MCGER, 19
MCGERK, 142
MCGLOTHIN, 3 202
MCGLYNN, 178
MCGOWAN, 14
MCGRATH, 114 166 171
MCGREEN, 25
MCGREGOR, 166
MCGRUDER, 142
MCGUGHEY, 188
MCGUIRE, 80 147 153
MCGUMS, 20
MCGURN, 120
MCHALL, 26
MCHENRY, 53
MCHUGH, 178
MCININCH, 190
MCINTOSH, 1 53
MCINTYRE, 71 92 187
MCIUTINE, 166
MCKARLE, 3
MCKAY, 53
MCKEE, 194
MCKEEVER, 162
MCKENNEY, 53
MCKENZIE, 128
MCKILLIP, 53
MCKIM, 214
MCKIN, 187
MCKINLEY, 109
MCKINNEY, 3 66 153 189
MCKINNIE, 193
MCKNIGHT, 1 16 195
MCKORLE, 4
MCKOWN, 4-5 162
MCKUNE, 53
MCLAIN, 3 53
MCLARKEY, 121
MCLAUGHLIN, 178 205 210
MCLAUGHLING, 25
MCLEAN, 137 170
MCLEOD, 116
MCLOYGHLIN, 53
MCLUNEY, 31
MCMAHAN, 28 32 34 36 153 175
MCMAHON, 4 121
MCMILLAN, 142 197

MCMINN, 30
MCMINUS, 84
MCMULLEN, 170
MCMURRAY, 185
MCMURRY, 3
MCMURTRY, 126
MCNAIR, 53
MCNALLY, 53 114
MCNAMARA, 118 120 167
MCNEAL, 109 162
MCNEALEY, 178
MCNEALY, 53
MCNEELEY, 153
MCNEESE, 142
MCNICHOLAS, 118
MCNUTT, 131
MCPHERSON, 92
MCPIKE, 3
MCQUAID, 125
MCQUEEN, 4
MCQUISTON, 53
MCRAE, 53
MCRENSEY, 26
MCRIGHT, 26
MCSHANE, 7 187
MCSPADDEN, 27 102
MCSPEEN, 89
MCUMBER, 3
MCVICKER, 199
MCWATT, 26
MCWHORTER, 53 196
MCWILLIAMS, 205
MEAD, 51 124
MEADOR, 215
MEADOWS, 29 153
MEAGHER, 124
MEAK, 142
MEALS, 142
MEANES, 142
MEANS, 30 34 153
MEARS, 190 215
MEDER, 69
MEDLEY, 207
MEEGAN, 120
MEEHAN, 118
MEEK, 37 109
MEEKS, 25
MEENEN, 51
MEERS, 162
MEIER, 51 204
MEILERT, 118
MEINHARDH, 169
MEININGER, 134
MEISSNER, 124
MEISTER, 77
MELLER, 204
MELSON, 2
MELTON, 35 195
MENDEKA, 119
MENDELL, 124
MENDENHALL, 51

MENGERSEN, 113
MENKE, 185
MENKING, 51
MENKINS, 210
MENOWN, 125
MERCHANT, 187
MEREDITH, 142
MERGAWASKI, 76
MERNAGH, 118
MERRELL, 21
MERRICK, 124
MERRITT, 126
MESANT, 78
MESLER, 185
MESLY, 170
MESSENGER, 194
MESSENLEY, 142
MESSICK, 26 109
METHERS, 142
METZ, 170
MEYER, 37 51-52 172 178
MEYERBERR, 134
MEYERS, 52 175 187
MICHAEL, 162
MICHEL, 124
MICHELS, 52
MIDDLETON, 126 171 197
    199
MIELKE, 125
MIKSCH, 52
MILAM, 2
MILES, 126 187 195
MILFORD, 126
MILLAR, 52
MILLARD, 196
MILLEN, 142 162
MILLER, 2 13 26 31-32 34 36
    52 71 86 92 96-97 109 122
    124-125 142 147 153 162
    168 174 176 187 196-199
    204 211
MILLIGAN, 195
MILLION, 142-143
MILLS, 52 62 71 143 153 187
    196 205 207
MILNE, 52
MILNER, 33-34
MINDER, 185
MINER, 109 143
MINNE, 103
MINOR, 2 52 71 213
MINTER, 143
MINTLE, 52
MINTON, 102
MIRES, 2
MISEMER, 109
MITCHEL, 3
MITCHELL, 6 52 76 95 134
    153 162
MOCK, 27
MODREL, 153

MODRELL, 153
MOELLER, 125
MOELLMANN, 166
MOERS, 52
MOFFETT, 2
MOFFITT, 143
MOHRMAN, 176
MOLAN, 28
MOLE, 182
MOLES, 129
MOLING, 9
MOLKENBUR, 184
MOLL, 215
MOLLETT, 88 190
MOLLOY, 187
MONAGHAN, 102
MONG, 52
MONROE, 52 143 179 187
MONTGOMERY, 25 70-71
    143 147 153 198 215
MONTI, 124
MONTIETH, 2
MONTROY, 172
MOODEY, 208
MOODY, 31 195
MOON, 143 187
MOONEY, 102 128
MOORBY, 64
MOORE, 2 7 9 15 76 85 103
    124 143 147 153 162 175
    187 189 191 194-195 198
    215
MOOTRY, 5
MORAN, 125
MORE, 34 122
MORELAND, 147
MORELY, 187
MORGAN, 3-4 8 31 52 154 187
MORIARITY, 120
MORIARTY, 169
MORIS, 67
MORITZ, 52
MORLEY, 118 120 125
MORRE, 26
MORRIS, 4 23 52 109 143 154
    162 167 173 187
MORRISON, 24 37 80 136 143
    203
MORRISS, 109
MORROW, 34-35 52 99 114
    143
MORSE, 52 197
MORTENSEN, 52
MORTON, 3 5 21 74 128
MOSBY, 109
MOSCICKY, 121
MOSE, 115
MOSELEY, 162 210
MOSER, 18
MOSHER, 52
MOSIER, 205

MOSLEY, 52
MOSS, 3 143 154 162
MOTSINGER, 34
MOTT, 76 143 198
MOUINGES, 178
MOUTRAY, 147
MOUTRIE, 154
MOWREY, 187
MOXLEY, 187
MOYER, 52
MOYRES, 26
MROCKOWSKI, 116
MUDGETT, 154
MUEGGE, 176
MUELLER, 52 115 124-126
MUELLMANN, 125
MUES, 52
MUFLER, 4
MUFLY, 162
MUHLIMAN, 64
MUIR, 52
MULDROW, 3
MULEENEY, 125
MULKEY, 154
MULKINS, 75
MULLALEY, 125
MULLANE, 170
MULLANEY, 176
MULLER, 97 103 124 178
MULLHOLLEN, 103
MULLINS, 25-26 32 143 187
MULROONEY, 125
MULVANIA, 200
MULVIHILL, 214
MUMFORD, 1
MUMM, 173
MUNCY, 154
MUNDHENKE, 53
MUNDT, 215
MUNKERS, 4 154
MUNNS, 12
MURBICK, 24
MURCH, 215
MURE, 143
MURHPY, 143
MURPHEY, 143
MURPHY, 4 22 34 81 94 103
    109 117 119 167 170 173
    177 205 208 210 214
MURRANCE, 187
MURRAY, 33 53 74 121 177
    196 198
MURRELL, 109 187
MURRI, 35
MURRY, 3 29 143 187
MUSGROVE, 207
MUSSER, 215
MYERS, 25 37 53 67 143 187
    197 204
MYERSON, 181
MYNATT, 109

MYRTLE, 143
NADEAN, 83
NAGLE, 187
NAILOR, 37
NALLY, 25
NANCE, 162
NANSON, 143
NASH, 73 95 154 215
NATHAN, 135
NATOLI, 114
NAUMAN, 213
NAUN, 174
NAVO, 172
NAY, 190
NAYLOR, 3 143 213
NEAL, 4 27 36 82 143
NEALE, 124
NEALEIGH, 53
NEALIS, 118
NEARY, 116
NEDARF, 67
NEDDERHUT, 124
NEECE, 26 109
NEEL, 3
NEELY, 4
NEHEMIAS, 115
NEHL, 124
NEIL, 17 154
NEIMAN, 172
NEKULA, 122
NELLE, 172
NELSON, 15 25 29 33 53 143
    208
NERO, 79
NESMITH, 54
NESSLER, 178
NESTER, 143
NEUDORFF, 102
NEUFANG, 125
NEUMISTER, 20
NEVADA, 138
NEVILLE, 54 174
NEVINS, 126
NEWBERRY, 80
NEWBY, 154 182
NEWCOMB, 3 137 143 189
NEWDORFF, 65
NEWHOFF, 135
NEWMAN, 54 75 109 123 187
    208
NEWTON, 25-26 74 126
NICHOLAS, 54 109 196
NICHOLDS, 143
NICHOLS, 3 54 125 147 196
    212
NICKEL, 54
NICKELL, 128
NICKELS, 32
NICKMAN, 54
NICKOLS, 165
NICKSON, 143

NICOL, 3 54
NIEBRUGGE, 125
NIEDERSCHMIDT, 181
NIEDT, 166
NIEHANS, 165
NIEHAUS, 177
NIEHOFF, 178
NIEMAN, 54
NIES, 115
NIGHT, 143
NIVERT, 213
NOBLE, 154 184
NOBLET, 197
NOEL, 37
NOERENBERG, 54
NOGALSKI, 119
NOIS, 25
NOLAN, 88 95 124
NOLAND, 162
NOLEN, 128
NOLTE, 54
NOLTING, 179
NOONAN, 173
NOOTER, 118
NORDIN, 54
NORMAN, 5 109 162
NORRIS, 99-100 109 143 154
    162 205
NORTH, 28 125
NORTHCRAFT, 210
NORTHCUTT, 187
NORTHRUP, 90 187
NORTON, 54 176 178
NORVELL, 136
NORWOOD, 143
NOSKA, 126
NOTTROTT, 187
NOWLIN, 3
NOYES, 134 189
NULL, 187
NUNN, 54
NUTT, 54 129
NUTTER, 54 187
NYE, 176
OAKLEY, 3
O'BANNON, 154
O'BANON, 4
OBER, 143
OBERG, 70
OBERMEIER, 165
OBERMEYER, 176
O'BRIAN, 67 85 97
O'BRIEN, 125 174 182
O'BRINE, 2
O'BRYAN, 176
OCH, 103
O'CONNEL, 167
O'CONNELL, 64 118-120 125
O'CONNOR, 54 118 154 214
OCTKIS, 103
O'DANIEL, 214

ODEAN, 35
ODEL, 30
O'DELL, 166
ODELL, 33-34
O'DONNELL, 118 125
OELRICH, 179
OEUS, 24
OFFITT, 33
OFFOFY, 215
O'FLAHERTY, 171
OGAN, 126
OGDEN, 68
OGELSBY, 190
OGLE, 4 147 162
OGLESBY, 28 33
O'HARA, 16 94
OHLER, 182
OHLMANN, 54
O'KEEFE, 77 120
OLDFATHER, 15
OLDHAM, 25 27 154
O'LEARY, 118
OLENSTEAD, 165
OLIPHANT, 29-30
OLIVER, 54 129 188
OLLHAM, 167
OLMSTEAD, 3
OLSEN, 54
OLSHAUSEN, 124
OLSON, 54 135
OLTMANS, 54
O'MALLEY, 120 125 184
O'NEAL, 143
OPAL, 103
OPELT, 10
OPOCENSKY, 54
OPPERMANN, 170
O'REILLY, 120
OREN, 37
O'RILEY, 70
ORR, 9 26 74 143 204
ORRE, 35
ORTEMANN, 181
OSBERG, 54
OSBORNE, 78
OSCHAE, 179
OSSENDORF, 170
OSTERMAN, 54
OTIS, 130
OTOOLE, 154
O'TOOLE, 166
OTT, 125
OTTE, 54
OTTEN, 169 183
OTTENS, 54
OTTENSMEYER, 173
OTTMAN, 200
OTTO, 184
OUSLEY, 32-33 36
OUSTOLL, 129
OVERMAN, 54 187

OVERTON, 81 154 162
OVIATT, 54
OWEN, 3 13 26 54 138 143 162
OWENBY, 147
OWENS, 4 26 109 143
OWERMANN, 125
OXLEY, 125
PABST, 125 168
PACE, 22
PACKWOOD, 201
PAGDET, 143
PAGE, 75 143
PAGET, 54
PAGETT, 3
PAIN, 37
PAINTER, 187
PAIRISE, 121
PAJACES, 170
PALLMEIER, 167
PALMER, 6 98 129 132 136 182 187 192
PALMERTON, 54
PALMERTRE, 143
PALMON, 4
PALUCZAK, 119
PAMETICKY, 203
PAMFLNE, 171
PANAS, 54
PANCAKE, 54
PANGHORN, 23
PANTER, 187
PARADOWSKI, 121
PARCHER, 197
PARIS, 109
PARISH, 25
PARKE, 169
PARKER, 3 12 18 24 27 30 54 89 109 125 162 170 215
PARKES, 184
PARKS, 19 54 97 143
PARLIN, 143
PARMAN, 32 71
PARNELL, 80 162 188
PARR, 3
PARRAT, 179
PARRIS, 54
PARRISH, 3 196
PARSON, 137
PARSONS, 3 26 36 54
PARTEE, 133
PARTON, 143
PARTRIDGE, 126
PASTERNACK, 103
PASTOR, 117
PATRICK, 26 64 125 143 187
PATTEN, 19 109
PATTERSON, 3 13 16 27 54 109 143 162 195 198 213
PATTON, 26 31 129 143 162 199 203
PATTS, 184

PAUL, 3 28 31 34 54
PAULSON, 54
PAUST, 125
PAVELKA, 54
PAVEY, 17
PAVLIK, 117
PAYNE, 3 143 154
PAYTON, 3 7
PAYUE, 81
PAYZANT, 55
PEABODY, 191
PEACHER, 143
PEAHLE, 63
PEAKE, 3 208
PEARCE, 143
PEARSON, 4 76 154 162 198 212
PEATLING, 55
PECHEL, 170
PECK, 187
PECKA, 122
PEEKA, 55
PEELER, 143
PEERY, 18
PEEVE, 56
PEIFFER, 126
PEIRCE, 19 55
PELHAM, 188
PELINSKI, 114
PELKIER, 154
PELL, 162
PELLEGRINL, 178
PEMBERTON, 28-29 34 36 143
PENDERGAST, 132
PENDIGRAFT, 25
PENDLETON, 109 126 187
PENICK, 154
PENN, 129 187
PENNEY, 55
PENNINGTON, 13 80
PENNOCK, 25
PENNY, 4 154
PENTECOST, 133
PEOPLES, 3
PEPPER, 3
PERCEY, 24
PERCIVAL, 143
PERDEE, 34
PERKINS, 4 22 84 143 169 195 212
PERMAN, 31
PERRETEN, 9
PERRINE, 178
PERRY, 3 24 36 55 101 131-135 137-138
PERRYN, 143
PERSELY, 5
PERSLEY, 132
PERSON, 143
PETAM, 76

PETEEL, 25
PETERS, 22 55 125 130 132 134-137 162
PETERSEN, 55
PETERSON, 25 55 172 176
PETHOUD, 55
PETIT, 162
PETREE, 204
PETRI, 55
PETRICK, 55
PETRIE, 80
PETROVICS, 116
PETTIJOHN, 55
PETTIPIECE, 55
PETTIS, 143
PETTIT, 25
PETTY, 143
PEUGH, 24
PEYTON, 143
PFEIFFER, 166
PFITZNER, 109
PFLEIDERER, 76
PHARIS, 143
PHARISS, 110
PHARRIS, 15 26 143
PHELAN, 181
PHELPS, 191 209
PHILDIUS, 193
PHILIBERT, 124
PHILIP, 205
PHILIPS, 133 143 179
PHILLIBER, 3
PHILLIPPS, 187
PHILLIPS, 3 32 76 97 100 110 143 203
PHILPOT, 143
PHIPPS, 125
PICKENS, 187
PICKER, 124
PICKETT, 3 162
PIEPER, 55
PIERCE, 126 162
PIERSOL, 10 208
PIERSON, 147 154 162
PIES, 167
PIESCHKE, 55
PIESTER, 1
PIGG, 154
PIKESH, 116
PILCHER, 3 133 143
PILE, 154 162
PILKERTON, 110
PINEGAR, 55
PINKSTON, 29
PIPER, 55
PIPES, 143
PIPKIN, 29
PIRTLE, 110
PITMAN, 5
PITMORE, 143
PITNEY, 143 212

PITTMAN, 20 138 194
PITTS, 110 130 143 176
PIXLER, 187
PLACHT, 166
PLANK, 55
PLANT, 125
PLATE, 165
PLATT, 125
PLEASANTS, 29
PLUEMPE, 124
PLUMMER, 110
POAGUE, 216
POCOCK, 55
POCOCKE, 172
POGUE, 25
POHLMANN, 125
POINDEXTER, 110
POINTER, 16 129
POIOR, 82
POJAR, 55
POKREFKE, 113
POLAND, 110
POLK, 143
POLLARD, 3
POLLOCK, 189
POMEROY, 133 187
PONDNEY, 3
POOL, 55
POORTER, 4
POPE, 55 117
POPP, 181
PORCH, 184
PORTA, 114
PORTER, 3 14 32 132 143 154 197
PORTIS, 200
POSEY, 25
POSTWAITE, 137
POTARF, 13
POTEET, 162
POTTER, 143 162
POTTS, 3 36 143 199 213 215
POWE, 154 162
POWELL, 14 35 73 95 101 132 143 154
POWERS, 55 100 187
POYNTER, 37
PRAEDICON, 172
PRATEL, 132
PRATER, 55
PRATHER, 143 187
PRATT, 7 133-134 137
PREDDY, 201
PRESLEY, 125
PRESTON, 154 168 215
PRICE, 3 25-26 28 137 143 154 162 170 210-212
PRICHETT, 110
PRIGMORE, 35
PRILL, 55
PRIME, 55

PRIMUS, 125
PRINCE, 143
PRINE, 34
PRITCHETT, 163
PRITHOHETT, 32
PRITTIRI, 121
PROCKTER, 143
PROCTOR, 3 143
PRUETT, 34
PRUICE, 68
PRUITT, 24 94 110
PRYOR, 97
PUGH, 75 125 143
PULLEN, 215
PULLIAM, 143 187
PUNSHON, 184
PURCELL, 121
PURDIN, 187
PURDUE, 163
PURNHAGEN, 184
PURROTT, 154 163
PURTLE, 36
PUTBRESE, 55
PUTNAM, 110
PUTSKA, 122
PUTTMANN, 118
PYBUS, 125
PYLES, 82
QUAIL, 178
QUARLES, 71
QUARTZ, 55
QUEROLO, 124
QUIDOR, 138
QUIGLEY, 210
QUIMBY, 29
QUINEY, 143
QUINN, 55 119-120
QUIRK, 174
QUISINBERRY, 143
RAAF, 124
RABERTIN, 143
RADCLIFFE, 55
RADELL, 26
RADEMACHER, 55
RADER, 29-30
RADFORD, 33 35
RADOMSKI, 117
RAFERT, 55
RAFFERTY, 120
RAGAN, 25 34
RAGLAND, 55 214
RAGSDALE, 3
RAILSBACK, 55
RAINEY, 63 163
RALBESON, 33
RALFS, 103
RAMBACH, 184
RAMONI, 114-115
RAMSAY, 200
RAMSEY, 31 36 110 163 187
RANDAL, 205

RANDALL, 17 187 192
RANDOLPH, 187 197
RANES, 143
RANEY, 13 133
RANKIN, 30
RANLETT, 126
RANSOME, 74
RANSSER, 175
RANTEL, 154
RAPALJE, 197
RAPP, 95 188
RASCHY, 63
RASMUSSEN, 55
RATAY, 177
RATCLIFF, 124
RATHBUN, 55 215
RATHERS, 175
RATHRON, 62
RATTS, 30
RATZLAFF, 56
RAWLINGS, 30
RAWLINS, 143
RAWLS, 163
RAY, 25 56 110 126 134 143 147 154
RAYBOURN, 212
RAYMOND, 23 79 181
REA, 56
READ, 31
READLE, 56
READY, 187
REAMS, 9
REAMY, 3
REAVIS, 114
REBORI, 178
RECKLING, 56
RECTOR, 3-5 56 143 147 154 163
REDDING, 136
REDDINGTON, 194
REDFORD, 31
REDIGER, 56
REDMAN, 3 143 154
REDMOND, 124 169
REECE, 2 26 32-35 56 163 187
REED, 24 27-28 33 36 71 143 187 211
REEF, 31
REEL, 85
REESIDE, 3
REEVES, 25 77 143 154
REGAN, 93 110 182
REGISTER, 191
REHER, 56
REICHMANN, 173
REID, 3 8 187
REILEY, 174
REINERT, 64
REINHOLD, 166
REINMUTH, 56
REISBERGE, 101

REITZ, 132
REKMAN, 94
REKOUSKI, 116
REKOWSKI, 117
REMBOR, 171
REMIO, 133
RENCH, 31 207
RENFRO, 212
RENICK, 27
RENNER, 116
RENO, 202
RENSHAW, 187 195
RENZ, 126
REPP, 204
RESSELOE, 26
REST, 122
RETHERFORD, 56
REVIS, 35
REYNOLDS, 3 35 126 143 154 163 187 193
REYNON, 143
RHEA, 34-35
RHOADES, 199
RHOADS, 182
RHODES, 3 26 129 154
RIALE, 116-117
RICARDO, 3
RICE, 3 8 12 17 23 28 33 35 75 101 143 163
RICHARD, 26
RICHARDS, 3 56 85 126 133
RICHARDSON, 4 80 89 94 143
RICHERT, 66
RICHESON, 147
RICHEY, 36
RICHISON, 3
RICHMOND, 110
RICHT, 125
RICHWEIN, 179
RICKER, 56
RICKERS, 56
RICKET, 187
RICKETT, 187
RICKETTS, 143
RICKMAN, 110
RICKS, 84
RIDDLE, 25 36 67
RIDDLESBARGOR, 143
RIDER, 56
RIDGE, 154-155
RIDGEWAY, 147 179 197
RIDGWAY, 143
RIDINGS, 170
RIEBEL, 116
RIECK, 187
RIEF, 56
RIETZLAW, 91
RIFE, 214
RIGGLE, 24
RIGGS, 3
RIGHT, 3

RIGNEY, 25
RILEY, 24 79-80 91 114
RING, 56
RINGER, 99
RINGHOFFER, 126
RINGLING, 167
RINGS, 99
RINIMELINE, 172
RINKEL, 26
RIPLEY, 90 195
RISSEY, 25
RITCHIE, 155 163 170
RITEMEW, 4
RITTENBACH, 182
RITTER, 102 175
RITZDORF, 177
ROACH, 25 27 170
ROADERICK, 5
ROANE, 143
ROARK, 26
ROBB, 3 143 155 163
ROBBINSON, 187
ROBERSON, 110 155
ROBERTS, 3-4 18 23 29 33 56 63 87 101 110 130 143 147 163 191 208
ROBERTSON, 110 155
ROBIDOEX, 155
ROBIDOUX, 147 163
ROBINETT, 155
ROBINSON, 3 63 88 93 143 173 187
ROBNETT, 163
ROBYN, 131 134 137-138
ROCHESON, 26
ROCKHOLD, 155
ROCKLAGE, 124
RODDE, 190
RODEN, 214
RODENBAUGHN, 203
RODES, 3
RODGERS, 13 22 56 187
RODIE, 95
RODMAN, 76
ROEDDE, 73
ROEMMICH, 124
ROENTS, 99
ROETTO, 201
ROGERS, 3 14 18 25-26 70 103 147 155
ROGERSON, 178
ROGGETS, 3
ROHNBACH, 171
ROHRER, 124
ROLF, 167
ROLLER, 25 201
ROLLINS, 36
ROMANO, 130
RONEY, 196
ROOKER, 143
ROOKWOOD, 3

ROOT, 56
ROPES, 167
RORDEE, 69
ROSE, 56 74 93 187 189
ROSEBERRY, 143
ROSELIUS, 37
ROSENBERGER, 56
ROSENBOHM, 200
ROSENCRAFT, 3
ROSENTREADER, 56
ROSS, 29 143 155 173 196
ROSSINGTON, 137
ROSSITER, 170
ROTH, 190 197
ROTHSCHILD, 168
ROTTER, 56
ROUGH, 101
ROUNDS, 56
ROUSE, 1
ROUSEY, 4
ROWELL, 56
ROWLAND, 56
ROWLEY, 194
ROWNTREE, 155
ROY, 11
ROYAL, 167
ROYER, 56
ROZELL, 37
RUARK, 111
RUBERSON, 192
RUCHMAN, 26
RUCKER, 143-144
RUDD, 56
RUDDY, 120
RUDISILL, 138
RUE, 9
RUEGER, 184
RUFFING, 67
RUGGLES, 177
RUHL, 198
RUHS, 56
RULER, 172
RULEY, 212
RULY, 26
RUMBECK, 56
RUMMEL, 56
RUMPFF, 86
RUNBLEN, 30
RUNCIE, 97
RUNDELL, 175
RUNESTAD, 56
RUNGE, 56
RUNKEL, 144
RUNNELS, 144
RUNOLFSON, 56
RUNYAN, 187
RUPERT, 66
RUPINSKI, 117
RUPP, 99
RUPPERT, 56
RUPPORT, 56

RUSCHICK, 21
RUSEL, 155
RUSH, 120 135 174
RUSSEL, 3
RUSSELL, 3 37 56 64 76 79 96 98 111 126 144 155 163 175 187
RUSSO, 116
RUST, 3 57
RUTH, 85 171
RUTHERFORD, 57 187
RUTHSATZ, 167
RUTTER, 3
RYAN, 57 119 177 184 187 202
RYKER, 111
SAAL, 124
SAALI, 57
SAARE, 189
SABINI, 124
SACHSE, 175
SACHTLEBEN, 103
SACK, 57 168
SAEGER, 126
SAFFIER, 181
SAFFORANS, 144
SAGE, 3 191
SAGER, 155
SAGSTETTER, 122
SAINT HALL, 26
SAINT JOHN, 4 18 57
SALEMRNIG, 175
SALING, 144
SALISBURY, 57
SALMON, 15
SALORGNE, 126
SALTA, 187
SAMINGTON, 144
SAMPSON, 3 25 147 163
SAMUEL, 155
SAMUELS, 111 144 175
SANDER, 204
SANDERS, 3 31 35 57 102 111 144 155 172 202 211
SANDMANN, 116
SANDS, 215
SANGANETT, 155
SANGUINET, 172
SANKEY, 25
SAP, 203
SAPINGTON, 187
SARGENT, 163
SARTIN, 144
SARTORI, 174
SASSE, 57 117
SASSEN, 57
SATEREN, 57
SATTLER, 187
SATTLEY, 57
SAUM, 30

SAUNDERS, 3 36 57 93 155 163 197
SAVAGE, 3 35
SAWYER, 126
SAX, 131
SAYERS, 124
SAYLOR, 99
SAYRE, 3
SCALES, 87
SCANLAN, 171
SCANTLING, 197
SCARBROUGH, 155
SCARLET, 20
SCHABE, 124
SCHADT, 76
SCHAEFER, 115 179 184
SCHAEFFER, 124
SCHAFFERLE, 175
SCHAFNITT, 202
SCHALARMANN, 181
SCHARAPINSKI, 119
SCHATZMAN, 132-133
SCHAUER, 114
SCHEJBAL, 184
SCHELLENBERG, 57
SCHELTER, 125
SCHEMERHORES, 172
SCHENER, 187
SCHER, 114
SCHERDER, 125
SCHICK, 187
SCHIESS, 113
SCHILLER, 103
SCHILLIG, 125
SCHILLING, 57 125
SCHINDLER, 57 113 167
SCHIORNER, 185
SCHIRKOFSKY, 57
SCHIRTZER, 103
SCHLEIF, 57
SCHLEIS, 57
SCHLENKER, 114
SCHLEUFER, 57
SCHLUETER, 167
SCHLUTER, 124
SCHMALE, 57
SCHMETZER, 174
SCHMIDT, 3 11 57 66-67 88 124 167
SCHMITT, 125
SCHMITTE, 90
SCHMITZ, 184
SCHNACKENBERG, 24
SCHNEBLY, 206 210-211
SCHNEDDING, 172
SCHNEIDER, 3 96 100 126 166 169 183
SCHNEINED, 175
SCHNELKES, 169
SCHNELLE, 124
SCHNELLY, 206

SCHNERMANN, 176
SCHNITZ, 70
SCHNORR, 165
SCHOBER, 57
SCHOEDEL, 124
SCHOENECK, 189
SCHOENFELD, 179
SCHOENHAL, 203
SCHOENHALS, 203-204
SCHOENTHAL, 13
SCHOETTGER, 57
SCHOLTEN, 134 138
SCHONEBECK, 184
SCHOOLCRAFT, 25
SCHOOLING, 25
SCHOONOVER, 57
SCHOPPE, 185
SCHRAEDER, 165
SCHRANTZ, 37
SCHRECKHISE, 187
SCHREIBER, 189
SCHRINER, 57
SCHRINES, 30
SCHROEDER, 14 124 178
SCHROUDER, 178
SCHUENGEL, 171
SCHULER, 89
SCHULES, 124
SCHULTE, 103
SCHULTZ, 86 175
SCHULZ, 57
SCHULZE, 57
SCHULZKUMP, 57
SCHUMACHER, 103 124
SCHUTTEN, 183
SCHVAAR, 209
SCHWAEBE, 182
SCHWARNECK, 165
SCHWARTZ, 124 183
SCHWARZ, 181
SCHWEICKHARDT, 115
SCHWEIG, 215
SCHWENK, 215
SCHWENKE, 57
SCHWENKER, 167
SCHWENSEN, 57
SCHWER, 23
SCHWICHTENBERG, 57
SCOTT, 4 11 13 26 32 57 74 88 144 155 181 187 192 208
SCOTTEN, 144
SCOVERN, 211
SCOVILLE, 3 7
SCRAGGS, 27
SCRIVEN, 57
SCRIVENER, 187
SCULL, 192
SEARCY, 144 201
SEARS, 25 57 144
SEATON, 210
SEAVER, 3

SEBASTIAN, 113-114
SEBOLD, 57
SEBREE, 144
SEBURN, 111
SECHKER, 57
SECKEL, 125
SEDFORD, 78
SEEKRES, 103
SEELEY, 187
SEELIG, 167
SEEVER, 169
SEIBEL, 177
SEIBURT, 144
SEIDEL, 63 182
SEIDERS, 58
SEIGAL, 111
SEIMEARS THURMAN, 202-203
SEIMEARS, 203
SEIMERS, 167
SELA, 163
SELDEN, 124
SELDERS, 58
SELECTMAN, 89
SELF, 71
SELIGSOHN, 113
SELLERS, 4 194
SELSOR, 3
SEMER, 3
SEMPLE, 125
SENN, 58
SENNEWALD, 166
SENSENEY, 58 210
SENTER, 125 184
SENTOUX, 125
SENWOOD, 68
SERVIS, 64
SESTRUP, 91
SETTLE, 144 213
SEVCIK, 58
SEVIER, 126
SEWARINGIN, 144
SEWELL, 100
SEXTON, 144
SEYSTER, 58 198
SHACELFORD, 33
SHACKELFORD, 144
SHACKLEFORD, 27 36
SHADLEY, 58
SHADRICK, 191
SHAFER, 136 211
SHAFFER, 35 212
SHAFFNER, 29 58
SHAFFROTH, 144
SHANDY, 10
SHANE, 187
SHANNON, 36 119 126 163
SHAPERS, 20
SHAPLEIGH, 165
SHARE, 32
SHARP, 3 5 58 166 172

SHARRAT, 132
SHATTINGER, 138
SHAVER, 168
SHAW, 3 26 125 144 169
SHAWMAN, 144
SHAWN, 195
SHAY, 135
SHEA, 169
SHEAFF, 58
SHEARER, 155
SHEEHAN, 214
SHEETS, 2
SHEETZ, 3
SHELDON, 176 187
SHELTON, 3 23
SHEPARD, 172
SHEPHERD, 34 144
SHEPPARD, 111
SHERIDAN, 64 101
SHERLOCK, 175
SHERMAN, 3 67 69 97
SHERMER, 58
SHERRY, 3
SHERWOOD, 75 147 155
SHESTAK, 58
SHIELDS, 144 169
SHIFFLET, 144
SHIFLETT, 144
SHIFLITT, 144
SHINES, 171
SHIPLEY, 144
SHIPMAN, 111 129
SHIPP, 144
SHIRLEY, 3 90 111 144
SHOCK, 25
SHOEMAKER, 58
SHOEMAN, 210
SHOFORER, 81
SHOMSEN, 60
SHOOK, 187
SHORE, 187 205
SHORES, 144
SHORT, 7 25 144
SHOSTROM, 58
SHRADER, 87
SHRDTRIDGE, 58
SHRINER, 58
SHROCK, 58
SHROPSHIRE, 210
SHROUT, 3
SHROYER, 58
SHRYOCK, 125
SHUBERT, 3
SHUCK, 58
SHUFF, 33
SHUFFIT, 3
SHUGART, 144
SHULL, 11 58
SHULTS, 37 111
SHULTZ, 76 163 195
SHULZ, 101

SHUMAKER, 3
SHUMATE, 36
SHURTS, 15
SHUTS, 187
SHUTTS, 37
SIBERT, 187
SIBLEY, 3
SICKELS, 212
SIDLER, 163
SIDNEY, 136
SIDUS, 129
SIEG, 125
SIESEL, 125
SIFOR, 65
SIGLER, 3
SILER, 26
SILLASEN, 58
SILLIMAN, 36
SILVER, 58
SILVERS, 148 163
SILVERWOOD, 1
SILVUS, 155
SILVY, 144
SIMBALL, 215
SIMCOCK, 33
SIMCOCKE, 28
SIMCOCKS, 30
SIMCOX, 166
SIMMER, 32
SIMMERMAN, 27-28 31 58
SIMMERSON, 33
SIMMONS, 35 58 136 144 163
SIMON, 131 138 177
SIMONS, 144
SIMPLE, 3
SIMPSON, 28 32 58 187
SIMS, 5 9 135 187 199
SINCLAIR, 175
SINGER, 124
SINGLETON, 5 126 147
SINKO, 119
SIP, 117
SIPLE, 35
SIPPLE, 187
SIRUNK, 103
SISCO, 170 203
SISSON, 206 208
SKAGGS, 28
SKALA, 119
SKEED, 190
SKEELS, 37 58
SKEEN, 58
SKEFFINGTON, 120
SKEHAN, 118
SKELLY, 175
SKELTON, 25
SKIDMORE, 34 58 129 135 138
SKILES, 19
SKINNER, 5 144 155
SKOUTEN, 163

SKREDINSKI, 121
SLADE, 199
SLADER, 187
SLAINK, 86
SLANKARD, 111
SLATERWRITE, 31
SLATTERY, 119 120
SLAUGHTER, 144 187 206
SLAYBACK, 3
SLAYBAUGH, 155
SLAYTON, 177
SLEVIN, 121
SLEZAK, 168
SLIGER, 9
SLINEY, 79
SLIVER, 187
SLOAN, 207
SLOIDK, 86
SLONECKER, 58
SLUSSER, 195
SMALL, 3 85
SMALLWOOD, 144
SMARR, 144
SMEED, 14
SMELSOR, 28
SMITH, 3-6 8 10-12 15 21 25 28 30-32 37 58 64-65 70 72 82 86 92 95-96 98-99 111 115 119 124-125 132 144 147 155 163 166-167 177 181 184-185 187 190-191 193-194 196-199 201 204-206 209-210 212-213 215
SMITHURST, 18
SMUGAI, 119
SMURR, 183
SNATHEN, 144
SNAVELY, 144
SNEED, 73 129
SNELL, 3 68 144 177
SNELLING, 27 30 35
SNIDER, 58
SNIVELY, 196
SNODDY, 144 213
SNOW, 187
SNYDER, 22 58 144 155
SOLAVER, 26
SOLDYNSKI, 119
SOLLARS, 3 155
SOLLENBERGER, 58
SOLLER, 125
SOMMER, 190
SONNENSCHEIN, 6
SONTAG, 114-115 137
SORENSSEN, 59
SORG, 178
SOTHAN, 59
SOUCIE, 59
SOUDERS, 130
SOULE, 24
SOUTHERLAND, 84

SOUTHWARD, 147
SOUTHWORTH, 144
SOVAR, 118
SPAENLE, 125
SPAIN, 203
SPANE, 62
SPANGLER, 26 65
SPARGUR, 196
SPARKS, 32 131 215
SPAULDING, 91
SPEACE, 3
SPEAKE, 195
SPEAKMAN, 111
SPEAR, 155
SPEED, 3
SPEERS, 111
SPELLMAN, 59
SPENCER, 14 25 134 138 144 155 163 213
SPENGEMANN, 179
SPERNEY, 144
SPIESE, 187
SPILMAN, 111
SPINNER, 175
SPOERING, 59
SPORTSMAN, 187
SPOTTS, 144
SPRADLING, 14
SPRAGUE, 23
SPRATT, 155
SPRICE, 144
SPRINGLE, 3
SPROCKE, 103
SPURGEON, 75 144
SPURGIN, 6
SQUIBB, 59
STABENOW, 59
STACK, 184
STACKEY, 25
STADFELD, 59
STAENGEL, 126
STAFFORD, 59 90 103 163 197 205
STAHL, 59
STALCUP, 3
STALEY, 163
STALKER, 125
STAMPS, 177 201
STANBERY, 25
STANCELL, 170
STANDERFORD, 144
STANDIFORD, 144
STANDLEY, 187
STANDLY, 144
STANECK, 184
STANLEY, 25 59 81 144 163 187
STANLY, 4
STANSBURY, 181
STANTON, 114
STAPLES, 17

STAPLETON, 144
STAPP, 144
STAR, 34
STARACHAWICZ, 122
STARK, 115 130 134-136 207
STARKJOHAN, 59
STARKS, 98
STARR, 33
STARRET, 3
STARS, 102
STATTON, 18
STEARNES, 189
STEBINS, 175
STECHFORD, 171
STECK, 184
STEEG, 172
STEEL, 103 155 164
STEELE, 18 59 81
STEEVER, 189
STEEVES, 59
STEFEL, 173
STEFFES, 59
STEFFEY, 213
STEFFLER, 199
STEIGER, 125
STEIN, 25 85 187
STEINBAUGH, 102
STEINBUCK, 22
STEINIUGES, 175
STEINKRUGER, 59
STEINMEYER, 183
STEINS, 171
STEMONS, 144
STEPHAN, 63
STEPHENS, 5 27 37 59 155
    174 187
STEPHENSON, 5 7 35 144 155
    187
STERLING, 27-28 30 187 192
STERN, 59 115 144 170
STERRETT, 89
STEVENS, 1 24-25 29 93 135
    137 205 207-208 215
STEVENSON, 7 23 25-26 164
    213
STEVER, 201
STEWARD, 35
STEWART, 3 6 31 34-35 59 76
    78 88 94 102 144 168 170
    188 193-195
STICE, 144
STICKLEY, 59
STIERLIN, 134 136
STIERMAN, 138
STIFFEL, 167
STIFFONS, 77
STILES, 144
STILL, 112
STILLS, 172
STINDT, 59
STINNET, 25

STINSMAN, 190
STIPE, 144
STIRLING, 28
STIZESEWSKI, 120
STOBAUGH, 155
STOCKDALE, 59
STOCKER, 124
STOCKTON, 23 25 28 33-34
    112 148 196
STOKES, 5 37 59 112 118
STOLL, 165
STOLZENBURG, 59
STON, 12
STONE, 3 25 33 36 59 112 144
    187
STOOPS, 59
STORBECK, 181
STORY, 59 187 208
STOUT, 11 98 125
STOVEALL, 212
STOVER, 3
STRABEL, 59
STRACHAN, 3
STRADEL, 168
STRAIT, 26
STRANDT, 59
STRANG, 33
STRANGE, 27 36 178
STRATTON, 59 189
STRAUSS, 215
STRAWN, 59
STREET, 144
STRIBLEN, 95 191
STRICK, 119
STRICKLAND, 155-156 213
STRIKELIN, 4
STRINGFELLON, 144
STRINING, 170
STRODE, 3
STROETER, 215
STRONG, 26 97
STRUBEL, 178
STRUBER, 187
STRUMPLER, 59
STUART, 3 27
STUBBLEFIELD, 26
STUBLMEYER, 184
STUCKEL, 187
STUCKERT, 19
STUCKY, 59
STUDEVANT, 187
STUECKLER, 125
STUEVE, 167
STULL, 59
STULTZ, 156 164
STUMPFF, 32-33
STUP, 85
STURGEON, 196
STURGES, 187
STURGIS, 3
STURMA, 116

STURTZ, 204
STUTZMAN, 59
STYLES, 3
STYRN, 144
SUBOVITZ, 215
SUDER, 187
SUEHL, 59
SUESS, 179
SUGAR, 187
SUGRUE, 214
SULLINGER, 202
SULLINS, 144
SULLIVAN, 7 112 120-121
    125 164 178 211
SUMMERS, 187 195
SUMNER, 129
SUNDELL, 59
SUNDERLAND, 125 144
SUPICH, 117
SUPPLE, 199
SUSWELL, 79
SUTER, 206
SUTHERLAND, 59
SUTLER, 190
SUTTON, 22 59 173
SVANDA, 59
SWAIN, 183
SWAN, 10 213
SWANE, 144
SWANSON, 24-25 59 114
SWARINGIN, 144
SWARTOUT, 59
SWATZEN, 26
SWEARINGEN, 3
SWEARINGER, 112
SWEAZER, 144
SWEENEY, 20 59
SWEETEN, 16
SWEETT, 59
SWETNUM, 144
SWIFT, 30 183
SWINFORD, 199
SWINGFEE, 26
SWINNEY, 144
SWITZLER, 144
SWOPE, 144 183
SYNDE, 31
TAAKE, 174
TABLER, 187
TAGGARD, 144
TAGGART, 35
TALBOT, 144 164
TALBOTT, 156 164
TALENT, 84
TALLEUR, 125
TALOT, 132
TANDY, 32
TANEY, 112
TANNER, 89
TAPSCOTT, 28 33
TARBELL, 3

TARREYRENA, 119
TART, 60
TARWATER, 164
TASSEMEYER, 113
TATE, 21 78 102 199
TATUM, 144
TAUTPHAEUS, 124
TAYES, 62 148
TAYLOR, 3-4 12 26 35-37 60
    82-83 116 144 156 164 166
    179 181 187 193
TEAGADON, 75
TEAGUE, 1
TEBBINS, 16
TEBBS, 36
TEDD, 25
TEDWELL, 26
TEELE, 22
TEETER, 34
TEHLE, 194
TEICHMANN, 178
TEMPLE, 23
TEMPLETON, 5 200
TENBUELT, 124
TENNER, 131 138
TEOESCOMB, 184
TERREL, 112 144
TERRELL, 60 144
TERRETER, 117
TERRILL, 144
TERRY, 14 26
TETER, 144 187
TETRICK, 77
TEXTOR, 125
THAGGS, 27
THARP, 144 187-188
THAXTON, 32 36
THEIN, 167
THEIRAUF, 170
THEIS, 76
THERENS, 60
THERMON, 144
THIEBES, 134 136 138
THIEMAN, 24
THIES, 125
THISTLE, 29 31 33
THOMAS, 2-3 25 60 74-75 78
    89 91 101 112 144 156
    164 166 173 176 181 189
THOMAZIN, 60
THOMPSON, 10 25-32 34-35
    60 79 90 124 126 134 144
    156 164 167 171 188 197
    209
THOMSON, 200
THORN, 3
THORNBURGH, 126 164
THORNTON, 27-28 30-33 36
    164 203
THORP, 3 156 164
THORTON, 126

THOUROUMAN, 5
THRASHER, 144
THULL, 60
THURMAN, 164 203
THURNAGLE, 60
TIADEN, 12 60
TIBBETH, 68
TIBBS, 28 77
TICHE, 125
TIERNAN, 132
TIGHE, 60
TILDEN, 60
TILFORD, 144
TILL, 112
TILTON, 60
TIMERSON, 189
TIMMERMEYER, 9
TIMMIS, 171
TINDALL, 34 144
TINDLE, 144
TINGLE, 3
TINNIN, 129
TINSMAN, 205
TIPPIE, 198
TIPTON, 156 200
TISTHAMMER, 60
TITTLE, 3
TITUS, 144
TIVY, 171
TOALSON, 144
TOBERMANN, 114
TOBEY, 131
TOBIN, 3 148 164
TOCCO, 120
TODD, 3 125 144 193 200 211
TOFTE, 115
TOLES, 144
TOLLE, 21
TOLLEY, 177
TOLNER, 26
TOLSON, 144
TOMILSON, 188
TOMLIN, 32
TONEY, 26 164
TOOF, 134 136
TOOLEY, 144
TOOLY, 144
TOOTER, 64
TOPPER, 97
TOREY, 60
TORRANCE, 188
TOTTEN, 84
TOWAS, 188
TOWN, 112
TOWNSEND, 60
TOWNSLEY, 29
TOY, 155
TRABER, 124
TRACY, 37 60 119 144 192
TRAGDON, 188
TRANTINA, 121

TRAP, 34
TRASK, 215
TRAVIS, 4
TRAXL, 125
TREAT, 60
TREFNY, 177
TREICHLER, 167
TRENT, 25
TREW, 60
TRIBBLE, 144
TRIGGS, 60
TRIMBLE, 14 60
TRIPLETT, 3 16 60 188
TRIPP, 137
TRIPPEER, 188
TRODE, 145
TROLLOPE, 60
TROTE, 24
TROUCH, 25
TROWER, 164
TROY, 97
TRUAX, 7
TRUETZEL, 184
TRUITT, 26
TRULLINGER, 60
TRUMBO, 188
TRUMPETER, 3
TRUSCOTT, 60
TRUSTY, 194
TRUXEL, 133 135 137
TUCK, 188
TUCKER, 25 35 69
TUDDER, 2
TUDOR, 145
TUFTS, 3
TUGGLE, 27
TULLARD, 183
TULLIS, 19
TURNER, 3 12 20 28 33 60 87
    112 124-126 145 148 156
    164 173 178 188 214
TURPIN, 3 188
TURRELL, 145
TURTLE, 211
TUTTLE, 60
TUXEL, 134
TWIST, 60 172
TYER, 145
TYLER, 4 32-34 103 164
TYSER, 60
UFFORD, 60
UHL, 81 190
ULAN, 33
ULINSKI, 124
ULLRICH, 125
ULMAN, 195
ULMER, 60
ULRICH, 183 188
UMGELTER, 184
UMLAND, 60
UNDERWOOD, 16 24 145 164

UPRIGHT, 30
URBAN, 125 179
URBANO, 115
UTT, 33
VABLE, 177
VACIK, 60
VAIHINGER, 3
VALENTA, 60
VALLANINGHAM, 174
VALSTIN, 181
VAN BUSKIRK, 37
VAN CLEEF, 176
VAN CLUF, 173
VAN DYKE, 112
VAN HOOSIER, 73
VAN HOZER, 84
VAN ORMAN, 60
VAN SCHOOTEN, 60
VAN VLEET, 61
VAN VOLKENBURGH, 191
VAN WORMER, 37
VAN ZANDT, 203
VANCE, 102 124 188
VANDEREN, 3
VANDERGRIF, 112
VANDIKE, 10
VANGUNDY, 1
VANHOOZER, 164
VANHORN, 145
VANLANDINGHAM, 3
VANMETRE, 3
VANOSDEL, 29 36
VANOUGER, 66
VANSICKLE, 2
VANSKOIKE, 3
VANT, 61
VAUGHN, 3 35 71 81 90 102 145 175 190
VAWTER, 3
VEAL, 171 188
VEIGEL, 61
VEJSICKY, 119
VELMONS, 4
VENDERAU, 125
VENDERHAGEN, 168
VENLEMANS, 156
VENNEMANN, 121
VERDI, 133
VERMEERSCH, 173
VERMILLION, 112
VERMILLON, 25
VERNOY, 61
VESPER, 19
VESPERMANN, 125
VESPERS, 7
VESSAR, 5
VESTAL, 164
VETTER, 173 177
VICK, 3
VICTOR, 26 133
VIERSEN, 61

VIGUS, 192
VILET, 28
VINCENT, 86 188
VINES, 145
VINYARD, 64
VIOLET, 27
VISE, 61
VIT, 121
VIVEON, 145
VIVION, 145
VOELKER, 168
VOGE, 10
VOGELSANG, 117
VOGT, 61
VOHS, 61
VOLLAR, 116-117
VOLLBERG, 125
VOLLING, 181
VOLLSTEDT, 135
VOLZ, 113 183
VON CLOSSMAN, 172
VON HOFE, 130
VON LINDERN, 61
VON WEBER, 136
VOORHIES, 156 164
VORTMAN, 61
VOSIKA, 61
VOSS, 61
WADE, 3 29-30 126 145 156 164 188 207-208
WADKINS, 112
WADSWORTH, 91 164
WAELE, 114
WAGELEIN, 172
WAGGONER, 25 61
WAGNER, 3 172
WAID, 112
WAILES, 3
WAINSCOTT, 30 33 145
WAIT, 61
WAITE, 61
WAKELAM, 130 133
WALDEN, 61 145 215
WALDON, 168
WALDRON, 69
WALEUP, 145
WALFORD, 29
WALGREN, 61
WALICE, 33
WALK, 195
WALKENDORFER, 83
WALKENHAUST, 19
WALKER, 3 10 29 31-33 36 61 77 98 101 135 138 145 176 181 194 199 206
WALL, 124
WALLACE, 3 61 79 145 156 164 199
WALLENICK, 173
WALLER, 102 112 164
WALLERSTEIN, 132

WALLING, 130
WALLINGFORD, 164
WALLIS, 137
WALLOVER, 10
WALSH, 125 132 176 188 214
WALTER, 37 200
WALTERS, 26 61 188
WALTON, 129
WAMEKE, 16
WAMINGTON, 93
WAMSLEY, 65 75
WANGER, 189
WANMER, 61
WANMOUTH, 145
WARBURTON, 102 190 192
WARD, 137 145 188 199 201 208
WARDEN, 145
WARE, 112 145 188 213
WARHURST, 189
WARNER, 8 61 99 126 134 188
WARNICK, 32
WARNINGTON, 26
WARREN, 25 27-29 34-36 61 63 125 134 136-137 145
WARRICK, 33
WARTZ, 3
WASHBURN, 25
WASHBURNE, 129
WASHINGTON, 86 98 179 189
WASTIER, 125
WATERS, 188
WATKINS, 4 188 210 212
WATKINSON, 61
WATMORE, 61
WATSON, 3 7 68 85 103 145 172 188
WATTS, 26 33 145 188 215
WAVRA, 116
WAYLAND, 145
WAYMIRE, 3 164
WEAR, 28-30 33
WEATHERFORD, 214
WEATHERMAN, 10
WEATHERS, 145 201
WEATHERSPOON, 112
WEAVER, 21 61 74 89 135 171 194 198 204-205 210 212
WEBB, 11 25 148 201-202 209
WEBBER, 26 67 132
WEBER, 130-138 172 212
WEBERM, 130 133
WEBSTER, 31
WEDDLE, 164
WEDE, 30
WEDLE, 174
WEDLER, 173
WEEDEN, 7
WEEKLEY, 28
WEFFERLING, 171

WEGRZYN, 61
WEHMER, 198
WEHMUELLER, 126
WEHRENBERG, 126
WEICHEL, 61
WEIDLE, 124
WEIDNER, 101
WEIGEND, 113
WEIKART, 179
WEIKEL, 188
WEIL, 130
WEILE, 138
WEIMANN, 168
WEINREICH, 184
WEIPERT, 190
WEIR, 164
WEIS, 118
WEISE, 3 181
WEISS, 125
WEITER, 184
WELCH, 3 61 103 125
WELDEN, 15
WELDON, 129
WELLEMEYER, 124
WELLER, 37 99
WELLMAN, 188
WELLS, 88 138 156 168 200 206-207 210-211
WELSH, 61 73 112 171
WENDA, 85
WENDEL, 168
WENDT, 78
WENZL, 61
WERNER, 61 124 133 165
WERTS, 3
WERTZ, 15
WERZ, 125
WESOLONSKI, 117
WEST, 27 29 31 34 61 98 112 201
WESTAPHER, 61
WESTERHOFF, 16
WESTERKAMP, 103
WESTHOLT, 126
WESTLAKE, 182
WESTMANN, 166
WESTON, 176
WESTPHALING, 93
WETHERALL, 64
WETTEROTH, 95
WETZEL, 61 164
WEUGES, 93
WEY, 16
WHALEN, 214
WHALEY, 112
WHANN, 112
WHAPPLE, 26
WHEAT, 112
WHEELER, 61 112 129 131 135 179 188 190
WHELAN, 120 172

WHISMAND, 188
WHITAKER, 176 188 204
WHITE, 6 10 26-27 33 35 62 77 79 83 87 112 127 129 131 145 164 170 172-173 177 179 184 188 196 204 208-209
WHITEHEAD, 156
WHITEMAN, 124
WHITESEL, 62 188
WHITINORE, 168
WHITLEY, 112
WHITLOW, 135
WHITMYER, 64
WHITNEY, 12 145 195
WHITSELL, 4 62
WHITSET, 103
WHITSETT, 27-28 32 34
WHITSON, 188
WHITSUN, 156
WHITTEMORE, 13
WHITTENBURG, 6
WHITTINGTON, 156
WHITTOCK, 145
WIBBING, 124
WICK, 62
WICKHAM, 11
WICKS, 26
WIDAMAN, 62
WIDENER, 167
WIDENSOHLER, 126
WIDNER, 164
WIEBERG, 103
WIEBUSCH, 125
WIEDEBERG, 22
WIEDNER, 172
WIEHL, 190
WIENECKE, 167
WIESEN, 125
WIETHUCHTER, 178
WIFERS, 167
WIGGINGTON, 145
WIGGINS, 12
WIGHT, 112
WIGHTMAN, 215
WIGREN, 62
WILBERTON, 4
WILBUR, 62
WILBURN, 156
WILCOTT, 62
WILCOX, 4 199-200
WILCOXEN, 31 145
WILDEISON, 126
WILDON, 212
WILDS, 145
WILEY, 31 34 145 165 179
WILFLEY, 156
WILHAUS, 188
WILHELM, 165
WILHOIT, 145
WILKENS, 62

WILKENSON, 145
WILKERSON, 4-5 145 156 215
WILKES, 184
WILKINS, 175
WILKINSON, 62 181
WILKS, 62 112
WILLAIMS, 202
WILLARD, 156
WILLEN, 114
WILLETT, 66
WILLHITE, 112
WILLIAM, 188
WILLIAMS, 21 25-26 30 62 75 83 89 94 96 103 112 134 145 156 165 170 173 181-182 188-189 213
WILLIAMSON, 3 26 183
WILLIGHAM, 127
WILLINGHAM, 127
WILLIS, 3 91-92 165 170
WILLMAN, 62 70
WILLOCK, 26
WILLS, 26 145
WILLY, 3
WILMS, 124
WILMUTH, 82
WILSON, 2-3 7 9 14 19-20 23 34 62 64 70 72 90-91 97-98 101 124 135 145 148 156 165 174 178 188-189 192
WIMMERSTEDT, 130
WINBORN, 145
WINCHESTER, 19
WINDSOR, 27-28 33 36
WINFREY, 62
WING, 26
WINGATE, 135
WINGER, 3
WINGFIELD, 27
WINKLER, 166
WINLOW, 26
WINN, 18 145
WINNTER, 124
WINSHIP, 188
WINSON, 145
WINTER, 62
WINTERS, 25-26
WIRTH, 24 125
WISCOM, 145
WISDOM, 145
WISE, 112 189
WISELY, 27
WISEMAN, 145
WISHER, 69
WISHON, 112
WISKERGER, 165
WISKIRCHEN, 165
WITHERBEE, 3
WITHERS, 83 113 145
WITHERSPOON, 3
WITHREN, 63

WITHROW, 70
WITT, 4-5 89 145 148
WITTEN, 192
WIXAM, 3
WOBLEWSKI, 120
WOFF, 13
WOHLERS, 62
WOLDRAN, 3
WOLF, 17 24 62 188 200
WOLFE, 3 21
WOLFENBARGER, 202
WOLFER, 3 192
WOLFOLK, 98
WOLFORD, 27
WOLFSKILL, 145
WOLLENBERG, 119
WOLVERTON, 193
WOMACK, 165
WONDERLICK, 82
WONDERLY, 156 165
WONG, 176
WOOD, 3 25-26 28 31 63 82 93 156 165-166 200 205 214
WOODARD, 25 145 198
WOODEN, 104 209
WOODEY, 182
WOODGATE, 62
WOODLAND, 29
WOODMAN, 3
WOODRUFF, 28 69 113
WOODS, 20 25-26 87 113 145
WOODSON, 87 145 215
WOOKMAN, 62
WOOLCOTT, 132 135
WOOLEN, 156
WOOLEVER, 113
WOOLEY, 113
WOOLF, 188
WOOLFOLK, 3

WOOLRIDGE, 62
WOOSTER, 98 215
WOOTEN, 31 201
WORCHLEY, 12
WORDS, 74
WORKMAN, 145 165 188
WORKS, 96
WORLES, 72
WORLEY, 213
WORMINGTON, 25
WORNEHUSON, 25
WORTH, 136 184 188
WORTHINGTON, 208
WRIGHT, 12 19 24 26 62 65 70 74 77 83 124 129 145 188
WRINKLE, 148 156
WRITE, 27
WROBLESKI, 202
WUHL, 78
WULBER, 200
WULFEMEYER, 126
WUNDERLICH, 125 166
WUNSCH, 177
WYANDECKER, 145
WYATT, 3 177 188
WYLIE, 188
WYSS, 199
YAEGER, 184
YANCEY, 145
YANKEE, 32
YANT, 62
YARNELL, 3
YATES, 131
YAUCK, 204
YEAGER, 145
YEATS, 126
YOCUM, 165
YOESEL, 62
YORK, 9

YOST, 62
YOUNG, 3 9 24-27 35 37 73 97 103 113 126 137-138 145 156 166 188 190-191 197
YOUNGER, 73 113
YOUNGMAN, 188
YOUNGQUIST, 62
YOUNT, 188
YOWELL, 145
ZACHARY, 26
ZACHRITZ, 185
ZARZENRSKY, 113
ZATORSKI, 182
ZAUCKER, 199
ZEHR, 62
ZEIGLER, 81
ZEIS, 125
ZELLER, 124 206 211
ZEMAN, 83
ZENGBRANNER, 63
ZIB, 117
ZIELINSKI, 116
ZILHARTT, 145
ZIMMERMAN, 21 62 129 145 170 200
ZIMMERMANN, 145 175
ZINK, 16
ZIRKLE, 81
ZODOCK, 86
ZOLLIKOFER, 121
ZOOK, 37
ZOPFI, 116
ZUMBRUN, 8
ZUNKEL, 193
ZURHEIDE, 125
ZUZAK, 116
ZWINGMANN, 103

Other Heritage Books by Sherida K. Eddlemon:

Missouri Genealogical Records and Abstracts:
Volume 1: 1766-1839
Volume 2: 1752-1839
Volume 3: 1787-1839
Volume 4: 1741-1839
Volume 5: 1755-1839
Volume 6: 1621-1839
Volume 7: 1535-1839

Missouri Genealogical Gleanings 1840 and Beyond, Volumes 1-9

1890 Genealogical Census Reconstruction: Mississippi, Volumes 1 and 2

1890 Genealogical Census Reconstruction: Missouri, Volumes 1-3

1890 Genealogical Census Reconstruction: Ohio, Volume 1
(with Patricia P. Nelson)

1890 Genealogical Census Reconstruction: Tennessee, Volume 1

A Genealogical Collection of Kentucky Birth and Death Records

Callaway County, Missouri, Marriage Records: 1821 to 1871

Cumberland Presbyterian Church, Volume One: 1836 and Beyond

Dickson County, Tennessee Marriage Records, 1817-1879

Genealogical Abstracts from Missouri Church Records and Other Religious Sources, Volume 1

Genealogical Abstracts from Tennessee Newspapers, 1791-1808

Genealogical Abstracts from Tennessee Newspapers, 1803-1812

Genealogical Abstracts from Tennessee Newspapers, 1821-1828

Tennessee Genealogical Records and Abstracts, Volume 1: 1787-1839

Genealogical Gleanings from New York Fraternal Organizations Volumes 1 and 2

Index to the Arkansas General Land Office, 1820-1907 Volumes 1-10

Kentucky Genealogical Records and Abstracts, Volume 1: 1781-1839

Kentucky Genealogical Records and Abstracts, Volume 2: 1796-1839

Lewis County, Missouri Index to Circuit Court Records, Volume 1, 1833-1841

Missouri Birth and Death Records, Volumes 1-4

Morgan County, Missouri Marriage Records, 1833-1893

Our Ancestors of Albany County, New York, Volumes 1 and 2

Our Ancestors of Cuyahoga County, Ohio, Volume 1
(with Patricia P. Nelson)

Ralls County, Missouri Settlement Records, 1832-1853

Records of Randolph County, Missouri, 1833-1964

Ten Thousand Missouri Taxpayers

The "Show-Me" Guide to Missouri: Sources for Genealogical and Historical Research

CD: Dickson County, Tennessee Marriage Records, 1817-1879

CD: Index to the Arkansas General Land Office, 1820-1907 Volumes 1-10

CD: Missouri, Volume 3

CD: Tennessee Genealogical Records

CD: Tennessee Genealogical Records, Volumes 1-3

www.ingramcontent.com/pod-product-compliance
Lightning Source LLC
Chambersburg PA
CBHW060559230426
43670CB00011B/1892